IBSEN & MEANING

James McFarlane
IBSEN & MEANING

STUDIES, ESSAYS & PREFACES 1953-87

Norvik Press
1989

Other Norvik Press books:

Michael Robinson: *Strindberg and Autobiography*
Irene Scobbie (ed.): *Aspects of Modern Swedish Literature*
Egil Törnqvist and Barry Jacobs: *Strindberg's Miss Julie: a Play and its Transpositions*
Sigbjørn Obstfelder: *A Priest's Diary*, edited and translated by James McFarlane
Annegret Heitmann (ed.): *No Man's Land* – An Anthology of Danish Women Writers
Bjørg Vik: *An Aquarium of Women*, translated by Janet Garton
Hjalmar Söderberg: *Short Stories*, selected and translated by Carl Lofmark
P.C. Jersild: *A Living Soul*, translated by Rika Lesser

Our logo is based on a drawing by Egil Bakka (University of Bergen) of a Viking ornament in gold foil, paper thin, with impressed figures (size 16 x 21 mm). It was found in 1897 at Hauge, Klepp, Rogaland, and is now in the collection of the Historisk museum, University of Bergen (inv.no.5392). It depicts a love scene, possibly (according to Magnus Olsen) between the fertility god Freyr and the maiden Gerðr; the large penannular brooch of the man's cloak dates the work as being most likely 10th century.

Cover illustration: *Vinternatt i Rondane* (Winter Night in Rondane), 1901, by Harald Sohlberg, Nasjonalgalleriet, Oslo.
Cover design: Andy Vargo

British Library Cataloguing in Publication Data
McFarlane, James Walter.
Ibsen and Meaning: Studies, Essays and Prefaces 1953–87.
1. Ibsen, Henrik – Criticism and interpretation
I. Title
·839.8′226   PT8895

ISBN 1-870041-07-0

First published in 1989 by Norvik Press, University of East Anglia, Norwich, NR4 7TJ, England

Managing Editors: James McFarlane and Janet Garton

Norvik Press has been established with financial support from the University of East Anglia, the Danish Ministry for Cultural Affairs, the Norwegian Cultural Department, and the Swedish Institute.

Printed in Great Britain by the University of East Anglia, Norwich.

Contents

Preface

This book is no palladian edifice. Rather a stretch of dry-stone walling. The materials which have gone to the making of it have been collected from widely scattered locations: articles in learned journals, discussion papers for various symposia, public lectures, introductions to books, and the like. Although the various items exhibited certain natural affinities among themselves, there was no sense in pretending that, by re-working them, they could be chiselled into dressed blocks of masonry ready for bonding and mortaring together in some grand design. What did seem possible however was to arrange them in rough mutual support of one another—to stack and layer and prop them in a way that would lend some coherence and stability to their overall statement. Inevitably there would be overlapping; there would be gaps in the fabric, holes in the argument; the separate pieces would fit only where they touched. But if, by this arrangement, it proved possible at least to demarcate an area of rewarding enquiry, then that (I felt) would be *raison d'être* enough.

I make no excuse for including a chapter on 'Modes of Translation' as the opening piece in the book. Long before I began the actual work of translating Ibsen, I had been interested in the theory and semantics of translation, and had set out my ideas in a number of published pieces. It seemed to me appropriate that, alongside the critical assessments which had grown out of the work on *The Oxford Ibsen*, I should include a statement setting out those ideas about the nature of translation which had served me during the practical work of putting Ibsen into English.

September 1988   JWMcF

Sources

Chapter 1: first appeared as 'Modes of Translation' in *Durham University Journal*, vol.xlv, no.3, June 1953, pp.77-93.

Chapter 2: first published in *Ibsen and the Temper of Norwegian Literature* (London, 1960), pp.52-72.

Chapter 3: was delivered as the 2nd Popperwell Memorial Lecture in the University of Cambridge, April 1987.

Chapter 4: was presented as a paper to the First International Ibsen Seminar, Oslo, 1965, and published in *Contemporary Approaches to Ibsen 1* (Oslo, 1966), pp.35-50.

Chapters 5 to 12 were published as Introductions to the individual volumes of *The Oxford Ibsen* (London, 1960-1977) in eight volumes: vol.1 (1970), vol.2 (1962), vol.3 (1972), vol.4 (1963), vol.5 (1961), vol.6 (1960), vol.7 (1966), vol.8 (1977). I am grateful to the Delegates of Oxford University Press for allowing me to reprint these items here.

Chapter 13: was originally delivered as a public lecture at the University of Exeter in Feb 1978 and published in the *Journal of European Studies*, vol.ix, 1979, pp.155-173.

Chapter 14: was presented as a paper to the Seventh Burdick-Vary Symposium held at the University of Wisconsin-Madison in March 1984, and reprinted in *Scandinavica*, vol.23, no.2, Nov 1984, pp.101-118.

Prolegomena

1

Modes of Translation

And every translator is to be regarded thus: that
he acts as mediator in this commerce of the mind,
making it his business to further this intellectual
exchange. For whatever one might say about the
inadequacy of translation, nevertheless it is and
will remain one of the most important and
worthy occupations in the general intertraffic
between peoples. — *Goethe*

I

There is a sad irony in the way translators protect themselves
and their art from humiliation. Like Flaubert, who sustained
the reputation of literature, at a time when its prestige was
threatened, by an endless grumble over the difficulties of the

'problème du style', they claim the immunity enjoyed by the virtuoso and the juggler and the acrobat and all those whose skills we at least recognize as being in themselves difficult. Running in advance of ridicule and indignity, they call out over their shoulders: 'Say what you like about what I do, you must surely admit it's not easy.' But whereas Flaubert was making a desperate tactical throw at a moment of crisis, translators have incorporated this manoeuvre into their permanent strategy; the status of their art, which is under perpetual threat, has been protected only by a sustained Flaubertian grumble about the problems, the difficulties, and indeed the impossibility of translation. Committed to this attitude, with one eye for ever on sentry-go, translators have inevitably left themselves with less than their full attention for pondering just what it is they are at.

True, it is not everyone who means to pluck at them with taunts and gibes. In a predominantly hostile world, they nevertheless have their friends and supporters who, while possibly deploring the misdirection of so much talent, nevertheless see in their activities a pardonable folly. 'Translation' as an act or process is admitted to have educative virtues as a mental discipline and has been granted the respectability of the examination paper. The practice of translating, even from English into Basic English,[1] has been recommended as a suitable initiation into the mysteries of semantics. And it is agreed that 'la version est l'exercice du style par excellence', that translation from a foreign tongue 'is the time-hallowed method of acquiring skill in the use of English' and one that our great writers have followed.

In the same safe and decorous way, society is quite ready to acknowledge the vaguer services of translation as a constituent of world culture. Respect is paid to the translator for his work in furthering international understanding, for his 'seeking to metamorphose strangers into acquaintances, acquaintances into friends, friendship into knowledge[2] and this world into a better world of men.' One joins with Goethe in gratitude for the stimulus which the translator gives to creative rivalry between nations and to intellectual barter between peoples.[3] One acknowledges his services towards the prevention of linguistic

decay, the conservation of language and — since 'every translation is commissioned, as it were, by the instinct for self-
preservation of a language community'[4] — the autonomy of
language taste. One welcomes his linguistic innovation, for 'it is
by means of translation that one language can be enriched by
others, can create unimagined new possibilities of linguistic
expression.'[5] And one salutes his work in literary eugenics,
preventing the danger of in-breeding by the importation of
ideas from abroad. These paths to the shrine of translation have
been trodden bare by heavy and purposeful pacing.

Nor is it rare for the translator to find his work judged
primarily by reference to his success or failure in respect of
these things. T.S. Eliot is seen rejecting Gilbert Murray's
translation of Euripides on the grounds that 'Greek poetry will
never have the slightest vitalizing effect on English poetry if it
can only appear masquerading as a vulgar debasement of the
eminently personal idiom of Swinburne.'[6] Not that such discussion is in any way improper; only that if we limit ourselves
to it, it is as though we might judge the merit of tables and
chairs purely in the light of the influence of carpentry on social
manners. We honour the ultimate and neglect the proximate.

Happy to see the translator as a self-educator pursuing
private gain, happy also to see him as a public servant contri-
buting to some remote community well-being, we are quick to
take refuge in perplexity when confronted with the individual
and concrete product of translation. Not always, admittedly,
but distressingly often. For many of the things we conveniently
classify as 'translation' — things queried by diplomats, commissioned by industry, or solicited by agencies — there is a ready
and tolerant understanding; they are recognized as being valuable to the extent that their ultimate results are valuable, results
that we can measure by the severely practical standards of
dividends, spheres of influence or production figures. They are
an inescapable part of our material civilization, opening a
market here, making a wheel go round there; and in this sense
there is no quarrel with Karl Vossler's claim that the purpose of
the overwhelming majority of translations is an economic
saving of labour.[7]

But when the talk is of poetry and imaginative literature, the discussion becomes clouded with a sediment of doubt, cynicism and scepticism. Even abuse is not unknown: 'Translation, sheer travesty! Translators, traitors! Give them a violet and they cast it into a crucible!' Harsh though this may be on a group of people dedicated by the very nature of things to a selfless task of doing their best by others, yet it is not so much the open hostility, the disparagement and depreciation, the charge of Philistinism, or the direct attack on personal integrity that has been so damaging to the standing of translation; rather it is the half-pitying, half-scornful attitude that informs the translator that *what he is trying to do is impossible.* The translator, whose own apologia is already aimed in this direction, is only too ready to agree — so ready, indeed, that there is scarcely translation published without some public wringing of hands, without some apologetic preface pleading the impossible nature of the undertaking. He admits to approaching his task as an 'inevitably unsuccessful exercise'; compromising, sacrificing, he is reconciled even before he starts to an ultimate falling short; judged by the highest standards (he pleads ingratiatingly) all translations are failures: 'The question is not, What translator is perfect?'[8] wrote Newman in reply to Matthew Arnold, 'but, Who is least imperfect?' Indeed, as von Humboldt put it, all translation is merely the vain attempt to solve an insoluble problem.[9]

This doctrine, the Doctrine of Imperfectibility as we might call it, has taken a firm hold on our ways of thinking about translation and deserves our best attention. Expressed in summary fashion, this doctrine is: that the impossibility of 'perfect' translation is the impossibility of reconciling the irreconcilable. It is accepted as axiomatic that a translation must stand in some distinct relationship to an original; that there must be some comparison, some putting together to see how one thing is like another and how unlike; that there must be some minimum essential quality that makes translation translation and not an adaptation, a variation on an original theme, a plagiarism or a completely independent composition. Let us call this thing Accuracy. On the other hand, a need is traditionally felt in translation for some minimum quality of elegance, some element of vitality, some ease of composition before translation can qualify for serious attention at all. Let us call this Grace. To achieve any high degree of Accuracy, the argument runs, is *necessarily* to write gracelessly; to produce genuine poetry is *necessarily* to play fast and loose with the original text. Which is paramount, it is forever being asked, and what combinations may we be permitted? Are we to make translation primarily accurate or primarily graceful? to make it literal with a certain admissible clumsiness, or sacrifice precision to ease and grace of composition? to be literal at all costs save that of absolute violence to our language, to strive to reproduce the known original, or to create for the reader the illusion of reading an original work? Because it is felt however that 'perfect' translation ought to possess both qualities in the highest degree, and because these qualities are considered to be by their nature in conflict and mutually exclusive, it is concluded that 'true' translation is impossible.

At times, a cynic might even feel that there is now only one accepted *point de départ* for any discussion of translation: remarking that the B.B.C. at one time introduced a new translation of *Faust* as something that 'reads and sounds more like some new masterpiece of English poetic drama than a translation of the greatest poem in German', and realizing that this is meant not as condemnation but as praise, he concludes therefore that that is best which seems to be anything but what it is, that the best translations are those that seem not to be translations. We make of 'translation' something that succeeds only if its proper demands are neglected. A line of thought is started which leads easily to the claim that the 'best' translations are the 'worst', and from there even more easily into delirium.

More than anything we lack a clear and unambiguous pronouncement on Accuracy, that which really makes translation what it is. The heritage of past theory shows a number of obsessions: with mysticism, with analogy, and with the delights of paronomasia. To address oneself to the 'psychic' aspects of language, to invest language with body and soul whereby in translation the soul remains but the body changes, or to hypostatize upper and lower levels (or inner and outer forms) of language, the one of which is and the other not 'translatable' — these are invitations best declined. To assert that translation is

15

like an engraving or a drawing after the life,[10] or a pouring out of spirit (whereby some essence will evaporate) is diverting and even in some special way enlightening, but alien to a sober curiosity. To juggle with meaning, to claim for example that 'nothing moves without translation' and then attach all sorts of consequences to *verbal* translation is to play a semantic parlour game. Exhortations to commonsense, moreover, smothering the affair with phrases, neither define nor necessarily even clarify our ideas of Accuracy: 'Be faithful, neither deviating, amplifying nor falsifying ... Be neither baldly verbatim nor periphrastic ... Be correct ... Be true to the original in quantity as well as quality ... Make the translation commensurate with the original ... Give the letter where possible but in any case the spirit ... Respect the individuality of the author ...' The terms used and their explanations have a drowsy appeal and wear an air of conviction; but they stifle discussion; they trade on the fact that they are assured of a favourable welcome and incline us to forget that they contribute more to our gratification than to our enlightenment. 'Let us commit any blasphemy of laughter and criticism,' says one of Virginia Woolf's characters, 'rather than exude this lily-sweet glue.'

Before we can begin systematically to attack or defend our assumptions, we need first to lay them bare. This act of exposure is probably the most difficult part of any investigation. Using for the moment the most general of terms, we might say that the pursuit of Accuracy has meant the search for an equivalent 'content' or 'sense'. This is not to say that translators have been satisfied with what might be called the merely substantial meaning, i.e. that which is common to 'Shut the door' and 'The wooden guardian of our privacy Quick on its axle turn', wherein it appears there in shirt-sleeves and braces and here in a Sunday best. In seeking Accuracy, translators have generally been at pains to respect both the substantive and the stylistic meaning; and these, it is suggested, are best served by taking the words one by one and finding and arranging their separate equivalents. 'By a translation', write Ritchie and Moore, 'we mean such a version as shall before all things make it plain that the translator (i) has grasped the sense of *each individual word* as used in the original (ii) has selected to

16

render *it* the nearest equivalent which the genius of our language permits, and (iii) has so arranged and welded together these equivalents that the whole becomes an exact English counterpart of the French passage . . .'[11] [my italics].

Let us break into the tangle of thought and opinion at this point and follow the thread through the various refinements of 'word-for-word' accuracy, from the 'literal' onwards, before we ask whether there is room for other alternatives.

II

It will help our reconstruction of the meaning most usually attached to Literal Accuracy if we use the common spatial image of 'keeping close', whereby (it is said) the closer we approach the greater is the accuracy as also the clumsiness, while the more 'distant' we are the more likely are we to write genuine poetry but only at the expense of accuracy. It is this territory between extreme proximity and extreme distance that has been so confusedly and strenuously mapped. Von Humboldt, who saw Accuracy and Grace as two cliffs threatening destruction, denied that there was any navigable way between them. Most reports however tell of an area of acceptable compromise, close but not too close to the original, where the translator is able to reproduce his original not *exactly* — for that is held to be impossible — but most nearly. The crux of the argument comes with the identification of 'literalness' as the point where the approach is closest, a literal translation then being — according to an extraordinarily interesting definition by J.P.Postgate — 'the nearest intelligible rendering of the words of the foreign original whether it would have been employed in the circumstances by a native writer or not.'[12] It is not then that 'literal' translation is in some way *over*-accurate, any more than 'free' translation is *over*-poetic. Literalness is rather considered to be the nearest approach to an ideal accuracy, acceptable in respect of its precision even if unacceptable on other grounds.

Such a definition invites us to picture the translator free to move along the path of Accuracy, approaching ever nearer, but seeming to encounter a series of check-points through which he may pass only by surrendering part of his freedom to act in a manner appropriate in other respects to the occasion. Thus, if his business is with poetry, he wishes 'in the circumstances' to write poetry in translation; but the arrangement of things is apparently such that, beyond a certain point, he can come closer to his original only by writing un-poetry. Stefan George has been accused of taking these extra steps beyond the bar in his translation of Shakespeare's sonnets. His work, it is said, contains 'all the absurdities that result from an unchecked invasion of imaginative realm by the rationalistic precept of "literal" translation':[13]

> Music to hear, why hear'st thou music sadly?
> Sweets with sweets war not, joy delights in joy . . .

> Musik dem ohr, was hörst du musik traurig?
> Süss kämpft mit süss nicht, lust ist froh mit lust . . .

The couplet does not entirely outrage the conventions of language but the translator has nevertheless written something which, all things considered, is judged unsuited to the occasion, in that he has rendered great poetry by verse which, whilst acceptable as German, is unacceptable as poetry. If the translation then approaches 'nearer' his original, he meets a second barrier in Idiom. Confronted with, shall we say, 'j'ai faim' or 'Sehr geehrter Herr Direktor', he is prevented from going beyond 'I am hungry' or 'Dear sir' unless he agrees to surrender his credentials as an idiomatic writer; whereupon he is then able to achieve the 'closeness' of 'I have hunger' or 'Very honoured Mr. Director'. Ultimately he reaches the last frontier, namely that marked Intelligibility. Beyond it he can enter a region where he is nearer than ever before but only at the expense of being almost or completely unintelligible, of writing English that is not-English. Margaret Schlauch quotes the following as an 'extremely literal' translation:

Die Vollständigkeit der Formen des nicht realen

Bewusstseins wird sich durch die Notwendigkeit des Fortganges und Zusammenhanges selbst ergeben.

The fullstandingness of the forms of the not-real beknowingness gives itself through the needturningness of the forwardgoing and the togetherhanging itself.[14]

The objection to these representative literal translations is then, as I interpret it, not that they are 'too close' in themselves, but that they are variously 'too close to be intelligible', 'too close to be idiomatic', and 'too close to be poetic'. They are, to go back once more to Professor Postgate, renderings which *in the circumstances* a native writer would not have written. But although inappropriate or incommensurate, they are all nevertheless regarded as having this in common: being 'literal', they are by definition all 'closer' than they would otherwise have been.

But *how* are they closer? What is the element common to them all that would explain their 'literalness'? Is there a consistent theory of meaning at hand to account for the 'nearness' of these three examples? What basis is there for thinking that 'needturningness' would — if it were not unintelligible — be nearer to 'Notwendigkeit' than 'necessity' is? Or that 'Very honoured Mr. Director' is a nearer translation than 'Dear sir'? Or George's lines nearer than, say, those of Karl Kraus:

Der selbst Musik hat, dich verstimmt Musik?
Dein süsses Wesen weigert sich der Süssen . . .

lines which, according to the same critic as above, have 'a richness and a beauty . . . which Stefan George's verses lack, but it is the beauty of a free rendering, . . . not of translation'?[15]

To arrive at these variously literal versions, the translators have plainly taken an integrated utterance of greater or less complexity and split it up into smaller constituent elements: the word 'Notwendigkeit' into the parts 'Not', 'wendig' and 'keit'; the phrase of address 'Sehr geehrter Herr Direktor' into its separate words; and so on. The motives underlying this are doubtless well-intentioned; and even Ritchie and Moore have, as we have seen, allowed into their statements phrases that seem at some levels to encourage if not prescribe exactly this: grasp the sense of each individual word (they write) and render it by the nearest equivalent. Possibly it is felt that each part on its own can then be observed more closely, more dispassionately; that this achieves a simplification whereby the parts will yield their true significance more easily in isolation than in a clutter of other words. But the breaking up of utterances in this way can only achieve precisely the opposite effect to that seemingly intended: a single word on its own is an infinitely less precise thing than the same word in a sentence; and an isolated sentence more diffuse than the same sentence in a poem. Instead of clarifying and simplifying the meanings of the separate parts, this act of dissection only obscures and complicates them.

'Not', when removed from its setting within the word 'Notwendigkeit', acquires in place of a specific and concrete context one which is completely generalized and conventionalized, one which is more comprehensive but essentially vaguer and yet which is felt in some way really 'belongs'. This new context offers itself as one associated in some loose way with the idea of urgently requiring something, or of lacking something, or of wanting some relief; with states or situations that are difficult or critical or perilous; with conditions of constraint or compulsion or destitution. The English word that best seems to fit this wider amalgam of contexts is judged to be the word 'need', and is accordingly selected as the 'nearest' rendering of 'Not' for whatever linguistic context it may appear in. The same procedure lifts 'geehrter' out of its environmental 'Sehr ... Herr Direktor', removes it from its implicit situational context of correspondence-by-letter, and establishes its wider associations with certain intrinsic affections or personal attitudes derived from the opinions or feelings of others, with the dignity of the individual, with marks of esteem and the paying of compliments, with the expression of regard, with various ceremonial. The more specific association with the paying of initial respects in letter-writing is not entirely absent from this more diffuse context, but it is at best only one small and remote part of it. But because 'honoured' seems to be the best verbal complement to these ideas, we persuade ourselves that it is the 'nearest' translation of 'geehrter' in all circumstances.

Every branch of linguistic science, however, insists at every turn on one thing: that a word acquires meaning only within a concrete linguistic and situational context. 'What a word means is the missing parts of the contexts from which it draws its delegated efficacy' is I.A.Richards' way of putting it.[16] 'Semantics . . . recognizes meaning as inherent in an entire context, not as the property of a word itself' stated the American MLA Committee on Research Activities.[17] And J.R.Firth has insisted that 'the use of the word meaning is subject to the general rule that each word when used in a new context is a new word.'[18] Both the immediate linguistic context as well as the wider social and cultural context do not therefore distract, they define. They *are* the meaning, or at least determine a large part of it.

Two elementary examples may show how this affects our criterion of Accuracy. Part of the meaning attaching to a word by virtue of its linguistic context has been aptly called 'meaning by collocation': a mode of meaning not directly concerned with the concept symbolized but which is rather 'an abstraction at the syntagmatic level'.[19] Thus, where there is habitual collocation of one word with another — say, 'silly' with 'ass' or 'dark' with 'night' — one of the *meanings* of a word is its 'collocability' with certain others. If we apply this test to 'Herr Braun' in German and 'Mr. Brown' in English, we find in the case of the former there is habitual collocation with 'Sehr geehrter'; but that in the latter case 'Mr. Brown' has no habitual collocation with 'Very honoured' — at least not today — but rather with 'Dear'. A greater accuracy of equivalence at this level of meaning is therefore obtained by a translation palpably unliteral.

Let us take as our second example the word 'Läufer' in German. Since it may be used in a variety of contexts and situations, it is capable of bearing a variety of meanings, say *a, b, c, d, e*. The literal translation in English, working to the principles sketched above, would be 'runner', with a fairly close identity of meaning in the case, say, of *a, b,* and *c*. In a chess manual, however, where 'Läufer' is used in sense *d* the appropriate English word to fit its contexts would be 'bishop', which itself in different contexts is capable of bearing other meanings *p,q,r*. And for sense *e*, the appropriate English word might be 'half-back' or 'sweeper', which is itself also capable of other meanings *x,y,z* outside the football field:

Läufer *a b c d e*
Runner *a b c*
Bishop *d . . . p q r*
Half-back *e* . . . *x y z*

First, then, we may note that the question 'What is the translation of "Läufer"' is an improper one, and that we should rather, with greater justification, ask for its translation *in this or that context*. Secondly, there is no reason for claiming that 'runner', because it happens in a numerical majority of cases to fit those situational contexts for which 'Läufer' is the appropriate complement, is therefore *the* translation or even the most accurate. In other words, we must not fall into the error of regarding 'bishop' or 'half-back' as 'free renderings' deficient in accuracy. Thirdly, all senses of the word 'Läufer' — or even of words like 'esprit', 'Gemütlichkeit', 'Stimmung' or 'home' — are not necessarily *always* present in our minds whenever the word is used: the night clubs at three in the morning are full of people talking of 'home' in terms quite devoid of complex overtones. We might do well then to pause before always dismissing them as 'untranslatable'.

When we turn to the literal translation of a poem, the difference is surely only one of degree. From a literalness that translates the syllable without reference to the word, or the word without reference to the phrase or sentence, we progress to that form of literalness which translates the sentence without reference to the poem. But we have insisted that the separate parts of an utterance mean what they mean essentially by virtue of the roles they play within a more or less complex unity; and the unity of, say, a Shakespearian sonnet is no less tightly integrated than that of, say, a compound word. The view that the whole — whether that whole be a word, a sentence or a poem — is merely a summation of its discrete elements forms a very rickety foundation on which to build one's views of

Accuracy in translation.

'Literal' procedure has its uses, of course; but we do well to recognize what those uses are and what they are not. It is essentially a procedure that serves as a kind of guide to the linguistic habits of other nations, informing us in an oblique way that in a certain situation the foreign language will use a word loosely linked with one sort of associational cluster, whereas in English the appropriate word is part of an entirely different cluster. But we must not expect anything other than clumsiness and it is superfluous to remark on it.

The point that needs the strongest emphasis, then, is not that literal translation is 'bad', nor that for practical purposes literal translation should be avoided — since in any case it generally is — but that *we should not set up Literalness as a standard by which to judge the fidelity of a translation*, that we should not posit a 'literal' version as an ideal of accuracy to be approached as near as we may decently venture. That way lies misunderstanding, frustration and in the last resort despair. It must be clearly recognized that if, in the act of literal translation, the artificially fabricated contexts erected round the separate bits of the original are heterogeneous and imperfectly integrated, so the words or groups of words in the new medium that separately fit these contexts will be inconsistent one with another. The resulting 'accuracy' is unacceptable not because it happens to possess a certain awkwardness of expression but because it is positively false. It is the result of trying to translate one *set of words* into another without any reference to what one might loosely call the reality behind the words. Not only are the values of each individual word falsely determined but the close interdependence of word upon word is entirely neglected. Indeed the resulting awkwardness is surely the direct consequence of this falsity.

To allow oneself to accept any such concept of Accuracy as an ideal, and then to approach it as nearly as 'elegance' or 'idiom' or 'linguistic convention' or 'intelligibility' will allow, is to perpetuate a doctrine of meaning long since exploded.

III

It is of course an excessively naive approach to the problems of translation which assumes that meaning is always conceptual, that words function only as a substitute for pointing. In any purely referential use of language — if indeed such an abstraction ever exists in practice — an equivalence in meaning between utterances in different languages is almost always possible. Even the seeming disparity between what are generally called 'primitive' and 'sophisticated' languages appears not to be of very great consequence at this level of meaning. We have, for example, the testimony of Sapir, who was convinced that the language of a primitive society 'inevitably forms as sure, complete and potentially creative an apparatus of referential symbolism as the most sophisticated language that we know of.'[20] It is not absurd to say, he goes on, 'that both Hottentot and Eskimo possess all the formal apparatus that is required to serve as matrix for the expression of Kant's thought.'[21] Where equivalence in meaning at *this* level is not possible, it is generally not difficult to see why; and the problem is the comparatively simple one of comparing the respective powers of symbolic reference of the two languages.

Anyone who feels he must look for a *precise* equivalent between *precise* symbols is however doomed to disappointment. 'All language is more or less vague' said Bertrand Russell; and the great majority of our verbal symbols in their conventional use have a 'fringe' round their area of meaning where their application is doubtful. The word 'chair', for example, quite apart from the separate meanings it may acquire by virtue of its contexts — a 'chair of philosophy', to 'take the chair', and so on — is, as H.G. Wells showed, essentially a vague word: 'Think of arm chairs and reading chairs and dining room chairs and kitchen chairs, chairs that pass into benches, chairs that cross the boundary and become settees, dentists' chairs, thrones, opera stalls, seats of all sorts, those miraculous fungoid growths that cumber the floor of the arts and crafts exhibitions, and you will perceive what a lax bundle in fact is this simple straightforward term.'[22] When we consider that 'chaise' and 'Stuhl' and 'silla' and 'sedia' are all equally 'lax' but not necessarily so in the same way, it becomes obvious that any comparison between them will be at two removes from precision. We probably need in any blueprint of translation theory some concept similar to the engineer's 'tolerance', some term to describe that state of affairs where there are similarities that are fundamental and differences that are irrelevant, some limits of imprecision within which there is a satisfactory functioning.

An equal claim — indeed many would say in the case of poetry, a greater claim — on the translator comes with the realization that an utterance may not merely refer, it may also *move*. Traditional theory has frequently put this point with varying degrees of explicitness: that since 'poetry has upon the mind of man an unmistakable effect . . . it is that effect which the translator must attempt, half despairingly, to reproduce';[23] that 'a translation from French into English should produce upon an Englishman an impression as far as possible similar to that which the French original produces upon a Frenchman';[24] that 'translation is arousing in the English reader or hearer the identical emotions and sentiments that were aroused in him who read or heard the sentence as his native tongue.'[25]

No sooner is the discussion one of 'emotional response' than we are confronted with one of the crucial problems of linguistic analysis: the problem of Referential and Emotive meaning, and especially the relationship between them. This dichotomy or one something like it — symbolic and emotive, informative and dynamic, representative and expressive, cognitive and reflective, manipulative and declarative, enunciative and precative, positive and imaginative — lies at the base of most modern theories of communication; and this is not the place to debate them.[26] But they must necessarily obtrude into any deeper discussion of translation theory. There is nothing novel in the discovery that the 'tone' of the native word is rarely the same as the 'tone' of the foreign word of which it is the referential translation. We are alive to the fact that different nations, races and times have shown different attitudes to certain things: hospitality in Euripides and eroticism in Lucian do not mean the same to us as to the Greeks; eating is regarded among some peoples with displeasure, forgiveness considered ignoble. If we then *refer* to hospitality or eroticism or eating or forgiveness in

25

the English of here and now, the impression or emotional response cannot but be different. An adequate translation of the referential meaning might therefore conceivably be grossly 'unfaithful' to the emotive meaning.

But the argument can bear pushing along a little further. Suppose we say that the main function of much language is not the giving of information but rather 'the raising of some passion, the exciting to or determining from an action, the putting the mind in some particular disposition';[27] suppose we go further and say that these things are directly stimulated by 'the perception of certain words, without any ideas coming between',[28] that 'many arrangements of words evoke attitudes without any reference between required *en route*',[29] and that 'a good deal of poetry and even some great poetry exists . . . in which the sense of the words can be almost entirely missed or neglected without loss.'[30] Then at once the problem for the translator is a different one. It is no longer, Why is the 'tone' of my 'translation' inevitably different from that of the original? but rather, Am I occasionally justified in employing a different referential symbolism in order to obtain equivalence in this all-important emotive meaning?

The mechanics implicit in this process at least seem feasible. George Rylands, who it is true was comparing not different languages but the same language at different stages of development, came to the conclusion that the *emotional* equivalent to the 'milk-white' of the ballads would for the Elizabethans be 'white-as-snow',[31] i.e., emotional equivalence is reached by means of different reference. And if the principle be thus conceded, the problem is then how widely it may be applied. May we, in a suitable context, translate the German 'Zimmerlinde' by the English 'aspidistra', knowing that the botany is all wrong but that national attitudes, associational complexes and so on are in their cases not dissimilar? And dare we, in certain extreme cases, write 'Thames' for 'Seine' on the grounds that although the geography is wrong the national affections are comparable? We have, after all, at various times seen Ibsen transplanted to Scotland and Chekhov to Ireland; might there not be more in this than the arbitrary whim of the translator?

A parallel form of argument might be applied to the third

kind of 'meaning' — or group of 'meanings' — inherent in words: that which derives from their nature as *things* with physical properties of their own. If we admit that there are 'forms of lyric poetry in which the auditory content and the rhythm are its chief reason for being';[32] if we agree that there 'are poets who aim at creating sheer word-music, who use words not indirectly as symbols of meaning but immediately as musical notes';[33] then strictly speaking we must recognize a form of translation that goes all out for equivalence of sound and lets the sense go hang. With this as our premiss, the argument becomes an appealing one: (i) all conventional language has both sense and sound; (ii) in a technical report, the vowel and consonantal qualities are without intrinsic significance, so the translator concentrates on the sense; (iii) in some poetry (it seems), the references can be neglected, so the translator addresses himself exclusively to the sound.

'Equivalence' of expressive sound must not of course be confused with 'identity' of sound. An exact repetition of the sequence of consonants and vowels would leave the original text as it was, i.e. untranslated; nor is it even the nearest possible approach to 'identity' of sound that a (perhaps nonsensical) string of native words will allow, as though 'Paddle your own canoe' were to be rendered 'Pas d'elles yeux haut ne que nous'; nor even a proper and conventional statement with as many of the original sounds in as much of their original sequence as ingenuity will allow. Even on the level of purely phonetic meaning, even in the case of onomatopoeia, there are differences in expressive sound between nations; to German ears, the cock crows to the sound of 'i', in England to 'oo'. And on what has been called the phonaesthetic level of meaning — that which has to do with 'the association of sounds and personal and social attitudes'[34] — it is undoubtedly true that that word which by virtue of its sound is felt to be particularly appropriate in its original setting may need translating (in terms of expressive sound) by a word with a quite different phonetic structure.[35] It is enough for the present that we draw the obvious conclusion: when we seek to criticize a translation, it is not always a valid reproach to select certain concatenations of sound quality in the original and remark on their absence in the translation.

It is generally agreed however that language rarely, if ever, functions exclusively on one level of meaning. Poetry in particular seeks to operate simultaneously and often ambiguously on a number of different levels — phonetic, phonological, phonaesthetic, collocative, emotive and referential — where the references assist in the evocation of emotion, where our attitudes are directed to certain things, and where the expressiveness of the sound both reinforces and is reinforced by these other functions. Sound and sense, it is then said, are structurally united and essentially indivisible. Stylistic devices, whether of classical rhetoric or modern semantics, are held to be intrinsic to the meaning rather than merely decorative. The pattern of the words, within which is included also what we earlier called Grace, *is* the meaning.

There seems now, in theory, nothing to prevent the translator, using the more sensitive instruments of modern linguistic analysis, from determining all the meanings of all the individual words. He may know the 'head-meanings' — the term is of course Empson's — of the words, and he may even by inductive inspection of their particular contexts discover also their esoteric meanings at the various levels in the poem. Why not then, like Louis MacNeice, set up as our ideal some hypothetic version that satisfies our demands of equivalence at all levels of meaning?

Ideally, what would the translator of a poem such as *Faust* wish to achieve? His first aim would be a broad pattern, a balance of masses, equivalent to that of the original . . . Then he would wish to achieve the following: (1) a literal faithfulness (denotation as distinct from connotation) — all the prose meanings of the German words to be brought out in English without addition or subtraction; (2) a connotative faithfulness — all the poetic colour, the suggestiveness, of all the German words to reappear in English in their identical shades and with no loss of lustre; (3) a line for line translation . . . ; (4) the retaining of the *order* of the words in general, and of images in particular . . . ;(5) an exact equivalent of the rhythmical patterns of the original; (6) an exact equivalent of the rhyme patterns; (7) an exact equivalent of what has been called the 'texture' (the sequence of consonants and vowels).[36]

Mr. MacNeice knew of course that his ideal of translation cannot possibly be achieved, and said so; his is simply the despairing cry of one who wants all things changed and yet nothing changed. He can separate out all the different bits of meaning and lay them side by side on the table, but he knows there is no one way of re-combining their English 'equivalents' into one coherent unit. When it comes then to the practical business of turning German into English, he is content if (shall we say) he makes an over-all average of 70% with not less than 50% on any one count.

His approach to translation is in some ways analogous to the Naturalist theory of literature. Art, said Arno Holz in Germany, ever tends to become Nature, and *does* become it in so far as the medium and the artist's skill permit. The equation 'Art = Nature-x' is the critical standard by which it is proper to judge, the greatest art then being found with minimal values for 'x'. Mr. MacNeice's mode of translation appears to assume an equation of similar pattern, namely 'Translation=Original-x'; and just as Naturalist art strives to reproduce but can never actually become identical with Nature, so translation strives to reproduce but can never actually become the original. The intransigence of the new medium exerts a steady inflationary force on 'x', and 'x' can be kept within limits only by the skill and ingenuity of the translator. The making of translations, it is then suggested, is a maddening puzzle, a challenge to ingenuity, like a game where one possibility is always being sacrificed to another and where the theoretical maximum score is never reached.

At a practical level, it seems that we disregard the intrusive 'x' in the equation only at the risk of psychological inhibition. The stutter that Karl Vossler fell victim to is surely the outward sign of this intellectual malady:

If we attempt to analyse (the) inner language form, we

see it as the form of language on the one side, and as sentiment or as inner meaning on the other. But nowhere are we able to find the crucial point at which the one passes over into the other; for the concept of the inner language form is precisely this identity of speech and meaning. Here translation is at an end. The inner language form is untranslatable, true, and always unique. The being that, in the external language form is called *cavallo* by an Italian and *horse* by an Englishman, in the inner sphere is an actual horse to the Englishman and an actual *cavallo* to the Italian, who here and now enunciates the name and means it to express something that has a meaning. That is to say, the name of the horse-being is by no means identical with the image, the picture, or even the concept of 'horse', but, if I may say so, it is the 'horse-horse'.[37]

Translation is thus indeed 'at an end'. If one demands that translation is to have the identical meaning of the original, and if one additionally insists on 'the identity of speech and meaning', then the original meaning is retained only by retaining the original speech, i.e. by not translating at all. How much more satisfactory for translators, he seems to suggest, if only the English and Italian names for the horse-being were not different, if only we of the different nations shared not merely the same concepts and images but also the same linguistic symbols for them. What purity of translation if only English were Italian and not English.

To deny merit to translation — to deny certain formulations even the right to call themselves translation — simply because there is not equivalence *in all respects at once* is a facile yet much practised perversion of criticism. Even reputable scholarship is not always entirely free from its taint: 'As soon as one has advanced beyond the first rudiments of a language,' wrote Louis H. Gray 'one begins to paraphrase: French *il y a* ('it has there') and German *es giebt* ('it gives'), where *a* and *giebt* are really impersonal, are in essence equivalent in meaning to but not translations of, English *there is (are)*.'[38] Move away from the literal 'it has there' (why not 'it there has'?) and you 'begin

to paraphrase' and forfeit the right to call 'there is' a translation. Scratch the surface of much of what passes for translation criticism today and one finds evidence of the fussy and
dogmatic Naturalist: 'Here is the so-and-so and the so-and-so
of the original,' he is fond of writing, 'but where is the so-and-
so?', as he picks his points from a list something like Mr.
MacNeice's. There will always be something different, something 'lacking' in the translation; and where the critic cannot
account for *all* things, there is little virtue in his dismissing the
translator out of hand or his reaching for the label marked
'untranslatable' in the mistaken impression that he is being
generous. The opportunities for irresponsible criticism are
limitless.

Mr. MacNeice's approach to the problem of translation is
therefore such that, in the words of Harley Granville-Barker,
one must 'decide what choice . . . one has, what it will be better
however regrettedly to lose, and what it is essential to
preserve.'[39] This the 'sacrifice', this the 'falling short' that must
be borne with because it is in the nature of things; this the
'impossibility' of 'true' translation. That such an ideal *is* impossible is not disputed; what is of greater interest is *how* it is
impossible. It is not the impossibility of running a three-minute
mile or writing the Lord's Prayer on a pin-head, where the skill
of the individual alone sets a limit to our achievement. Nor is it
even the impossibility of finding an exact value for '*pi*', so as to
fulfil one single external condition, namely that the product of
it and D should equal C. In kind, it is more like the impossibility of constructing a regular decahedron, of making a solid
body with ten uniform and regular surfaces. To fling several
conflicting conditions together in this way is to launch a purely
'noumenal' definition; and to criticize the translator for failing
to satisfy them all at once is as though we were to belabour the
geometer for having some surfaces too few or too lop-sided.
But then geometers very soon gave up looking for this non-
existent and non-existible thing; why should we then condemn
our translators to an eternity of similarly fruitless search?

It would surely be much more profitable then if we were to
quit all stale discussion of whether or not translation has
'travestied' the original because (inevitably) it is not equivalent

31

in all respects at once, and sought rather to say what we can about the 'x' quantity that must necessarily be reckoned with in this mode of translation — a quantity that is inseparable from any change in linguistic medium.

IV

Common to all these modes of translation is a procedure that devotes itself to an examination of individual words. A poem, it is claimed, is after all but a particular choice and arrangement of words. It is then the function of the translator to understand the meanings of these words, find suitable equivalents, and so arrange his own choice as to fulfil as many of the separate conditions as he is able. Argument in the past has generally concerned itself with the tactics of this undertaking; there may however also be room for questioning the wider strategy, for asking if we want translation to try to be like the original *in this way*.

Briefly, literal translation sees a poem as a plurality of discrete units, discursive translation (exemplified by Mr. MacNeice) as a summation of related units. The immediate objection is that the separate words in a poem are not merely symbols in contextual settings but are themselves equally contexts for each other, modifying each other and combining with each other to provoke a coherent response, so that the significance of the poem is always more than the sum of each separate signification, no matter how carefully these separate significations are determined; that the unity inherent in the poem may be so complete that to attempt to break it down into its constituent elements would, like the breaking down of a compound word, only lead us along the path towards literal, i.e. bogus, accuracy.

The objection may be put more astringently thus: may we not be mistaken when we assume that there is some unchanging and accessible thing of words, something we call 'the poem', which will allow itself to be fed through translation processes like those earlier described? A Crocean aesthetic, for example, would insist that 'works of art exist only in the minds that create or re-create them';[40] and it has been said that 'for art — and for aesthetics generally — objects do not exist, but only experiences.'[41] Should we not then rather say that a poem, being not a continuing *existent* but rather a permanent *possibility*,[42] becomes a poem only when it has been emotionally and synoptically experienced, and that any 'meaning' that may attach to it is inseparably connected with the events leading up to and away from it,[43] with the experiences of — to use Samuel Butler's terms — the sayer and the sayee.

For some translators this is no real problem; their defence is that they assume not an *impersonal* meaning but an *interpersonal* one. Like the lawyers with their 'reasonable' man and the economists with their 'average' man, they find it convenient to deal in terms of a normal reader whose interpretation of the symbols results in a signification shared by a majority of readers. This they accept as a norm, a genuinely interpersonal meaning; and they conclude that personal idiosyncrasies can without disaster be neglected. If on the other hand we pay strict attention to the objection and say, with Bloomfield, that 'the occurrence of a speech . . . and the whole course of practical events before and after it depend upon the entire life-history of the speaker and the hearer',[44] we are justified in supposing that the 'meaning' for two different hearers of the same utterance may well vary in proportion to the significant differences between their respective life-histories.

Lest it be supposed that these differences are always negligible in successful communication, we have but to remember the well-known divergent interpretations given by two suitably qualified readers to the closing lines of the Fifth Sonnet of Wordsworth's River Duddon series: the one which saw the last sentence 'as saying that the gloom of lonely nature, of sullen moss and craggy ground, however it might seem later on in life, had no oppressive effect upon the children'; and the other as saying that 'however barren and gloomy might be the scene, actually lonely nature there itself had no such character.'[45] These 'meanings' are so widely separate that if they were to be translated, recast in a different language, it is highly improbable that they would bear any great resemblance to each other.

On the same grounds, we must acknowledge the possibility of an equally great divergence between the sayer's 'meaning' and the 'meaning' that any sayee might give to it. This discontinuity of language, which is a problem even at the level of referential communication, assumes even greater proportions when the occasion is one of poetic utterance, where the 'meanings' are even more unstable. There is the meaning for one's own self, the meaning for others, and the meaning the author intended it to have; and there is no reason to suppose that in the case of poetry these will ever be identical or necessarily even very similar.[46] Since in these stricter terms we can never properly talk about *the* meaning, so we can never talk about *the* translation; there will inevitably be different translations deriving from different meanings, all of them perhaps equally valid but none of them an 'ideal' or a 'true' one.

This approach to the problems of translation might with some truth be called pragmatic in the sense that the total meaning of the poem is determined by reference to its function, that the poem is held to have a cause and effect of which it is the embodiment and only thus to have significance. Corresponding to this 'facing both ways' quality of the poem are two further modes of translation: the semasiological, where the meaning of the poem is taken as the effect it has on the *hearer* and where the act of translation consists in the hearer's making that which is provoked in him the cause of a further utterance in a new linguistic medium; and the onomasiological,[47] where the meaning is taken as that which the *speaker* is trying to communicate — some reference, emotion, experience, attitude, goings-on in the mind, or whatever it might be — and where the act of translation consists in repeating the genesis of the utterance with the substitution of one linguistic medium for another.

The objections to the first-mentioned kind of pragmatic translation are too well known to need lengthy rehearsal here. Wherever the hearer's meaning, in the sense of the total effect the poem has on him, is allowed to form itself freely and naturally in the new medium, there is unquestionably a very real danger of his producing not an equivalent poem but a meta-poem, i.e. a poem about a poem. If we characterize the original poem as a piece of declarative language expressing the effect on the speaker of his environment, then certainly translation is equally so, but the environment in the latter case is then not the concrete reality of experience but the aesthetic experience of Art. Too much of the translator himself is allowed in, it is said;[48] we run the danger of encouraging ungoverned subjectivism, for it is precisely when the translator responds most vigorously to the original poem that his own personality tends to reveal itself in what he writes. The end-result is then something that Vossler has called 'histrionic interpreting'[49] rather than anything properly deserving the name of translation.

There have been suggestions that a more satisfactory control might be established over the translator's intrusive personality by requiring him to make his interpretation of the poem not the *datum* of his version but the *aim* of it, by asking that there should be equivalence not between the original's effect and translation's cause, but between their respective effects; that, as Valéry put it, 'traduire, c'est reconstituer au plus près l'effet d'une certaine cause.' But the very making of this demand assumes that the translator, in formulating his new utterance, can predetermine and control the response of his readers. Indeed it seems to impose not merely an unorthodox but even an impossible function on language, in that it denies to the translator's initial stimulus the right to form itself naturally in language and instead demands that this stimulus must somehow so adapt itself that, when formulated, it will tend to produce some predetermined effect.

The problems are no less disconcerting in onomasiological mode. The character of this sort of translation is unique in that, in laboratory jargon, the variables are reduced to their severest minimum: it postulates a completely bilingual poet who, keeping constant his personality, mood, point in time and the thing he is endeavouring to express, writes the 'same' poem in two different languages. In short, it envisages genetic processes identical in all respects save that of linguistic medium. It is an approach to translation that is at least as old as Dryden, who in the *Preface to Sylvae* (1685) hoped the critics would feel that if the poet 'were living, and an Englishman, they [the expressions] are such as he wou'd probably have written.' And in our day, James Forsyth was bold enough to adopt this principle for his translation of Ibsen's *Brand*, and stated his creed thus:

> It is, on the best grounds, sheer nonsense to hope that poetry of one language will translate into poetry of another with any high degree of parallelism in the texts . . . In art any approach to the activity of copying seems to keep one's eye on the thing copied and not on the sources from which the original has sprung — which are the sources of vitality. It seemed it might be better *not* to try to imitate the thing — the text — but to imitate the human process — Ibsen's creation of it.[50]

But unless we know what in fact does happen in cases of simultaneous composition, we can have no secure standards to judge by. We must beware of taking a blind jump into pure theory. Specimens of such work must necessarily be rare, for even if we find a poet sufficiently competent to undertake composition in two different languages his poems will be inadmissible if one of them is merely the result at some later point in time of a translation which is literal or 'word-for-word' in inspiration. There are however scraps of circumstantial evidence here and there which are disturbing in their implications. After studying an English translation of one of his novels, Julien Green is reported to have praised the beauty and fidelity of the translator's work but confessed that had he written originally in English, the novel would have been an altogether different thing. When Albert Schweizer re-wrote in German his own book on Bach, which had originally been written in French, the resulting work was different in many ways and almost double its original length. Rilke, who possessed considerable poetic facility in French, did in fact experiment with simultaneous composition of this kind and we find in his correspondence evidence of his amazed reaction: 'Several times I attempted the same theme in French and German, and to my astonishment it developed on different lines in the two languages . . .'[51] His further remark — that this 'would seem to indicate that translations are not natural' — is an unexpected commentary on what we have come to expect conventional translation to be like.

The hostile analogy employed by Schleiermacher against such procedures as these is well known: Show me what the poem would have been like if the author had written in a different tongue, he expostulates, and I would be as grateful as if you had shown me the picture of a man as he would have looked if his mother had begotten him by a different father.

And yet is this not also just a little mischievous? Is it not also born of the desire to see all and yet nothing changed? If, as it seems we must in view of Rilke's evidence, we admit that language plays an active and formative part in poetic composition, can we still make demands on translation that assume precisely the contrary: that language is a passive and inert thing waiting to receive the stamp of the poet's inspiration?

Some consideration of what these 'different lines' were for Rilke — and what sort of thing we might therefore expect from any other exercise in this mode of translation — commends itself as something that modern linguistic scholarship might profitably concern itself with. Merely to assert that Rilke himself was 'different' when he wrote and thought in French is only a graceful way of dismissing the problem; it leads us into the same barren land we reach by wondering whether John drunk is the 'same' person as John sober. More forbidding but also potentially more rewarding is to re-state the problem as part of a wider question in aesthetic theory: to ask not so much how the medium affects the personality of the artist but rather how it functions in the creative act as a whole.

Let us, as a provisional aid to understanding, adopt an idea from Dewey and suppose that language in communication is capable of acting either as a *vehicle* or as a *medium*;[52] and then to these two categories add a third of our own — that it may also function as an *exhibit*. Where language is used as in a technical report, where the end — the conveying of the substantial or referential meaning — is the whole importance, where it is immaterial if other adequate means (pointing, demonstrating, etc.) are substituted, where the words are merely a kind of scaffolding to order and direct the thought, then language is what might be called a vehicle. We might therefore say, with Hönigswald,[53] that the 'thing' expressed belongs intrinsically to no language, not because it is something independent of each and every language but rather because it is a function of all possible languages. True, even at this level of meaning, an utterance may be linked indivisibly with the language 'within' which it is conceived; but the 'thing' expressed stands in a functional relationship to all languages; and translation then consists in the adjustment of one system of language structure to another with reference to this 'thing' which is a function of them both.

Where language is used as in an excessively simple pun, where the chance properties of sound and sense *alone* make possible the utterance, where the sayer is virtually passive or at best reveals an easy wit in recognizing the opportunity for display, then language is being used — or rather offers itself as an exhibit. At this level of communication, translation is never possible (except rarely and by chance) because the effect is inherent solely in the language.

A simple analogy need not mislead. Wood, shaped and fashioned for a utilitarian purpose as telegraph poles or window frames, is external to that which is achieved; the means and the end are separate, and the substitution of a different material would not substantially alter the situation; it is a vehicle. Wood, untreated by human agency, may nevertheless in itself display attractive qualities of colour and grain; the effect is completely at one with that which causes it, and no substitution is possible; it is an exhibit.

Assume now, however, that a sculptor takes a piece of wood and uses it as a means of artistic expression. His material is then neither a mere vehicle nor a mere exhibit, but — to follow Dewey — a medium. The act of expression is then no longer a unilateral act, since neither of the two constituent elements is wholly or predominantly passive; instead we have an *inter*action between those forces that reside in the artist and those that reside in the material, whereby *both* are shaped and formed. Sir Alan Gardiner has argued that the verbal formulation of all but the simplest things itself involves an alteration of them;[54] and as soon as we admit that the medium is not a merely passive thing waiting for the supervention of an inspiration already wholly formed but is itself a force active in shaping that experience, we begin to see clearer reasons for Rilke's bewilderment. We may go further and say that the greater the active part played by language, the less easily will the utterance submit to conventional translation. Karl Kraus, of whom it has recently been said that 'he did not write "in a language", but through him the beauty, profundity and accumulated moral experience of the German language assumed personal shape', and that 'he has no "command of words"; he is at their command, avenging their honour upon all who violate them',[55] defies all attempts at orthodox translation in spite of the fact that the bulk of his work is in prose.

Onomasiological translation seems then to embody an accuracy of an unusually pure if unconventional kind. 'What is peculiar to the poet' wrote C.S. Lewis, 'is not the thing he communicates, nor even the symbols whereby he communicates, but his power of finding them and using them.'[56] It is this unique element, this special skill and invention when applied to a new set of symbols that such translation strives to preserve. That the new version will be 'different', not merely in respect of its material but also its form, is an integral part of its special sort of accuracy.

Only the simple-minded would of course imagine that any such accuracy could be achieved by a second person though processes of reason or analysis. The inner workings of the mind are strictly inalienable and — in spite of advances in the science of psycho-analysis — it is a bold claim that seeks to explain the secret processes of the poet's mind on the basis of his works, his life-history or any other outer manifestation of his inner life. Probably the most one can ever hope for is a kind of sympathetic understanding, based on an informed intuition; it must also be said, however, that such instinctive methods are frequently no less valuable or trustworthy than excogitation and may sometimes even have a delicacy that rational methods lack.

V

He misunderstands the purpose of this essay who sees in it merely the substitution of one irritating paradox for another: the gradual drift from 'the best translations are the worst' to 'the freest are the most accurate.' Its intent is rather to underline the need for some new, provisional theory of translation: 'new' in the sense that it should be diagnostic rather than hortatory, that it should be concerned not with unreal ideals and fictional absolutes but with actualities, and that it should not hesitate to use the instruments of modern semantic theory; and 'provisional' in the sense that it should not so much attempt to impose a rigid pattern on the facts as we at present see them but rather serve as a device for the better understanding of them. It is not the principles of translation that need re-adjusting — it is presumptuous to suppose that one could — but rather our ideas about them. Translators will no doubt continue to do as they have always done, and rightly so; but if it were possible to establish reasonably stable critical standards and put an end to the superfluity of merely persuasive discourse, translators might at least find themselves better served by their critics.

'You can reduce everything to communication — yet communication is extremely complex,' it has been said.[57] The proposal implicit in this essay is that the time has come to act on this hint, in spite of its threat of the difficulties to follow: that we consider translation as a complex act of communication embracing two acts of speech, each with its own structure of speaker and hearer, 'meaning' and medium, and wherein the one speech act stands in some analysable relationship with the other; and that we must then consider what must surely be the chief questions: In *what* ways may an utterance in one linguistic medium be made 'like' another in a different medium, and what things are essentially within and what necessarily beyond the control of the translator?

In recommending a codification and analysis of these activities, in advocating an examination of what translation is and can be rather than what it ought to be but never is, we do no more than urge a measure that is being increasingly applied in other spheres. The physicist, instead of working to some speculative definition of 'length' is encouraged to suppose rather that the concept of length is fixed when the operations by which length is measured are fixed; and the philosopher demands — or at least some philosophers demand — that 'explicit' definitions be replaced by 'definitions in use'. Before we can begin to make value judgements about translation, we must know more about its nature, and it is suggested that analysis of *procedure* — in the belief that translation is as translation does — is the approach that promises best.

The methodology would then be that common to most forms of analysis: to conduct the discussion of translation not in terms of its synonyms (among which we might class metaphorical comparisons) but in terms of those things of which translation is the logical construction, considering not only the nature of the constituent elements but also the ways in which they mutually influence one another when compounded. That these things will in themselves be complex is inevitable, and an analysis of this kind may seem to many an over-sophisticated, even perverse, undertaking if at the end of it all we merely find ourselves left with a further set of even more forbidding problems: philosophical problems of meaning and communication; aesthetic problems of the function of media in artistic creation; psychological problems of mental patterns and their influence on style; ethnographical problems of national character and its influence on thought. But there will at least be some small achievement if we find ourselves dealing with concepts that have had close scrutiny in other fields of enquiry where there is a coherent structure of thought surrounding them. Inevitably, scholarly caution is at a premium; translation borders on too many provinces for the linguist to remain secure within his own proper territory or to survey the ground from one vantage point alone; a thorough exploration will compel him to make repeated approaches through the territories of his neighbours, and he will rely desperately on their guidance and advice.

Ibsen and the pursuit of truth

2

Ibsen and Ibsenism

A long familiarity with Ibsen has still not entirely succeeded in erasing the memory of his first introduction to England. One approaches him still, in the theatre and in the armchair, with certain strong if not always precisely formulated expectations that have their source in the 'Nineties; he is enmeshed in a web of association, he is part of a familiar local scene. In this one respect he resembles Baudelaire, of whom it has been rightly said that the task of dissociating what is permanent in his art from what is time-bound is partly the problem of detaching him from the associations of those English writers who first admired him, and partly a question of distinguishing the man from his influence.

A simple mnemonic fixes the general chronological pattern of Ibsen's work: his first drama *Catiline* was published pseudonymously at the age of twenty-two in 1850, and the corrected proofs of his final work *When We Dead Awaken* were delivered to the printer in the last December days of 1899; so that the span of his creative life corresponds almost exactly with the second half of the nineteenth century. In his fifty years of authorship he wrote twenty-five plays, the thirteenth of which, the enormous and ponderous 'double' drama *Emperor and Galilean* (*Kejser og Galilæer,* 1873), stands there as a watershed to his life's work — with the later and more characteristically 'Ibsenist' plays standing on one side of it, and the earlier and less characteristically so on the other. The immediate outward sign of the change in his work at this time is the deliberate adoption of a realistic prose dialogue as his dramatic medium in place of metrical verse. Edmund Gosse felt that *Emperor and Galilean* might have gained by being written in verse, and wrote to Ibsen to tell him so; Ibsen's reply of 15 January 1874 is forthright in its rejection of this idea:

> You think that my play should have been in verse and that it would have gained by this. On that point I must contradict you, for the play is — as you have noted — cast in a form as realistic as possible; it was the illusion of reality I wanted to produce. I wanted to evoke in the reader the impression that what he was reading really happened. If I had used verse, I would have run counter to my intention and to the task I have set myself . . . My new play is no tragedy in the old style; what I wanted to portray was people, and it was precisely for that reason that I did not allow them to speak with 'the tongues of angels'.

A considerable part of his earlier work had been written in verse. *Catiline* written in the winter months of 1848-49, and about which Ibsen later wrote that many of the things round which his later writings revolved -'the contradiction between ability and ambition, between what is willed and what is possible, that which is Man's and the individual's tragedy and

comedy at one and the same time — appear here faintly indi-
cated'; *The Warrior's Barrow (Kjæmpehøjen)* and *St John's
Night (Sankthansnatten)* from the years 1850 and 1852 respec-
tively but not published until much later; much of *The Feast at
Solhoug (Gildet paa Solhoug, 1856)*, for which Ibsen's reading
of Norwegian folk songs provided inspiration; parts of *Olaf
Liljekrans*, a romantic drama in three acts, performed at
Bergen in January 1857 but not printed until 1898; and *Love's
Comedy (Kjærlighedens Komedie, 1862)*, a drama which
contemporary criticism found both immoral and unpoetic, and
which Ibsen later regretted having published at that time in
Norway, saying that 'both time and place were an unfortunate
choice'.

Yet even at this early stage in his career, Ibsen seemed to
show greater assurance in prose: *Lady Inger at Ostraat (Fru
Inger til Østeraad)*, first performed in Bergen in January 1855
and published in 1857, is perhaps not particularly remarkable;
but *The Vikings at Helgeland (Hærmændene paa Helgeland,
1858)* was an accomplished piece of dramatic composition in
which, inspired by his reading of *Volsungasaga*, Ibsen
attempted with some measure of success to find a modern
approximation to the strong and purposeful language of the
sagas; and with *The Pretenders (Kongs-Emnerne, 1864)*, a
drama which contrasted the easy confidence of Haakon with
the complex and introspective nature of Skule, he produced
what is the profoundest of these early works.

The Pretenders, written in the summer months of 1863, was
performed in January 1864 in Christiania with moderate
success. But by this year Ibsen was if not an embittered then at
least a disappointed man. He had experienced financial difficulties; many of his plays had been met with indifference and
even outright hostility. The Norwegian parliament had refused
him the 'poet's pension' it had recently granted to Bjørnson.
Ibsen left Norway in April 1864 and for the next twenty-seven
years was resident abroad almost without interruption, in Italy
and Germany.

Brand, first conceived as an epic poem and then re-written as
a verse drama, was completed in the summer of 1865 at Ariccia
near Rome and published the following year in Copenhagen; it

47

was followed in 1867 by *Peer Gynt*. These two 'non-theatrical' plays complement each other: *Brand* takes as its hero a Kierke-gaardian figure, unbending, uncompromising, sternly dedicated to the principle of 'all or nothing'; *Peer Gynt* follows the fantastic career of a person wholly unprincipled, buoyant, yielding, and content to adopt as his motto 'To thine own self be — enough'; where the one is admirable but unlovable, the other is lovable but reprehensible; and yet both can justifiably be considered in part as portraits of the author. 'Brand is myself in my finest moments', Ibsen is reported to have said; whilst Bjørnson on the other hand later said: 'Not till *Peer Gynt* did Ibsen become himself; for Peer Gynt *was* him.' To the 1860s belongs also that other dramatic work which in part spoils the neat geometry of the mnemonic: *The League of Youth (De unges Forbund)*, completed in Dresden in 1869 and which in style and influence anticipates to some extent the later plays.

It was in the last quarter of the century, in the second half of his creative life, that Ibsen produced with almost metronomic regularity the series of twelve plays by which he was in England most generally known. These were the years in which the realistic 'problem' plays of Ibsen and Bjørnson gave Norwegian literature its leading position among the literatures of Europe, plays which appealed to a generation only too ready to receive them as exercises in social criticism. Beginning with *Pillars of Society (Samfundets støtter)* in 1877, Ibsen continued with those works whose titles alone are still redolent of the powder and shot of controversy: *A Doll's House (Et dukkehjem*, 1879), *Ghosts (Gengangere,* 1881), *An Enemy of the People (En folkefiende,* 1882), *The Wild Duck (Vildanden,* 1884), *Rosmersholm* (1886), *The Lady from the Sea (Fruen fra havet,* 1888), *Hedda Gabler* (1890), *The Master Builder (Bygmester Solness,* 1892), *Little Eyolf (Lille Eyolf,* 1894), *John Gabriel Borkman* (1896), and *When We Dead Awaken (Naar vi døde vaagner,* 1900).

It is clear from this chronicle that Ibsen arrived late in England, in the more public sense of arrival; and it is also noteworthy that England was much later than Germany with her welcome. In the 1870s no fewer than six of Ibsen's plays had been translated into German, and indeed two of them, *Brand* and *Pillars of Society*, each appeared in three different translations; this is as against one play (and a bit) in English, and none in French. By 1890 there were altogether twenty-seven different German translations, covering sixteen of the plays, plus also two separate translations of his poems; in England, there were seven translations of five of the plays; in France, two of the plays had been translated. Moreover it is recorded that as early as 1878 there were, in the month of February alone, five different companies in Berlin all per-forming *Pillars of Society*. In England, the first influential translations did not appear until 1888, when there was pub-lished (in the Camelot Series) a volume edited and introduced by Havelock Ellis and containing *Pillars of Society* and *Ghosts* (both translated by the daughter of Karl Marx, Mrs. Eleanor Marx-Aveling); in the following year *A Doll's House* was performed, in Archer's translation, at the Novelty Theatre, the first (shall one say) 'substantial' Ibsen production in England. By this year, however, Ibsen was over sixty years old and had been writing plays for nearly forty of them.

One should not conclude from this that Ibsen was entirely neglected in England before these events. There had been the efforts of Edmund Gosse, who in 1872 as a young man of twenty-two had been commissioned by the *Spectator* and *Fraser's Magazine* to visit Scandinavia and report on the state of the literature there; in one of his four short and unsigned articles that same year he described Ibsen as 'second to none of his contemporaries', and introduced him as a writer who was prevented from enjoying the European reputation he deserved only by 'the remoteness of his mother tongue'. A further article of his the following year in the *Fortnightly Review* succeeded in awakening rather more interest in Ibsen in certain circles; and in 1879 there appeared in volume form his *Studies in the Literature of Northern Europe* which marked the culmination of a decade's enthusiastic but often uncritical endeavour on Ibsen's behalf.

Meanwhile translations of a kind had begun to appear; the first — a most unexpected choice — was of *Emperor and*

Galilean by Catherine Ray in 1876; and in a book published the same year and bearing the title *Translations from the Norse* (thought to be by a certain A. Johnston) there appeared, along with a number of Ibsen's poems, the first Act of *Catiline* together with a summary of Acts Two and Three. The first ever London production of an Ibsen play was on 15 December 1880 at the Gaiety Theatre: a play called *Quicksands*, a much mutilated version of *Pillars of Society*, translated by William Archer. Of this performance a Danish theatrical critic reported to his Copenhagen paper that the audience gave the play an enthusiastic reception and called loudly for the author, a request which 'was readily met, without any reserve or trace of embarrassment, by Mr. Archer, the English translator'. *A Doll's House* also had a fitful life on the London stage about this time. It was first (and very eccentrically) translated under the title of *Nora* by a Dane in 1880, again under the same title 1883 by Henrietta Frances Lord, and yet again in 1884 by Henry Arthur Jones and Henry Herman, whose version was performed on 3 March at the Prince's Theatre under the title of *Breaking a Butterfly*. If this title seems by implication to show sympathy for Nora, there was to counterbalance it the selection the following year of the authentic version of the play — which as is well known ends with Nora leaving home and slamming the door on her husband and children — for a charity performance by an amateur group calling itself 'The Scribblers' Dramatic Society'.

So it was that often in rather unexpected ways Ibsen made progress in this country — one might also mention with affection the keen propaganda work of the Rev. Philip Wicksteed, who about this time made it his habit to take the texts of his sermons from the pages of *Peer Gynt*, and who in his enthusiasm for Ibsen had, at a Hampstead school, conducted classes through the Norwegian text of *The Vikings at Helgeland*. After the pioneering work of Gosse, however, it was William Archer who made the more solid contribution to Ibsen's English reputation. He had met Ibsen in the winter of 1881-82 in Rome, and he went on to devote himself to the translating, editing and arranging of Ibsen's works. The English collected edition began appearing in 1906; despite the hard things that are said, sometimes justifiably, about the quality of the translation, it remains a praiseworthy achievement.

It was not until the year 1891 that the storm broke, a year in which there were five of Ibsen's plays produced in London, including *Rosmersholm, An Enemy of the People* and, of course, *Ghosts*. The violence of the press reaction is well known. Ibsenism was then under way and under fire.

The official histories of the original Ibsenite campaign rightly pay close attention to the generalship of Shaw. From our present standpoint in time, one can delight in the vigour of his *Quintessence of Ibsenism*, in the thrustful aggressiveness of his defence, in the brilliant intuition that informed him of the weaknesses in the opposition and his cruel probing of them; but many are now ready to admit that his brilliance in this respect was a tactician's brilliance and that his strategy was misconceived. He elected, as is well known, to join the battle on the grounds that the plays are first and foremost the embodiment of a lesson, illustrations of a thesis, exercises in moral persuasion; he shared Archer's admiration for the plays as messages rather than imaginative creations, and even his assessment of Ibsen's technical achievement — the novelty of which he ascribed to the introduction of 'the discussion' — rests on this assumption. But the suspicion grew with time that this had been a false appreciation of what was vital to defend. What happened if one persisted in holding to Shavian criteria is shown very clearly in Spengler's *Decline of the West*, the first volume of which appeared in 1918. There Spengler trod the path of Shavian Ibsenism to its terminus, finally arriving at the conclusion that Ibsen would have to be banished to the lumber room, to be taken out and dusted down for the benefit of accredited researchers only. Spengler was another of those who saw the drama of the late nineteenth century primarily as a medium for agitation and debate. He placed Ibsen in a cyclic phase which began with Schopenhauer and ended with Shaw, which included the names of Proudhon and Comte, Hebbel and Feuerbach, Marx and Engels, Wagner and Nietzsche, Darwin and John Stuart Mill, the creed of which he defined as 'ethical socialism'. As for the plays themselves, he considered they were so tied to their own age that they would never be able to claim the attention of later generations; their merits, such as they were, were historical rather than intrinsic. By 1950, Spengler asserted confidently, Ibsen would be quite dead.

But although the ideas of Shavian Ibsenism are nowadays generally discredited, its influence on some Ibsen criticism is still potent. Few are any longer misled *into* it but many are still misled *by* it, provoked by it into views that are different but equally unacceptable. One imagines the argument going something like this: Ibsen is after all, on all the evidence, not dead but on the contrary very much alive; yet the things he wrote about — the themes, the ideas, the content of the works — no longer seem to concern us very closely; therefore surely his continued vitality can only be ascribed to his technique. It is, seemingly, not what he said but the way he said it. What indeed, it was once asked by H.L.Mencken, are those once famous ideas?

> That it is unpleasant and degrading for a wife to be treated as a mere mistress and empty-head; that professional patriots . . . are frauds; that success in business usually involves doing things that a self-respecting man hesitates to do; that a woman who continues to cohabit with a syphilitic husband may expect to have defective children; . . . that a neurotic and lascivious woman is apt to be horrified when she finds that she is pregnant; . . . that the world is barbarously cruel to a woman who has violated the Seventh Commandment or a man who has violated the Eighth.

Such remarks, which are of course meant to be in defence of Ibsen, claim a timelessness for his ideas only by insisting that they are unremarkable. The ideas are considered as neither adding to nor detracting from the real merit of the plays as honest, workmanlike, journeyman drama. The consequence is that, in post-Shavian criticism, Ibsen has often found himself taken out of the company of Schopenhauer, Darwin and Nietzsche and associated rather with Scribe and Augier and

Feuillet and Dumas *fils* and the tradition of the *pièce bien faite*. He is respected as one who found a successful solution to certain technical problems of dramatic composition.

It is the swing of the pendulum. Whereas the generation of Holbrook Jackson admired Ibsen as a man 'whose method of criticizing conventional morals by means of drama had a profound effect upon thinking people', the present generation is inclined rather to echo the words of the Angus Wilson character in *Hemlock and After*, who says: 'I admire Ibsen's stagecraft, but I find it more and more difficult to sit through hours of life in the raw.' His moral stock has slumped, but this has been balanced by the appreciation in the value attached to his craftsmanship; he maintains his position, it seems, although no longer as a leader of opinion but rather as a technician of the highest order. And a new orthodoxy bemoans the fact that such a talented writer lavished his gifts on such sadly perishable material.

Yet even Shaw, in the most confidently assertive book ever written about Ibsen, disarmingly admitted the folly of making confident assertion: 'When you have called Mrs. Alving an emancipated woman or an unprincipled one, Alving a debauchee or a victim of society, Nora a fearless and noblehearted woman or a shocking little liar and an unnatural mother, Helmer a selfish hound or a model husband and father, according to your bias, you have said something which is at once true and false, and in both cases perfectly idle.' This is no less true of the conflicting things that have been said about Ibsen himself; and it echoes a phrase from his own *Emperor and Galilean* first isolated and applied to Ibsen by one of his contemporaries in 1873 and equally valid today: 'What he is, that he is not, and what he is not, that he is' — a phrase of which the critical literature on Ibsen is in its totality an enactment. The first denials came with what the Ibsenites in their day said to those who felt that they knew only too well what Ibsen was; and having established to their own satisfaction what Ibsen was, were themselves in turn rebuked in the same terms.

The landscape of his authorship, once mapped by them as a high central plateau of problematic realism, a region peopled with pillars of society and enemies of the people and ghosts, approached through the bewildering thickets of *Brand* and *Peer Gynt* and falling away 'down among the dead men' — this landscape in more recent and more audacious reports is seen as one having as its main feature a triumphantly flowing poetic inspiration, moving in subterranean passages in mid-career, but emerging with enhanced power and sweep in its later reaches.

It becomes increasingly obvious that his genius is of a kind that demands a ceaseless, Forth Bridge-like surveillance, of which it is then meaningless to ask if it is complete but only what point it has reached: whether it is for the moment looking to the 'problems' or to the 'poetic vision'; whether it is concerned with the investigation of 'real people in real situations' or of certain themes, in the enunciation of which the characters are rather the central elements. Whether one calls his dramas the encoded abuse of a fugitive from humiliation, or the occasions for release of private passion, or the night thoughts of one who feared the light, or an audacious and defiant minority report on life; whether one interprets them as the fruits of a mind subtly elated by a sense of secret power or nagged by the possibility that on Sirius two and two might make five; whether one stamps them as visionary or inquisitorial, gnomic or punitive, venomous or introspective — the result is to draw too particular a distinction, is to make assertions that are all equally true, equally false, equally idle.

One thing inevitably emerges from any closer study of Ibsen, something rather unsettling to critical orthodoxy; and this is the realization that he does not seem to react very satisfactorily to any of the standard laboratory tests of criticism; further, that any account of his work that limits itself to what is positive and obtrusive in it seems destined to end in triteness; or else — something which is strange and astonishing in this seemingly so straightforward and uncomplicated author — it turns out that any generalization once made seems to demand reservation and qualification so drastic that the end result is little short of flat contradiction. Considerations of this kind lend significance to that other expression of admiration of the 1890s, less strident than the official Ibsenism, less partisan, less conspicuous but more durable and one suspects more influential in a rather indirect way — an admiration of which the defining figure is Henry James. To his friend Elizabeth Robins, one of the greatest Ibsen actresses of the decade, he once wrote: 'What an old boy is our Northern Henry. He is too delightful — an old darling.' What Ibsen might have meant to James personally is suggested by the entry in his Notebooks for 21 December 1896:

> I realize — none too soon — that the *scenic* method is my absolute, my imperative, my *only* salvation. The march of an action is the only thing for me to, more and more, attach myself to: it is the only thing that really, for *me*, at least, will *produire* L'OEUVRE, and L'OEUVRE is, before God, what I am going in for. Well, the scenic scheme is the only one *I* can trust, with my tendencies, to stick to the march of an action. How reading Ibsen's splendid John Gabriel a day or two ago (in proof) brought that, FINALLY AND FOREVER, home to me!

James's rather ambivalent admiration for Ibsen as it found expression in certain articles of his — one in June 1891 for the *New Review* on *Hedda Gabler* and another for the *Pall Mall Gazette* in February 1893 on *The Master Builder*, together with two shorter pieces from January and February 1897 in *Harper's Weekly* on *Little Eyolf* and *When We Dead Awaken* — is generally indifferent to those aspects of the dramas his contemporaries considered most worthy of remark; and it is also obvious that whilst he was impressed by Ibsen's technical mastery, it was not to this exclusively that he looked. There was, however, one thing that quite evidently bewildered him; commenting on what he called Ibsen's 'irritating, his bewildering incongruities', he went on: 'He is nothing as a literary personality if not positive; and yet there are moments when his great gift seems made up of negatives, or at any rate when the total seems a contradiction of each of the parts.' There is reinforcement for this idea also in the words of one of Ibsen's more perspicacious critics, Muriel Bradbrook, who when considering *The Wild Duck* writes: 'One day it will be read as a tragedy, the next as the harshest irony; parts of it are clumsy . . . So searching and yet so delicate is the touch that these flaws and vagaries seem in themselves to strengthen the work.'

Both these expressions of view — that a positive is in part made up of negatives, that weaknesses contribute to strength — seem to put certain qualities in Ibsen in an entirely new light. An absence of humour, an absence of free imagination, an absence of glamour, an absence of what is loosely called 'style' even, add up to nothing; but in the case of Ibsen they seem to multiply up to what has very suitably been called his 'spell'. It seems that you cannot mark him independently on, say, content and style with any hope that a conflation of the two assessments will give any adequate index of his achievement. The constituent elements in his drama are not items in a ledger but factors in a product; his technical skill not an additive but rather an exponent in the algebraic sense, his dramas an exponential series in which the plus and minus quantities function in a way altogether different from those that figure in an accountant's statement of profit and loss. One is encouraged to look at the dramas again, to look not at what is positive and obtrusive but at what is (so to speak) conspicuously unobtrusive and even assertively negative. One asks oneself whether this is the occasion to remember the positive significance of the nil return. Should one approach Ibsen as an occasion not for counting the heads but for calling the roll, where it is not the crude total that signifies but rather the meaningful silences and the absences of response? Always remembering, however, that those who seem to be playing truant may all the time be hiding behind the what-not or under the horse-hair sofa.

In the first place there are a number of things that are there but do not show. This is partly the case with his alleged lack of humour. There *is* humour there of a kind and there in abundance, but it is the solitary, unshared, suppressed laughter behind a desperately straight face; there is the tight-lipped fun that he made of contemporary Norwegian society; there is the encoded satire that he aimed at some of his more eminent contemporaries, a code which a study of the draft manuscripts, the letters and the life of the author help to crack; and not least there is the wry ironic detachment with which he turned many a private hurt into a public show. Nor is it so very different with his alleged lack of poetry or imaginative inventiveness. So often one hears the reproach that he is prosaic, uncompromisingly realistic, inveterately observed — a reproach that admittedly sees (say) *Pillars of Society* or *An Enemy of the People* or *Ghosts* as the purest and most characteristic expression of Ibsen's genius, and which is made only after uneasy glances over the shoulder at the luxuriant fantasy of *Peer Gynt*. In the matter of poetic content, one is once again dealing not with some innate deficiency, not with some lack of aptitude, but with a deliberate act of suppression or concealment. In middle life, after the completion of *Brand* and *Peer Gynt*, Ibsen took his resolve to renounce poetry in all its more extravagant or self-conscious forms, to avoid metre, to speak in the language of men talking to men; it was, as it were, the Preface to the *Lyrical Ballads* tightened up another notch. But the poetic vision was not so easily denied; the consequence was a poetry not of a surface beauty but of inner strength, not of fleshy contour but of bony structure, of controlled organization without any concession to prettiness or adornment, and as such it is something surprisingly modern in its assumptions about poetic communication.

As an architect of drama, Ibsen built with the materials of his age; he displays to view a great deal of grey, massive, solid masonry; but at the same time he appears to be doing astonishing things with his conventional material, to be reaching heights of sublime humdrum, to be performing abnormal feats of normality, to be operating within a style of extravagant sobriety. At times his drama seems tremendously firm and monumental, at other times recklessly audacious and topheavy; it is only on closer inspection, when one has worked out the hidden architecture, that one realizes how extraordinarily steely it all is, how spendthrift even in its strength. When one looks at the plans, sees from the drafts and sketches (especially of some of the later plays) the meticulous process of re-designing that went on, one realizes that behind and within the outer cladding there is concealed a frame of invention of the highest tensile strength; one discovers not only the pillars of load-bearing realism but also a steel skeleton of poetic imagination. One sees how he shored up the fabric with further devices: buttresses of precise and meaningful stage-direction, scaffoldings of symbolism, motifs that appear decorative but which on examination are discovered also to be taking part of the strain, until the whole thing is braced and strutted into complete rigidity. Only thus was Ibsen able to use so imaginatively such unimaginative language, to compose dialogue that is so unnaturally natural, to make such a vivid impression with creations so uncompromisingly monochrome. It was none other than Maeterlinck — one of the least likely, one might think, to find anything congenial in Ibsen — who detected this hidden thing; he listened to what he called 'the inner dialogue', those exchanges conducted unspoken behind the spoken word, so eloquently inarticulate.

These dramas suppress their poetry as Brand suppressed his love, and from the same wilful strength. What is love (another of those things so conspicuously absent in Ibsen), says Brand with bitter scorn, but a cloak under which men conceal their lack of will; and what indeed, one might further ask, is hate in these plays but love turned sour — 'If Mrs. Borkman had not loved her husband,' Ibsen wrote in explanation of this figure of hate, 'she would have forgiven him long ago.' It seems that absence, and absence alone, makes the heart grow fonder, as one learns from Solveig's example, or from that of Martha in *Pillars of Society*; conversely, the closer the relationship, the more inevitable and bitter the estrangement. How loveless a thing is marriage in Ibsen's world: like Mrs. Alving's to be endured in shame; like Hedda Gabler's, a career in frustration; like the Master Builder's; even the children, Oswald, Hedvig, Little Eyolf, are blighted. There is infatuation in this world, possessiveness, appetite, there is amiability, reasonableness, devotion even; but one will search in vain for any love scene of genuine proportions, for any delicate exploration of personality by two people growing fond of each other.

What of those other deliberately contrived absences, those bare patches in the landscape that were not just left unpopulated but depopulated by design, empty spaces not just left out but carved out? There is in particular that fatal lack which disables the lives of so many of the characters, their essentially negative potential, by which as the result of some insufficiency, some incompetence, some impotence or inherent disqualification, some inauthenticity in the control or direction of their lives, they are so to speak debarred. Never has there been a gallery of lives so dedicated and yet so flawed, so disciplined and yet so unfulfilled, so determined and yet so insensible; lives so dedicated to All or Nothing, to homes for humans, to the good of society, to freedom under responsibility, to the compact majority, finding answers everywhere but in their own hearts; lives that under the pressure of dramatic event reveal (to use Eric Bentley's phrase) not unexpected depths but unexpected shallows.

They are, shall one say, shut away — but from what? From fortune? from happiness? from the truth? from self-fulfilment? Should one for the moment rather say: from the Light? Think of the imprisoned ones: like Hedda in the stuffy cell of her marriage to Tesman, a captive to bumbling amiability, dreaming of an admirer with vine leaves in his hair, and of the thrill of beautiful death; like Nora, placed under doll's house arrest, sneaking a few forbidden macaroons and squandering her life in deceiving her indulgent warder; like Oswald, kept in the dark about his wastrel father the whole of his young life and moaning for the sun; or like Borkman pacing up and down in his gallery like a caged animal. Think also of those who take refuge in a darkness of their own creating, who dwell in the shadow of a phrase or a lie or a secret dream: like Hjalmar Ekdal, comforted by the thought of the photographic invention he will never make; like Consul Bernick, sitting snug in the illusion that he is serving the community; like Alfred Allmers, sustained by the grandiose scheme of writing a big book on Human Responsibility. And here already one can see something that is strongly characteristic of Ibsen's dramatic utterances: the Light is something to play both hide *and* seek with; the Dark is either a prison or a refuge, something that shuts in or shuts out. On the other hand there are those words of Brand who tells of certain ideas (recurrent in Ibsen) that used to send him into fits of laughter: what if an owl were afraid of the dark, or a fish afraid of water? How they would long for 'air and the glad flames of day'. And yet this (he says) is the lot of humankind, living between the fact of having to bear and the realization that it is unbearable; imprisoned. But then the Light, as well as being something to be yearned for, can also be something to be feared. In an early poem of Ibsen called 'Fear of the Light', he confesses that his courage drains away as the sun rises, that the troubles of the day and the claims of life drip cold terror into his heart so that he hides himself under a flap of the scarecrow veil of the dark, embracing night as a protective shield.

Ibsen's benighted are thus of two main kinds: those who long for release, from oppressive respectability, from the commonplace, from frustration, who yearn for something wonderful to happen; and those others who take refuge from the insistent demands of life, who build up an insulation against the torments of decision and the agonies of conscience, whose approach to life is a retreat from it, a withdrawal into a stronghold of personal fantasy. And between them stand those who try to fill the fatal deficiency in their lives by taking from others, who illuminate their careers with borrowed light; those who apply themselves earnestly to the business of living but are inherently disqualified, who are like the African Magician in the Aladdin myth who covets the lamp that will assure his fortune but is debarred from seizing it unaided. Either, like Brand, they adopt some impersonal directive and live by code or statute because they cannot trust themselves to live by rule of thumb; or like Skule, whose sense of uncertainty is such that he doubts the very doubt that nags him and who takes over the 'kingly thought' from his rival, they carry their deficiency about with them like a vacuum, desperately trying to fill it from without; but instead of filling it, they succeed only in encasing it in a shell of dedication, fastidiousness or borrowed authority; each stroke of the drama exhausts this vacuum a little more until at last the protective shell crumples under the pressure of external event.

What follows from this realization? The first thing is that these negative aspects of his work contribute materially to its achievement. It is certainly in part a technical *tour de force*, for it is in its own way as difficult to incorporate absent qualities in drama as it is to give examples of them in criticizing it. But it is also more. When Ibsen writes of the Light as something to yearn for and to flee from, of the Dark as something that oppresses and something that comforts, when he regards buildings as being both homes and cages, he is saying on the level of symbols what his dramas are often concerned to say dramatically: truth in *Pillars of Society* brings salvation, in *The Wild Duck* it brings destruction; a lie is synonymous with both an ideal and an illusion, something which for Hjalmar Ekdal makes life tolerable but which for Consul Bernick makes life intolerable. To ask for the essence of Ibsen, still more for the quintessence of Ibsenism, is to formulate a wholly misleading question; there is nothing to be got by boiling down, there is no extract of wisdom that would allow us to regard his drama as a linctus for the ills of mankind. If one must have an analogy, one might be a little nearer the truth by asking for the root of Ibsen; for just as the root of (say) 9 is not 3 but that more ambiguous entity mathematicians call ±3, so the root of Ibsen's view of life, however positively he may at times seem to express himself, conveys the impression of being similarly 'plus or minus'. The separate bits may not add up very satisfactorily, but they function.

The problem is then to determine what sort of questions the modern Ibsenite *should* ask. One notices that in an age when literature gave itself to the business of debate, Ibsen himself waited for question time and cast his dramas in an interrogative mould. 'I do but ask,' he was fond of saying to those who sought enlightenment from him about the meaning of his works, 'my call is not to answer.' His dramas are those of one who understood the strategy of the contrived question and the shrewd supplementary, who knew how much more could be achieved by implication and insinuation and by the manner and timing of the asking than by the mere forcing of some answer. Perhaps his critics could learn from his example and acknowledge that there is room for an approach to Ibsen that questions the questions we ask of him rather than competes for answers. He offers a problem in delicate handling in which the matter of whether questions can be found to yield definite answers is subordinate to that of finding a genuinely Ibsenite question with the rightly provocative degree of obliquity. For example: Is there any Thing that might be discovered as standing to Ibsen as the Wild Duck stands to *The Wild Duck*?

Contemplating such Ibsenist Things, one wonders: How symbolic are they, and how are they symbolic, and are they all symbolic in the same way — the Wild Duck, the white horses in *Rosmersholm*, the sea in *The Lady from the Sea*, the 'Indian Girl' in *Pillars of Society*, the infected baths, the orphanage, the high towers in *An Enemy of the People, Ghosts* and *The Master Builder*? What at one time it was sufficient to call a symbol (whether or not one felt inclined to add, like Arnold Bennett, 'deplorable, even in its ingenuity') is now a 'symbol', shielded by its quotation marks from any simple view that it might 'stand for' anything in some straightforward sense; sometimes it is credited with explanatory or elucidatory power, sometimes with cohesive or magnetic force; at times it is seen as 'a pressure point for all kinds of feeling', at times as a kind of appliance which gathers 'all the scattered lights of the play and focuses them in one': there is some suspicion that it is often attached to its play (and therefore 'detachable') rather than inherently of it, that it is centrally placed rather than nuclear, perhaps even that it is intrinsic and extrinsic at one and the same time.

The Wild Duck is no doubt in one sense a centre of attraction; but it might be thought to have other and possibly more significant functions as a kind of formula or code word for finding the centre of gravity, the point about which all the separate elements exactly balance one another. Asked to imagine the shape of the play to which it belongs, one might see it as something equivocal, like a boomerang perhaps or a question mark, where the centre of gravity lies not within but without; but if one were to hang it up at any point, at Hedvig, say, or Hjalmar or Old Ekdal or the 'life-lie' and allow things to find their natural equilibrium, this centre of gravity — although nothing more than a point in space — would come to rest immediately below the point of suspension; what one is not able to do is actually *balance* anything on this point of balance, this point which is detached and yet not strictly detachable, which is a function of the configuration of the piece rather than something of a piece with it. It would then be immaterial whether one hung the problem plays uppermost, or the visionary, or the poetic and non-theatrical; a private enthusiasm for, say, *A Doll's House* or *Ghosts* or *Peer Gynt* or even *Emperor and Galilean* (which would probably have been Ibsen's own choice) ought in theory all to point to the same spot.

Staring too fixedly, however, at the Wild Duck has its dangers; and in straining the vision, the analogy itself becomes strained. Looking round for a moment instead at the company it keeps, one becomes aware of another bird which has been strangely disregarded, one which along with Chekhov's Seagull seems to be — no matter what ornithology might say — a bird of a feather: Boccaccio's Falcon, that which appears in the ninth story of the fifth day of the *Decameron*. There is even some suggestion that the resemblance is not altogether accidental, the link between the two being Paul Heyse, German critic and author, whom Ibsen met in 1875 while living in Munich. Ibsen, it seems, occasionally attended the weekly meetings of the Crocodile Society, of which Heyse was a prominent member, and they saw much of each other without ever becoming close friends. A few years earlier, in 1871, Heyse had sketched his theory of the *Novelle*, his so-called *Falkentheorie*, derived from a study of Boccaccio's story; and it would be surprising if this did not on some occasion provide the society with something to discuss. Heyse had summed up his argument in the words: 'Der Leser wird sich überall fragen, wo der Falke sei: also das Spezifische, das diese Geschichte von tausend anderen unterscheidet', i.e. look for the falcon, that which in some recognizable but not easily definable way focuses, particularizes, concretizes the work and gives it identity. A simple translation of Heyse's formula provides a paraphrase of the question implied above, a question in which Ibsen might have found quiet amusement, where the inner ramifications are everything and the answers largely incidental: Where is Ibsen's Wild Duck, that which distinguishes him from a thousand others?

The immediate past is not lacking in suggestions, many of which resemble each other only in their determination not to flatter. For James Joyce's Stephen Dedalus the differentia was cathartic: 'You have,' he said to the Ibsenite, 'connected Ibsen and Eno's fruit salts for ever in my mind.' For Arne Garborg it was demonic, suggesting to him the figure of Trollman White-beard who spoke in riddles and acted so wise and turned the whole country into a madhouse by his magic. For Oxford's Professor of English Literaure it was swinish: 'I send you Zola and Ibsen', wrote Sir Walter Raleigh in a letter accompanying two very ugly cabinet photographs, '. . . they seem to me to embody modern earnestness, crankiness, gloom and stupidity in their speaking countenances . . . I think we must frame them with the legend Modern Pigs underneath.' And Ibsen himself provided ammunition for his detractors by his reference to the Scorpion which preserved its health by injecting its poison into a piece of soft fruit: 'Is there not a similarity,' he wrote, 'between this and writing poetry?' Many of the lyric poems, as well as the dramas themselves, make a contribution to the discussion, embodying in particular many of those more obvious and generally acknowledged qualities of their author: the profound and wholly pitiless psychological insight, the complex subtleties of organization, the stern judgement of individual responsibility, the scorn of inauthentic living and thinking. In these poems, the Strange Hunter on the *vidda* forces mortals to contemplate their lives 'steel-set'; the Miner hammers his way into the secret chambers of the heart, seeking the answer to life's riddle, foregoing even the consolation of the light; and there is the suggestion of the Judge who holds doom sessions on the soul. Ibsen's astonishing technical skill invited identification with the Master Builder; and in view of Rubek's sardonic remarks in *When We Dead Awaken*, this might well be extended to include also a Master Sculptor:

> There is something equivocal, something hidden within and behind these portraits — something private that the others cannot see. I alone can see it. And I find it intensely amusing. Superficially there's the 'striking likeness', as it is called, that people all stand gaping at in astonishment — but deeper down it is . . . just the dear old barnyard.

Nor should one neglect the Amazingly Clever Dog, the one which in any case fished up the Wild Duck from the depths — a Dog who (to put too fine a point on it, no doubt) was at first treated like a cur but lived to have the day the proverb promised him, who was fierce and bristling but who, if tossed a decoration by some crowned head, could be placated.

All these things are, however, too partial, too explicit, too 'symbolic' in the sense that the Wild Duck is not; and when they are asked to accommodate some of the other less obvious but no less pervasive elements in these dramas, they fail. Where is the relevance to the incessant self-analysis of those characters who, as Hofmannsthal said, are forever thinking about thinking, feeling themselves feeling and conducting autopsychology; who think in slogans and long for the miraculous; who decorate their egocentric lives with secret dreams, subordinating all about them in private illusions of grandeur; whose lives are the deeds they have left undone, whose speech is the words they have left unspoken? Granted, these explanations belong to the study, not in the theatre; and many sensitive critics have insisted that only in the theatre should Ibsen properly be judged. It is not good, they suggest, to go trudging down long avenues of reference every time Ibsen points his finger; there is, in the theatre, no time for digression, the pace has to be maintained. This was the view of James Joyce, whose early enthusiasm for Ibsen led him to teach himself Norwegian, the better to read the plays, who in March 1901 in his newly acquired foreign tongue wrote Ibsen a moving letter of homage and admiration, and who in an enthusiastic article on *When We Dead Awaken* in the *Fortnightly Review* of April 1900 claimed that 'appreciation, hearkening, is the only true criticism':

If any plays demand a stage they are the plays of Ibsen ... They are so packed with thought. At some chance expression, the mind is tortured with some question, and in a flash long reaches of life are opened up in vista, yet the vision is momentary unless we stay to ponder it. It is just to prevent excessive pondering that Ibsen requires to be acted.

The real answer seems to be therefore that there is no answer; or rather that there is an infinity of answers too stark and stiff to fit anywhere but where they touch — which makes the modern Ibsenites' search for enlightenment a matter not of discovering some single secret truth but of rejecting a multiplicity of explanations which under scrutiny turn out to be inadmissible. Not even the precise ambiguity of the paradox nor the ambiguous precision of the 'symbol' serve in the last resort to break down the complex unity of his art. He is irreducible.

3

Drama in the Making

My purpose in this lecture is to look again at what we know or what we can discover about Ibsen's working methods, about his highly personal approach to the business of writing drama; and then to ask one very innocent, wide-eyed question: What use is this knowledge? Does it contribute to our understanding of the plays? Does it have anything significant to say about the mechanism of dramatic composition in general? Or is it merely a pointer to what the work might have become but never did? If, at the end, we find that there are no tidy, round-figure answers, then (defensively) I would have to say that this would be entirely in the spirit of Ibsen who — in one of his better known utterances — insisted that he saw his own mission in life as that of asking questions rather than of finding answers.

Popular curiosity about Ibsen's working methods was quick to manifest itself once his reputation had begun to spread. But in those early days, in the 1880s and 1890s, it was largely the more journalistic or human-interest details that were recorded and given circulation. These were accounts based mainly on anecdote about his daily routine, about his personal habits, and on opportunist interviews or conversations with the author himself.

One of the first to sound him out in this way was William Archer who, in the summer of 1887, braved the stormy sea-crossing of the Skagerak to call on Ibsen who was holidaying in North Jutland. As he later explained to his brother Charles[1], what he was really after was 'to get at the genesis of a piece in his head.' But the fear of seeming to cross-examine a man who was already notorious for his irascibility prevented him, he confessed, from getting at anything very explicit. Archer suggested to Ibsen that seemingly the *idea* presented itself before the characters and the incidents. This however Ibsen flatly denied; what he did apparently admit was that there was a certain stage in the incubation of a play when it might just as easily have turned into an essay as a drama.

> . . . He has to incarnate the ideas, as it were, [Archer reported] in character and incident, before the actual work of creation can be said to have fairly commenced. Different plans and ideas, he admits, often flow together, and the play he ultimately produces is often very different from the intention with which he started. He writes, and re-writes, scribbles and destroys an enormous amount before he makes the exquisite fair copy he sends to Copenhagen.

Their conversation reads a little like a rehearsal for the longer conversation on the same topic which Ibsen had later that summer holiday with his biographer Henrik Jæger. Jæger was able to supply one or two further anecdotal embellishments which were quickly taken up into the popular view of what kind of writer Ibsen was in essence:

When he has chosen his material [Jæger subsequently reported], he ponders it carefully for a long time before he sets pen to paper. Much of this thinking takes place on his long walks; moreover, the long time he takes over dressing is also given over to this preparatory thought. When he has thought the thing through in broad outline, he writes an outline sketch. I asked him: Presumably you work out your outline so carefully that you could just as easily write the last act first and the first one last? No, he answered, many of the details do not emerge until during the work of composition, as I begin to make progress. On the basis of this outline, he then sets about giving the thing shape, and this goes relatively swiftly. He also takes care, when he has finished for a day, still to have some pieces of dialogue ready in his mind which he can begin with the next day. He believes this helps him to keep going ... In this way the first manuscript grows from day to day until it is finished. But this manuscript is then for Ibsen nothing more than a preliminary. Only when this is complete does he feel he is familiar with his characters, knows their natures and how they express themselves. Then comes the revision in the second manuscript, and finally the fair copy in the third. He does not allow the work to leave his possession until there is a complete fair copy in existence.[2]

He said much the same thing to a German visitor the following year, asserting that before he wrote a single word, he had to have his characters fully under control:

I must see into the inmost reaches of their minds. I always start from the character; the context, the setting, the dramatic ensemble, they all take shape of their own accord just so long as I have first assured myself of the character in its human totality. I also need to visualize his appearance right down to the last button — how he stands and walks, how he gesticulates, what his voice sounds like. I don't loosen my grip on him until his destiny is complete.[3]

There were many similar reports during these years, each with its own claim to exclusive and heavily reverential detail; and slight though they are in themselves, they were not without some historical significance in that they set the first outlines of a received view of the man and his creative methods which has shown itself to be unusually persistent. In their general detail, they built up into a composite picture of a man, the most distinctive feature of whose life and authorship was that of ordered, disciplined, even inflexible routine: one whose daily constitutional walk was an event by which one set one's watch; whose daily perusal of the newspaper at his regular table in the city's best-known café had become a scheduled public spectacle; whose books — it was early realized — were to appear throughout the Eighties and Nineties with predictable and strictly biennial regularity, shrewdly timed to catch the Christmas book market.

Good order and literary discipline, it followed, were not only the supremely distinguishing features of those hours which Ibsen spent at his desk but were also the main merit and sign of the works themselves. Those contemporaries — and they were many — who felt that true genius belongs rather to the uninhibited outpouring of endlessly spontaneous insights were clearly uneasy. Whilst those who in any case disapproved of Ibsen felt justified in putting about the notion that Ibsen was nothing but a writing machine: not a man (as Bjørnson once said) but a pen.

The year 1909 gave a new dimension to this arena of enquiry, the greater part of which until then had been directed towards satisfying a largely idle public curiosity. This was the year of the publication, in three volumes, of Ibsen's *Efterladte Skrifter*, his literary remains. This allowed wide public access for the first time to his working drafts and other foul papers. I am now conscious that I begin to navigate here in contentious waters; and I am anxious on this particular occasion not to be drawn into any protracted discussion of the general merits of the place of 'foul papers' within the general field of literary interpretation. You will be aware — as I am — of the existence of a broad spectrum of opinion and belief: from, at the one extreme, the view that awards ready prima facie recognition to almost any scrap of incidental documentary material of this kind as a source of usable evidence by which our reading of the finished work is refined and sharpened — a belief which, incidentally, has loaded the archive shelves of certain Texan libraries with vast amounts of expensively acquired paper; to the view at the other extreme which insists on the total autonomy of the finalized text — a text within which, it is claimed, all relevant meaning is held, and to which all else is extraneous.

Without attempting to plot my own position on this spectrum with any precision, I would have to acknowledge that the fact that I was ready to give my best attention over a period of some twenty years of middle life to this *Nachlass* betrays something of my own standpoint.

Compared with certain other collections of surviving papers, its bulk is I suppose not overwhelmingly large, though it is quite substantial. On my own study shelves, it occupies in photocopied form something not far short of two metres. In terms of chronological spread, it covers the whole span of Ibsen's creative career, from his first play *Catiline* of 1850 to his last 'dramatic epilogue' of 1899, with only very few gaps of any significance. It comprises notes, jottings, scenarios, drafts, fragments of trial dialogue, marginal annotations, occasional pen and ink illustrative drawings, all for the most part sequentially numbered and/or lettered and physically sorted and arranged, and often additionally encoded to preserve their essential sequentiality. Compared with many another *Nachlass*, there is virtually nothing in it which the jargon might call 'bulk filler' — material which fails to offer evidence of compositional decisions of greater or lesser significance. Very few of the amendments recorded in these papers are without some direct relevance to the shaping of the final text and the ultimate determination of its meaning. Taken separately, their impact may seem slight, but cumulatively they interact upon each other to yield a semantic significance much greater than the mere sum of their parts.

Moreover the care which Ibsen habitually gave to dating his papers, often furnishing precise dates both top and tail, makes it possible in a great many instances not merely to sort and order with confidence the various and separate fragments into a coherent succession of events, but also to place them with rare precision in time: by year, month and day.

If dramatic (or indeed any kind of literary) composition may be thought of as an infinitely complex set of branching decisions in respect of choices thrown up by the inventive mind, then one recognizes in such papers an opportunity to reconstruct — crudely perhaps, coarsely, haltingly, but in the best instances profoundly revealingly — something of the original creative process. In homelier terms, it possibly allows one (as the phrase has it) to 'get into the mind' of the original creator, to follow its insights and recognitions and revisions and changes of direction in the sequence in which they uniquely occurred, and to participate (however indirectly and however imperfectly) in a creative process of high distinction, following the progress of a piece from the very first seed of an idea, through the successive stages of development right through to (in Ibsen's case) the meticulously timed despatch of the flawlessly handwritten fair copy to the printer to make the optimum deadline.

Seen as a problem in the aesthetics of drama, these working papers admit an intriguing new complexity: they set up a new axis, an extra time coordinate, by which each of these draft works can be individually plotted. Taking one's cue from Lessing who, in the *Laoköon*, defined poetry (and by extension drama) as the art of what is successive in time (in contrast to painting and sculpture which are arts of the coexistent in space), one sees in these drafts a special though admittedly rather cerebral mutation of drama. Superimposed upon an art form which itself is constituted of articulated signs or symbols at successive moments in time there is a further time grid, namely the days and weeks and months of their own actual composition. The action of this meta-drama as it moves from its own definable point of departure by way of invention and revision through to the final and definitive text shows in itself many of the elements of high drama. I venture to suggest that for anyone who has himself or herself ever cherished hopes of writing original drama — and I wonder how many literary scholars or academics would, if pressed, deny having at some time held such an ambition — the act of tracing, step by astonishing step, the genesis of a major play (such as all these plays are) from the first tentative thematic beginnings, through the various intermediate and developmental stages by which those themes are bodied forth in speech, gesture, setting and action until their final realization — this is, in my view, an intellectually exhilarating experience without parallel.

One immediate consequence of the publication of these papers was that — at a superficial level, at least — they seemed to substantiate many of the popular views about their author and his methods, and — by extension — about the cast of his creative mind. They revealed him as an apparently obsessionally methodical writer; they provided documentary evidence of the deliberate pace at which he worked; they testified to what seemed like the laboured care with which the adjustments and amendments, the refinements of the dialogue, the re-alignment of parts, the re-allocation of emphases, and the not infrequent excisions were made in the pursuit of effective dramatic communication.

More than that even, they seemed to indicate a kind of production formula, a drill to be followed which — it once having demonstrated its efficacy — was pressed into service as a methodological pattern to serve for play after play.

What nevertheless emerged with the greatest clarity from the sum total of these papers was abundant evidence that, in Ibsen's case, dramatic composition emphatically did not mean the mere supervention of language on an inspiration which was already complete. They left no doubt that the writing of an Ibsen play was a highly interactive occasion, a dynamic process full of shifts and retreats and advances and semantic flux as the creative invention of the author, the imperatives of the linguistic medium and the hidden potential of the thematic material acted upon one another throughout the period of active composition.

Sometimes the re-appraisal imposed by one or the other of

these factors at a particular stage in the composition of a piece was such as to entail an almost total abandonment of the draft in hand at a relatively advanced stage and its replacement with what was virtually a new play. I cite but one quite well-known example of this: The play which we now know as *Rosmersholm* began as a play about a widowed clergyman, his two daughters and their governess; the fact that he was called not Rosmer but Boldt-Rømer, and she was called not Rebecca West but Miss Radeck is one example of a feature of these drafts that I shall also want to take up in a moment. This draft was abandoned part of the way through Act 1 to be replaced by a new play, called 'White Horses', wherein this time the clergyman is presented as already having recently married the housekeeper; and in which they are visited as newly-weds by the clergyman's brother-in-law, here called not Kroll but Gylling, and later by a vagabond writer and agitator called not Brendel but Rosen-hjelm. Midway through Act II of this draft, however, Mrs Rosmer is discovered reverting to unmarried status in the name of Miss Dankert. This draft was then abandoned halfway through Act III; to be followed by a full four act draft, quite close in many respects to the *Rosmersholm* with which we are now familiar, except that those distinctive scenes involving Brendel (here called Hetman) are still only imperfectly realized.

I will not itemize in detail the other kinds of changes represented here, but simply catalogue some of the kinds of change to which these papers testify. There are plays, of which *Pillars of Society* is one example, which go through multiple starts and re-starts as the potential within the theme progressively begins to reveal itself to the dramatist: in this case through five different drafts of varying lengths. Or other plays where the need for logicality and coherence of exposition demanded a fundamental repositioning of various constituent passages and elements; others where the balance of the masses, their distribution and relative weighting, called for major re-adjustment. And some — and these have an extra entertainment value for the reader — where the quality of some of the draft passages was by any standards so bad that the only course open to a sensitive author was to cut them. I think, for example, of one excruciating passage in one of the drafts of *A*

Doll's House where Dr Rank delivers himself of a piece of ill-digested Darwinism on the subject of Nora's new carpet:

> My word, just look at this new carpet. Congratulations! Well now, what about a nice new carpet like that, for instance? Is that a luxury? I say, no it isn't. A carpet like that pays for itself, ladies. With a carpet like that under one's feet, one has finer and sublimer thoughts, nobler feelings than one would have in a comfortless room with cold, creaking boards. Especially where there are children in the house. People are ennobled by beautiful surroundings . . . It has to do with psychological statistics. But that's a science that hasn't been very much developed yet. . . .[and so on]

There are also plays — and *Little Eyolf* is possibly the supreme example — where Ibsen eventually discovered after some time that he wanted to say something quite different with his play from what he first set out to say. But instead of starting all over anew, he completed Acts II and III to the new design and then set about the task of re-writing Act I to fit the new situation. Much that is otherwise puzzling or obscure about this difficult play does — it seems to me — fall more satisfactorily into place when it is known that the end was finalized before the beginning.

One brief comment in parentheses I can perhaps allow myself at this point. The kinds of textual change I catalogued a moment or two ago as being identifiable in the papers were all what might usefully be called macro-changes: modifications to the play's dramatic structure, alterations to the naming and inter-relating of characters, the transposition of parts, changes in the sequence of events and scenes, the inclusion or exclusion, the addition or deletion of major references or of passages of substance. But one must not disregard the microchanges: the linguistic fine-tuning of the dialogue. Ibsen repeatedly claimed that this aspect of dramatic composition was one that greatly pre-occupied him. With, for example, *A Doll's House* virtually ready for fair-copying to go to the printer, he nevertheless and characteristically decided to award himself one further complete revision, and wrote to his Publisher: '. . . In order to give the language and the dialogue generally the greatest possible precision, I propose to write it out once more with improvements, corrections and alterations before I finally send you the fair-copy.' Similarly on a later occasion with *The Wild Duck*: after pronouncing it completed, he then immediately qualified that remark, and added: 'But now comes the finer revision, the more vigorous individualization of the characters and their modes of expressing themselves.' He even claimed on one occasion that the way any given character spoke at night would be different from the way he would speak during the day.

These microchanges caused me a good deal of anguish when I was working on The Oxford Ibsen, an edition which attempts to make available in translation for the English reader the more important parts of this draft material, and to fit them in to a chronological framework. You will not expect from me here any ponderous exemplification of the way in which many of these subtler linguistic emendations — all of them carrying some larger or smaller charge of semantic energy within the whole — proved to be too fine, too language-specific, and thus too elusive to be trapped by the coarse mesh of the translation process. The degree of literal precision which would in most cases have been required to signal these changes from, say, the penultimate draft to the final text was in constant conflict with the need to preserve that minimum level of idiomaticness or 'speakability' necessary in an English text meant to be read easily and played successfully. Nobody, then, is readier than I to acknowledge that, beyond a certain stage of sophistication, the rigorous study of Ibsen is possible only by addressing oneself to his original Norwegian text.

Let me leave abstractions for a moment and turn to the more prosaic details of what actually happened when Ibsen sat himself at his desk and began to put pen to paper; and to look at how he then paced himself, knowing his self-appointed deadline.

Think, if you will, of the Ibsenist creative cycle as one which habitually extended over two years, typically from the successful autumn completion of one play to the autumn of the next year but one. Two years each, between 1875 and 1881, went to the writing of *Pillars of Society, A Doll's House* and *Ghosts.* Then came, exceptionally, a rush of blood to the head, in consequence of which he angrily wrote *An Enemy of the People* within a brief twelve months. Then, at precise two-yearly intervals for the next fourteen years, there came that astounding succession of plays which took Europe and the world by storm: *The Wild Duck, Rosmersholm, The Lady from the Sea, Hedda Gabler, The Master Builder, Little Eyolf* and *John Gabriel Borkman.* Finally came an untypical three years over his 'dramatic epilogue', *When We Dead Awaken.*

Let me then start, by way of example, in the autumn of 1877. Ibsen had recently completed *Pillars of Society*; a little over twenty-four months later he sent off the completed manuscript of *A Doll's House* to the printer. The first twelve months of this period very obviously went on thought: searching, brooding, examining, rejecting, and pondering what the theme of his next drama might be. Little of this process seems ever to have been committed to paper. I have a feeling that a great deal of his attention went — as always, but perhaps with greater intensity than usual during these periods — to a study of the newspapers and periodicals that regularly found their way into his house in his search for usable material.

Eventually, in the October of 1878, he committed some of his thoughts to paper for the first time on the subject of his new play, writing down, in a careful hand, certain ideas which he sensed might lend themselves to dramatic treatment. They were not intended as aphorisms, nor should they be judged as such; they were certainly not intended for publication. Their sole intention seems to have been to define a point of departure, to serve as a kind of internal memo to himself as a declaration of intent.

It is perhaps not too fanciful to think that — both at this stage in the play's composition and in the later drafting stages — the size, shape and format of the paper he used played a small role. Practically the whole of Ibsen's *Nachlass* — certainly that part relating to the so-called modern plays — shows him using a form of folded quarto sheet, or sheets, giving him in its simplest form a rudimentary form of booklet of four sides with an octavo sized page. Frequently he augmented this — as indeed he did in these Notes to *A Doll's House* — into an interleaved set of two such folded sheets, which then gave him a unit of eight sides; on other occasions he would create for himself what were virtually small booklets of twelve or even sixteen sides, the leaves of which were numbered serially, and the whole sewn or stitched together to keep them ordered and to preserve their sequence.

Ibsen clearly felt that it was more conducive to ordered thinking to have something with even this modest element of structure and form than to have a plethora of loose single sheets with all the attendant threat of disorder. He also found that, at times of major revision, this kind of make-up facilitated the interleaving of new sheets and the interpolation of new material.

The preliminary Notes to *A Doll's House* — and I doubt if it would serve any useful purpose for me to read them in their entirety — begin as follows:

Notes for the tragedy of modern times.

There are two kinds of moral law, two kinds of conscience, one in man and a completely different one in woman. They do not understand each other; but in matters of practical living the woman is judged by the man's law, as if she were a man and not a woman.

The wife in the play ends up quite bewildered and not knowing right from wrong; her natural instincts on the one side and her faith in authority on the other leave her completely confused.

A woman cannot be herself in contemporary society; it is an exclusively male society with laws drafted by men, and with counsel and judges who judge feminine conduct from the male point of view.

The next stage of composition consisted of putting together a short scenario of an opening act. In the notes to *A Doll's House* there is as yet (and this is typical) no title to the play. Typical too is that there is no naming of characters — only references to 'he', 'she', or at most 'the mistress of the house', 'the friend', 'the debt-collector', and so on. A typical scenario might additionally offer the chance for a brief snatch of dialogue, or a key phrase, and maybe some indication of the *mis-en-scène*. In these earliest Notes to *A Doll's House*, one remarks the conspicuous absence of any reference to 'a doctor' among the dramatis personae: Dr Rank seemingly was not in Ibsen's plans at the earliest stages. In this instance, these Notes occupy the first side and part of the second of the eight-sided booklet.

To make changes in the characters' names was a regular and integral part of the process of composition. Occasionally one senses that the changes were made in order to achieve some closer accord between the name and the nature of the character, so that — as one might say — it sounded 'righter' to call the Doll's House family Helmer rather than Stensborg, and so on. This is however a difficult thing to prove. Perhaps more relevant was the consideration that to change a character's name at the point where there occurred some major revision in the concept or direction of the play itself was to build into the draft a kind of marker (rather akin to colour-coding) where Ibsen was immediately helped in identifying those passages which belonged to some earlier strategy and which would therefore need particularly close scrutiny if inconsistencies in the action were later to be eliminated.

His routine then turned, for its third stage, to the listing of the characters of the play by name. *A Doll's House* has a list of eight characters (not counting Nora's children). The Helmers are at this stage called Stenborg; Mrs Linde is unmarried; and Rank (who now *does* figure) is called Hank. They are given no detailed description other than their profession or status (eg. wife, nursemaid, etc). The list in this instance was inserted on the lower part of the second side of the document.

The possibility of one other listing of some significance must be allowed for at this stage: a list of the real-life people who were intended to serve as models for the characters under creation. There is in fact only one actual instance of this type of list extant: in the papers relating to *The Wild Duck*. Whether this was part of the regular routine of composition or not cannot now be shown with any confidence. Certainly it was a very sensitive category of document, and it may well be that any others of this kind were destroyed. What the existence of this one document does show, however, is that to work from such models could on occasion be part of his practice.

Not until the beginning of May 1878, it seems, was the work of transposing these ideas into dialogue form begun: in other words, some 19 or so months of the allocated 24 had gone on preliminaries of one sort or another before what the world would think of as the 'real' work of composition was put in train. Following which, in three months of intense and concentrated work, a complete draft of the three acts of *A Doll's House* (what we might call the 'Ur-Doll's House') was worked out in detail, using a succession of scenarios, and involving a repeated scanning and a detailed working and re-working of the text.

The result was a version prickling with inconsistencies, and which embodied a number of major modifications, a re-naming and re-vamping of several of the characters, and a succession of corrections to the navigational plan.

This was the version to which Ibsen then allotted the better part of the August and September of that year for adding what he called the final 'improvements, corrections and alterations'. The changes that he made are much too numerous, the detailed changes too textually pervasive for me to attempt to summarize them here; but one or two of the more striking things serve a more general truth, and act as indicators of where meaning in this play, and in his plays in general, is to be sought. More obviously, they demonstrate how many of the quintessentially Ibsenist things could (and did) regularly enter the text at a very late stage in the work's composition. One point of interest is that the innuendo-ridden conversation between Rank and Nora where she teases him with her 'flesh-coloured silk stockings', and which adds a whole new sexually charged dimension to their relationship and to the entire domestic set-up, only now enters the dramatic scheme of things. The second is that Nora's feverish dancing of the tarantella at the tense end of Act II — one of the most memorable events in the whole of world drama — is only now brought in triumphantly to substitute for what would have surely been a monumental slackening of tension: an accompanied rendition by Nora of 'Anitra's Song' from *Peer Gynt*. And thirdly, it is only at this late stage that Ibsen contrived, by a simple switch of personal pronouns, that moment of delicious shock that re-echoed round Europe in its day: by his turning Torvald's cry of relief, on reading the Krogstad letter, from the solicitous but dramatically low-charged 'You are saved' of the draft into the devastatingly self-condemnatory 'I . . . I am saved.'

All three of these changes, taken together with those many others which I have left unremarked, skilfully honed the cutting edge of the drama. It may well be that the text had to reach this particular degree of finality before these and similarly devastating insights presented themselves to the mind of the dramatist.

In all three instances, what happened was that certain elements already resident in the drama were given emphasis and enhanced definition by selected *coups de théâtre*. Nevertheless, it is noteworthy that, as Ibsen moved on through his career to late maturity, he frequently used these revisionary opportunities not so much to block in the meaning, not to firm up the outline, but rather to blur, in the interests of the overall composition, certain contours which he doubtless felt were too emphatically drawn. The precise nature of the earlier liaison between Gina and Old Werle in *The Wild Duck*, and that between Rebecca West and her foster-father in *Rosmersholm* were, for example, deliberately taken slightly more out of focus in the later stages of revision; and other examples are not hard to find.

In all this, there is everywhere evident a compulsive need to *consolidate* each successive stage in the composition by careful re-writing, usually in a painstakingly deliberate hand. It is almost like an act of ordered occupation of newly won territory in a planned campaign of advance. It probably also meant that many of the more rapidly written revisions were discarded and destroyed at the time — and it could well be that those early witnesses who commented on Ibsen's heavy consumption of paper were right.

I have left to the last one aspect of these papers which would normally merit only low priority: the calligraphic evidence. Even a casual reader leafing through the body of this *Nachlass* would be aware of a distinct change of handwriting sometime in the late 1860s, and perhaps be prompted by this to remark that, when we speak of Ibsen's career, we are wrong to think of it as limited to the modern 'Ibsenist' plays.

It then comes as a shock to realize that nothing of what I have just been saying about Ibsen's tightly disciplined regime applies in any way to the dramas that occupy the earlier part of Ibsen's career. If one examines the genesis of *Brand* and *Peer Gynt*, it is only too evident that the circumstances attaching to their formative stages bear absolutely no resemblance to the later routines.

The *Ur-Brand* — if I may call it such — was not a carefully drafted drama arrived at by the deliberate and measured processes of the kind that produced *A Doll's House*, but (altogether improbably) a long epic poem in no fewer than 212 eight-line stanzas, rhymed and metrical. The agency which then transformed this epic poem into the completed drama was no careful campaign conducted in line with a defined strategy, but one single, overpowering, overwhelming moment of inspiration. Ibsen has described it:

> One day I went into St Peter's, Rome . . . and there, suddenly, the form for what I had to say came to me, forcefully and clearly. Now I have thrown overboard the thing that has been a torment to me for the whole of the past year without my having got anywhere; and in the middle of July I began on this new thing, which then progressed as nothing has ever progressed for me before.[4]

The huge five acts of *Brand* were then completed in a matter of some four months, between July and November 1965, in what was clearly a kind of raptus.

Brand was followed shortly afterwards by *Peer Gynt*, also long and also in verse. It was for its part written in a period of about nine months, between the January and the October of 1867: a vast free-ranging invention, audacious in its imagery, uninhibited, undisciplined. But Ibsen himself saw the signs and heeded the warning. Shortly after it had appeared, he called it 'reckless'; in later life he described it as 'wild and formless'[5], and confessed how he had written both *Brand* and *Peer Gynt* at very high pressure, amounting to nervous overstrain, writing verses the whole time, even when asleep or half awake, thinking them capital for the moment but realizing later that they were the veriest nonsense.[6]

As one then contemplates these works, and as one recalls the otherwise innocuous handwriting change from a spindly, forward-slanting scrawl to the later bold, upright and firmly formed hand of the later years, and remembering too those other outwardly visible signs of change in Ibsen's life-style — the more formal dress, the greater fastidiousness in his personal grooming, the greater *gravitas* of manner, the dignified demeanour — and putting all these things together, one begins to suspect that beneath all these externalities there was possibly some wholly profound change in Ibsen's life and attitudes.

And of course one would be right. To examine this change in any detail would require at least one other lecture, and I must resist the temptation to pursue it further here and now. Let me — inadequately — merely say that what was happening here, at this turning point in his career, was the willed imposition of discipline and control upon a creative talent that otherwise threatened to get frighteningly out of hand. Rather like — dare one say — capping an oil-gusher.

The springs of invention, the great reserves of creative imagination which were so prodigally exploited in *Brand* and *Peer Gynt* remained vigorously active throughout Ibsen's later career of authorship. But equally formidable, and in its own way equally impressive, was the control — the iron, unrelenting control — to which they were subjected.

4

Meaning and Evidence

What I have to say on this occasion does not pretend to be anything more than an invitation to share a private obsession I have
fallen victim to: an obsession with three separate and not
obviously related bits of Ibsen. All three things seemed to me to
have the kind of significance we conveniently but loosely call
symbolic, a significance that reached beyond the immediate
context; even more tantalizing was the suspicion that together
they seemed to enjoy some kind of inter-relevance, something
which did not reveal itself immediately but which I had the
feeling further reflection might reveal. I am asking you, then, to
bear with me as I very tentatively work through these things in

the hope of finding some way of resolving them into something less fragmentary.

The three things I find so obsessive are:

(a) an intuition bearing on the final moments of *Pillars of Society;*
(b) a fascination with the mechanics of the Brendel episodes in *Rosmersholm;*
(c) a particular phrase which, although it only occasionally passes the lips of Ibsen's characters (in *Emperor and Galilean*, for example, and in *The Lady from the Sea*) nevertheless in a great many instances seems clearly to be passing unspoken through their minds.

Let us begin with the intuition. I had long felt uneasy at the generally accepted interpretation of *Pillars of Society* as a drama of simple and sentimental moral triumph. As you will know — and to this audience I can dispense with any ponderously full documentation and content myself with a representative selection of critical opinion — it is generally held to deal with the career of a man who, when his guilt and deceit are brought home to him, purges himself by full confession, clears his soul of evil, and by his conversion demonstrates the victory of right over wrong: 'It is possible to admire the ingenuity of the plot,' Raymond Williams has written, '. . . but in spite of its skilful carpentry, *Pillars of Society* is crude. Everything in it is a simplification of the order of Lona's last cry: "The spirits of truth and freedom — *these* are the pillars of society." '[1]

Bravely, some critics have sought to resist the obvious charge of 'sentimentality' by a flat denial; but more often than not, their phrases themselves amount to a kind of admission of it, as in the case of Emil Reich:

Here everything turns out for the best, a little too much so, as in *The League of Youth*. One set of glad tidings succeeds another, to be followed by general reconciliation . . . What led Ibsen to make such a finale were not external considerations but a triumphant and dominant belief in a better future — which we too would want to call good, not out of any flabby sentimentality but in defiant pleasure at this chivalrous battle against corruption and decay.[2]

The dismay widely felt at this play by Ibsen's critics — even the most sympathetic of them — tends to find a refuge in the idea that *Pillars of Society* must somehow be seen to be 'different'. Halvdan Koht claimed that this play was the only one of all Ibsen's works that made a direct appeal to the emotions and called forth tears:

> *Pillars of Society* is the only one of all his works which directly touches the emotions and calls forth tears. Otherwise his plays usually close in such a way as to disturb the conscience, temper the mind, or incite the will; one may become angry or afraid, one may oppose or agree; there is only one thing one never becomes, and that is soft-hearted or tearful — with one exception, *Pillars of Society*.[3]

And the ultimate step from seeing this play as merely different to seeing it as different *and inferior* is a short one, and one often and quickly taken — as (for instance) Roman Woerner did, who thought it the least successful of all Ibsen's modern plays, and so different that it was unworthy to be compared with the others:

> Here Ibsen wanted to drive the moral home with a sledge-hammer . . . And for its conclusion a finale in the family circle of such sentimental earnestness, such dubious gaiety, such universal self-satisfaction in optimistic platitudes, that it is only by virtue of its brevity that it is to be preferred to the Fourth Act of Bjørnson's *A Bankrupt*. [It is] . . . in artistic terms the least of Ibsen's modern dramas . . . It is Ibsen's one *Tendenz* play. This has to be stressed, not so much to distinguish the play from its successors, but the reverse: so that the latter are not put together with it as similar in kind.[4]

My own reaction to this — an instinctive one, I admit, in the first place — was to feel that if any error of judgement *had* been made in this instance, the error probably lay not with Ibsen himself but with his interpreters. My own intuitive reading of the play was that it was not the simple, crudely sentimental thing it generally passed for, was not a mere *Tendenzstück*, and was not to be dismissed out of hand as inferior — as immediately and unquestionably inferior, at any rate — to the other plays as it was generally held to be.

I felt that there were other possibilities that at least merited scrutiny: that, for instance, the play might conceivably be construed as a deceptively but nevertheless mordantly ironic piece in which simple honest virtue, far from triumphing at the end to a chorus of sentimental moralizing, is on the contrary seen to be once more duped and deceived, manipulated, hoodwinked, led by the nose by a very smart operator indeed who knows all the tricks. There is no doubt that in the end Bernick leaves himself sitting very pretty — prettier, probably, then he has ever sat before — and taking full advantage of the domestic and public sympathy that an apparently repentant sinner who knows how to play on the heart-strings can count on.

To play with such possibilities brings us then to the first term of the title I have given this address: it suggest that the play might be capable of sustaining a very different *meaning* from that conventionally attached to it. My own students, to whom I held out the possibility of such a reading, were naturally and very properly not content with unsubstantiated intuitions of this kind, and demanded *evidence*. Which led — and could lead *us* if I do not with resolute cowardice stick to the shallows — into very deep and very treacherous waters indeed.

Even, however, if one limits one's notion of 'evidence' to things overt, intrinsic, and directly communicated within the play, there is much that might be thought of as speaking for an ironic reading. It is clear that Bernick confesses only that which can no longer be concealed, and only after he has been driven into a very tight corner from which no other escape is feasible. Having once decided on confession, he instinctively seeks for ways of turning the situation to advantage; and the very words he uses, from which it appears that he is even then calculating

in terms of what *profit* might be extracted, provide an involuntary betrayal of the way his mind is working:

> But let us not decide anything tonight. I ask each one of
> you to go to his home . . . to compose himself . . . to look
> into his heart. And when we have all calmed down, it
> will be seen whether I have lost or gained by speaking
> out.[5]

This same speech, as it continues, makes it clear that although he
has confessed to his youthful peccadillo, and to having sheltered
behind the magnanimity of his brother-in-law, he is nevertheless very careful to keep quiet about the most monstrous thing
of all: that he had been ready to send a whole ship's company to
their deaths in the 'coffin ship' merely to save his own respectability. All he is ready to say publicly about this is:

> Goodbye! I still have much . . . very much . . . to repent
> of, but that concerns my own conscience alone.[6]

He manages still, we are led to understand, to retain personal
control of the railway, and succeeds furthermore in eliminating
any further interference from his three earlier business associates. And all in all, he is seen playing on the sentiments of
the two women at the end of the play in a thoroughly shameless
way. One could well imagine a production of the play which,
using only the most economical of devices — a particular
emphasis or intonation here, the hint of a gesture there — could
subtly but surely convey something of the bitterness of the
message behind all the sickly sweetness of the smiles and
embraces and sloganizing of the final curtain.

However, I do not want to turn this present occasion into a
simple though detailed analysis of *Pillars of Society*. Nor am I
in this instance particularly concerned with trying to persuade
you of the possible validity of the ironic ending I have briefly
proposed. All I am asking of you now is that you share my
astonishment that the *possibility* of such an interpretation has
gone so completely disregarded. One might have supposed that
somebody or other would have held up this reading before now

to be looked at, even if only to discard it after examination.

For what is it, after all, that informs this reading but dramatic irony of the very simplest and basic kind: a secret shared by one character with the audience, a secret from which the other characters are excluded, a secret which thus lends extra meaning to every remark that passes on stage? And one asks: Why, in this most ironic of authors, has this ironic potential been overlooked? Why, despite all the dismay, the disappointment, the head-shaking, over the inadequacies of the play that go with a simple surface reading, why had the possibility that some things in it might have more than a face value not previously commended itself?

Let me make clear what it is I am asking. There is, of course, small merit in seeing in this one further (though previously unsuspected) instance of the fact that things in Ibsen are not always as they seem. It is not that appearances are often deceptive in Ibsen — this we know already — but that on the evidence of *Pillars of Society* this deceptiveness can itself prove to be deceptive.

The really interesting and much more difficult and complex question is therefore: *How* may things in Ibsen not always be what they seem? Are there in his dramatic technique any kinds of evidence which make special or unusual claims on the spectator, things peculiar to Ibsen, or at least in their subtlety or frequency peculiar? Can we identify in his drama any principles at work affecting the nature of the dramatic evidence he presents his audience with? And if so, how is this evidence then to be assessed? What adjustments and revisions are to be made, what distortions and deviations allowed for in the surface reality of things before one can arrive at a valid meaning?

Before I pass from the first to the second of my obsessions, from *Pillars of Society* to the Brendel episodes, I need first to set up some very rough scaffolding for the ideas I shall be dealing with. I shall be asking you to try to reserve some kind of distinction between

(a) what the characters say — and by 'say' I mean anything the characters overtly communicate by their words, their gestures, posture and movements, their visible reactions, and the like;

(b) what the characters think — and by 'think' I mean such views, ideas, prejudices, pieces of knowledge as can reasonably be supposed to be in their minds; and

(c) what is actually the case — and by 'actually the case' I mean the state of the fictional world as it really is, somewhat in the sense of Wittgenstein's opening statement in his *Tractatus logico-philosophicus:* 'Die Welt ist alles, was der Fall ist.'

Any disparity between (a) and (b) provides one kind of basis for an ironic situation. Re-sketching the Bernick situation in these terms, for example, we might write:

Bernick: says $\neq$ thinks = the case,

i.e. knowing the full truth about the 'Indian Girl', he knows (and we know) what is 'the case', but his words do not wholly reflect this knowledge; there is a clear discrepancy between what is in his mind and what he says; there is suppression with intent to deceive.

This pattern is of course commonplace not only in Ibsen, but in dramatic literature in general, though many variations are possible. Engstrand, for example, must clearly be supposed to know what is 'the case' in the matter of the candle and the wood-shavings; we, the audience, do not 'know' with any certainty what this 'case' is, though our suspicions are of course strong, and we take it that Engstrand's words represent a departure from this reality. Another very characteristic and very moving variation on this basic pattern is the conversation between Borkman and Foldal, where Borkman — either from a spirit of altruism towards his friend or from his own need for reassurance — has in the past forborne to say what he has long known to be 'the case' about his and Foldal's friendship:

Borkman: says $\neq$ thinks = the case.

Foldal meanwhile has in a more genuine sense been deceiving himself about their friendship all these years, though his speech faithfully reflects what is in his mind; so that in his case the pattern of irony corresponds rather to the kind I shall be discussing in a moment or two.

Only one other variation have I time to call your attention to at this point; and that is where the basic pattern remains as above, but where there is a built-in time delay and an inversion of orthodox dramatic irony. I am thinking of those instances — like the conversation between Kroll and Rebecca in the opening moments of *Rosmersholm* — where instead of the audience sharing a secret to the exclusion of certain characters, the characters share a secret concealed from the audience, until time uncovers it. Thus we may still write:

$$\text{Kroll/Rebecca: say} \neq \text{think} = \text{the case,}$$

i.e. they both know the reality of their own past relations, but suppress or disguise this beneath what at first hearing seem to be the conversational banalities of everyday politeness: 'Have you settled in?' 'How is your wife?' 'How nice you've got the place looking!' and so on. All of which has to be reviewed and revised in retrospect from a later point in time when 'the case' — the details of the past, the savage reference by Kroll to Rebecca's 'bewitching' powers — is made clearer to us and the implicit significances are released.

Complementing this basic pattern is the further kind of situation where

$$\text{a character: says} = \text{thinks} \neq \text{the case,}$$

i.e., where speech and behaviour faithfully reflect what is generally *thought* by a character to be 'the case', but where these thoughts and ideas are at some remove from a sober appraisal of actual reality. This pattern is particularly richly represented in Ibsen: where a character, because of some delusion or mis-apprehension or prejudice or ignorance or mental sickness or hypnotic suggestion cannot or will not grasp the realities of the

case. Hjalmar, Fru Alving, Helmer, Rosmer, Ellida, Solness —
a great many of Ibsen's characters are those whose lives at some
time or another fit this state of affairs.

But — and I fancy I have now reached the nub of the argument — these two kinds of ironic disparity can only be properly
assessed if we have available to us some reliable or convincing
or plausible way of determining — from the evidence the
dramatist presents us with — what 'the case' is. Only then have
we something against which to measure the validity of what a
character 'says' or 'thinks'. And the problem of *how* to determine
what is actually 'the case' is one that is central to any discussion
of the meaning of the plays.

What are some of these ways in which 'the case' is made
known to us?

In some instances, of which *Pillars of Society* is an obvious
example, 'the case' is woven into the narrative of the play, presented as a series of dramatic events, as are the facts of Bernick's
career.

At other times 'the case' can be the subject of comment within
the play by a character whom we are prepared to accept as a
reliable witness, e.g. Borkman's impatient rejection of any
further mutual self-deception, or Relling's explicit analysis of
the 'life-lie'.

Occasionally, though the occasions are rare, Ibsen himself
seems ready to instruct us, through some remark or other
altogether extrinsic to the play proper, on how we should
conceive 'the case' to be. These remarks offer their own peculiar
kind of enlightenment — peculiar not so much because of the
contribution they make to certain precise and select points of
difficulty, but rather because of the glimpses they give into the
ways in which Ibsen expects us to interpret his dramatic
evidence.

There is profit in looking at one of these instances in some
small detail. Take, for example, the Tesman/Thea episode near
the end of *Hedda Gabler*, where these two characters settle down
with the notes of Løvborg's book to try to reconstruct what has

been lost. There have been those who have seen in this the same triumph of simple goodness generally ascribed to *Pillars of Society:*

> Thea is not thinking of herself, but only of the man she loves. . . . The prospect of devoting her life to glorifying his memory carries with it a healing strength. The virtues that are Thea's — self-abnegation, loyalty, blind faith, the quiet strength of service — are out of fashion in our day and age, but that does not prevent them from existing still . . .[7]

Certainly, there is nothing *explicit* within the play itself which would contradict a reading of this kind; and one is often tempted to think — rather maliciously perhaps — how many other critics of the play would have been inclined to take the sentimental view of things here, had it not been for those acid remarks in Ibsen's notebooks where he speaks of the 'irony', and even more damagingly of the 'burlesque element' in the Tesman/Thea situation:

> Then H. [Løvborg] is brought to his death. And then those two sit there with the manuscript they cannot interpret . . . What an ironic comment on human striving towards development and progress.[8]

And later.

> Tesman reads in the posthumous documents about 'the two ideals'. Mrs Elfsted cannot explain to him what E.L. [Løvborg] meant by it.
> Then comes the burlesque element: Both T[esman] and Mrs E[lf]sted] dedicate their future lives to solving the riddle.[9]

In parenthesis, it should also be said in all fairness that even among those critics familiar with Ibsen's notebooks there are still some who consciously and knowingly reject too ironic an inter-pretation of this incident; Arild Haaland, for example, writes:

93

> Despite Ibsen's strange comments, the real moral heroes — lightly caricatured — are no less than Jørgen Tesman,Mrs Elvsted and the incomparable Aunt Julle.[10]

Indeed, the problem of establishing what is 'the case' in such instances is really the problem of how far to admit extrinsic evidence of this kind into one's deliberations, or whether to hold exclusively to such evidence as is intrinsic to the play — which is a very big question indeed, and not one which can easily be contained within the framework of these present remarks.

More modest-seeming but very relevant to our present purposes is another example of such outside prompting from Ibsen himself — an example which has only recently come to light. Faced with the characterization of Arnholm in *The Lady from the Sea*, one asks what is 'the case' here. Taking certain internal evidence in the play at its face value only, and accepting unmodified the testimony of Bolette and Hilde, one might take him for an *old* man. But Ibsen, as he very clearly pointed out in a letter to the Christiania Theatre of 18 Dec 1888, obviously intended an ironic discrepancy to be evident here, intended that certain necessary adjustments and allowances should be made by the spectator, that the girls' testimony should not go untreated:

> Herr Hansson must not be misled by Bolette's and Hilde's remarks about his appearance into portraying Arnholm as a really old or decrepit man. It is only to these young girls that he appears so. His hair has grown somewhat thin, and schoolmastering has taken it out of him — that is all.[11]

Thus, as above, the girls say honestly what they think, though what they think is not 'the case'. And Ibsen's strictures constitute a serious warning that what the characters say, *even when the situation is not markedly ironic*, needs interpreting with the greatest care.

It has taken me some considerable time to reach the second of my obsessions: the Brendel episodes; though now, I think, from what I have said, the relevance can be made clearer.

The problem it bears on is: How, apart from the more straightforward and obvious instances I listed earlier of direct narrative, embodiment in the dramatic texture, plausible comment or incidental author's directive, is 'the case' defined in dramatic terms, in order that we as audience should be conscious of the ironic disparity between what is and what seems, whenever a valid meaning depends upon our being aware of it?

Let me remind you of what takes place when Brendel is announced. Into a situation in which the relationship of three people to each other is being worked out, a new and previously unannounced element is introduced: the figure of Brendel. All three minds swing round to bear on this phenomenon before it ever appears:

ROSMER [*with a start*]. Ulrik Hetman! Was that it?

MRS. HELSETH. Yes, Hetman, that was it.

KROLL. I seem to have heard that name before . . .

REBECCA. Surely that was the name he used to write
    under, wasn't it, that strange man . . .

ROSMER [*to* KROLL]. It is Ulrik Brendel's pen-name.

KROLL. That waster Brendel. So it is.

REBECCA. So he is still alive.

ROSMER. I thought he was on tour with some
    theatrical company.

KROLL. The last I heard of him he was in the workhouse.

rosmer. Ask him to come in, Mrs Helseth.

MRS. HELSETH. Very good, sir. [*She goes out.*]

KROLL. You are not really going to let this man
    into your house?

ROSMER. He was once my tutor, you know.

KROLL. Yes, I know that he went and crammed your
    head full of revolutionary ideas, and that your
    father drove him out of the house with a horse-
    whip.[12]

Three separate bearings on this yet unknown thing, with a whole range of possibilities: for Rebecca, he is 'strange' and associated with authorship; for Kroll he is 'prodigal' and a trouble-maker, and associated with the workhouse; for Rosmer he is the one-time tutor, and associated with the theatre. All these views betray a certain built-in deflection from what is actually 'the case', like a compass one must make an allowance for. To rely on any one of these alone would yield a misleading picture, like Bolette's and Hilde's view of Arnholm. One notes that it is not necessary for the expression of view to be 'wrong' before a discrepancy can enter in; so perhaps in this case we ought to write:

$$\left. \begin{array}{l} \text{Rebecca} \\ \text{Kroll} \\ \text{Rosmer} \end{array} \right) \quad \text{say} = \text{think} < \text{the case}$$

i.e. they all say without dissimulation what is in their thoughts, but their thoughts represent a good deal less than the whole truth. Nevertheless, when taken together, these three references mark out an area within which one must suppose the truth about Brendel might be found.

The process is however by no means complete with this. Brendel himself makes his appearance; and between what he 'is' as he presents himself in person, and what in his view he says he is, there are further tensions:

Brendel: says = thinks $\neq$ the case
Brendel: is ------------ the case

In the main body of the play, between his two appearances, there are more references to his behaviour in town which contribute further to the circumstantial evidence offered on Brendel. Until, finally, Brendel appears in person once again to give a new and revised estimate of himself which, while still shot through with self-dramatization, is a much more clear-sighted view of what is actually 'the case' about himself than his earlier self-estimate had been; thus, in a very large degree:

Brendel (2): says = thinks = the case.

The Brendel episodes are useful because they constitute a small and relatively easily analysable sample of a method of presenting 'the case' which in many different and complex ways recurs again and again in Ibsen's work. The essence of it is that the audience is offered a series of multilateral references, each of which is liable to be biased or coloured or distorted in some way, and from which we are invited to reconstruct the reality of the situation. The factors that distort the references may in some instances be innocent ones, in others less so: time, age, personality, prejudice, preoccupation, deception, illusion, excessive idealism, self-deception, experience, upbringing, frustration, and so on.

It is of course not always that 'the reality' presents itself either in person as with Brendel, or in some comparable tangible form; it is not always that we have some direct, non-allusive form of representation against which we can measure the various references. Within *Rosmersholm* itself, for example, one recalls how the personality of Beate — a key element in the structure of the drama — is wonderfully and exclusively built up by multilateral reference of this kind.

I have, for ease of argument, so far spoken of this thing as though it were a one-way (even though often very complex) operation. Now, however, is the time to remind you that in essence the process is a dialectic one, that there is a constant and progressive reference *back* from these referents. It is this that constitutes what is perhaps the most demanding claim on the attention of the audience — demanding because it requires doing in retrospect and often on the basis of interim judgements which are subsequently seen to require revision. As soon as 'the case' begins to take on shape and definition by this process of multilateral reference, certain remarks which earlier served to *define* now are seen to *betray*: a remark by A about B serves first to contribute to our knowledge about B, but as soon as B is more precisely and reliably determined, the original remark then functions as something that reveals something about A, in that A is then seen as the kind of person who was prepared to make a remark of that nature about the phenomenon we now know as B.

Again, time prevents me from giving more than one brief example of this, though it would not be at all difficult to find many, many more. In Act II, Rosmer speaks to Kroll about Beate:

> I told you, didn't I, about her uncontrollable, wild fits of sensual passion — which she expected me to respond to.[13]

At first one files this remark away in one's mind as a statement that contributes towards a definition of Beate's nature; but as a truer picture of Beate emerges from the multilateral references later in the play, when rather fuller circumstances are known, this remark is reviewed and reinterpreted as a statement that *betrays* something of Rosmer's nature. (The similarity between this piece of dramatic architecture and the situation in *Ghosts* is one that I can simply draw attention to in a kind of parenthesis: how Mrs Alving's account of Captain Alving as a dissolute reprobate first serves to represent the husband, but is later more eloquent of Mrs Alving's joyless puritanism of those years, her distrust of 'livsglæde'. It is not always that commentators of this play, in assessing the meaning of it from the dramatic evidence, make adequate allowance for the fact that Mrs Alving's remarks about her past married life are both strongly biased and largely uncorroborated).

The final complication comes when it is realized that what I have so far been attempting to analyse is something corresponding in large measure to the atomic structure of Ibsen's dramatic technique; and that when these multilateral references are seen operating not as separate and discrete entities but as things interlocked and inter-linked in molecular chains, the full complexity of the structure becomes evident. Instead of a simple *accumulation* of multilateral references, with each set serving to define an individual referent, these things are seen rather to form complicated lattices of cross-reference, forever changing under the press of time's revelations.

Which finally brings me to the third of my obsessions; the phrase that seems to me to echo so persistently through Ibsen's dramatic world.

In Act III of the first part of *Emperor and Galilean*, in the famous seance scene with Maximos and Julian, when the latter is desperately seeking to interpret what he has just seen and heard, when he is trying to resolve the conflicting and ambiguous evidence offered to him by circumstance and prophecy, when all seems balanced in a torment of doubt and uncertainty, he says half-sadly, half in despair: 'Tegn imot tegn' — 'Sign contra sign'.

Fifteen years and seven plays later, when Wangel and Arnholm are trying to explain the curious fascination which the Stranger has for Ellida, when they try to account for the nature and the timing of the puzzling events, when they review the commonsensical as well as the more mystical explanations of things, Arnholm comments half-sadly, half in despair: 'Altså tegn imot tegn.'

The reality of this dramatic world, what I have here been calling 'the case', towards which and from which the audience must work if it seeks to arrive at a valid interpretation of things, is — as I have tried to show — a composite construction of signs: signs coexistent and signs successive, signs seemingly contradictory, often apparently irreconcilable, signs reliable and deceptive: 'tegn imot tegn'. These signs and references are rarely simple indices of an evident truth, but are themselves in many instances 'interpretations' of what is actually 'the case'. He who then seeks for meaning in Ibsen's drama must always be ready to allow for the deceptively deceptive nature of these signs, if his grasp of the realities of this fictive world is to be what Ibsen requires of us.

Continuity and change

5

Early Plays

Catiline; The Burial Mound; St John's Night; Lady
Inger; The Feast at Solhoug; Olaf Liljekrans

The merit of Ibsen's earliest plays lies not in what they are but
in what they presage. He is greatly disappointed who comes to
them in the expectation of finding unregarded masterpieces of
world literature; even the hope of discovering a body of intrinsically significant though apprentice work is only partially and
uncertainly fulfilled. The essential fascination of these plays is
that which is born of our own hindsight, of the impulse to identify in embryo those qualities which in time made Ibsen uniquely great. There are, here and there, rewarding glimpses of things
prophetic of the disciplined power, the bleak poetry, the
psychological penetration of works then unwritten; there is
pleasure and indeed insight to be gained from observing the first

stirrings of that stupendous talent which eventually erupted into *Peer Gynt* and *Ghosts* and *Hedda Gabler*. In this, one takes a cue from Ibsen himself who, a quarter of a century after completing his first play *Catiline*, recognized in it much of what his subsequent work had been about: 'the clash of ability and aspiration, of will and possibility, at once the tragedy and the comedy of mankind and of the individual.' Nevertheless by any standards, let alone when measured against the towering stature of his later dramas, the achievement of these early works was modest indeed, and very uneven. All was promise.

As things primarily of historical rather than of intrinsic worth, they betray a great deal about the pressures to which their author was subject in these years of early manhood: the social inducements, the cultural constraints, the obligations and duties, the impositions and the embargoes that were active in shaping his life and career. They document the early stages of a protracted and difficult and at times painful process of spiritual and artistic emancipation. They help to define the nature of a kind of intellectual bondage from which it took him long years to break free. Summarily expressed, the two things that mainly held him fettered were the Norwegian Myth and the *pièce bien faite*. His allegiance to the one, his ambivalent disdain for the other were mutually reinforcing, a push-pull effect. Consolidated, they not only determined the essential features of his dramatic endeavour in these early years but also left traces on the whole of his later work.

In 1850, the year in which Ibsen made his debut as a dramatic author, Norway was a country wholly preoccupied with finding, or more accurately reasserting, its identity. And in seeking to define what it felt it was and hoped to be, its eyes were ever and again drawn to its own distant past and to what at one time it had impressively been. The Norwegian Myth, the sense of vanished glory and of what had constituted it, was the chief sustaining factor in a people freshly conscious of its destiny and of the promise that lay in its new social and political and cultural opportunities, in its role as a re-emergent (rather than simply emergent) nation.

For four centuries following the Treaty of Kalmar in 1397 Norway had — or, equally significantly, believed it had — been deliberately held in social and intellectual subjugation to Denmark. A popular phrase spoke of the 'four hundred year night', an image within which is contained the notion that the once heroic impulses of the people — impulses powerfully expressed in its ancient myths and legend — had been merely slumbering. Now, with the removal of the 'Danish yoke' and with the challenge of a new political freedom and a new constitution, the nineteenth century offered an extension of spiritual horizons and a new destiny. Norwegian culture was conceived as having been a continuing but latent and quiescent thing; it lived on, persistently, in the remote valleys of this distant part of Europe. What matter if in certain urban centres it had been overlaid by the metropolitan culture of Copenhagen? The people, the 'folk', had surely remained inviolate. No opportunity was to be neglected of re-creating a sense of proud nationhood, of proving to the world and to oneself that the new Norway was no whit inferior to the Viking old, that the embers of artistic and intellectual talent within the people could once again be fanned into bright flame wherewith to forge a nation that would be a shining example to the world.

By mid-century, Norway had entered upon a period of second generation nationalism. The extreme Danophobia of the years immediately following the new constitution of 1814 had in some measure diminished; nevertheless the problem persisted of how best to create and foster a distinctively Norwegian culture in a land where Danish traditions were so deeply entrenched, where Danish language still contaminated the work of government, of the church, of the professions, and of the theatre. It was a problem not by any means restricted to politics and public life. It invaded all aspects of living; and in particular no artist or writer could expect to be exempt from its demands.

There was thus a firmly defined framework of reference within which Ibsen as a young dramatist was expected to work; and for long years he found himself exposed to forces and pressures of a very distinctive and peculiarly localized kind. This was something to which Ibsen was always especially sensitive: 'The locale has a great influence on the forms within which the imagination creates', he declared many years later in explanation of why there was so much reminiscent of Germany, of 'Knackwurst und Bier', about his later play *The League of Youth*. The cultural climate in which he wrote these early plays was one of intense patriotic aspiration, of chauvinistic endeavour. To express pride in one's nationhood, and to put one's abilities at the service of 'the people' was obligatory on all who played any kind of public role.

In all this, the Bergen Theatre occupied a unique place. Itself established in 1850, the same year that saw the publication of Ibsen's first drama *Catiline*, it was intended to serve as the focal point of specifically Norwegian theatrical enterprise in a land where after nearly forty years of political separation from Denmark, the theatre in all its branches still remained almost entirely dominated by Danes. The 'new' theatre — 'new', alas, only in its corporate existence, however, for it had to make do with an old and inadequate building — was to serve as the instrument for revivifying and rejuvenating the innate creative spirit of drama that had for so long lain dormant in Norway.

When therefore Ibsen, as a young man of twenty-three, was engaged in 1851 by the most single-mindedly nationalistic theatre in the land to assist it 'as dramatic author', the normal expectations that he would serve the national myth were immeasurably reinforced. Commonly assumed as it was that the role of the modern poet, like that of his skaldic predecessor, was to serve as the mouthpiece of the people, making articulate what lay closest to the hearts and minds of the 'folk', how much more assertive this obligation was in this special context of Bergen. Ibsen soon showed himself to be in no doubt where his duty lay. The Prologue he wrote for the fund-raising festival evening in Christiania was a clear articulation of this sense of duty; and in it he fulsomely expressed what he felt was the poet's mission: to proclaim the nationhood of the people, to affirm its glorious past, to praise the noble simplicity of its way of life, to extol the glories of its tongue. The Prologue speaks of that heroic society long ago when the warrior's sword was an instrument of great eloquence, carving powerful images upon the features of his enemies, and of the age when the skald, in whom this same heroic spirit found gentler personification, transposed these selfsame things into a minor key. But then, Ibsen reminded his hearers, a sleep fell upon the land; the voice of the skald was silenced and 'a hush fell on all things, as on the barren strand when the shipwreck's splinters are rocked back and forth by the waves, rolling soundlessly upon the white sand'. At length the people broke their bonds, and art once more began to fulfil its rightful role as a sounding board for the vibrant strings of the people's soul, echoing the vanished splendour of the past and of the rich new life that only now was beginning to assert itself.

It is a view of life and art conveniently defined by the term 'national romanticism': romantic both by its insistence on pastoral ideals — the notion of the sturdy little people of natural piety which Ibsen was to castigate so fiercely in *Brand* — and by its essential reliance on the past, its indifference to new ideals, to any new social or moral engineering, or to any sense of radical innovation. And strongly emphasized within it all is the notion of the stage as a moral institution, as an agency with which to warn and flatter and encourage and exhort, as a formative influence in the creation (or re-creation) of a people and of a nation. Literature in these years for Ibsen was chauvinistically didactic in much the same way as it was for his Swiss contemporary Gottfried Keller who said that just as beautiful portraits were held up before a pregnant woman that her child should be influenced for the better, so on the national level the artist had to present to the ever-pregnant 'people' an enhanced and idealized portrait of what it might in time grow to be. The theatre was to have the same 'moral' purpose — part personal, part political — that Schiller had urged before the end of the previous century: 'Had we but a national theatre,' he had written in 1783, 'we would become a nation.' A measure of oblique flattery of the people was obligatory. The poet was expected to tell of the strong and simple pieties of the people, its pagan courage, the poetic vigour of its language, the virility of its native Northern culture in contrast to the effete sophistication of Southern lands. Popular delight in folk superstition and the inhabitants of the Nordic supernatural world — trolls and nisses and hulders and hill-people and goblins — was clearly something that called for literary exploitation. Inevitably, the ancient saga and the medieval ballad, the folk song and folk tale, history and legend were all energetically explored in the search for inspirational material. The result was a literature nationalistic in sentiment, romantic in its preoccupation with the past, folksy in its outlook, pastoral in its values, and yet for all that heroic in its aspirations.

Upon this basic groundwork of pre-empted loyalty and of conflict between skaldic duty and individual talent were super-imposed other factors that both complicated and yet also in some respects unexpectedly reinforced the prevailing chauvinistic pressures. Dominant among these is the practical experience of his work in the Bergen Theatre between 1851 and 1857. For a young and ambitious author to be invited at the age of twenty-three to join this exciting new enterprise was on the face of it a stroke of amazing good fortune; even today it is difficult to believe that the effect on his career was other than wholly beneficial. At the moment of his appointment, he was the author of two plays, one of which had been published but not performed, the other performed but not published. How impressive this was in its day may be judged from the fact that no Norwegian play had been published at all during the previous seven years. The job that Ole Bull in his impetuous way offered him in Bergen must have seemed heaven-sent. The post not merely encouraged him to write for the theatre — it positively required him. In addition it offered enviable opportunities for having his work staged. He could in a most immediate and direct fashion familiarize himself with all practical aspects of dramatic production and gain valuable experience of the peculiarities and potentialities of the medium. He could build up an unrivalled knowledge of those plays from many different countries that formed the popular European repertoire of the day. Such things brought real and immediate benefit. But it was not all gain. What should not be underestimated is that for long years these things helped to coerce him along paths that ran counter to his natural bent, sadly delaying the moment when he finally realized where his true dramatic talent lay. How?

The Bergen theatre had been launched on a wave of patriotic fervour: at last the theatre in Norway was to have a truly Nor-wegian home. One almost insuperable obstacle stood, however, in the way of full triumph: there was in Norway no existing corpus of native drama adequate to sustain in performance the nationalistic aspirations of the people. There was admittedly a considerable repertoire of Danish drama, much of it based on impeccably Nordic themes; but this, alas, was the work of a nation from whose cultural hegemony the Norwegians were desperately trying to free themselves. Such plays were of course included in the theatre's programme; but they were neither numerous enough to prevail, nor Norwegian enough to give entire satisfaction. A glance at the annual lists of plays performed in Bergen in these years shows the extent to which even the nationalistically motivated Bergen theatre was forced to rely on the French *pièce bien faite* and on German and Danish imitations of it. (Relatively very few English plays were put on in these years in Bergen.) It is names like Scribe, Mélesville, Dumanoir, Bayard, and Ancelot which preponderate. There is no Racine, no Corneille, no Molière, no Goethe or Schiller, no Kleist or Grillparzer or Hebbel, and no English works of any prime significance except one Shakespeare — *As You Like It*.

Ibsen was under no illusions when it came to judging the quality of the plays he was asked to produce. As early as April 1851, while still in Christiania, he was prepared to make disparaging remarks about the Scribean style of drama. In a dramatic notice of a German play by Gutzkow, he commented that a surfeit of plays from France and Copenhagen had left the Christiania public unable to stomach this different German fare: 'When, year in and year out, one has grown accustomed as our theatre-goers have to Scribe and Co.'s sugar-candy dramas, well spiced with suitable quantities of various poetry substitutes, it is only natural that the more solid German fare must strike even the ostrich stomach of our public as somewhat indigestible.' And the following month, commenting on a performance of a play by Duvert and Lauzanne, he remarked on the public's complaint that nothing but warmed-up dishes were being served up: 'Something new must be found. . . We ourselves produce nothing, nor do the Danes. Scribe has become stale.' He rejects what he thinks of as the alien morals of the French plays that dominated the theatre of his day, morals that were wounding to the ethical and aesthetic sensibilities of many a patriotic citizen, cloying morals that spoiled the appetite for 'det Nationale', truly 'national qualities'. He cites *L'homme blasé* as an instructive example of what a play should *not* be like. But in rejecting

French drama, he is nevertheless wary of advocating a straight adoption of the German mode. German drama was to French, he claimed, as a *tableau vivant* is to a painting, i.e. a stylized form of reality instead of illusion. The essentially undifferentiated reality of the German mode is unacceptable because it fails to acknowledge the necessary economy of dramatic expression, the need for some minimum measure of abstraction, to simplistic blacks and whites, to a denial of the subtleties and complexities of reality.

How, then, is the genuinely 'national' author to pick his way among these hazards? Not by tricking out his plays with superficially national things, like folk dances, 'funny' dialect, strange oaths, rhyming contests, and the like; merely naturalistic copying, like the *tableau vivant*, was inadmissible. There must be some measure of abstraction, some attempt to capture, symbolically perhaps, those less easily definable qualities that echo the spirit of the people, 'those undertones which ring out to us from mountain and valley, from meadow and shore, and above all from our own inner souls'.

For the six years or so that he was in Bergen, the plays of the Paris 'drama industry' tended to represent 'the theatre' for Ibsen. Apart from his brief study trip to Denmark and Germany in 1852, and his previous eighteen months in Christiania (where the fare offered was very little different in kind from what his own theatre was to offer), the repertoire of the Bergen theatre represented practically his whole familiarity with living theatre. Not that this experience of the *pièce bien faite* was wholly without positive value for him. Inevitably these plays must have taught him something about the composition of a logical and consistent dramatic statement, about the fundamental syntax of the theatre. More important than these considerations, however, was the polarity these plays induced in his own dramatic philosophy. At one end of the axis were to be found the realistic, contemporary, prose plays of Scribe and Co.: superficial, ephemeral, contrived, contemptible. At the other was the more deliberate artistry of the Danish 'national' plays: measured, distanced, stylized, lofty. These two categories presented themselves almost as an Either/Or of dramatic composition; and in rejecting the one, he gave himself so much more completely to the other. It also appeared to exclude compromise: realistic prose dialogue, even of the mannered Scribean kind, seemed to be inimical to serious art; modernity, the exploration of contemporary themes, seemed indivisibly linked with superficiality. Serious drama apparently demanded some rather obvious kind of distancing: displacement into history or legend or myth; an archaic or otherwise heightened idiom; the medium of verse. The one thing that these two modes could apparently share, however, was a conventionally contrived dramatic structure. It is the application of Scribean *structuring* techniques to nationalistic themes and motifs that produces the unfortunate synthesis characteristic of Ibsen's work in these years.

Of the early plays in this volume, *Catiline* — the first — stands in some measure apart from the others, and also to some extent apart from the above generalizations. Written in the backwater of a provincial coastal town in the dark Northern winter of 1848-9 before Ibsen came to live in the capital city of Christiania, it is based on a concept of drama derived very largely from his matriculation syllabus, when his familiarity with the theatre proper was minimal. Although its setting is remote in time, although it is cast in verse, it is as yet free of the obtrusive nationalism that was very shortly to overwhelm his work.

It might be thought of as representing its author's own brief Sturm und Drang. Like Goethe's Egmont, Catiline is possessed of that irrational demonic driving force that spurs him on to great and daring deeds, but within which are contained the seeds of his own destruction. Like Schiller's earliest and turbulent drama of 1781, *Die Räuber*, this first play of Ibsen's might equally well have borne the motto 'In tyrannos' on its title page. Here is the Ibsenist version of the 'Kraftkerl', the charismatic figure who by personal magnetism and the imperious sweep of his vision leads the fight against petty-minded self-seeking and the corrupt and corrupting ways of society. Here, too, is something of the Schillerian notion of the 'sublime criminal', the man who though himself guilty of monstrous crimes nevertheless stands like a giant of fearful rectitude among his fellows, an object of admiration and fear together, loved and hated at one and the same time.

The drama was the product of two quite improbably matched stimuli: the widespread revolutionary fervour of the turbulent year of 1848; and the presence on the list of Latin set-books for the current matriculation examination of Sallust's *Catiline* and of Cicero's speeches. Ibsen's later preface to the 1875 edition of his *Catiline* dwells on these two matters. The February revolution, the uprisings in Hungary, the war over Schleswig were all aspects of the general unrest that deeply affected the young twenty-year-old. In the course of the year he wrote poems of passionate homage to the Magyars, composed a series of rousing patriotic sonnets to King Oscar urging him to take action in support of the Danes, and inspired by the news from abroad he startled and shocked the locals of Grimstad by the (to them) outrageous though sometimes unintentionally comic antics and outbursts to which these events provoked him.

Predictably, scholarship was quick to concern itself with the question of how far Ibsen had departed, in his portraiture of Catiline, from historical accuracy — or at least from what was at that time conventionally accepted as the historically accurate picture. One of the very earliest critical studies of Ibsen, that by Vasenius in 1879, attempted to measure the discrepancy between what history had made of Catiline and what Ibsen had seen in him. As the latter himself pointed out in a note to the first edition of 1850, there was in fact precious little in common: 'The factual background of the present drama is too familiar for it not to be immediately obvious how far it differs from historical truth, and also that history has only to be utilized to a limited extent, so that it must be considered primarily as a vehicle for the underlying idea of the play.' In line both with Lessing's firm declaration of nearly a century earlier, and with Hermann Hettner's more recent exhortation, Ibsen in his capacity as dramatist had made himself 'master over history'; and in aiming instead at the kind of truth that a purely imaginative reconstruction gives, Ibsen was perhaps trying to do for Catiline very much what Schiller had earlier done for Wallenstein, and for much the same reasons: to compensate for the fact that so many of the contemporary or near-contemporary reports were the work of opponents and detractors, whose accounts were therefore suspect. Although Ibsen 'lapped up' — to use his own phrase — Sallust and Cicero, he was greatly concerned not to take over uncritically their estimate of Catiline. He particularly mistrusted the testimony of Cicero; and in scornfully categorizing him as 'the indefatigable spokesman of the majority', Ibsen associates him with the role he was later to assign to the contemptible Aslaksen in *An Enemy of the People*, whose attachment to 'the compact majority' is one of the more nauseating manifestations of life as it is lived in a small-minded community. Catiline on the other hand — a Stockmann-like figure as the man who stands alone — is given a character in strong contrast to that which his detractors had created for him, and one which (as Vasenius points out) is much more in line with the one that more recent historical research has established.

The 'idea' was thus the sustaining force in the play, not conventional historical accuracy. The two chief historical sources, of whom Ibsen is thus openly suspicious, portray Catiline as a dissolute and corrupt and repulsive character; yet the suspicion remains that he must clearly have had great natural authority to be able to exert such unquestioned command over his followers. Not that Ibsen has created a wholly idealized character, and many of the warts are there: the crimes against the individual and society, the seduction of the innocent, sacrilege, bribery, arson. But by giving his attention to the *extraordinary* qualities in Catiline's make-up, to the destructive elements that made of him one of the influential figures in the development of history, Ibsen concentrates on what was for him the 'idea'; and in diverging thus from the usually accepted interpretation reveals more clearly than he would otherwise have done those things that were uppermost in his own mind. Equally, by fundamentally altering the original characters of Fulvia, Aurelia, and Curius, he was at pains to emphasize a pattern that continued to absorb him throughout most of his later career: the pattern of the man juxtaposed between two women who — here, as in innumerable guises in the later plays — represent Ibsen's conception of the two basic kinds of Woman: the terrible and the gentle. So insistent does this become in the play — and by extension, presumably, for Ibsen — that the struggle in the play between the two women for possession of the man becomes sheerly allegorical, with the women becoming unambiguously allegorical forces of Good and Evil.

Already in *Catiline* one becomes aware of two features that showed themselves to be remarkably persistent in its author's later career — though there were periods, notably in the 1850s, when they tended to become overlaid by other somewhat contingent considerations. The first of these was a deep-seated revolutionary cast of mind, an attitude to social change that in later life led him to declare — explicitly in his letters to some of his correspondents, and obliquely but powerfully in certain of his dramas — his readiness to support a revolutionary cause. One remembers, for example, his letter to Georg Brandes of 17 February 1871: 'The state must go! That revolution I shall join. Undermine the concept of state, set up free choice and spiritual kinship as the one decisive factor for union, and that is the beginning of a liberty that is worth something. Changing the forms of government is nothing more than tinkering by degrees, a little more or a little less — rotten, all of it. Yes, my friend, the main thing is not to allow oneself to be terrified by the venerableness of the establishment.'

The other was the conviction that, superimposed upon contemporary society's innate resistance to change, there was additionally a peculiarly Norwegian kind of social inertia that derived from the country's general geographical remoteness and from its consequent lack of social awareness. Ibsen himself has confessed that built into the drama there is a sense that although great things may have been happening in 1848 in the wider world, only the faintest ripples of this reached the remote and infuriatingly smug community in which he found himself living. Furthermore the very straitened economic circumstances in which he lived threatened to dull even his own sympathetic responses. This was a point he made in 1870 in a letter to Peter Hansen, in which he explained that *Catiline* had been written in a little provincial town where he was not in a position to give vent to everything that was fermenting in him, except by playing mad practical jokes that drew upon him the wrath of all the respectable citizens who were completely remote from the world that occupied him in his isolation. Five years later he returned with even greater emphasis to this same point when he phrased the preface to the second edition of the play: 'The long and the short of it was that, while big things were happening in the tumultuous world outside, I found myself at loggerheads with the small community in which I lived, cramped as I was by private circumstance and by conditions in general.' This is of course not unlike the circumstances that finally broke Captain Alving, as his wife was in time to realize: 'There was this lively happy boy. . . having to eat his heart out here in this little provincial town; pleasure of a kind it had to offer, but no real joy; no chance of any proper vocation. . .' Whilst much the same considerations are at the root of Ellida Wangel's anguish as she feels herself deprived of contact with the open sea and all the promise of great and distant things it seemed to symbolize.

Catiline was written in time doubly hoarded: from the few leisure hours that remained over from his working week in the chemist's shop he first had to find time for matriculation study; and from these hours he then had to steal yet a further few — mostly night hours — to write this first youthful drama. The inner compulsion that drove him to it found an immediate correlative in Catiline's opening words: 'I must! I must! Deep down within my soul a voice commands, and I will do its bidding.' And it is here perhaps that the deeper identity between Ibsen and his subject matter is to be sought: in the sense of conflict it explores between on the one hand a calling, a mission, the author's conviction of his own innate ability or potential, and on the other an awareness of the constricting forces of society, the straitened economic circumstances, the long and tedious hours of work. The fate that he feared was expressed more directly in a poem of these years, which he also wrote in Grimstad — 'By the Sea' — which puts the question whether, like the wave that beats in vain against the cliffs and falls back to be absorbed into the undifferentiated sea, he might not also have to submit to a similar defeat and be lost in oblivion.

Already before Ibsen left Grimstad there were clear indications that he had taken a decision to put his authorship at the service of popular nationalistic sentiment. This showed most immediately in his poetry. Lyric poems whose structure was immediately reminiscent of certain well-known folk songs and whose themes were based on popular legend began to displace the more subjective and confessional kind of poetry he had inclined to earlier. In the winter of 1849-50 he began work on a prose narrative with the title of 'The Prisoner of Akershuus', a piece which Ibsen himself described as 'a nationalistic Novelle'. He completed the first act of a drama he referred to at the time as 'Olaf T.' — almost certainly 'Olaf Trygvason' — which would have indicated a highly nationalistic theme taken from Norwegian history; and he drafted a one-act drama provisionally entitled 'The Normans', which was the play that later in revised form became *The Burial Mound*.

Thereupon to move, a few months later, from the relative isolation of Grimstad to the infectious atmosphere of Christiania was to become exposed to a much more virulent form of cultural nationalism than he had ever encountered tucked away in that little provincial coastal town. There was the heady atmosphere of life in the capital city; there was the exhilaration of the new student environment; there were journalistic enterprises to join; and there was the theatre. The shift from the markedly individualistic character of *Catiline* — derivative in many of its aspects though it was — to the tired conventionality of *The Burial Mound* gives some measure of the extent to which he fell victim to current enthusiasms. This second play of his marks an almost complete surrender to the received ideas of the day: determinedly nationalistic, as though to defy anyone to repeat the criticism made of his first play that 'because it was not national and relevant' it did not deserve much recognition; safely Oehlenschläger-like in language and style to ensure its appeal to a theatre management that had proved so unreceptive to *Catiline* and its Roman motifs; popularly Viking in it subject matter with its blond and blue-eyed heroism, its skaldic portentousness, its blood revenge and sacred oaths and warrior deaths; and a reach-me-down dramatic structure that based all on unsuspected identities astonishingly revealed.

Such 'meaning' as the play has polarizes out about a

North-South — and thus, by extension, a pagan-Christian — axis. By accepting as the initial situation the circumstance that a Viking warrior, wounded on a raid far from his Northern home, is saved from death by the tender care of a local girl, the play is able to contemplate — 'explore' would be too forceful a word — the notion of the reciprocal influences of Nordic strength and Southern gentleness. The growth of his understanding of Christian humility as he sees it practised by her, and the growth of her passion for the Northern lands and peoples as she hears them described by him — these things herald the kind of reconciliation of opposites that the final curtain speech proclaims. And finally, after all the vicissitudes of the plot, the union of the gentle Southern maiden with her warrior husband is blessed by the ageing Viking in terms that very obviously underline the symbolic meaning: in speaking of 'this pact combining Nordic strength with Southern mercy', he enjoins the girl to 'plant Southern flowers there in the pine trees' haunt, and spread the light of truth throughout the North'. It was the first dramatic treatment of a polarity that appears again and again in Ibsen's later work in different guises; one has only to think of Rosmer and Rebecca, of Hedda and Tesman, of Solness and Hilde to see this dialectic re-enacted with varying degrees of complexity and in subtly differing variations.

Despite the flattering device of putting the praise of Nordic life into the mouth of a Southern girl, many of the public and some of the press were far from satisfied with the general image of Viking man conveyed by the work. In Oehlenschläger they had become accustomed not only to a more fulsome kind of praise for the Viking tradition but also to a more rigorous denunciation of the effeteness and flaccidity of Southern ways. When Ibsen came to re-write this play for performance in January 1854 — and his revision was quite far reaching — among the adjustments he made was to give the North-South opposition rather more forceful expression. The setting, which for the 1850 version was Normandy, is displaced further south to Sicily. The 'South' becomes more languidly and lushly Mediterranean. The sense of a decayed civilization is emphasized by the new opening speech, a monologue by the girl Blanka, who sees in the dead marble monuments around her merely the remnants of a vanished world, the epitome of the decrepit or 'sunken' South; by contrast, the life of the North is bright and vigorous and alert. In the South, she complains, all is but a crumbling ruin, drowsy, slothful, heavy and dull, whilst in the North life is a plunging avalanche, the coming of spring and the death of winter. Her dreams, in the revised version, became much more vividly idealized, and she tells of her vision of a youthful hero, a copper helmet on his blond hair, with blue eyes and a deep and manly chest, and gripping in his mighty hand a sword. Ibsen's determination to fashion something to the popular taste, to make the play acceptable at all costs to the Norwegian public, strikes one now as rather pathetic, perhaps even somewhat distasteful. In mitigation, one might perhaps remember that in 1854, after the resounding failure the previous year of *St. John's Night* to win favour with the public, he was desperately anxious to achieve a popular success. He was disappointed.

It takes no great effort of imagination to recognize that 2 January 1853 was a crucial day in Ibsen's early career. This was the date on which his first *commissioned* drama was to be performed. This was the first chance, since he had been invited fifteen months earlier to 'assist the theatre as dramatic author', that his employers would have of assessing the creative talents of the man they had appointed. It was the first opportunity for the Bergen public to gauge the quality of their young playwright. The management loyally laid out a little extra on new costumes and props. The public bought tickets in encouraging numbers for the first night. Ibsen chose to write a 'fairy tale comedy', *St. John's Night*, which in its own way was both 'national' and 'romantic'; and to that extent was thus in the current idiom. Alas, the play was a resounding failure. Ibsen's audience left him in no doubt that the writing of *such* plays was decidedly not how they viewed his poetic mission; and public opinion brought him very sharply to heel. The bitterness of his disappointment must have been profound.

Why, one wonders, did the Bergen audience turn so single-mindedly against the play? Probably not because of any dismay at the creaking complexities of the plot — a highly contrived story of denied inheritance, long-lost documents, a scheming widow, a comically senile old man, and two pairs of lovers who re-align themselves to affirm a kind of elective affinity of true love — a plot which was no better but no worse than those of a score of similar dramas current in the theatre of the day. Nor was it likely to be impatience with the obtrusive fairy-tale elements; after all, the fairy-folk — the goblin, the mountain king, the elves and the rest — were of impeccably Norwegian origin, and therefore acceptably 'national', and the by-play with the magic potion had been a not unfamiliar device in plays that had found a ready acceptance. (Some commentators, incidentally, have been encouraged by the midsummer-night setting of Ibsen's play and by the superficial resemblance between the goblin's pranks with the potion and Puck's antics to draw parallels with Shakespeare's *Midsummer Night's Dream*; but the cross-reference seems to offer little reward.)

Doubtless, what principally upset the Bergen audience was the fact that Ibsen had allowed his naturally irreverent cast of mind too free a rein in treating what was for those days a very sensitive range of topics. On the other side, Ibsen probably failed to realize just how dangerously two-edged irony is as a weapon, and that careful handling is essential. It is not improbable that a number of things that were meant as comically grotesque nevertheless succeeded in giving serious offence. It was far from obvious to Ibsen's contemporaries — something which is surely clear enough today — that the transposition of this highly conventional subject matter into a satirical key was the most individual and in a sense the most original thing about the entire play. Without it, the play might well be nothing more than a simple variant of a pattern which a number of well-known plays of the day had combined to create: plays like Heiberg's *Day of the Seven Sleepers*, for example, or Hostrup's *Master and Apprentice*. With it, and despite Ibsen's own later protestations to the contrary, the play is a recognizably Ibsenist thing.

It is worth stressing — although the point was very largely lost on his public — that Ibsen's intent was not to mock the nationalist ideal, only spurious nationalism; not the romantic spirit as such, only bogus romanticism. And in pursuit of this, his creation of the ludicrous Julian Poulsen was a considerable achievement. Casting himself as a Byronic figure, intent on impressing others as a wild and dark and demonic poet, Poulsen nevertheless betrays the most commonplace and unimaginative of minds. His account of his struggle to remain 'primitive' and 'national' is hilarious; he explains how he was devoted to that 'most national of all things national', the hulder, holding it to be the ideal of feminine beauty until by chance he discovers that hulders, despite their more apparent allurements, have tails, whereupon he suffers a great crisis of conscience. Is he to abandon his nationalist convictions because of this? He tries to revive his nationalist zeal, to recapture some of his earlier audacious primitiveness by taking to wearing a sheath knife, starting to spell phonetically and writing nouns with small initial letters (i.e. in bold defiance of the traditional Danish practice), but all in vain: 'Weltschmerz' seems the only refuge. So there, in his own self-dramatization, he stands like a typical Romantic 'Zerrissener', his nationalistic Self at war with his aesthetic Self, his primitive nature in conflict with his sophisticated mind, rustic ideals with urban, anxious on the one hand to show fitting allegiance to the hulder and other nationalistic fairy-folk, yet quick to explain them away as merely 'symbolic concepts', and mis-identifying the Mountain King as a member of the Festival Committee.

It is at this point, possibly, that Ibsen can be seen making a genuine though in the event largely unsuccessful effort to give depth to the otherwise largely two-dimensional quality of his play. If he had indeed read Hettner's *Das moderne Drama* in the summer of 1852 when at work on *St. John's Night*, he must have been struck by what was said there about the nature and purpose of the 'Märchenlustspiel'. (Ibsen calls his own play on its title page an 'Eventyrcomedie', a close equivalent.) Briefly, Hettner's argument is that this particular genre best fulfils itself by exploring, in its own distinctive and idiosyncratic way, the relationship between illusion and reality, truth and fiction. There must be an interpenetration of the real and the fairy-tale world, whereby each sheds light on the other. Ibsen, instead of using the device of the magic potion merely to increase the surface complexity of things, makes of it an instrument for interrelating illusion and reality. The potion, the goblin explains, will allow a glimpse of things beyond any merely outward appearance; for those who drink it, the mists that cloud the vision will be dispelled by the leaping flames of dreams; and a true sense will be vouchsafed of those inner forces that reign in the hidden chambers of the mind; he whose mind is empty, however, will remain as blind as ever before, and sleep. When, in the following Act, the visions on Midsummer Hill are seen poetically by Birk and Anne, prosaically by Julian and Juliane, the dramatic discussion is at once, by implication, widened to embrace the limits of rationality, the validity of the visionary, and the nature of reality.

For some years after its production in Bergen (it was played for only two nights, on the second occasion to an almost empty house) Ibsen continued to include reference to it among his works when making official applications for fellowships and grants and the like. But in later life, with his reputation assured, his repudiation of it was complete; he not only refused to contemplate having it included in a collected edition of his works, but he also denied that he was in any real sense the author of it. It has been constructed, he said, upon a rough, botched-up sketch which he had received from a fellow student called Berhoft; all he had done was re-draft this and put his name to it; but he could not possibly acknowledge it as his own.

Certainly it would be going too far to suggest that *St. John's Night* is in any way an impressive play in itself; but it does display certain qualities of freshness and naturalness that immediately mark it off from the other plays of these years, which by contrast give the impression of having been commissioned by a public looking for cultural reassurance and a measure of oblique flattery of themselves. It may well be that the fiasco of its reception determined him not to try to be so 'clever' another time; that his policy must be to assess popular demand and to write for it; to play safe, and to experiment only within cautious limits; not to yield too readily again to his delight in satire; and to hesitate before again adopting a contemporary setting.

Nationalistic fervour struck a rather more strident and more overtly polemic note in Ibsen's next play. *Lady Inger*, written probably in the summer and early autumn of 1854 and played in Bergen on 2 January 1855, is a historical drama in prose, a play not merely assertively Norwegian in theme but also pointedly anti-Danish in its implications. By its preoccupations it echoed the tradition of patriotic literature associated with Wergeland and his supporters of the earlier generation of the 1830s, the keynote of which in its turn had been struck by Nicolai Wergeland, the poet's father, with his book of 1816 entitled *A True Account of Denmark's Political Crimes against the Kingdom of Norway from 955 to 1814*. In this he had claimed 'that Norway, having suffered the insult of Denmark through the course of generations, had gained nothing and lost all. . . lost its kings, its freedom, its courts, its fleet, its flag, its language, its territories, its resources and its name in the political and literary world.' Like reformist movements everywhere, the new spirit that followed the adoption of the Eidsvoll constitution of 17 May 1814 was never happier than when being reminded of the bad old days.

Lady Inger did just that. The action of the play is set in 1528 when Norway's fortunes were at their nadir, and when her subjugation to Denmark was at its most humiliating. Henrik Jæger in his biography of Ibsen of 1888 put it succinctly: 'The Danish nobles sat firm in the land; they took command of the best regions, took possession of the richest estates by marriage or by other less honourable methods, and did virtually as they pleased. Conditions were almost completely lawless: violent feuding, robbing, annexing of land, plundering, even small-scale wars made up the order of the day. Things never looked so black in Norway as they did then; and if one holds to the old image of "the four hundred year night" as a description of Norway's age of subservience, the beginning of the sixteenth century must be characterized as the midnight hour.' Stimulated as it may well have been by the publication in the spring of 1854 of Paludan-Müller's two-volume history of the conflicts of these years, *Lady Inger* is nevertheless more invention than history. Whether Ibsen took his cue here from Hermann Hettner's *Das moderne*

Drama (which he is thought to have read on his study tour to Dresden in 1852) is unsure; what is certain, however, is that in discussing the nature of historical drama, Hettner makes his point very firmly: 'What then, in poetry, does history mean for us *qua* history? From the moment it enters the realm of poetry does it not forfeit all independent rights?' Ibsen's play is very much in the spirit of this declaration.

Again it was Jæger who was one of the first to catalogue the many divergences in the play from the established facts of history; and both Georg Brandes and William Archer, in their introductions to the German and English translations of the play respectively, made much of these: Lady Inger, though an able and wealthy woman in her day, was never in any real sense a focus of anti-Danish activity in Norway; she quite happily married her daughters into the Danish nobility, motivated probably by simple social ambition; the notion that Nils Stensson, the 'Dale-junker' was Lady Inger's own son is purest invention, and in actual fact Lady Inger betrothed one of her daughters to him; Nils Lykke was in real life married to Eline, one of Lady Inger's daughters, and after her death he took her sister Lucia as his mistress; this in the eyes of the day was incest, however, and he was arrested and executed in 1535. There was thus no real attempt in this drama to re-create the events of history, tempestuous enough though they were; rather, as Archer puts it, 'the Fru Inger of Ibsen's play is, in her character and circumstances, as much a creation of the poet's as though no historic personage of that name had ever existed.'

The plain events of history deserved, and indeed invited, the kind of treatment that was stark and simple. Instead, Ibsen succumbed to the allurements of the play of intrigue. The result was a play of daunting complexity. Improbability follows implausibility in wilful, relentless progression. The characters are herded towards their contrived fate by misunderstandings of almost unbelievable artificiality. Identities are mistaken; documents fall into wrong hands; the wildest suppositions are formed on the flimsiest of evidence and then used as the basis of the extremest of actions; relationships — of blood, of marriage, of liaison — are asserted, denied, anticipated, renounced; oaths are imposed, silences enforced, events concealed, confidences betrayed, all within a shifting pattern of dramatic irony bewildering beyond belief. Even the sympathetic Brandes was unable to conceal his dismay: 'Right at the beginning of the play Olaf Skaktavl knows for example that he is to meet a man at Østråt, but does not know who that man is. When Nils Lykke, who hopes to find Count Sture there, hears of the arrival of a stranger, he presumes Skaktavl to be Sture; whilst Skaktavl for his part, who is to meet Nils Stenssön, naturally takes Nils Lykke for Stenssön. Although therefore the Danish knight does not know whom he is dealing with in the person of Skaktavl, he nevertheless very skilfully gives the impression that he himself is the man the other person is to meet. Then Nils Stenssön arrives. He too is to meet a stranger at Østråt who has not been described to him in detail but to whom he is to hand over papers and documents. By cunning, Nils Lykke succeeds in getting documents intended for Olaf Skaktavl handed over to him thereby gaining access to secrets, knowledge of which gives him advantage over the others. This advantage is enhanced when Lady Inger involuntarily reveals to him the crucial secret of her life. Nils Lykke learns that Nils Stenssön is the son of Sten Sture and Lady Inger; he reveals to the young man the identity of his real parents of which he was previously unaware. It might then have seemed possible to lead the plot to its conclusion without any complications other than those arising from the situation and the characters — but the obscurity which has scarcely begun to clear is once again increased. Namely by the fact that Nils Stenssön, as the result of an oath into which Nils Lykke has inveigled him, finds his lips so firmly sealed that he cannot reveal himself even to his own mother as her son, with the result that Lady Inger — who beyond all probability has never seen her own darling child and believes instead that Stenssön is her son's rival for the throne — kills this son of hers from ambitious mother-love.' (The passage is strongly reminiscent of the famous occasion in the *Hamburgische Dramaturgie* where Lessing pours scorn on Corneille's *Rodogune* for much the same reasons as here: for absurdly complicating a dramatic situation that was immeasurably more powerful without the complications.)

If only, one feels, Ibsen had heeded the warning uttered else-where in Hettner — that a basic law of all tragedy is that Chance has no place in it — much might have been saved. As it is, however, the play is not wholly devoid of genuine dramatic power, despite its obvious deficiencies. The inner conflict within Inger herself, for example, is authentic and moving. Bold and yet fearful, confident and yet strangely uncertain, she is recognizable as a typical Ibsenist creation, even though as yet the draughtsmanship is crude. The final Act contains in Inger's own words the central tragic theme: 'I am hated there on high, because I bore you into the world. . . I was born with wealth and brains and a famous name that I should be God's standard-bearer on earth. But I went my own way. . . and that is why I have had to suffer so much and so long.' It is a recognition that she has failed in her duty, her mission, because of human weakness — because she 'went her own way'.

When Ibsen himself looked back fifteen years later at what he called the 'inner history' of the play, he passes over the literary patriotism in silence; what remains in his memory is the emotional background to the play. The play, he said, 'is based on a quickly formed and violently broken love affair, to which are linked also a number of minor poems, like "Wild Flowers and Pot Plants", "A Bird Song", etc.' The reference is doubtless to Rikke Holst, whose company Ibsen enjoyed in these months until her father rather firmly set his face against the association; though it must be admitted that the immediate relevance of this affair to *Lady Inger* is not very obvious, apart from the fact that the love scenes between Nils Lykke and Eline have a spontaneity about them that might well be supposed to have derived from Ibsen's own experience.

No other play of Ibsen received such exhaustive and formally authenticated commentary from its author as *The Feast at Solhoug*. Not that this occurred immediately: at the time of its first performance, in 1856, Ibsen was glad to let the audiences of Bergen, Christiania, and Trondheim show by their applause the extent of their appreciation; in Bergen, indeed the citizens actually serenaded Ibsen after the performance. It was the first ever of Ibsen's plays to be performed outside Norway: Stockholm saw it in the autumn of 1857; and the occasion of its performance in Copenhagen four years later made of it the first Ibsen play to be produced in Denmark. The succession of hostile press notices was something that Ibsen was for the moment prepared to suffer in silence; whilst for the theatrical success, long delayed as it had been, Ibsen was deeply grateful and much sustained.

Yet in 1870 he was quite prepared to disown it. In his letter to Peter Hansen of 28 October 1870, he dismissed it in an after-thought as 'a study I no longer acknowledge', though even at this point in time he was anxious to add that 'also this play had a personal origin'. By 1883, however — perhaps because of the attention Vasenius accorded the play in his dissertation of 1879 and his book of 1882, based in part on personal discussion with Ibsen — he was anxious to bring out a second revised edition of the play, for which he suggested a preface 'like that for *Catiline*' written by himself.

This preface is in many respects a precise and detailed document. In it Ibsen records his application to the study of Norwegian medieval history that had accompanied the writing of *Lady Inger*; how this had led him first to the study of the kings' sagas — which he found too cold and too distant for immediate dramatic use — and subsequently to the Icelandic family sagas, notably in N.M. Petersen's translation, with their emphasis on personal conflict and confrontation, 'man and man, woman and woman, person and person'; how this subsequently led to the first vague shaping of *The Vikings at Helgeland*, whereupon various factors (including his discovery of Landstad's collection of *Norwegian Folk Songs*) had once again led him back to medieval romance. This encouraged him to incorporate these early tentative plans for a Viking drama into a different kind of lyrical historical play, to transform first Hjørdis and Dagny into the figures of Margit and Signe, and then Sigurd into Gudmund, and to ameliorate the starkness of the original tragic mood.

The motives that led Ibsen, exceptionally, into giving such a *compte rendu* of the genesis and growth of the play seem on the surface obvious enough. He had been greatly irritated by the dismissive way in which the critics and the press had received his play, in contrast to the approval accorded it by the theatre-going public. Published criticism, with few exceptions, had marked it down as a merely derivative piece within the general tradition of the Danish romantic drama; some critics indeed went further, and labelled it a simple imitation of the manner of Heiberg and Hertz; whilst Georg Brandes, in company with several others in both Norway and Denmark, declared in 1868 that the play was 'nothing more or less than a colourless imitation of [Hertz's] *Svend Dyring's House'.* Ibsen's preface of 1883, and especially his bitter comments in the opening pages on those qualifications that apparently served to make a critic, are evidence enough of the depth of the hurt this criticism occasioned him.

To this extent, the preface is explicit enough. But in some important respects, the document is neither greatly persuasive nor wholly candid. Anxious though Ibsen was to defend himself against the imputation of 'literary influence', in effect the preface merely substituted one kind of literary influence for another: not Heiberg but Petersen's translations, not Hertz but Landstad's folk-song collection. And where he might have more vigorously defended himself against charges of being derivative and secondhand by spelling out the personal statement his play might claim to make, he is unexpectedly evasive. Writing of the switch in plan from a saga-type tragedy to a lyric drama, he is disappointingly uncommunicative about concrete details: 'At the time I had not drafted any complete and consistent plan. Yet it was clear to me that some play of that kind was the first I should now have to write. But then many things intervened. Most of these were indeed of a personal nature and were, I presume, decisive in a most forceful and immediate way; but then neither do I believe that it was entirely without significance that just at that time I was also engaged on an intensive study of Landstad's collection of *Norwegian Folk Songs*. . .' This emphatic though enigmatic insistence that personal experience of some crucial kind had intervened at a key moment in the composition of the play has bothered commentators ever since. The usual refuge has been to link it to Ibsen's brief affair with Rikke Holst; not only is the chronology of events awkward here, however — he had broken with Rikke Holst in 1853, and *The Feast at Solhoug* was probably written in the summer of 1855 — but the relevance of that affair to the play is far from obvious.

Many years later, when Ibsen was an old man, Brandes wrote another preface to his play for the German collected works edition; his phrases give the impression — whether deliberately or not, it is hard to say — that not only was it right to emphasize the fact that associated with the play there was some distinctly personal experience, but also that he (Brandes) could possibly guess what it was, though friendship with the author and natural scruples were perhaps preventing him from revealing what it was. Discussing the remarks Ibsen had made in his preface of 1883, Brandes commented: 'The personal element, of which moreover we learn nothing, was therefore the main thing. One could already guess this from the content of the play, especially since variations on this theme are frequently found in Ibsen's youthful works, and most importantly in *The Vikings at Helgeland* which appeared two years later. Where this personal nucleus lies must be left unsaid by a critic who has received no confidential communication from the author. . . Here one finds the contrast between on the one hand the violently passionate married woman, distraught, seductive, and prepared to use criminal methods, and the wholly naive and devotedly loving woman on the other. The chief male character, finally, is a poet. . . *The Feast at Solhoug* shows in fictive form how fate frees the young knight and minstrel from the net in which he has enmeshed himself. . .'

The facts of Ibsen's life as we have them do indeed suggest an association here. The only awkward thing is the chronology. For instead of life inspiring art, art seems to realize itself in life. It is recorded that among the audience on the first night of *The Feast at Solhoug* on 2 January 1856 were the Rev. Johan Thoresen and his (third) wife Magdalene. As they were making their way home, Magdalene apparently persuaded her husband to invite the young dramatist to their home. Five days later he came; there he met and fell in love with one of the daughters of the house, nineteen-year-old Suzannah; within weeks he was formally engaged, and the marriage took place two years later.

Our attention today is, however, drawn mainly to Suzannah's step-mother, Magdalene. She was at the time thirty-six years old, some nine years older than Ibsen, of striking appearance with dark eyes and a fine Mediterranean complexion. From her earliest days — and she was of humble origins — she had determined to be a writer. After a turbulent youth and a tempestuous love affair with a brilliant but poor young Icelandic poet, she eventually gave her life some stability by accepting an offer of marriage from a widower, the Rev. John Thoresen. She made no secret of the fact that she was marrying not for passion but for companionship and security; and her new husband was happy to accept this arrangement. There is no very good reason to suppose that the party she gave after *The Feast at Solhoug* was the first time she had met Ibsen. She had both written and translated for the theatre, and three at least of her plays — *The Princess's Plea* and *A Witness* in the season 1852-3 and *Herr Money* in 1853-4 — had been played at the Bergen Theatre. She has left behind a brief pen-portrait of Ibsen in his early years in Bergen, in which she stresses his reserve, his awkwardness in company, and adds that 'even towards the woman who approached him with ready admiration he appeared to lack the ability to yield to her charms'. Equally, one cannot be wholly sure that Ibsen and Suzannah had not met before. Certainly she had already seen some of his work performed in the theatre, for she apparently spoke to him of her admiration for *Lady Inger*; and there is significance, possibly, in the fact that after what is claimed to be their second meeting, only three weeks or so after the first, Ibsen sent her a proposal of marriage in the form of a poem.

There are grounds for wondering what precisely it was that led Magdalene, in the January of 1856, to decide that the time had now come to invite the young Ibsen to her home. Ibsen's own daughter-in-law, writing nearly a century later, must also herself have wondered; for she wrote: 'It must have both amazed and annoyed popular Magdalene Thoresen when young Ibsen gave all his attention to her stepdaughter instead of to herself.[1]' It is wholly consistent that when Ibsen left Bergen, Magdalene transferred her attention to the young Bjørnson who replaced him; and that in later years she took an equally close interest in the still younger Georg Brandes. When, after leaving Norway and after some years of silence, Ibsen took up again with Magdalene by correspondence, his letter (of 3 December 1865) is full of the kind of portentously veiled and ambiguous phrases he was inclined to use when writing to women who had figured significantly in his life:

> Dear Mother-in-law!
> I decided some time ago that I wanted to write to you; for now I can. Previously I was really never wholly myself *vis à vis* you. What I had to say from my real inner self always found a false expression; and as I myself was only too conscious of this, I closed up. . . . Your finest work *Signe's Story* [sic] we have down here; when we meet again, I can talk to you about it; previously it was as though something came between. That was surely what you meant when you said, as we parted, that things would be different and get better. I already understood you well enough then; but these things have to happen before they can be fully and completely understood. Yes, you may believe me when I say that I now understand you as you deserve to be, and as you always have deserved to be; but I had to get away from the swinishness up there in order to become in some measure cleansed. . . . Suzannah has written you two letters. . . . If there is anything about these letters that prevents you from answering them, at least answer this one!. . . With this I must conclude for this time. I am sure I can count on your replying with a few words. As you will understand, Suzannah will not be allowed to see this letter. . . .

Magdalene survived her husband by some forty-seven years, and continued to exist as a presence in the life of the Ibsens. She is generally regarded as having contributed many details to the figure of Ellida Wangel in *The Lady from the Sea*. One could make a claim for her having been one of the most influential women in Ibsen's entire career. One final footnote is possibly not out of character. When, in the spring of 1895, Suzannah wrote from Italy accusing her husband of contemplating divorce, Ibsen was moved to fury: 'It made me extremely sad to read your last letter of 1 May. And I hope that after considering things further you now regret having sent it to me. It's that stepmother of yours, that damned old sinner, who's been at it again, trying to make mischief by setting us off against each other.'

At the very centre of the play itself, in among all its folksy importations, its ludicrously contrived misunderstandings and misinterpretations, its cups of cold poison variously raised and set down again, its hasty operetta-like resolution by way of violent death, swift repentance, magnanimous withdrawal, timely restitution, and the promise of marriage bells — in among all this is the genuinely moving history of Margit. (In parenthesis, one may remark that although the scene involving the poisoned goblet 'perhaps now reads like a parody', as one perceptive modern critic[2] has written, 'yet it is instructive': instructive in that it illustrates — though without the disciplined control of the corresponding scene in *Hamlet* — a method whereby action as a separate and self-sufficient thing can, by means of such objects as the goblet, manufacture a whole succession of exciting situations. Our impatience with the scene as it now reads in *The Feast at Solhoug* is rather because Ibsen's 'dramatic speech. . . is deliberately contrived to increase the confusion', since the author wanted no more of the language 'than that it should keep the confusion of the action going.') Hers is the history of the proud, impassioned woman who has 'sold' herself in marriage to the wealthy, insensitive, and weak-willed Bengt, and who, finding herself in competition within her own household with a younger unmarried woman for the love of a young poet, bitterly regrets 'the wealth' of happiness she has lost.[3] There seems to be in all this — in the character of Margit as also in the situation itself — something observed, something direct and immediate, something that impresses one as not to be explained by reference to merely literary sources. For the accusation of plagiarism from Hertz is nothing short of ludicrous. 'Literary influence' there still is in the play, admittedly; for Ibsen here is still deep in the toils of the tradition of the play of intrigue: the kind of play that Ibsen, month in and month out, was being required to produce almost to the point of nausea. But in some of its aspects — the torment of Margit particularly, and the slightly grotesque ineffectualities of Bengt, for example, though not the reaction of the two young lovers who are merely pasteboard figures — there is conveyed a sense of genuine feeling.

In 1856, and for the second time during his years in Bergen, Ibsen took out from among his papers one of his earlier manuscripts in order to help him meet his annual deadline: the requirement that he should complete a new play every year for performance on the anniversary of the theatre's foundation day. In 1853, when *The Burial Mound* was the play in question, he had been able to start with a complete play to re-work, and one moreover that had already seen the boards. This time he had at his disposal only a fragment — an act and a half — of a play originally planned in four acts, entitled 'The Grouse in Justedal' and written in 1850. The new play that he made of it, *Olaf Liljekrans*, was performed in Bergen on 2 and 4 January 1857. In most of its essentials it became a very different play from the earlier fragment, and none of the original dialogue was retained. Nevertheless, enough of the earlier piece remained residually in the completed work to give it in a number of respects an air of being strangely out of place in the strict chronological order of Ibsen's dramas. This — the residual romanticism that lingered on from the play's original design — is the first of three constituent elements that can be separated out from the play without great difficulty. The second is related to the enthusiasm for folk poetry as a possible source of dramatic material that Ibsen conceived in these years, and in particular his interest in that collection of *Norwegian Folk Songs* published by M.B. Landstad in the early fifties. The third is linked with the instruction Ibsen had accepted — unconsciously perhaps, unwilling even — from those Parisian dramatists and their imitators to whose plays he devoted so much of his time and energy as producer in the theatre.

'The Grouse in Justedal' was an early product of Ibsen's surrender to the spell of national romanticism. Drafted probably some time in the second half of 1850, it was explicitly defined on the title page of the manuscript as a 'national play'. Taking for its starting point the myth of the unspoilt child of nature, a descendant of survivors from the Black Death living a primitive and idyllic life deep within the mountains and far from the corrupting society of men, it at once proclaims its link with that folk tale on the same theme in the collection of *Norwegian Tales* published by Andrea Faye in 1844: even the place names of Justedal and (with slight emendation) Birkehaug are taken over from the tale into the drama. It embodied a myth that carried an immediate appeal for Norwegian society of this mid-century, incorporating as it did the notion that Norway's mountains constituted some great safe-deposit of cultural values; that their isolation and remoteness provided a simple but effective protection against the contagion of social evil; and that simple goodness endured, though (as presumably the unfinished fragment would have gone on to show) it was sorely vulnerable if abused or insensitively treated. The trials and possible triumphs of such a fey creature are presumably what the drama would have been concerned to show in a plot clearly designed to trace the clash between romantic love and dutiful marriage — a theme which, in infinitely subtler fashion than here, was to become a constant preoccupation of Ibsen's dramas in later years.

Noteworthy too at this early stage is the introduction of the Minstrel. Here he is given the conventional form of the skaldic or bardic figure: prophetic, in league with the mysterious forces of nature, attuned to the world of the supernatural, dedicated to poverty and the simple life but of a powerful natural dignity, to offend which is to invite dire retribution. It represented for Ibsen a persona he would have been glad himself to adopt. Not only are variants of it to be found in the works of these years — in the figure of Hemming in the two versions of *The Burial Mound*, for example, or in the poem 'Møllergutten' ('The Miller Boy'), written probably in 1850 — but also in the later Jatgeir (in *The Vikings at Helgeland*), Falk (in *Love's Comedy*), Maximos (in *Emperor and Galilean*), and even Rubek (in *When We Dead Awaken*), though the connections admittedly become more tenuous as the years pass.

Superimposed on these early elements from 1850 is first the influence of Landstad's collection in particular and of the medieval ballad in general. In Landstad, Ibsen found the ballad of Olaf Liljukrans. The theme of the young man struck down by the elves whilst riding in the forest the evening before his wedding is one that recurs with a range of variations in the folk poetry of many lands — one finds the Scandinavian version transposed into German in the poem 'Erlkönigs Tochter' in Herder's *Stimmen der Völker*, for example. Apart from this isolated element of plot and the adoption of the name Olaf Liljekrans direct from the Landstad volume, the final drama has little directly in common with the corresponding ballad. Of the more important but more diffuse effect that Ibsen's ideas about the ballad form had on this play, the theories he outlined in his essay on 'The Heroic Ballad and its Significance for Literature' offer the best commentary.

Basically, then, what Ibsen did when he took out this early fragment in 1856 was to fuse the Alfhild theme of 'The Grouse in Justedal' — the myth of Innocence Survived — with the new theme of Olaf the Spellbound ('pixilated' is a word that also suggests itself) taken from Landstad. Ibsen also seems to have been concerned to diminish the rawness of the supernatural element by relegating it to the safer confines of merely superstitious belief. Finally, however, he took pains to interweave all these mythical and folk elements into a framework of intrigue and complication and contrived misunderstanding which in its pattern would not have been out of place in the most representative Parisian play of the age.

Again there is the basic tension, of a highly conventional type, between an arranged marriage and the unpredictability of romantic love. The arrangement is for Olaf to marry Ingeborg, whereby the man provides a solution to his family's economic problems, the girl raises her family's social status, and the enduring feud between the two families is settled. But shortly before the wedding day, Olaf's heart is captured by Alfhild, the fey innocent girl of the mountains; Ingeborg, meanwhile, is being wooed by her father's lowly-born servant Hemming. The man's domineering mother Kirsten, and the girl's bluff father Arne complete the mirror-image nature of the design. Thereupon there follows a plot in which misunderstanding, double talk, wilful ambiguity, theatrical trick and surprise twist succeed each other in earnest succession: first to tie a formidably complicated knot and then to shake it free again with artificial and deceptive ease. The conversation between Lady Kirsten and Alfhild in Act II, for example, with its asides to the audience and its painfully contrived misunderstandings, is an excruciating example of dramatic intrigue of a deservedly discredited kind.

If one nevertheless moves on from its (very deficient) intrinsic worth to its importance as a document of Ibsen's development as a dramatist, it can be seen as a significant item in the tireless exploration which Ibsen conducted into the conflict between the claims of illusion and reality. The 'happy ending' — almost like a musical comedy in the bathos of its resolution — is nevertheless totally out of harmony with the nature of the shock which is felt when naive idealism meets deceit and self-seeking and the harsher edges of reality. One of the earliest critical commentaries on this play — that of Henrik Jæger in 1887 — defined 'the idea' of it as 'the struggle between reality and romanticism'. The piquant thing is that, even at this early and unsophisticated stage, the play considers this from two opposing points of view. The destruction of innocence is seen as a double-edged thing: in one light pathetic, and in the other satirical. Georg Brandes saw a clear link here with *Love's Comedy*: both the earlier and the later play, in their inquiry into love and marriage, betray a scepticism about romantic values, however much they may seem to be in their toils. On the one hand there is Alfhild, the embodiment of simple, untutored romantic innocence, who comes into sad conflict with the painful realities of the real world. The 'Dichtung' of her father's account of death is shattered after its encounter with the 'Wahrheit' of a real funeral, of a mother's actual grief at the loss of her child, of the stark significance of the coffin; her daydreams of the distant world, of the nature of society, and of community living are roughly dispelled when she leaves her mountain fastness; and the hurt she feels at the deceptions of love drive her in the end to murderous deeds. Olaf's warning to her is urgent:

'Tis often so
That life itself turns out like this!
Don't come too close — it's so easily done —
You may find you have burnt your fingers.
In truth it may shine like the stars of heaven,

But only when seen from a distance.

This is balanced by the irony in Ingeborg's and Hemming's reaction to the demands of the simple life. Theirs is the Alfhild situation in reverse. They flee from the complexities of community living to the supposed delights of a simple cottage life, but their awakening is both rapid and comic: Hemming declares he will hunt and fish, but remembers with dismay that he has brought neither bow nor fishing rod with him; Ingeborg, who is to pick berries and see to the house, realizes that she now has no servants at hand to do her bidding. She has no clothes but the outrageously impractical wedding dress she stands up in; and Hemming refuses to go back for others, fearing he will be hanged for a thief. And at once reality has imposed itself:

> INGEBORG . . . What about when the long winter comes? No people up here, and never the sound of singing or dancing. Hemming! Should we stay here, or. . .?
> HEMMING. Where else could we go?
> INGEBORG [*impatiently*]. But nobody can live here.
> HEMMING. Of course they can.
> INGEBORG. You can see for yourself they are all dead! Hemming! I think it would be best if I went back to my father.
> HEMMING. Then what will become of me?
> INGEBORG. You shall ride to the wars!
> HEMMING. To the wars! And be killed!
> INGEBORG. Certainly not! You shall perform some famous deed, and then you'll be knighted, and then my father will not stand against you.
> HEMMING. Yes, but what if they do kill me?
> INGEBORG. Well, we can always think about that. . .

It is only at such times — like also the delicious moment when Lady Kirsten finds comfort in the notion that Alfhild, too, probably can expect to inherit extensive lands, and will therefore make an acceptable daughter-in-law — that the play really comes to life in among the rather dreary progression of pasteboard figures through the creaking plot. When one of the contemporary newspaper critics complained that he found it impossible to sort out the sense of this confused play after only one performance, and accused the author of lacking knowledge both of the world and of human nature, Ibsen was very cross and wrote an angry letter to the newspaper in his own defence. But even today one sees what the critic meant, and one has sympathy.

As one more product of the struggle for ascendancy between the romantic tradition and Ibsen's individual talent, *Olaf Liljekrans* helps to define the path of artistic development he was following. Though diffuse, slack, contrived in its structure, clumsy in its motivation, shallow in its psychology, the play nevertheless has something of significance to say to the present-day reader as a further variation on the theme of the authenticity of individual existence, and the necessity to search for it; though at the time of its composition Ibsen was apparently not prepared to give serious consideration to the relevance of this to his own search for dramatic form.

Among the pressures — social, political, professional, and others — acting from without to impose shape upon a creative talent in its most formative years, two are thus conspicuous: the obligation to serve the Norwegian Myth; and the requirement to confirm to the skaldic image. Like some monstrous piece of corsetry, they constricted and contorted Ibsen's talent to a sadly unnatural shape; and it took sheer physical release — an escape by voluntary exile from Norway in 1864 — before this talent was allowed to find its natural configuration. Only great resilience of mind and spirit could have survived; and inevitably one speculates whence it was that this resilience drew its strength.

The notion that emerged from a discussion of *St. John's Night* is helpful again here: that of Ibsen's natural irreverence. Perhaps not one of the more obvious, more immediately striking qualities of his work and personality, it is nevertheless always recognizable, not only in his early years but also in later life beneath the layered accretions of decorum, as an enduring element in his make-up. His childhood friends repeatedly testify to his delight in tricks and practical jokes; he has himself confessed that his antics as an apprentice shocked the bourgeois society of Grimstad; alongside the highly conventional love poems of his youth there are many lampoons of great exuberance; against the solemn pieties of his occasional poems and prologues one must set the irreverent satire of his journalism; and countering the high-flown sentiments of *The Burial Mound* there is always the dry mockery of *Norma*. Almost always, in literary debate and polemic, he is at his most effective when flicking at his target with scorn rather than when taking an earnestly argued line of rectitude.

Nowhere is this duality between Ibsen's natural irreverence and the conformist pressure of the Zeitgeist so graphically illustrated — in the strictly literal sense of these words, indeed — as in his paintings and drawings of these years. From his earliest boyhood days in Skien and all through the years he spent in Grimstad, Christiania, and Bergen, Ibsen was greatly devoted to drawing and painting. From the very beginning — to judge from the testimony of his boyhood friend Boye Ording — his work seems to have fallen into two quite distinct categories: on the one hand there were romantic landscapes in water-colour; and on the other there were cartoons, caricatures, and satirical sketches. Few works have survived from these earliest years; but characteristically one is a tight, stiff, and formalized landscape water-colour painted in 1842 (the year before he left home), in which conspicuous in a primitively composed picture of green and blue vegetation with red and white farm buildings is a flag-pole carrying the Norwegian flag; whilst two of the other extant works are caricatures painted in oils on wood, said to be of his two brothers: one as a fox and the other as an ape.[4] In Grimstad he continued to paint earnestly: mainly portraits and landscapes in oils, views of deeply cleft fjords and waterfalls and log houses and snow-covered pines in sunset glow. But alongside these more contrived pieces he also — as the reports of at least two of his contemporaries in the town bear witness — indulged his more private passion for cartoon and caricature. Christopher Due, one of his closest friends, writes admiringly of the quick and ready pencil Ibsen had when it came to caricaturing and satirizing those with whom he came in contact. He tells of the wicked pleasure it gave them in the long evenings in the apothecary's house to write comic verse which Ibsen would then illustrate: 'Ibsen had an astonishing facility for writing free-flowing verse, and he had a great talent for drawing. His pencil could make the point swiftly, deftly and tellingly when something had to be conveyed by an illustration.'[5] This same gift found later outlet in the satirical drawings he contributed to the periodical *Manden/Andhrimner* — works which though primitive in their technical quality (they are printed from crude woodcuts) nevertheless have an animation and a simple directness that is largely lacking from his more ambitious landscapes. When he finally came to Bergen, he appears to have concentrated mostly on the more conventional kind of work, producing landscapes of a generally naturalistic though sentimentalized style, in which the influence of his teacher Johan Ludvig Losting — a painter whose enthusiasm and versatility outran his talents — is very marked.

In these pursuits as elsewhere he was clearly under strong compulsion to do, to say, to write, to draw, and to paint what was expected of him. But beneath it all was the dedicated joker. Throughout his entire career, even as the top-hatted, frock-coated, much decorated dignitary of his later years, he was in the habit of referring to his plays as 'galskaber' — monkey tricks, practical jokes, pieces of tomfoolery.

Finally, it would be a mistake to imagine that Ibsen's eventual flight to Italy in 1864 betokened a mere closing of the chapter. It was not a simple escape from this conflict between literary convention and individual talent, with a new start. There was an enduring consequence: and it assumed the proportions of a revelation. It did not take long — as many of his letters from Italy testify — for him to reach an awareness of the full significance of what it was he had undergone; and how, generalized, it was relevant to vast areas of life. The experience of those years — it would not be an exaggeration to call it 'traumatic' — then invaded his later dramas in a multiplicity of guises. In essence, what emerged was the conviction that any submission to conventional 'duty', any surrender to traditional or institutional or social pressure was an affront to the integrity of the individual and therefore something to be passionately resisted in the interests of genuine self-realization, which alone justifies our existence. It is a notion with which few of his maturer dramas are not in some way preoccupied, sometimes even obsessed. Duties and responsibilities call for detached scrutiny and subjective evaluation. Only 'the call' or 'the mission' — which might be thought of as a Self-orientated 'duty' — can properly claim our attention. Duty to the Self, responsibly defined and responsibly pursued, must always come first. To Theodor Caspari on 27 June 1884 he wrote: '. . . I believe that none of us can do anything other or anything better than realize ourselves in spirit and in truth.' In a hundred different ways his mature dramas offer a commentary on this view: to subordinate one's life to the effort to meet the obligations of family or state or church (they say) is to turn one's back on authentic living, is to be absorbed into pattern and routine and stereotype, is to fall victim to drab conformity. Only by throwing off these con-straints and escaping into a condition of life that allowed the unforced realization of one's potential, that allowed one to follow a natural bent and develop innate talents, obeying inner imperatives unhampered by the dictates of organized society and guided only by an individual sense of responsibility and pro-priety — this alone (the later dramas insist) must be the motive force of genuine living. This is the common factor that informs many of the key phrases of these works — notions like 'the joy of life', 'the man who stands alone', 'nobility of mind',' freedom with responsibility', 'the robust conscience', 'the miraculous'. Individual fulfilment following some independent recognition or act of courage is the aim; and 'duty' ('pligt' in Norwegian) is — as Hilde Wangel declares — a nasty word both in sound and in implication.

Not until Ibsen had quit the North, however, had put a con-tinent between himself and that overpowering sense of Nordic duty, and had set aside the skaldic persona he had so eagerly assumed in obedience to the call of the age; not until he had known at first hand the liberating experience of Mediterranean skies, of brilliant light and classical art and all the life of the South — it was not until he had done all these things that he became fully aware of the nature of the bondage under which he had suffered. The essence of his release and the extent of his emancipation then became clear to him. Many years later, in 1898, he described this revelation: 'I travelled South, through Germany and Austria, and crossed the Alps on 9 May [1864]. The clouds hung like great dark curtains over the mountains; we drove in under them and through the tunnel and suddenly found ourselves at Mira Mora, where the beauty of the South — gleaming strangely like white marble — suddenly stood revealed to me. It left its mark on all my later work, even though not everything there was beautiful.' It was, he said, like 'a feeling of being released from darkness into the light, escaping through a tunnel from mists into sunshine'.

6

Years of Crisis

The Vikings at Helgeland; Love's Comedy; The Pretenders

Ibsen's later and better-known dramas confer on his earlier works an importance which, by themselves, they might hardly seem to deserve. It is difficult, when approaching works like *The Vikings at Helgeland, Love's Comedy,* and *The Pretenders*, not to be distracted by a sense of anticipation, by some expectation of finding there, extra to any quality the plays may have in their own right, features that can be recognized as prophetic of things to come. Hindsight in its usual complacent manner begins to take over; inherent worth and documentary significance tend to merge, particularly with the realization that these three works were the products of a time of real crisis in Ibsen's life: the seven agonizingly difficult years during which he lived in Christiania, between giving up his appointment in Bergen in the summer of 1857 and his ultimate departure from Norway into voluntary exile in the spring of 1864. Intrinsic or extrinsic evaluation alike, however, invariably confronts the critic before long with three rather improbably associated concepts, the roles of which in Ibsen's thought and work and life in these years were crucial. Those concepts were nationalism, 'aestheticism', and — perhaps not, as yet, the most obtrusive but certainly the most fundamental and persistent — realism.

In a sense, preoccupation with these things built up early in Ibsen. In *St John's Night* — a comedy he wrote in 1852 and later entirely disclaimed — there is a young man called Julian Poulsen who combines great patriotic fervour with exquisite sensibility. Demonstrating his rugged Norwegianness by wearing a sheath knife and spelling all his nouns with small initial letters, in contrast to the effete Danish practice of using capitals, he falls urgently in love with the *hulder*, the 'most national' of all Norwegian fairy creatures; but when he discovers that the *hulder* has a tail, his mental anguish is great. 'I cannot tell you how I suffered', he cries. 'Aesthetics and nationalism fought a life and death struggle in my breast.' This describes exactly the difficulties Ibsen had in writing *The Vikings at Helgeland* later that same decade. The earliest compulsions attaching to this play were nationalistic. By mid-nineteenth century, constitutional independence in Norway was still a comparatively recent thing; the people craved reassurance that despite the political youthfulness of the nation they nevertheless belonged to an ancient kingdom; they wanted to be reminded of their long history and their great traditions; and the tendency was often to judge things, including works of literature, by the contribution they made to the processes of national consolidation. From this general attitude Ibsen was in no way exempt, as is only too clear from the form of the petition to Parliament he drafted in October 1859 on behalf of the Christiania Norwegian Theatre. After pointing out that national pride was now everywhere recognized as an essential factor in the development of the country's cultural life, and insisting that political liberty alone did not make a people wholly free in spirit and in truth but that a nation must first be able to shape its ideas in a way native and natural to it as a people, uncontaminated by foreign prejudices,

143

he went on in the rhetorical style thought suitable to public petitioning:

> This fight in the service of a higher freedom is fought here, as elsewhere, mainly by our artists and authors, the spiritual eyes of the people . . . Our writers have, by their works, taught the people to love the past with all its vicissitudes; they have presented to our gaze an image of the life of the people in forms both true and noble; and for all the variety, for all the divergent features and characters, they have taught us to see and recognize behind it all one characteristic thing — a way of thought common to the entire people, a peculiarity of outlook belonging to us and nobody else, because vis-à-vis the rest of the world we form a whole, not merely as a result of political unity but by reason of common origins, common traditions, common language and a common destiny through times good and bad — in a word, because in the true sense of the term we make up a nation.

Clearly, with this as the current view of the role of the writer in society, there was an inescapable obligation on a young and ambitious dramatist to look to Norway's past history for the stuff of his plays. Yet although the initial pressures on Ibsen to write a 'saga-drama' were thus nationalistic, he very soon — like Poulsen with his *hulder* — found himself up against an aesthetic problem. It seemed to him that the two elements involved — the special quality of the saga material and the peculiar nature of drama — were irreconcilable; and that only by forcing things, perhaps beyond the limits of tolerance, would it be possible to combine the two. He was inclined to think that the sagas, particularly by contrast with the mediaeval heroic ballads, were too remote, too cold, too monumentally self-contained and self-sufficient to lend themselves easily to dramatic treatment; their characters were too magnificently statuesque, the whole genre was too rigorously and too objectively epic to be taken over without drastic modification. Only by some measure of *lyric* adulteration would it be possible, he believed, to make them amenable to dramatization: 'If the poet is to create a dramatic work out of this epic material,' Ibsen stated in a paper, entitled 'Concerning the Heroic Ballad and its Significance for Literature', read to a Bergen literary society on 2 February 1857 and printed in *Illustreret Nyhedsblad* the following May,

> . . . he must necessarily introduce a foreign element into the given material; he must bring in something of the lyric; because the drama, as is well known, is a higher combination[1] of lyric and epic. But by so doing, he disturbs the original relationship between the material and the beholder; this epoch and these events, which previously had been represented to us through the beauty of their abstract plastic form, are now offered to us by the writer as a painting, with colours and with light and shade; and the content of it, to which we had become accustomed through the agency of a wholly different medium, we now find difficult to come to terms with. Admittedly, by such dramatization the saga age comes much closer to reality; but this is precisely what must not happen. A statue does not gain by being given the natural colour of flesh, or hair and eyes.

It must have been reasoning of this kind that had persuaded Ibsen to turn for the time being away from the sagas and look instead to the heroic ballads as possible sources of dramatic material; for in them he found, strongly represented, that lyric element which in his present view was so essential to successful dramatic composition; there would be no need, he felt, to do any great violence to *this* material. Instead of going ahead with the drama that eventually became *The Vikings*, he therefore addressed himself instead to the (closely related) *Feast at Solhoug*, which he completed in 1855. The problem of how to reconcile saga material with dramatic form was not abandoned, however, only shelved. When he had first talked of the need to 'bring in something of the lyric', his immediate idea seems to have been to write the play in verse. Whether or not in fact any of the earliest drafts were in verse is not known for certain, but he did at least give the matter earnest thought. Indeed, the more general problem of the nature of the relationship between literary content and linguistic medium, with all its wider implications, exercised him greatly. At one point, he declared himself against the use of iambic pentameters for the dramatization of saga themes, claiming that it was too foreign a metre to serve for such an expressly national content; on the other hand, he seems to have contemplated using a metre reminiscent of Ancient Greek tragedy, on the grounds that the essentially heathen nature of the saga themes demanded some form of pre-Christian linguistic vehicle. (This seems to have been one of the reasons why he considered Oehlenschläger's *Balder the Good* — which he mistakenly refers to as *Balder's Death* by confusion with Ewald's drama of that name — to be this author's most successful drama). But the most significant remark of all, perhaps, was little more than an aside: it was his incidental reflection, in his paper on the heroic ballad, that he could imagine an 'Earl Haakon', for example, from the pen of Oehlenschläger being just as poetic in prose as in verse. This is to be put alongside the fact that, despite Ibsen's previously declared belief that some lyric element was indispensable to drama, *The Vikings at Helgeland* was nevertheless written in prose. Quite clearly with this play he had decided that 'poetic quality' did not necessarily mean 'lyric quality'. This play offers residual evidence of the shifts that took place in Ibsen's interpretation of the terms 'lyric', 'poetic', and 'dramatic' — shifts that helped to bring his theories into line with his own compulsively changing practice and, for the duration of this particular enterprise, into some kind of stability with each other. It was, moreover, an acknowledgement that he had been phrasing the problem back to front: whereas earlier he had supposed the problem to be that of how to adapt and trim the saga material to fit the nature of drama as he then believed it to be, he finished by having to modify and enlarge his conception of the nature of drama to allow it to meet the challenge of this intractable material. In a career which in its entirety might be defined as a tireless search for new sources of dramatic poetry, *The Vikings* marks a crucial step: a recognition of the genuinely poetic potentiality of prose dialogue. It is thus not unduly fanciful to see *The Vikings* as a kind of exercise in applied aesthetics which Ibsen set himself to work through: a technical problem, the result of which would allow him to see in concrete terms whether there seemed to be in that direction any promise of further things.

It would, however, be entirely false to presume that the adoption of prose as his dramatic medium betokened in any direct sense an anticipation of the later realism of the social plays; *that* realism was a much more complex growth altogether. At the time of writing *The Vikings*, Ibsen had nothing but scorn for the contemporary mode of 'realism' in the theatre, for the virtuoso pieces, the technically accomplished but in his view vapid and essentially meaningless 'well-made' plays that the Paris workshops were turning out, as he put it. A dramatic notice, which he wrote almost certainly while busy on *The Vikings* and published in *Illustreret Nyhedsblad* on 11 October 1857, makes a startling document for the kind of modern reader who thinks of Ibsen merely as a social realist, moving with a photographic sensitivity through the 'tasteless parlors' of the spirit. For here, in his utter and explicit rejection of the 'photographic' realism of contemporary drama, in his conviction that drama cannot be divorced from literature and poetry, there is an astonishing anticipation of T.S. Eliot's famous diagnosis of the 'ruin of modern drama — the distinction between drama and literature', and its associated assault on that 'exact likeness to the reality which is perceived by the most commonplace mind.'[2] After Ibsen, in his notice of the play, had pointed out that it had running beneath it a note of genuine poetry — which in itself, he noted wryly, at once made the general public very suspicious of it — he went on:

> There are many quite reasonable people who believe that this play must with good reason be called both untrue and unwholesome, since it does not stand in photographic relationship to reality. For these people, reality and truth are synonymous: unless the first is copied, the second cannot be present. Yet in approaching art in this way, the public is at least behaving consistently. In the National Gallery, or on reading a work of literature, etc. the self-same remarks are heard: a landscape is appreciated only when the beholder recognizes the view, when — as

147

the saying goes — there is a likeness. The same is also true of the stage; people crave only what reality has to offer, neither more nor less; the notion that art should display some power to uplift is one that few are prepared to admit; how much more often do people demand to be instructed to be taught all sorts of 'useful things'. That the theatre should be educative is a statement understood by the mass of the people only as they would understand it of an encyclopaedia.

There was only one serious deficiency about photography, he went on with heavy irony, which was that it was still only capable of an abstract reproduction of the actual colours of reality; but ingenuity and inventiveness would soon put that right, so that a new and 'improved' realism would result, and with it a new stimulus to realism in art and literature — and doubtless, he added, this would add greatly to their popularity. Finally, an appreciation he published the next month of Anton Wilhelm Wiche, one of the leading actors of the day, confirmed his lack of sympathy with the aims of realism; and the same hostility as before informed his phrases, especially where he spoke appreciatively of Wiche's 'deep feeling for the sacredness and the significance of art, his inspired striving not for crass reality but for truth, for that higher symbolical representation of life, the one thing in the world of art that really deserves to be fought for, and which nevertheless is acknowledged by so few.' These critical comments reveal an attitude on Ibsen's part to his art that no attempt to pass informed judgement on the dramas of these years can afford to ignore.

Ibsen's intent with *The Vikings* was thus not merely non-realistic (which is obvious) but positively anti-realistic; and the completed drama carried with it an invitation to judge it not by its success in reproducing 'crass reality' but rather by its efforts to communicate some 'higher symbolical representation of life'. In the first place, he made very formalized use of his sources, in no way attempting to make the play 'representational' of any one saga; instead, he adopted a markedly eclectic and abstractive approach, amalgamating features selected from a number of different sagas, chiefly — as Ibsen himself acknowledged in his preface to the later German edition of the play — *Volsunga Saga, Egils Saga, Njåls Saga,* and *Laxdœla Saga.* In this, his practice was also entirely consistent with his current views on the proper use of history in drama: 'We have no real right', he wrote in December 1857 when reviewing Andreas Munch's drama *Lord William Russell,* 'to demand of true historical tragedy that it give the historical facts, but only historical possibilities; not the evident persons and characters of history, but rather the spirit and temper of the age.' The implication was that a dramatist should aim at achieving a measure of abstraction rather than at accumulating a mass of verifiable detail. Something of the same attitude showed also in the language of the play: a prose dialogue which stood back from the conversational rhythms of contemporary speech and which instead by its mannered terseness, its deliberate use of archaisms and its stylized idiom — which, incidentally, many critics dismiss as mere saga-pastiche — struck a kind of harmony with the play's formal non-representational nature.

It is in the structural pattern, however, that the formality of the play is most evident. Laid out at the centre with scrupulous geometry is a quadrilateral of relationships: two men and two women joined by sets of overt relationships, yet secretly attached in other ways by hidden cross-ties. The two men are joined by ties of blood-brotherhood, the two women linked by the intimacies of foster-sisterhood, whereby the basic design starts with two sets of 'homosexual' relationships, each of them in the form of an adoptive kinship and arranged in parallel. Thereafter these four individuals are paired off heterosexually by matrimonial ties, thus cutting across the already existing attachments to mark out a rectangle of alliances within which their *Wahlverwandtschaften,* their elective affinities, are worked out. And whilst the contribution within this framework of some of the other characters, particularly Ørnulf, is quantitatively great — pointing up the social fabric, detailing the prevailing code of conduct, and by the motif of Ørnulf's funeral lament drawing attention to the relief from pain that poetic composition brings — it remains essentially ancillary. No less four-square is the pattern to which the individual temperaments of the four corner characters are constructed: Sigurd, the manly man, set off against Gunnar, the womanly man; Dagny, the womanly woman, set off against Hjørdis, the manly woman. They are — to apply Ibsen's own phrases to them — not 'likenesses' but 'symbolic representations', and exemplary rather than idiosyncratic. Taken together they spell out a paradigm of human conduct; they are part not of the chit-chat but of the rhetoric of existence. Ibsen makes no sustained attempt to make them psychologically interesting as individuals; their dramatic potency lies not in what they might do, but in what they must do, and will; their individual conduct, because they can all be relied on to act predictably, remains intrinsically unexciting. Even by pairs, their destinies remain unremarkable; there is no build-up of any tragic potential in their married careers, for any tension there might be seems to drain away in boredom and frustration. Life together for Sigurd and Dagny, whatever its outward successes, has meant only that the man fell short of his secret ambitions, while the woman waited patiently for the day when they could settle down quietly at home; for Gunnar and Hjørdis, life has brought only frustration to a woman who yearns for heroic deed and conquest, and torment to a man who asks only for a quiet life. Gunnar is content to live his life, like Carsten Bernick in *Pillars of Society*; and Sigurd, like Johannes in the same play, is ready to keep silence; until, that is, their hands are forced. What forces them, in the last analysis, is the mere fact of their coming together; they join company in such a way that their interlocking destinies become a closed system, the escape vents are sealed, and passion builds up within the perimeter of their relationships from which no escape is then possible except by an explosion.

It is the secret and diagonal cross-tension between Sigurd and Hjørdis that ultimately provides the play with its axis, however; and it is along this axis that the three significant revelations within the play are disposed — it being characteristic of the play's special atmosphere of inevitability that the tension is sustained not by any unexpected surprise *developments* but by a succession of revelations of things already irrevocable. The first revelation makes known the true identity of the man who had killed the white bear and carried off Hjørdis; the second is Sigurd's admission that he was in love with Hjørdis, and always had been; and the third, which is intended retrospectively to put much of what has gone before into a more meaningful perspective, is Sigurd's dying confession that he had embraced the Christian faith — something which finally and rather abruptly depersonalizes what was earlier referred to as the Sigurd-Hjørdis axis into an abstractly and ideologically Christian-heathen one. Sigurd's sense of obligation towards Gunnar, his unwillingness to hurt Dagny, the disciplining of his passion for Hjørdis, his willed self-control are in the end revealed as manifestations of Christian virtues; Hjørdis, on the other hand, who ranks strength and courage as the highest of human qualities, who has no scruples about abandoning her husband and who has only contempt for the gentle Dagny, whose will is an instrument to be used on others in the interests only of herself and her man — she is the embodiment of a Viking philosophy of life. Although one tends to think of Hjørdis as possessing a fierce will of her own, it is rather the reverse that is true: she is the one possessed. She is dominated by the idea of domination, seeing everything in terms of power: power of will, strength of courage, physical prowess. Even her womanly appeal takes its stamp from it. She deliberately translates the act of courtship into an ordeal of strength; her image of marriage to Sigurd is of a triumphant alliance of power in which the fact of her sex is a matter of little consequence: 'I love you', she tells Sigurd, 'and I can say that now without feeling ashamed. Because my love is not a soft thing, like the love of weak women. If I were a man . . . by the powers, my love for you would still be just as strong.' The sense of outrage she feels when she hears of Sigurd's fateful personation of Gunnar is not because she feels she has been violated but because she was not; she feels defeated because her appeal had been powerless to break down Sigurd's loyalty to his friend; just as she is angered, also, after Sigurd has confessed his love for her, because this time she is equally powerless to break down his loyalty to Dagny. Her love, seeking as it does its consummation not in happiness but in greatness, has almost nothing to do with affection, and everything to do with ambition; it is a passion not unlike Rebecca West's, which Shaw once described as 'the cold passion of the North — that essentially human passion which embodies itself in objective purposes and interests on behalf of others — that fruitful, contained, governed, instinctively utilized passion which makes nations and individuals great, as distinguished from the explosive, hysterical, wasteful passion which makes nothing but a scene'.

For all the intensity of feeling communicated, the result was a 'cold' drama — 'cold' not in any pejorative sense but descriptive rather of that wholly deliberate quality that chills and distances, which has always been one of the legitimate aims of art, and particularly of tragedy. It was never intended that the ordering of incident in the play should be judged from merely naturalistic premisses; nor that the characters should live by the richness of their psychological plausibility. It happened, for example, that two of the key elements in the play — an instance of mistaken identity and a rather blatant example of misunderstanding — were stock devices found regularly in the farcical pieces fashionable in the day, and as exploited there quite repugnant to Ibsen. But the personation by Sigurd of Gunnar which we hear about and which is so important to the motivation of the play is far too stark and elemental a thing ever to be judged on the same level as *Charley's Aunt*, and the wilful ambiguity of Thorolf's words too boldly posited, too fate-laden to be open to dismissal on crude common-sense grounds. The same might also be said of the — by naturalistic standards — extreme coincidence that collects all the characters together at the same time on a remote and barren shore, so that the drama may begin. These are devices which, however lightweight they may be in the context of the salon-drama, possess an inherent gravity, take on a kind of archetypal inevitability in their special setting. That the whole drama has an experimental look comes perhaps from its almost neo-classical treatment of a theme drawn directly from national romanticism; its longer-term significance, however, lies in the fact that it reconciled Ibsen's conception of the drama as something essentially colourful and painterly with his image of saga material as a sculptured, plastic thing — without, as Ibsen had feared might be the case, having to stoop to using false moustaches. Above all, it is a drama which, perhaps for the first but certainly not for the last time in Ibsen, sought its poetry elsewhere than in the more obvious sources of lyricism.

The Vikings was a kind of sublimated *Hurrapatriotismus;* and never again was Ibsen to exploit the appeal of nationalism as openly — or, indeed, as naively — as he had done there. In the years that followed, he gradually discarded his more expansive notions of national pride; a growing sense of *le malheur d'être norvégien,* engendered over a number of years by the wounding treatment he received at the hands of both government and public, finally culminated in a spasm of disgust at his country's refusal in 1864 to come to the help of the Danes against the armies of Prussia and Austria. The angry terms of his letter from abroad to Bjørnson on 16 September 1864, denying the modern generation of Norwegians any right to claim their traditional historical greatness, give an index both of his one-time ardour and of his sharp sense of betrayal: 'We can cross out our ancient history,' he wrote, 'for the Norwegians of our own day clearly have no more to do with their past than have the Greek pirates with the generation that sailed for Troy . . .'

What nationalism had been to *The Vikings* — a factor giving initial momentum — 'aestheticism' was to *Love's Comedy.* The quotation marks are a warning to take the term not in its generally philosophical but in its more specifically Kierkegaardian meaning, the meaning Ibsen clearly intended it to have when, three years after completing the play, he wrote on 12 September 1865 from Italy to Bjørnson about his own past obsessions:

If I were to say now what the most valuable result of my leaving [Norway] has been, I should say that it consisted in the fact of my having rid myself of aestheticism [det Æsthetiske], the isolated kind that seems to demand an independent validity, and which had so much power over me before. Aesthetics in that sense now impresses me as being as big a curse to poetry as theology is to religion. You yourself have never been encumbered with aestheticism in this sense; you have never gone about

153

looking at things through your hollowed hand.

This last allusion provides the clue to what Ibsen was trying to say; it points in the first place to his poem 'On the Heights' (Paa Vidderne), in which the phrase occurs, and beyond it again to the five difficult years following the completion of *The Vikings* which left an indelible mark on *Love's Comedy*. 'On the Heights' tells how a young man is schooled to contemplate the things of life with the lofty detachment of the artist, of one who is 'steel-set'; he is encouraged to admire the purely aesthetic qualities of sights that in any normally sentient person would wring the heart and blind the eyes with tears, and learns to shade his eyes with his hollowed hand 'to get the perspective right'. Explicitly linking this poem with *Love's Comedy* is a letter Ibsen wrote in 1870 to Peter Hansen: 'Only after I was married did my life acquire a weightier content. The first fruit of this was a longish poem 'On the Heights'. The urge for freedom running through this poem did not find full expression however until *Love's Comedy*.' Fitting the pieces together, one might therefore shape the implications thus: *Love's Comedy*, the product of a certain 'urge for freedom' of which 'On the Heights' is an earlier and less fully articulated expression, grew out of an 'aestheticism' related in some way with the start of married life and the assumption of new and weightier responsibilities.

The gap between *The Vikings* and *Love's Comedy* was not merely the longest interval between major works in Ibsen's entire career, but also came at a stage in his life that should perhaps have been one of the most productive: those years between the ages of twenty-nine and thirty-four. These are the years of which 'On the Heights', written in 1859, is the defining product. A lyric cycle of nine poems which fall into three quite clearly defined sections of three, four, and two poems respectively, each section having its distinctive metre, stanza form, and mood, it follows the initiation of a young man into a new and sterner mode of living and feeling. After spending a summer night with the girl he loves, he leaves for the mountains to live there for a short time in solitude, away both from her and from his own mother. There he encounters a stranger whose cold eyes are like ice-fed pools, whose laughter is full of tears, and whose lips are eloquent even when they are silent; he exercises an uncanny fascination over the young man and seems to steal his will. As time passes, the young man overcomes his longing to return to the life of the valley. On Christmas night he looks down and sees his own homestead ablaze, watching as his mother is burnt to death; while the stranger, shading his eyes with his hollowed hand, points out the splendid play of light from the flames as the moon shines on the conflagration. The final test the young man passes alone, when from the heights he sees the girl he loves riding to her wedding with another man, and without prompting he shades his eyes with his hollowed hand to get the perspective right, admiring the colourful effect of the bride's red skirt against the white birch trees. The price he pays for this remote detachment, this dedication, this freedom from sentimental involvement, is the slow petrifaction of his soul.

Ibsen's encounter in this poem with his own unhappy *Doppelgänger* brings out clearly the two claims he was exposed to at this time. On the one hand there was life down on the level where 'others' lived, the life of family ties and women's love, the warmth and comfort of the valley and the participation in 'life' with all its distractions, its responsibilities, and its human claims. Up on the heights of art, however, the feelings were subject to a severer discipline; there was remoteness, solitude, dedication; such an existence brought with it a distancing, a rarefaction, a freedom from the demands of sentiment, an escape from embroilment in material things. This conflict, a variant merely of the eternal conflict between life and art, did not need inventing. Ibsen, who had married in 1858 on precious little money and on prospects that showed little sign of fulfilling themselves, was awaiting the birth of the first child of this marriage at the time he was writing the poem; he was learning at first hand the bitter truth of what Julian Poulsen had once joked about in *St John's Night*: 'In your courting days you take a theoretical view of love; engagement and marriage, on the other hand . . . these, you see, are practical matters, and you cannot always make theories work in practice.' His work in the theatre involved him in trying to make a financial success of an institution too poor to contemplate putting on anything very much other than popular farce and vaudeville: 'For a writer,'

155

Ibsen once wrote to Bjørnson in later years, 'theatre work is like a daily repeated abortion.' Both domestic and professional obligations bore down on him so heavily that he found it almost impossible to do any creative work. Worse was to come later: his financial position grew desperate; in 1861 he fell seriously ill; and in 1862 the theatre he worked for went bankrupt and he lost his job. It needs no great effort of imagination to picture how the desire to be free from *such* claims of life became obsessive, how the kind of withdrawal he incorporated in 'On the Heights', an escape to 'aestheticism', exercised a fearful fascination. Yet although it is often (and with some truth) suggested that Falk might well be regarded as having stepped 'off the heights' into Mrs. Halm's tea-party in *Love's Comedy*, there was in this later work — later by some three years — a profound and significant change of attitude. The heroic became mock-heroic, the sublime bordered on the ridiculous, and the obsession with freedom that filled the poem now in the play became itself the thing to be fought free from. The claims of 'life' seemed by implication to reassert themselves; Ibsen found an instrument of salvation in satire; and the product was a splendidly comic rehearsal of *Brand*.

Despite the vast difference between *The Vikings* and *Love's Comedy*, the plays have at least two things in common: one positive, in that the same real-life model served (from what Ibsen said) for both Hjørdis and Svanhild, by which he is generally thought to have meant his wife Suzannah; the other negative (though no less important for that), in that the two plays shared the same hostility to Scribean realism, to the photographic triviality of the pieces that Ibsen was compelled by his appointment in the theatre to produce, but for which he continued to cherish the greatest contempt. In the earlier play, his anti-realism had manifested itself in a mannered formalism of structure; in the later play it expressed itself in the decision, ultimately, to cast the play in verse.

The shifts from tragedy to comedy, from prose to verse, from the historical to the contemporary, from solemnity to levity, from the objective to the subjective, from nationalism to 'aestheticism', from characters as planned symbols to characters as caricatures — all these are obvious enough. But they are merely tangential to what was perhaps the most important change: the switch from a severe and controlled directness to a complex and exuberant sophistication, from a kind of melodic linearity to a mode of dramatic composition full of disturbing vertical harmonies. By contrast with the lean, spare muscularity of *The Vikings* with its simple loyalties and established codes, *Love's Comedy* trades in subtleties and ambiguities, attempts to capture what is elusive and unexpected in human conduct, finds a hidden paradox in love and picks out those flaws in the institution of marriage that society conspires to conceal. *Love's Comedy* reverses the normal pattern of boy and girl comedy romance, allowing the wealthy middle-aged suitor to carry off the girl, sending the hero off jilted yet triumphantly claiming to find victory in defeat, dispossession as the only true possession, and eternity in the moment's memory. The aim of *The Vikings* had been, by nourishing the nation's craving for solidarity and reinforcing its pride, to aid the processes of national consolidation; the intent of *Love's Comedy*, by contrast, was socially subversive, and so plotted as to administer a deliberate affront to received ideas. Instead of gathering the patriotic sentiments of the onlookers together in unison, it broke up the simple harmonies with a distractingly and discordantly satirical accompaniment.

Three principal characters — Falk, Guldstad, and Svanhild — stand out against a variegated background of minor, and mostly grotesque, figures; and the fact that Guldstad has less to say than the other two does not in any way diminish his importance as an element in the *pattern*; indeed some producers are reported to have made him the central figure in the play. Fundamental to the whole design, certainly, is the contrast between Falk the poet and Guldstad the business man: the one living for the day, the other saving something for later; the one looking for excitements, the other for security; individuality is set against social conformity, idealism against practicality, the romantic against the realistic. (And must one catch at some significance, in the light of Ibsen's subsequent career, in the fact that the *realist* appears to triumph?) Between them stands Svanhild who, Candida-like, is faced in the end with choosing between them, and in doing so pronounces in effect the play's judgement on the name and nature of love and marriage, and on the proper relationship between them. Superimposed upon this are certain further complications, consequent upon the secret dreams and aspirations, the attitudes and the illusions of the people most closely concerned in this choice. All is worked out in a series of encounters involving the three principals as well as the minor supporting figures, of which, however, three are crucial: the scene in Act I where Falk proposes marriage-less love to Svanhild, and is rejected; the scene in Act II where Svanhild swings round so far as to invite Falk to join her in marriage, and is accepted; and the scene in Act III where Guldstad interposes himself between Falk and Svanhild, and in love-less marriage claims the girl for himself.

The first of these scenes comes as the culmination of a satirical assault on the institution of marriage which has been sustained throughout the Act. Grotesque exemplification is given of the laming effect of marriage on talent, the tainting effect on the soul: on the 'genius' of Straamand, now a windy clergyman-politician with a family of twelve daughters; on Styver's talent for poetry, once his secret enthusiasm in office hours but now forgotten in a seemingly interminable engagement; and so on. To Svanhild, Falk offers love without marriage as a chance to defy the world, as a way of striking a blow for freedom, as an escape from the crippling influence of marriage on the personality, and as a declaration that they are not to be tied down by the outworn constraints of convention. Unfortunately Falk combines this appeal with another motive which he is unwise enough not to keep hidden: the notion that Svanhild's love will act as a needed stimulus to his poetry. He thinks of her rather as he thought of the little song bird he had killed with the stone — 'aesthetically', as something sent only to inspire him. He reduces her to a pre-condition of poetry — give me, he had cried earlier in the Act, either some great consuming sorrow, or else give me a bride. Either would provide him with a useful course in spiritual gymnastics, he declared. Svanhild, unimpressed, rejects him.

The next time Falk is shrewder, and takes care to cast his appeal in a more fetching mould. He puts on a new self, and this time it is Svanhild's secret fantasies that are gratified, not his own. Electing to express himself through public deeds and not private words, doing battle over the tea-cups and putting his adversaries to rout, he plays the bold knight of Svanhild's day-dreams. She is dazzled by the brilliance of his exploits; she pictures herself as his 'squire', loyally helping him in a career of similarly splendid deeds, marching into the future under the banner of truth. She proposes — and it is here that the resemblance to Hjørdis is clearest — an alliance with him, a matrimonial alliance, by which they agree to join together and wage glorious battle against the outworn forces of convention.

The final encounter involves a much more formidable opponent who wields a terrifying logic; he has a sure aim, and knows the vulnerable point. This is their confidence in their own distinction. Neither Straamand nor Styver, who appeal to Falk each in their own way, succeed in moving him; but Guldstad wins his bout almost nonchalantly. He does it by persuading them that, despite their belief to the contrary, they are not in essence different from others, and therefore cannot expect the course of their marriage to run any differently. Their hidden flaw is that they are both concerned not so much with being themselves (which is always sure of Ibsen's approval) as with being different from others (which is not). It was this quality of seeming to be 'different' that had first attracted Falk's attention to Svanhild; he saw her in among the company sitting 'silent, utterly apart, like a bird on a roof', and like minted silver among common coin. And in confessing this, he betrays something of the inner standards by which he measures the worth both of himself and others. To win esteem means being different, and being different leads one to expect exceptional treatment; it is the undermining of this belief by Guldstad, the realization by Falk that he cannot forever count on being exceptional, that brings the shock of defeat. It is this that makes Falk the *victim* of the comedy.

There is, however, one extra complication to be allowed for in interpreting Falk's words and actions, one further ironic factor. He is not always what he seems. Svanhild responds strongly to this, and quite early on tells him he is like two people who cannot agree; and Falk, in admitting the truth of this, explains that it was because he hated to wear his soul indecently exposed. Sometimes it seems that he is as he is, as in his opening and more candid exchanges with Svanhild, perhaps; at other times, and these are less certainly defined, he is acting a part, protecting himself against injury and hurt, and putting a brave — or a deceptive — face on things. In both roles, however, he inhabits a markedly egocentric world. When he does not dissimulate, he reveals himself as one for whom all things are there only to be possessed, who is ready to subordinate the lives, the privacy, the spirit, the happiness, and the trust of those about him to the demands of his art, using his love as source material and exploiting the confidences of others. Equally, however, when he plays a part, he is indulging in a very private game, hugging his secret and smiling inwardly. His aggressiveness is an aspect of vulnerability; he is impetuous and wary at one and the same time. Lind is another one who comes close to realizing the truth, and in the last Act tells Falk that he seems, like Janus, to have two different faces; whilst Falk's own last speech admits that the instrument of his own inner self had a kind of twofold resonance, and a double note.

Inevitably this affects our reading of the play. A measure of the possible ironic discrepancy between what the play says and what it implies is provided by the finale, which seems to leave everybody satisfied — everybody, that is, but the onlooker. The final chorus of engaged and married couples naturally shows delight at the defeat of this young upstart who had threatened to expose what was private and sacred in their lives; *they* are in no doubt that truth and sanity have prevailed. Guldstad — an incipient Mortensgaard with his realist's sense of what can and cannot be done — is content at the victory of sound common-sense. Falk is (or seems to be) glad to keep the memory of love unsullied by coarse matrimonial realities, and discovers an exquisite happiness in unhappiness. Svanhild takes pleasure in the chance to play the very role in Falk's life that she had earlier indignantly rejected: that of being the little song bird, the agent of inspiration, expendable once the task was complete. The only difference this time is that she is not disqualified from life for ever; indeed, to her joyous astonishment, she discovers that the one decision complements both men's lives: one for whom rejection preserves the purity of love, and the other for whom acceptance means the opportunity to share the security of wealth. Thus, as Guldstad had forecast, *three* lives seem to be saved for happiness. Amid the laughter and cheers and singing at the end of the play, the reason why the spectator is uneasy is that he knows from Ibsen's later plays of the terror that lies in marriage between a Svanhild and a Guldstad. Love is not love, the play seems to say, unless it does alter when it alteration finds; and in its world the marriage of convenience alone makes sense. But the menace in such a marriage is no less real for being muffled; one recalls the terrible revenge Ibsen took in his later works not merely on possessive, 'doll's house' marriages (such as that to Falk would probably have been), but also on loveless marriages; one thinks of the hollowness of all the other calculated, politic, socially arranged and financially inspired marriages, of the careers of Bernick and Mrs. Alving and Hedda Gabler and Borkman. Only then does something of the true savagery of the irony in *Love's Comedy* become apparent, making it impossible to share the view, often expressed, that Guldstad had somehow been given his author's endorsement.

Ibsen never attempted to conceal his habit of writing himself free from things he had on his mind or his heart or his conscience or his nerves. This was particularly evident in the case of *Love's Comedy*: 'As for *Love's Comedy*', he wrote on 10 August 1863 to Clemens Petersen, 'I assure you that if ever an author felt the need to disburden himself of a mood and a theme, that was the case with me when I took up with that work.' That this labels *Love's Comedy* as 'subjective' is one thing; but to say how it — or indeed any work of literature — is subjective is another. One understands, for example, how tempting it must have been to Ibsen's contemporaries to assume that his own marriage, so recently contracted, coincided substantially with the image of marriage that the play is concerned to create; so persistent and so excessive were these attempts to demonstrate a parallelism, indeed, that Ibsen was forced to protest. Another of the similarities quickly seized on was that between Falk's lines in the opening Act:

Give me — if only for a month on loan —
a harrowing, overwhelming, crushing sorrow,
and all my poems would palpitate with joy

161

and the passage in Ibsen's letter to Carl Johan Anker of 30 January 1858: 'I ardently longed — indeed almost prayed — for some great sorrow that would properly complete my existence and give my life meaning.' Too often, however, the timing of these two passages is insufficiently regarded; the letter was written more than four years before the play was complete, and even then it was speaking of the past, dismissing the idea as 'absurd', though the memory of it (he went on to say) would always remain. This realization encourages the view that with *Love's Comedy* Ibsen was cutting himself free from a part of his own past, pronouncing sentence on some part of his own earlier self, ridiculing what he had once persuaded himself were deeply held convictions and which he now suspected of being only moments of attitudinizing — 'suspected' only, for to talk of any permanent recognition of them as such is, in the light of what *Brand* had to say, no doubt rather premature.

The defining influence in all this is of course Kierkegaard. Ibsen was never very ready to admit that he had drawn much inspiration from Kierkegaard; but it is known that some familiarity with his works came to Ibsen very early in his career — in the 1840s in Grimstad — and that his ideas were very much in the air in Scandinavia in this age. Indeed, the opening words of what is probably Kierkegaard's most influential work, *Either-Or* (1843), could quite easily be taken as an anticipation both of Ibsen's letter to Anker and of Falk's lines in the play:

> 'What is a poet? An unhappy man whose lips are so formed that his sighs and shrieks are transformed into beautiful music, while secret torments lie hidden in his soul . . .'

The same work also explored the divergent natures of 'romantic' and 'marital' love, and argued the relationship between love and marriage in the following terms:

> Just because one must never enter into marriage does not mean that life need have no element of eroticism. The

erotic may even contain in itself some element of infinity — poetic infinity, that is — which may just as well be concentrated into an hour as into a month. When two people fall in love and feel that they are meant for each other, what is needed is for them to have courage enough to break it off; for if they go on, there is everything to lose and nothing to gain. This seems to be a paradox; and to the emotions it is, but not to the reason.[3]

More than anything else, however, what Kierkegaard provides is a possible insight into the complex relationship between Ibsen and Falk. On the one hand there was the real-life Ibsen, attracted by the detachment and dedication of the Kierkegaardian 'aesthetic', by the possibility of liberation it seemed to offer from the claims of practical living; and on the other hand there was Ibsen's created character, the dedicated aesthete, who emerges from *his* crisis by burning his manuscripts, pleading to be given a 'mission', and determining to give up his art for life. Falk reverses the direction of flow. Whereas Ibsen by his drama was turning his life into poetry, Falk decides that his poetry must be turned into life: 'My poem shall be *lived!*' he announces. Once again the cross-reference that suggests itself is to *Either-Or*, to the section entitled 'The aesthetic validity of marriage', where Kierkegaard has an intriguing explanation of the essence of the relationship between dramatist and dramatized, between poet creator and created poet. Remarking that the 'Aesthetic' is something realizable only in terms of life and not in terms of poetry — and using, incidentally, the same rather unusual passive verb form 'at det leves' (that it be lived) that Ibsen himself used in his play — Kierkegaard goes on:

. . . In truth, he who has sufficient humility and courage to submit himself to aesthetic clarification; he who feels himself to be a character in that play which the godhead is writing, where there is no difference between dramatist and prompter, and where the individual like a well-rehearsed actor who has lived himself into his part and into his words is not put off by the prompter but feels that what is being whispered to him is what he

himself wants to say, so that it is a matter of some doubt
whether he is putting words into the prompter's mouth or
the prompter into his; he who in the profoundest sense
feels himself to be creating and created at one and the
same time, who at the moment of creating has all the
original pathos of the words, and who at the moment of
being created has the erotic ear that catches every
sound — he and he alone has realized what is highest in
the Aesthetic.[4]

The occasion for the release of creative energy that resulted in
The Pretenders is not far to seek: the choral festival in Bergen
which Ibsen attended in company with Bjørnstjerne Bjørnson
between 14 and 18 June 1863. After six years of frustration,
hostility, misunderstanding, and growing artistic isolation, after
months of worrying financial difficulties, after *Love's Comedy*
had flopped with the public and Ibsen was beset with doubts
about his own adequacy as a dramatist, the four days of festivity
brought him a great flood of warm, human sympathy, of gaiety
and cordiality and appreciation and companionship. His letter of
thanks to his host, Randolph Nilsen, after his return home to
Christiania, betrays how deeply he was moved by the contrast
Bergen had offered with his unhappy life in Christiania:

. . . Heaven be praised, I still bear within me the festival
mood, and I hope I shall keep it for a long time yet. My
warmest thanks to you and your dear wife for all the
inexpressible kindness and goodness you showed me. The
festival there, and all the many kind people I met and
shall never forget have had the same tonic effect on me
as a good visit to church, and I greatly hope this mood
will not wear off. Everybody was so kind to me in
Bergen. That is not the case here, where there are many
who try to hurt and harm me at every turn. Common to
all visitors at the festival was, I think, a powerful sense
of being uplifted, a feeling as it were that one's thoughts
were being ennobled and elevated; indeed, his would be
a hard and evil soul who could keep such impressions at
a distance from himself. It is perhaps here that the most

deeply beneficial effect of the festival lies.

Ibsen had arrived back in Christiania on 21 June 1863; the above letter was written on 25 June; by the beginning of September of the same year, he was walking along the main street in Christiania with the fair copy of *The Pretenders* under his arm. How much of the play had existed in draft form before that summer — for it is believed he first started work on it as early as 1858 — is in the present state of our knowledge not easy to say; but it seems reasonably clear that a great part of the work on it was done in that July and August, in the mood that lingered on from the Bergen festival.

But this is only one element in the chemistry of the play that calls for examination. The other was, of course, the residual effects of six years of not conspicuously successful endeavour in the theatre in Christiania. Some years later, in a letter to Peter Hansen of 28 October 1870, Ibsen commented on this:

> *Love's Comedy* . . . gave rise to a lot of talk in Norway; people mixed my own personal affairs in with the discussion, and my general reputation suffered greatly. The only person who approved of my book at the time was my wife. . . None of my countrymen understood anything of this, and I had no inclination to confess myself to that crowd. So then I was outlawed; they were all against me. The fact that everybody was against me — the fact that I no longer had anyone standing by, of whom I could say that he had faith in me — all this, as you can easily imagine, could not help but create in me a mood which found its release in *The Pretenders*.

Two distinct 'moods', it seems therefore, contributed ultimately to the composition of this play: one of despondency, of doubt, of sombre forebodings about his ability and talents; the other of pleasure, of well-being, and — deriving particularly from renewed contact with his great contemporary, Bjørnson — of a sense of buoyant confidence. The resulting reaction between these two things, the interplay of mood and attitude, was the thing that gave *The Pretenders* — Ibsen's first real and incontrovertible masterpiece — its distinctive quality.

There is little reason to doubt that the character of Haakon Haakonsson took life from Bjørnson. Ibsen and Bjørnson were of course no strangers to each other when they met on the occasion of the festival and their paths had crossed a number of times in the twelve years or so since they had attended the same 'crammer's' in Christiania to prepare for their matriculation examination. They had never felt particularly drawn to each other in the past, although they had often championed each other in print, and associated themselves with the same causes; a marked ambivalence continued to characterize the relations between them for the rest of their lives, even when in later years the two families were drawn closer together by the marriage of Ibsen's only son to Bjørnson's daughter. Always, and on both sides, it seemed as if their attitudes were composed of the oddest mixtures of admiration, envy, gratitude, exasperation, affection, contempt, and at times plain hostility. But during the four days of the festival Ibsen was completely taken by Bjørnson (who had just returned from three years' residence abroad), wholly captivated by his generous personality, his infectious enthusiasm, his dashing and extrovert self-assurance, by his outspoken contempt for the cultural apathy he saw all about him on his return to Norway, and not least by his public declaration in a great banquet speech of the identity of purpose he felt with 'his friend', Henrik Ibsen. Yet the sense of rivalry between them was not, at least as far as Ibsen was concerned, in any way diminished by this; and when Ibsen compared their careers up to that point, it cannot but have seemed to him that Bjørnson, five years his junior, had indubitably been the more successful. Indeed, Bjørnson impressed more than anything else as the living embodiment of confident success. The 'Peasant Tales', beginning in 1857 with *Synnøve Solbakken*, had been an immediate triumph; Bjørnson had been everywhere accepted as the spokesman of the new generation; he had been eloquent and active in many causes; and in 1863 he was awarded an official literary bursary at the same time as Ibsen's application was — largely because of the 'scandalous' remarks in *Love's Comedy*

about the institution of marriage — humiliatingly refused.
The very personal relevance to Ibsen's own career of the thirteenth-century rivalry between Haakon Haakonsson and Skule Baardsson for the throne of Norway may well not have struck him until a comparatively late stage in the genesis of the play. About *Emperor and Galilean* — a work in many respects close to the spirit of *The Pretenders* — Ibsen once said that not only was there a great deal of 'self-anatomy' about it, but also that 'the historical theme chosen has a closer connection with the movements of our own age than one might at first suppose'. So also with *The Pretenders*. Long before he turned with any sense of real urgency to its composition in 1863, he had been familiar with the historical events and characters that provide the substance of the drama; but when, in the preface to the second edition of *The Feast at Solhoug*, he spoke of his activities in the year 1854, he admitted that at that time the material had had little interest for him:

. . . The Kings Sagas and the more strictly historical accounts from that distant time did not attract me; I was not able, for my literary purposes of that time, to make any dramatic use of the conflicts between kings and chieftains, between parties and factions. That did not come till later.

Some impetus was given to his plans in this direction by the publication in 1857 of P.A. Munch's *History of the Norwegian People,* which among other things gave an account of the period of internecine war in Norway in the late twelfth and early thirteenth centuries. It is known that Ibsen found much to fascinate him in the work; but doubtless his interest at this stage was still largely nationalistic, and the theme of progress towards the establishment of a united Norway must have had a ready fascination for one who was still in these years very susceptible to patriotic suggestion. The moment when the material really took possession of him and demanded to be dramatized was delayed, it seems, until the moment when by a kind of revelation Ibsen recognized both the essential modernity of the theme and its clear relevance to his own personal situation.

As with the two previous dramas, one of the more urgent problems concerned the choice of linguistic medium. In the middle of his most intense work on the drama, on 10 August 1863, he wrote to an acquaintance that he was working on an historical play — 'but in prose,' he stated, 'I *cannot* write it in verse'. But there was not to be any mere repetition of what had served for his earlier saga-historical drama, *The Vikings*; there the prose had been deliberately archaic, purposely reminiscent of the language of the sagas themselves; now, perhaps encouraged by the policy Bjørnson had adopted for his drama, *Sigurd Slembe*, the previous year — of which Ibsen in a review of it noted that the tone of the language was not, and indeed should not be, that of the sagas, because 'any particular historical quality in the language would only be a mistake where the writer has, as here, given himself the task of depicting an inner conflict valid and intelligible for all time' — the dialogue in *The Pretenders* was in a less time-bound idiom, closer to modern rhythms without ever being aggressively 'contemporary'. The victory for prose on this occasion was a splendid one; the artistic success of the play proved to its author that he need not forever feel compelled to adopt either metre or conspicuous mannerism to find a medium commensurate with the dignity of his art. But that the victory for prose, although memorable, was still not a decisive one is of course at once shown by the choice of verse for his next two great dramas of the 1850s, *Brand* and *Peer Gynt*.

It was to prove to be the last of Ibsen's historico-nationalistic plays. By giving a reasonably prominent place to the idea of the unification of Norway — the 'kingly thought' as it is, in literal translation, called in the play — Ibsen made at least a minimal gesture in the direction of the patriotic aspirations of his age. But this remains something almost incidental to the main concern of the drama, which is with psychological types. The complementary creations of Haakon and Skule — the one self-confident and Bjørnsonian, the other vacillating, uncertain both of himself and his cause, and (with certain important reservations) Ibsenian — come almost exactly halfway in time in a tradition that begins with Schiller's distinction between 'naiv' and 'sentimentalisch' (perhaps best translated 'reflective'?) and ends with Jung's typology, in which the concepts of 'extravert' and 'introvert' are used as factors of differentiation. Georg Brandes, the great Danish critic, linked the two figures most interestingly with the Aladdin myth, particularly as it had been given dramatic shape by Adam Oehlenschläger, in his *Aladdin* (1805). To this, Oehlenschläger had himself added an epilogue which offered a symbolical interpretation of the work: Aladdin is the child of nature, the naive genius, uncomplicated, direct, who seizes the magic lamp with never a moment's hesitation about his right to do so; whereas Nureddin, for all his shrewdness, his profundity, is somehow disqualified from within, so that when he reaches out for the lamp, his courage fails him and his plans collapse. This distinction it was that Brandes later elaborated.

It is the insistence with which the play dwells on the factors of *inner* qualification and disqualification that makes it more than just a drama of doubt and faith — which is how it is often described. Its deeper implications are not with faith alone, but with the faith that is given to faith; not with doubt alone, but with the doubt that bears on doubt; not with right, but with the right to have the right. It goes beyond the consideration of ways of thinking to an exploration of ways of being; and it is here in this play that one first begins to detect the authentic tones of the Ibsen who later startled the world by the pitiless penetration of his psychological insights. One consequence of this approach is that interest is focused proportionately rather less on Haakon and rather more on Skule. To have the kind of faith in one's faith that Haakon exhibits so inspiringly is simply to increase the potential of that faith, is to raise it to the next highest power in a process capable of such faith: 'Pray to the Lord thy God, Haakon Haakonsson!' his chaplain commands in the opening moments of the play at the trial by ordeal, to which Haakon — with his very first words in the play — characteristically replies, 'There is no need. I am sure of Him.' His confidence is something that radiates out from him affecting others; he has, as Bishop Nikolas admits, what the Romans called *ingenium*, the quality of the man 'on whom fortune smiles, who feels the needs of the times on his pulse, whose intuition outstrips his reason and points a way for him he knows not where, which nonetheless he takes, and *must* take, until he hears the people shout with

169

joy, and looking round him with dazed eyes, perceives he has achieved a noble deed'. In Skule's case, the path instead spirals inwards, infinitely receding, towards a kind of dead centre of paralysis. To doubt the doubt that nags one is to be what Jatgeir, the bard in the play, calls an 'unsound doubter'; it is to torment oneself with the possibility that one's uncertainties are themselves dubious, whereby the mind starts off on an endless quest for external proofs to substitute for one's lack of inner conviction. It means, for Skule, to search desperately yet despairingly for the crucial document, to attend to omens and signs, to crave legitimation; it is to try to enlist the beliefs and doubts of others, to urge others to denounce Haakon that his own disbelief might be reinforced, and to annex the faith of others (his son Peter's, for example) to make up the deficiencies in his own; it means wielding borrowed power by holding on licence the seal of authority while lacking the reality of power; it means stealing the 'kingly thought' from a rival; until the final picture is of one who, equally unable to prove his doubts as to trust his proofs, allows indecision to set hard into a way of life, and accepts uncertainty as a delicious torment.

The third protagonist — and potentially perhaps the most fascinating of all the characters — is Bishop Nikolas. He stands as an image of the power-seeking impotent, the man of violent lusts incapable of gratifying them, ambitious yet cowardly, sensual yet emasculate, dedicated to the establishment of mediocrity because he cannot bear to be himself outdone. He pictures himself as a man living beyond good and evil, far above all guilt, and a rigorous sceptic; yet even in this he is disabled. He sustains the murderous balance between Haakon and Skule, working through muttered hints and betrayed confidences, pulling the strings that would reduce the others to the level of his puppets, and thereby feeding his illusions of power; he exults in the chance to extend his baleful influence beyond the grave, to set going his *perpetuum mobile* of strife and distrust for Norway's future woe, to win an unenviable immortality. Very much to the detriment of his own fictive career, however, and many would say detrimental also to the drama as a whole, he dies in the third of the five Acts, reappearing only momentarily in what William Archer (surely with much justification) called 'the great and flagrant artistic blemish of the Ghost Scene in the last act . . . a sheer excrescence on the play'. What reduces the Bishop's artistic stature within the play, however, is not so much this act of truncation as the fact that he is not fully realized in dramatic terms; the greater part of what we know about him is merely *declared*, not embodied. He announces himself too much for what he is — especially in his death scene — without ever having adequate opportunity to enact all that he says he is. His portrayal is too much enumeration; he is too obviously a set of notes, self-enunciated, for a character rather than a fully contoured thing. But what there is of him, the basic conception, has a wonderful fascination.

To Ibsen, in 1864, it must have seemed as though events were determined to add substance to the spirit of Bishop Nikolas; in the last Act of the drama, as a ghostly apparition, the Bishop had threatened to spread cowardice, evasiveness, mediocrity, and pettiness of mind throughout Norway all down the long years; and the (to Ibsen's mind) shameful policies on the part of Norway that left the Danes to fight their hopeless war alone seemed to him to epitomize just such a spirit as he had ascribed to the Bishop. To the contempt Ibsen felt on a domestic level for the ways of organized society within Norway (so clearly evident in *Love's Comedy*) was now added a burning sense of shame at his country's international conduct. He left Norway — financed partly by an official travelling scholarship but mostly by the proceeds of a whip-round among his friends which the big-hearted Bjørnson had organized — while the crisis was at its height; he was in Copenhagen while the crucial battle of Dybbøl was being fought; and on his way south through Europe, he was in Berlin for the Prussian victory parade, and saw how the crowds spat on the Danish cannon captured at that battle. As he later reported, it seemed to him like a portent of the way history would spit in the faces of Norway and Sweden for their shameful part in that affair.

It is unlikely that, on his departure, Ibsen had intended to make his absence from Norway so permanent; the fact that he did stay away, that within a few months he sent for his wife and child and remained in almost unbroken exile for over twenty-seven years, is due in no small degree to an extension of the two

171

factors that had played so important a part during his years in Christiania: 'aestheticism' and nationalism. The detachment he had once been tempted to try for philosophically, he finally achieved geographically; the distance exile gave him was the distance 'aestheticism' had often seemed to promise: the opportunity to take a long, resolute view of things, to 'get the perspective right'. And what he looked at most critically and most particularly were the qualities that went to make up this defective nationhood of his own people, the way in which the spirit of Bishop Nikolas was threatening to despoil what, deep within, was for him a source of fierce pride. Thus the two things, the perspective of 'distance' and the complacencies of nationalism, coalesced: 'The most decisive and significant thing that has happened to me,' he wrote to his mother-in-law on 3 December 1865, 'is that I got a sufficient distance away from home to see the hollowness behind all the self-made lies in our so-called public life, and the piteousness of all the big talk, never at a loss for words when it comes to talking about "a great cause", but never with either the will, the power, or the sense of duty to perform a great deed.' They coalesced into a passionate urgency that heralded a wholly new phase of endeavour for him — a mood that prompted him, when writing at this time to the King, to speak of his 'life's mission' and to define it as that of 'waking the people up and making them think big'.

7

Epic Poetry
and Poetic Drama

Brand; Peer Gynt

Brand was many things before it finally received the stamp of
drama: a cry of shame; an act of exorcism; an accusation of
wrongful inheritance; an admission of guilt and complicity; a
call to expiation; a shudder of repudiation; a spasm of disgust.

It began, improbably, as an appeal for urgent sanitary measures: 'I see a corpse,' Ibsen wrote in the very earliest stages of
the work's composition, 'monstrous as Ymir's body, lying and
spreading its pestilential air over field and fjord, infecting rich
man and beggar alike. Wrap the corpse in all the flags of
Norway: Help, youth, to sink it deep in the sea!'

It was a cathartic discharge of venom: 'While I was writing
Brand,' Ibsen reported, 'I had standing on my desk an empty
beer glass with a scorpion in it. From time to time the creature

became sickly; then I used to throw a piece of soft fruit to it, which it would then furiously attack and empty its poison into; then it grew well again. Is there not something similar to that about us poets?'

It spat in the faces of his countrymen. Writing of the moment of *Brand*'s conception, of those pregnant days when the work began to grow within him 'like a foetus', he declared: 'I was in Berlin when the victory parade took place [in early May 1864 after the Prusso-Danish War], and I saw the mob spit into the mouths of the [Danish] Dybbøl cannon, and it seemed to me a sign of how history will one day spit in the faces of Sweden and Norway for their part in the affair.'

In its origins, *Brand* was above all else an act of repudiation and disavowal, a passionate denial of earlier assumptions and beliefs. Compounded of distaste, guilt, contempt, and frustration, it represented a breakaway from what was now seen as a whole world of false values and spurious ideals. It cut away from the past, away from inauthentic living and writing. For twelve months and more Ibsen strove to give shape to the inchoate amalgam of passions and recognitions and attitudes that now obsessed him. When the solution did eventually present itself, it came swiftly and with all the force of a revelation. It was a day in July 1865, by which time Ibsen had already been struggling with his material for a year. He found himself in Rome on an errand (he wrote to Bjørnson) and he walked into St. Peter's: 'There, suddenly, the form for what I had to say came to me, forcefully and clearly.' He abandoned the narrative poem on which he had been working and which had caused him increasing torment; the new work grew under his hands as never before. In under four months, and before the end of the year, *Brand*, a dramatic poem in five acts, was complete.

What he had struggled so long and in vain to communicate, and for which he now suddenly found the appropriate vehicle, was thus a thing of some complexity. The same letter to Bjørnson admitted that whilst the form of the work was new, the 'content and mood' of it had been hanging over him like a nightmare 'since those many unhappy events back home'. Ibsen had sailed from Christiania on 5 April 1864, and arrived in Copenhagen the following day. Some time after the middle of

April he left Denmark for Italy, just about at the time of the
Danish defeat at Dybbøl; he travelled via Lübeck to Berlin,
where on 4 May he witnessed the Prussian victory parades. He
was seized with anger and shame — shame not only at the
betrayal by the Norwegians and Swedes of their Danish brothers,
but also at the cowardly blow which was thereby dealt to the
whole stirring notion of Scandinavian solidarity which had
recently been the subject of so many reverberant speeches, so
many high hopes. 'If I had stayed any longer in Berlin,' he later
stated, 'where I saw the parades in April, saw the crowds surge
round the trophies from Dybbøl, saw them ride on the gun
carriages and spit on the cannon — those same cannon which had
received no help and which nevertheless kept on firing until
they burst — I don't know how I would have kept my reason.'

Closely following these (to him) shattering Berlin events came
another experience that moved him almost equally deeply,
though it was a very different kind. Travelling south from
Berlin, through Austria, he crossed the Alps into Italy on 9 May.
This too was a revelation, an experience that remained vivid in
his memory until the end of his life. He drove from the north
under the great curtain of cloud and into the tunnel, and
emerged at the other end into the gleaming white world of Mira
Mora; many years later he recalled 'a feeling of being released
from darkness into light, escaping through a tunnel from mists
into sunshine'. All the beauty of the South suddenly stood
revealed — something which, he himself admitted, left its mark
on all his later work. In the months that followed, his letters tell
repeatedly of the joy he was taking in his work, the peace of
mind which he now found he could bring to his writing. The
great monuments of classic and Renaissance art brought delight
and insight. The whole spirit of life in this Mediterranean land
was different.

The letter to Bjørnson nevertheless does not stop short at the
reference to the 'many unhappy events back home'. Ibsen went
on to say that he had been impelled by these events also to look
deep within his own soul, to look hard and long at many things
in the Norwegian way of life that he had earlier simply accepted
unthinkingly, and to take stock of life anew. It was therefore
only in an immediate and limited sense that *Brand* derived from

the public and political events of the day. At a deeper and more significant level, the new work drew on whole areas of his earlier life and career: on his own childhood, and on his relations to parents, brothers and sister; on his earlier authorship, its aims, its purposes, and its disappointing achievements; on the frustrations and humiliations of his professional life in the theatre, 'a daily repeated abortion', he was later to call it; on the realization of his earlier unthinking acceptance of conventional beliefs and current ideas; and on his new and increasing awareness of standards and values fundamentally different from those that served his contemporaries back home. He was moved to contrast he realities of his Italian experience with the defensive fictions of the Norwegian Myth, with the 'life lies' — to use his later term — of Scandinavian national romanticism: those notions, to which he had himself shamefully given currency by his pen, of the decay and effeteness of Mediterranean culture when compared with the gale-swept, invigorating strength of the North. He began to see the crippling provincialism of that way of life which had been his lot for half a lifetime — he was now thirty-six — and which he now recognized as hollow and empty and based on cruel delusion. Now he was in a position to measure the extent of that smug self-deception which sought to sustain local morale by a kind of xenophobic denigration of others. He squirmed when he recalled the active part he had played as a writer in preserving these illusions, in promulgating these lies: notions of Nordic supremacy, of the staunch courage and clear-sighted virtue of this brave little race, of the latent poetic and artistic skills that were supposed to be slumbering in the people, waiting to be roused. He was filled with resentment at the realization that social and cultural forces had somehow manipulated him, had exploited his talents in the interests of a spurious and lying ideal.

The distaste, revulsion even, that he began to feel for much of his own earlier work — things which, with notable exceptions here and there, had in servile fashion propagated the very Myth he was now determined to repudiate — took command. His previous rather solemn dependence on folksy elements, the preoccupation with goblins and trolls and nixies and the fairy folk of mountain and stream, was something he was determined to get away from in this first work of his exile. He relived his earlier exasperation at the public's disapproval of anything that had poked fun at their sacred belief — especially he recalled the reception given to *Love's Comedy*, 'a forerunner to *Brand*' as he himself described it. It took little effort to persuade himself that he had left behind a country of big mouths and timid hearts; a people given in their cups to fierce Viking cries but who, when challenged, quickly changed their adopted *persona* to one of 'a little people', wholly absorbed in the daily struggle for existence, ploughing their fields and fishing their Northern seas.

Those passions which the Norwegian defection of 1864 roused in him, deeply felt though they were, were thus important less for their own sake than as a kind of fuse that set off a veritable explosion of thought and feeling in his life. Things he had suffered and proved on his own nerves, things he had himself 'lived through' — a phrase Ibsen was very explicit about to a number of correspondents, as something to be distinguished from his merely having witnessed, or experienced from the outside — now combined to impose upon him a fundamental reappraisal: the social pressures, the cultural impositions, the received ideas, the wishful thinking, the public hypocrisy, the individual self-deception, the false assumptions, the spiritual chauvinism, the empty phrases, the little-Norwegian attitudes, and all the sickening *Hurrapatriotismus* on which he could now look back across the entire length of Europe, all were now distanced, and seen for what they really were.

The immediate consequence of this turmoil of feeling was the astonishing poem 'To my fellows in guilt'. In the most forthright and uncompromising way, it announced that its author was breaking with his own past. In this poem Ibsen declared that he was turning away from earlier sentimentalities, away also from ineffectual dreams of the future, in order to face the realities of the present. It represented both an analysis and a manifesto; and as such it stands as one of the most important programmatic statements about his work and beliefs that Ibsen ever made.

In effect, the poem was a call to Ibsen's fellow countrymen to repudiate the lying pretence that had been infecting all levels of public and private life. The past, he insisted, was dead; the Viking spirit upon which the people so pathetically prided themselves, apostrophizing it at every Independence Day celebration, was no longer a living thing but a rouged and embalmed corpse, pestilential; it spread a plague that sapped the strength and drained the initiative of all men along the length and breadth of the fjords; the ancient grandeur had vanished, and the modern generation was too puny even to attempt to wear the trappings of that earlier heroic age, too feeble to be worthy of the inheritance. (One compares this with the phrases he used when writing to Bjørnson on 16 September 1864: 'We can cross out our ancient history; for the Norwegians of our own day clearly have no more to do with their past than have the Greek pirates with the generation that sailed for Troy . . .' It was obviously a notion that had taken firm root in his mind, for he used it again almost word for word over eighteen months later when writing to John Grieg). Geography, far from being a beneficent factor and acting — as the Myth claimed — to preserve uncontaminated the pure strain of traditional virtue, was in reality a malevolent force, an inhibition, an obstacle to movement, a barrier to free flight, blocking the sun and making narrow the spirit. The one paramount thing, the poem insists, is to be honest with oneself and to face realities, to explore the mist-ridden world of the present in all its wind and rain and discomfort, with a single mind.

Essentially what this poem bears witness to is a fundamental change in Ibsen's conception of the role of the poet. In his earlier career he had been quick to cast himself for the role of skald in the traditional mould: praising heroism, idealizing events, sustaining morale. Now, he declared, he had sung his last song in his capacity as bard. Now he saw his duty as that of the solitary observer, recognizing the realities of life, taking distant views, getting the perspectives right, showing honesty and courage in putting the truth, however unpalatable it may be. When about this time he was asked, by one who had in fact volunteered for service at the front, why he had not himself enlisted, he answered, 'We poets have other tasks.' The remark should perhaps not be regarded wholly as the defensive reply of one whose conscience on this point was uneasy, for from now on Ibsen's work took on much more clearly the character of a campaign: assaulting errors of thought and conduct, storming the citadels of prejudice, holding high the banner of truth.

'To my fellows in guilt' was eventually incorporated as the first section of that work which has come to be known as the 'Epic Brand', the extended but still fragmentary narrative poem that long occupied Ibsen's attention and energies before he finally, in July 1865, threw it over in favour of dramatic form. In its role as prologue to this long narrative poem, 'To my fellows in guilt' warns the reader not to overlook the hidden meaning in what was to follow: 'My lute is tuned to play a muted song; but deeper strings lend colour to the chords. A poem is thus concealed within the poem; and he who fathoms *this* will grasp the song.' Initially, these lines were doubtless meant to alert the reader to the symbolic attack which the poem was to mount on the Norwegian Myth; but other things too came crowding in as the work progressed, and it is rewarding to try to identify the stages in the composition of the 'Epic Brand', one by one, in an effort to follow the changing pattern of intent. Each of the successive stages has left a kind of deposit, not only within the poem itself but also, though less distinctly, within the drama that supervened.

Assuming that 'Over the great mountain' — ultimately the third section of the 'Epic Brand' — was the part of the work that next occupied Ibsen's attention, the inference seems to be that he was anxious in the early stages to set *en face* two opposing philosophies of life, to permit one spokesman for each to present a case, and for any inherent didacticism to emerge from this confrontation. The two ways of life represented were, as stanza 97 puts it, the way of the pulpit and the way of the palette.

As promised in the introductory section 'To my fellows in guilt,' the whole of 'Over the great mountain' is heavily, even portentously, charged with secondary meaning. The initial encounter itself takes place in a markedly symbolic landscape, at the very watershed of Norway's east and west, 'that place on the wasteland's broad breast where, out of the marsh, the river trickles out to east and west', towards the gently, undulating, sunlit valleys in the one direction, and to the mist-laden, precipitous, rocky steeps in the other. From the sunlit east come Agnes and Einar — actually in the earliest drafts called Dagmar and Axel — to represent the idea of *carpe diem*. Life for them is a game, the play of butterflies; they exist in the present, with no regret for the past, and no care for the future; sorrow is formally outlawed from their union, and they live for art and beauty. Not that 'beauty' was in any sense a merely decorative adornment to life; it was a guiding principle, a vital force, a power that seemingly had proved itself more efficacious than even the science of medicine itself. Einar, seeking beauty as a painter among the mountains and the moor's pines and the forest rivers, discovered its real power only after he met the ailing Agnes. 'Then he painted his best masterpiece', said the doctor. 'He painted healthy roses on your cheeks; two eyes he painted radiating happiness, and then a smile that laughed its way into the soul. I soon realized that I, your old doctor, was superfluous to such a cure. His songs worked better than any medicines, better even than bathing in God's nature.' Einar and Agnes dance and sing their way towards the west, and their song is like transmuted laughter. By contrast, Brand's song resounds through the hills like a mighty organ in the church of Nature, deafening the river's roar and the thunder of the falls. It halts the happy couple in their tracks by its fearsome power, by the terror of its stern demands. Brand's song is an appeal for pain and suffering and prayer, for strength to resist the temptations of the flesh, for the enrichment of life through sorrow.

As it stands in these drafts, the confrontation is one not so much between personalities as between personifications, between the representatives of two conflicting *Weltanschauungen*: the hedonist and the puritanical, the ecstatic and the ascetic, or (to use Kierkegaardian terms much current in these years when *Brand* was being written) the aesthetic and the ethical. Striking about *this* version is how very much more evenly matched the two are as spokesmen for their ideologies than they are in the final drama. The arguments are more evenly weighted, the eloquence not nearly so one-sided as was to be the case later. In the drama, Einar is crushed and virtually silenced by the vehemence of Brand's outburst; in the narrative poem, although the two lovers are frightened and subdued by Brand's outburst,

Einar is nevertheless permitted to score some shrewd points —
arguments which were ultimately cut from the drama. How little
Brand is capable of grasping the mystery of beauty, Einar
accuses: 'Do you think a flower's right to blossom is greater if it
holds medicinal properties in its sap or leaf than if it simply has
scent and colour? Do you think that a bird should sit silent in the
forest unless its song can ease somebody's grief?' In the narrative
poem, until Brand shifts his ground and attacks what Einar is
actually in no way concerned to represent, the implication is
indeed that both views might well claim equal justification, that
the palette can surely serve God's ways as properly as the pulpit.
Not until Brand directs his strictures away from the purely
aesthetic mode of life and on to the hypocrisy that grows out of
it — that hypocrisy of big talk and cowardly deed which had
figured as the target in 'To my fellows in guilt' — not until then
are the two lovers left crushed and the victory in the battle of
words goes, rather unfairly, to Brand.

Next in the genesis of the narrative poem seems to have been
a decision to try to establish plausible antecedents for the two
spokesmen; and things are traced back to the formative influences of their childhood. The two men had already been described
as 'a pair of schoolboy friends' who met thus in later life. What
Ibsen now apparently did was to develop this notion by introducing into the poem an equally dualistic encounter between the
two while they were still boys, an episode in which Agnes too is
allowed to appear in a subsidiary role. In the new section,
entitled 'From the time of ripening', the treatment was no less
heavily symbolic than before. Unexpected, however, is that, in
attempting to trace back to childhood experience those attitudes
and values that dominated the adult lives of the two spokesmen,
the poem becomes boldly and even crudely naturalistic,
Darwinian almost, in its simplistic emphasis on the role of
heredity and environment.

Once again the leading figures occupy a geographical halfway stage, a ridge in the landscape that offers a vantage point
for surveying two ways of life: to the South lie the houses in the
sun, the gaily beflagged ships in the bay, the islands in the open
fjord; while to the North lies the wilder landlocked country, the
dark forests, the inland lakes. Two boys sit in the evening light:

one, the Einar of the later episodes, is blond, open-featured and gay, with his gaze (literally) turned to the sunny side of things; the other, Brand, has his back to the sun, and his face turned to the North, looking and yet somehow not seeing, *committed*. He seems 'to look *beyond* what he saw, as though something unseen lay hidden beyond the view' — an oblique invitation to the reader once again to do what the opening section of the poem had enjoined him to do: to look for the hidden meaning, for the poem within the poem. And beyond the two horizons, one to the South and one to the North, lie reminiscences — symbolic reminiscences which pivot about a North-South axis in a way not wholly unexpected in an author who so recently had quit a memory-filled North for the inviting South.

The two narratives, Einar's and Brand's, again pivot about the basic dichotomy. The former's account is of Sunday mornings in summer in his childhood home to the South, an account that stresses all that is colourful, healthful, loving, companionable, and is full of the joy of life; the latter's is of the events of a winter night far to the North, where all is black and frostbound, a tale of sickness and death and bitterness. It is a tale so full of terror, indeed, that the teller of it has to pretend not only that it happened to some third person and not to himself, but also that it happened only in a dream. Mother-love in the one is terrifyingly matched by mother-hate in the other — a duality that Ibsen was eventually to work out in elaborate detail in the dramas of *Brand* and *Peer Gynt*.

Still, as yet, there was in the work no real indication that the centre of interest was eventually to become the figure of Brand; still less any hint that the poem might seek to enlist sympathy or admiration for him. He emerges from this stage of the work as a distinctly repellent figure: twisted in mind, cruel and even sadistic in his responses. The incident where he cruelly beats his dog to death in order to be able to torment his mother by his knowledge of her secret conduct is a peculiarly contrived and grotesque incident. Brand seems at this stage not merely untouched by any kind of loving or human impulse, but positively evil. Not until the next stage was it that Brand, as a character with individual as distinct from typical characteristics, began to emerge as a central figure. In the first five stanzas of the succeeding section of the 'Epic Brand', entitled 'Two on the way to church', there is a new and significant development. (There are, incidentally, also technical reasons — partly to do with the change of name from Koll to Brand, and partly relating to a change in the ink of the manuscript — why these five stanzas draw attention to themselves.) Up to this stage, the characters in the narrative rather obviously *represented* certain philosophies of life, philosophies which themselves were somewhat crudely delineated. Now, for the first time in the poem, one detects a distinct concern for psychological light and shade.

As Brand makes his way along the edge of the abyss after parting company from Agnes and Einar, his eye is now turned *inward*; and, matching this, the poem's eye now allows itself to penetrate beneath the surface of outward event to explore the complexities and paradoxes of the individual heart and soul. The poem is not content merely to remark the 'crusading zeal' transfiguring Brand's face; it also reveals his curiously mixed inner feelings, the fact that he 'revelled in the agonized delight which a soul can draw from the word "regret" — poised between embracing and condemning.'

In the earlier draft version, Ibsen made no fewer than four attempts at the last line of this stanza to get it right; and in following the line of 'reported thought' — in which Brand recognized that he had deadened the song of the summer-glad singer by his own words, and had turned the man's eyes from the sun to the ground — the draft originally allowed Brand to admit 'that he had committed evil and craved remorse', before reaching the final formulation that 'he saw what he had done and writhed in his remorse'.

The access to the inner thoughts of Brand which the poem now permitted itself was not only new; it was also symptomatic of the shift of focus away from a simple clash of ideologies, aesthetic and ethical, and towards a livelier interest in the character and fate of Brand himself. Brand now becomes a more complex creature than he was earlier when cast for the role of 'scourge of the world' taking a simple pleasure in chastisement; and it marks an intermediate stage in the development of Brand towards what the next section defines him as: 'the midwife of the age'.

From now on, Brand's inner reactions to things are given more precise attention: the sight and memory of familiar scenes, the recollection of the boy who amputated his finger, the spectacle of the village congregation on its way to church, the encounter with the gypsy girl. He is assailed by memories from the past, by 'the terror of home', as a consequence of which he feels his strength shrink and his determination weaken. His thoughts, 'half-spoken aloud', reveal his contempt for the hypocrisies of Independence Day oratory. The train of his thought as he observes the people making their way to church is essentially an inner monologue, though convention allows the explanation that 'compulsively, the words come in a low voice from his breast'. His anguished self-questioning is opened up to the reader. His encounter with the gypsy girl brings long-forgotten things once more to the surface of his mind, where they too are laid bare for inspection: 'A name flashed like flickering lightning through the night of his memories, coming and going, hissing and beckoning . . . Gradually its features grew familiar . . . He remembered a remote valley . . . .'

By stages the whole section builds up to an *argued* inner conflict (stanzas 185-189): his deeper desires, his memories, his instinctive reactions, his inner visions, his fears, all announce themselves, until finally the three things that clearly disturb him and threaten to deflect him from his high mission of redeeming the whole world are enumerated: 'What concern to him was that churchgoer up in the snows? Or those two who chose the way to church through joy? Or the crowd that crept along the deep and narrow valley? *He* was to cure the whole world's pain! *His* voice was to ring out for all.' Three menacing distractions: the Ice Church and all it stood for, its natural grandeur, its severe demands, its bleak immunity against the impious work of little men; aestheticism, with its attendant meekness and humility, its love and its charity, its search for God through joy and the pursuit of beauty; and the dumb appeal of those helplessly weak mortals creeping to church, deprived of spiritual leadership, dependent (it seemed) on somebody like himself with his strength of will and forceful personality if ever they were to be helped to salvation.

With this, the central conflicts of the work moved to a different plane. Externalized ideological clash was superseded by inner psychological and moral tension; things outgrew their earlier declamatory stage and became problematical. The focus and the grouping of figures within the composition underwent alteration: Brand was moved much nearer the forefront of things, and grew bigger — almost as though the author had heeded the words he gave to Agnes: 'But did you see how, as he spoke, he grew?' And to accommodate Brand, and to admit those new elements which, by their relationship to him, were to reveal his true dimensions, the others — Einar and Agnes — were set further back. Brand began to dominate the work as never before.

Declamation — even the murmured declamation of inner brooding — proved to be increasingly inadequate to the changed circumstances of the work as Ibsen tried vainly to make progress with the final section 'By the church'. Here at last Brand literally does mount the pulpit. But words, oratory, *declaimed* character no longer served for what the work had become. It had moved too far in the direction of drama; it required not rhetoric, but action. The sermon which Brand begins in the poem was seemingly never completed. Four stanzas were enough to persuade Ibsen that the material was beginning to burst the limitations of the epic form. He recognized that the new patterns of conflict within it craved dramatic treatment — not theatrical treatment, necessarily, but a form that would accommodate the developing range of relationships he now found himself faced with. It is possible — though the evidence is scant — that Ibsen at one point might have contemplated a more ritualized and rhetorical mode of drama than the form he eventually adopted. One surviving scrap of dialogue in stanza 104 —

First: See, she stares carefully at him,
             Spying as though at an enemy camp.
Second: Now she seeks her friend's eye,
             Waiting silently for the victorious answer.

— contains lines which, as drafted, might have been meant to be spoken by detached, even unnamed, observers, by some chorus-like figures standing outside the drama's world of space and time. But nothing else seems to have survived to sustain the notion that this ever got beyond a passing idea; and no trace of this has persisted in the final form of the drama.

The moment in the narrative poem, therefore, when Brand feels a 'crusading zeal', when a hot tear burns on his cheek, when he opens wide his arms and calls out Einar's name as though in dread, when he finds himself poised between embracing and condemning and discovers the sweet anguish of remorse — this moment not only marks a new departure in the total conception of Brand, but also anticipates the final shattering moments of the drama that was still to be written. 'What is this?' Gerd asks him those tense moments before the avalanche descends. 'You are weeping . . . weeping hot tears that turn to smoke upon your cheeks . . . Man, why have you never wept before?' The strict answer was that he *had*, but not as the Brand of the drama; and the drama itself is open to definition as an exploration in depth and in detail of those factors that eventually brought a man like Brand to the point of tears.

These same lines in the narrative poem also contain other phrases that find a different echo elsewhere — an echo no less significant in its own way than the other. The parallel this time is with Ibsen's own phrases when, in a letter to Bjørnson of 4 March 1866, he recalled the zest he had brought to his work on *Brand*: 'Last summer, when I was writing my work, I was so indescribably happy despite all the shortages and difficulties; I felt within me a crusading joy, and I cannot think what I wouldn't have had the courage to attack.' The terms he uses here of himself — 'Korstogsjubel' and 'lykkelig' — are immediately reminiscent of the 'Korsdragerlykke' he ascribes in the narrative poem to Brand, and betray the growing identity of purpose that began to emerge between Brand and his creator. The tight-lipped and cruel attitude to life of the earliest Brand, with his warped mind and disbelieving refusal to admit warmth and love and companionship as things with any real part in life, now for the first time showed an unexpected vulnerability to feeling. Conscience now became a factor; and the earlier starkly drawn and even rather grotesque figure of hate and cruelty and vindictiveness acquired more humane dimensions. 'Brand is myself in my best moments', Ibsen later admitted. It is not the kind of remark he would have readily made if Brand had remained as he was in 'From the time of ripening', or even in 'Over the great mountain'.

This crusading zeal is intimately linked with what they both, creator and created, spoke of as their 'call' or 'mission'; for both Brand and Ibsen were greatly conscious of possessing one. In the narrative poem, Brand's 'call' is still uncertain, and Einar recognizes here a chink into which he drives one of his more wounding arguments; whereupon Brand is forced to admit to some degree of uncertainty in his 'call': 'Like the moon it waxes and wanes; I rise and fall like a ship at sea.' By contrast, the Brand of the drama shows inflexible confidence in his 'call' from the very first moments. This confidence, this unshakeable conviction, is matched in the phrases Ibsen himself used in his grant application to the King of 15 April 1866, not long after completing *Brand*, in which he wrote: 'I am not seeking to claim any kind of carefree existence; I am battling for the mission which I implicitly believe in and know that God has placed upon me — the mission which is for me the most important and the most necessary in Norway; that of rousing the people and getting them to think big.' Brand's mission was Ibsen's mission at one remove.

The chronology of events is nevertheless important. From Ibsen's own account, it was seemingly in July 1865 that he finally found the form that would allow him to say 'what he had to say' — fifteen months after leaving Norway, and about a year after first starting work on the narrative poem. The question that immediately obtrudes is whether 'what he had to say' had altered very much in the meantime. If one takes 'To my fellows in guilt', presumably written not later than the summer of 1864, as the programmatic statement it obviously was, one needs to ask how far it was still a valid programme for 1865. To what extent, if any, had the emotional and intellectual 'mix' of his mind undergone change? The evidence is necessarily indirect, and the arguments speculative.

In the first place, it is clear from his correspondence and from the testimony of friends who shared his company in these months that his feeling of revulsion for the life he had put behind him remained undiminished, though perhaps as time passed it lost something of its original rawness. His disgust with the more official sides of life in Norway, with state and local politics, with organized religion, with the empty public phrases; and his impatience with the supine acceptance of these conditions of life, the pusillanimity, the pretence and the hypocrisy — these things persisted, as the finished *Brand* bears witness. Secondly, the impact of Mediterranean culture had gone even deeper in the months following those earliest impressions, had permeated the very fibres of his thought, and left an enduring mark on both his ideas and his authorship. The astounding experience of classical art and of ancient monuments, the growing familiarity with the works of the Renaissance artists, and — finally, mysteriously, overwhelmingly — the towering achievement of St. Peter's itself gave new dimensions to his work, encouraged him to a sublimer rhetoric, to contemplate the grander emotions, to venture a bolder symbolism. Along with this, and despite his very real economic worries, his life in Italy gave him new confidence in his powers as a writer, and he exulted in his new-found freedom. No longer the drudge of a bankrupt theatre, no longer the servant of a despised and dispirited society, he was a free agent under an open sky, answerable only to his artistic conscience. His vision grew clearer, his horizons wider, his powers suppler.

Thirdly, Ibsen's righteous indignation came in time to be tempered by a somewhat uneasy conscience. Though he had known anger and shame at the events of early 1864, he came to realize that he had in effect turned his back on the situation, had run away from his obligations. In Italy he found himself very much in the company of the close relatives of Christopher Bruun — his anxious mother, his sister and brother. Bruun himself was at the battlefront, having volunteered for military service. Later they were all joined in Italy by Bruun himself, a one-time theological student and an impressively dedicated and single-minded young man. Though quick to deride others' inaction, Ibsen himself was doubtless uneasily conscious of having himself *done* nothing. All he could bring himself to do — for he made no secret of the fact, either to himself or others, that when it came to physical confrontation he was not the most courageous of men — was to try his best with words. But from its initially rather obvious purpose as a vehicle of denunciation

and reproach, *Brand* more and more became the means whereby
its author wrote himself free of a condition of life in which not
only public anger and shame were prominent, but private
defensiveness and an uneasy conscience also played their parts.
Brand 'developed in its day as the result of something lived
through — not merely observed', Ibsen wrote to a correspondent
some four years after the publication of the book. 'It was
imperative for me to free myself in the form of literature of
something which, inwardly, I was finished with; and when by
this means I had rid myself of it, my book no longer had any
interest for me . . .'

Finally, and growing out of all this, there was the fascination
which the whole personality of Christopher Bruun began to exert
on Ibsen. One feels no sense of surprise that a dramatist like
Ibsen would soon cease to find artistic nourishment in the
merely symbolic clash of ideologies which the earlier forms of
Brand represent; and that he would seize avidly on the rich
potential of this model, on its human fascinations, on its
psychological complexities. The emergence of Brand as the
dominant figure of the work seems to have kept pace with the
growth of Ibsen's admiration for the person of Christopher
Bruun. That this admiration was grudging, or at least qualified,
merely served to enhance the fascination. Brand began to take
form as a dedicated but essentially *driven* man, a fanatic whose
spirit is endlessly willing, but whose flesh — though in no sense
weak — is only finitely strong, only limitedly capable of meeting
the demands of his relentless will; whose determination is greater
than his physical or mental powers, and who — to use the
awkward but expressive literal translation of the original terse
Norwegian phrase — *wills* more than he *can*.

Brand, as a character, therefore came to serve a double purpose for Ibsen. On the one hand he made a splendid instrument
with which to castigate Ibsen's contemporaries and compatriots-
— obliquely now, and through the mouth of an invented
character, rather than directly and in hortatory fashion as in the
epic. But also, and more importantly, Brand offered a further
and absorbing opportunity to explore that theme which had
obsessed Ibsen ever since the days of his earliest drama *Catiline*:
'the clash of ability and aspiration, of will and possibility, at

once the tragedy and the comedy of mankind and of the individual' (Preface to the Second Edition of *Catiline*, 1875).

Some of the targets Ibsen selected for attention in the drama — particularly the more public figures like the Dean, the Mayor, the Schoolmaster and the Sexton — were in the event so heavily and so devastatingly satirized that it really did not require the invention of a Brand for denunciation to work. They condemn themselves out of their own mouths; they act as agents for their own contemptibility. Brand's role in his relations with *them* is very largely limited to that of *agent provocateur*; though, admittedly, when these pillars of society are in the end allowed to enjoy a popular victory over Brand, the satire ceased to be merely bitter and become bloody. By contrast, the condemnation of society as represented by the Peasant, by Einar, and by Brand's Mother required a Brand if it was to be mounted effectively. Only when judged by the stern principles, the palpable courage, the unyielding standards, the flint-hard integrity of a Brand is their conduct judged deficient. Essentially, their culpability in Brand's eyes lies in their readiness to come to terms with life, to haggle, to adjust, to compromise. Brand's Mother, in the event, is prepared to go not half but fully nine-tenths of the way to meet Brand's demands; and the Doctor, speaking with the sturdy commonsense and realism that members of the medical profession are so often ready to display in Ibsen's dramas, urges that for all practical living and in the name of common humanity this is surely sufficient. Even the Peasant is censured in Brand's terms not because of any real vice of which he might be held guilty — to be so positive would in Brand's view almost redeem him — but because he is merely partial even in his virtues, 'a vulgar fraction of evil, a fragment of good'. (In parentheses, it is noteworthy that whereas the English phrase 'the spirit of compromise' has a sufficiently obvious pejorative overtone to make it a not unnatural target for attack by a much less single-minded reformer than Brand, the Norwegian phrase 'Akkordens Aand' [lit. the spirit of accord] tends to emphasize even more the stern rigour of Brand's own criteria.)

Nature also brings her own peculiar and symbolic reinforcement to the drama's general sense of hostility. She is here almost

190

entirely stripped of those blander and more reassuring features
that characterized the Norwegian landscape of national romanticism: the rippling streams, the nestling valleys, the protective
hills, the magnificent peaks, those custodians of art and virtue
and of a proud way of life which had with Nature's help
remained inviolate for centuries. Even in the 'Epic Brand' a
sense of the sunnier, kindlier, gentler aspects of the landscape 'to
the east' had been allowed to coexist on almost equal terms with
the awesome landscape of the west. Now, in the drama of *Brand*,
there is but a momentary glimpse of the sunlit heather that had
served as the setting for the butterfly game of Agnes and Einar,
and even that ends abruptly and terrifyingly on the edge of the
abyss. From the opening moments, Nature in *Brand* reveals itself
as a menacing, hostile force: storm and gale and brittle ice, and
precipitous steeps. Her elements whip the fjord to a fury where
few men dare venture; she severs the land routes, and cuts off
men from help even in the extremities of their distress. The
valleys seem to have grown narrower than they were before. 'It
all seems to look greyer now,' Brand comments, 'and smaller; the
mountain's suspended avalanche of snow hangs over . . . and has
narrowed even more the valley's narrow sky. How it glowers,
threatens, overshadows, robbing us of the light of the sun.' The
sunlessness and the freezing cold bring sickness and death; the
mountains and the sea fill the churchyard with the bodies of
men who have died a violent death. The repudiation of
Romanticism's Nature is abrupt and vehement.

What life as lived by Brandian principles is like — in terms of
sacrifice, dedication, and the cost in human happiness — is
movingly told by the history of Brand's marriage to Agnes: the
loss of their child; her anguish, intensified as it is by Brand's
harsh imperatives; and her own eventual death. After the initial
sense of terror and compassion, however, the spectator is left
with two rather more enduring recognitions: that no obvious
positive achievements, certainly no lasting satisfactions, seem to
follow this regime; and that, paradoxically, Brand's is in a most
important sense an easy road to follow. There is no difficulty
about knowing the path; only the *going* is hard. He stands not so
much for a way of life as a code of conduct — a code, indeed,
of easy three-word brevity: 'All or Nothing.' The difficulties and

anxieties of this mode of life lie not in the usual anguish of deciding what to do for the best, not in resolving a series of difficult alternatives, but simply in doing as one's code requires. Life is lived by a single, portable yardstick which is offered up to all life's problems and a decision read off. The pain lies all in the doing, not in the deciding. The degree of self-discipline required is formidable, but the instructions are always clear; one commandment is universally applicable, eternally valid. It is a categorical imperative without feed-back; the inner voice speaks, but with a one-track insistence. There is no dialogue within the soul, only endless reaffirmation of the sovereignty of the code. Brand's mind is shut, or it at least derives such strength as it has from being shut. (The one mind more tightly and more terrifyingly closed than Brand's is that of Einar on his last appearance, where the extremity of his bigotry and his 'holier than thou' attitude parody the denunciation he himself suffered earlier at the hands of Brand.) Those moments when Brand's mind seems open to alternative instructions are for him moments of weakness. Right and wrong are curiously matters of quantitative not qualitative concern: all or nothing.

Although the admiration Ibsen felt for his character was real, it was — as was said above — also qualified. As a scourge, as an instrument of correction, as a crusading force Brand might well be necessary in what Ibsen was at pains to demonstrate was an imperfect world; yet the drama also seems to imply that his view of life was flawed by a fatal deficiency. This aspect of Brand Ibsen explores in that other series of encounters within the work: those with Gerd — encounters which are of a very different order from, for example, those with the Dean, with Brand's Mother, with the Peasant and the rest, and which make their eloquent point in a different and almost metaphysical way. Brand meets her on a number of different occasions within the drama, in Acts I, III, and V; and the *spiritual* distance he moves, the extent of the shift of sensibility which he undergoes, is well measured by the first and last of these encounters. Initially, Gerd is in Brand's view merely mad, with her prattle of the Hawk and the Ice-Church; and he marks her down — or, at least, what she stands for — as something to be combated. As he prepares to descend into the valley, he identifies three targets, three states of mind which he feels he must vanquish if he is to fulfil his mission: one is the frivolity of mind [*lettsind*] represented by Einar; the second is the dullness of mind [*slappsind*] represented by the Peasant; and the third is the madness of mind [*vildsind*] represented by Gerd. Together they constitute the 'triple threat' against which he must do battle:

I now behold the nature of my mission on earth!
The downfall and death of those three demons
Would cure this world of all its sickness.

At this point, Brand distinguishes no real difference in kind among these three phenomena; indeed, the terminological similarity emphasizes the identity they share, and their comparability. They invite a common hostility.

By the end of the play, two things of deep significance have occurred. On the one hand, Gerd's utterances which Brand once thought merely mad he now recognizes as visionary; *she* recognized, long before it occurred to any of the others to comment on it, the meanness and ugliness of the man-built church, of the established and official religion; she was the first to point out, *à propos* of Alf, the element of idolatry in the worship of the Child. Like Ellida Wangel of a later play, she thinks in images; and Brand himself comes in time to see that rational discourse is not the only nor even necessarily the best path to truth. What Agnes calls 'knowing without knowledge', and what Brand acknowledges as the 'vision in the dreams people dream' sometimes leads straighter to the heart of things than the way of reason and commonsense.

The other thing is that Brand, at the end of his career and without willing it or having consciousness of it, finds himself in the Ice Church — that which he had earlier dismissed as the ravings of a deranged mind. Insistently, in those final moments, Gerd asks him: 'Do you know where you are standing now?' And as the mists lift, and Brand realizes where he is, she underlines the significance of it all: 'So you came to *my* church after all.' Such is the outward index of the deeper insight that Brand finally works his way towards, and which informs the closing moments of his life: the ultimate realization that his 'All' had been a deficiently quantitative thing, a thing of commonsense and commonplace dimensions. The 'All' that he had demanded of his mother was something that could be counted and assessed; even the 'All' that he demanded of his fellows — that of total self-sacrifice, of the commitment of one's very life — was something terminable and finite. It is only when Brand, after having committed his 'All' — his wife, his child, his career, his happiness, his material and spiritual well-being — to the symbolic project of rebuilding the village church, is left deeply dissatisfied, that doubts about the 'All' of his code, as he has hitherto understood it, begin to assail him. There stood the church, splendidly rebuilt; and all Brand's resources, human, spiritual, and material, had gone into the rebuilding. Yet the result was mean, the organ discordant; and it seemed to him that the Lord himself was greatly displeased. He begins dimly to see on the one hand that 'All' was somehow independent of scale, and realizable in both the large and the small, the familiar and the remote. Only now he sees how wrong he was to suppose that 'All' could be achieved by crying 'Double it . . . that will do! Five times greater . . . surely that will do!' He sees that man must strive for a 'greatness' that cannot be measured in conventional units, but which instead 'beckons towards the realms of dreams and wonders, and towers over us like heaven ablaze with stars'. The 'All' that he has sacrificed has been in vain; the result has been no more than one monstrous compromise with dogma and narrow faith. Now he announces:

> The church is infinite and without end.
> Its floor is the green earth —
> Mountain, meadow, sea and fjord;
> The Heavens alone are vast enough
> To span its great and vaulted roof.
> There you shall live your active faith . . .

He urges the people up and into the high mountains, the frozen wasteland, to the cleaner air, there to set up God's image anew in *life's* great church. Unconsciously he is echoing Gerd's words to him on their first encounter when she speaks of *her* church of ice and snow, a *real* church where the wind prays from the

194

glacier cliff, and mass is sung by avalanche and waterfall.

So that when, stoned and abandoned by the people, torn and bleeding, tormented in spirit, Brand is brought to the realization that, without knowing it, he has made his way to the Ice Church, he knows too that his Will has driven him to the limits of endurance, to the frontiers of madness. He occupies the same territory, is a worshipper in the same church, as Gerd, the wild-eyed, visionary girl. Her vision of him is of Christ the Saviour, with the blood on his brow from the crown of thorns, the wounds in his hands from the nails. He too knows a kind of self-identification with Christ, and his vision of the Tempter in the Wilderness is transposed by his tormented mind into a very Brandian nightmare. His quest to relate the code of 'All or Nothing' to his own life has brought him in the end to breaking point, that point which must inevitably mark the end of the road for any man 'who *wills* more than he *can*'. Cumulatively, the experiences of grief, death, isolation, rejection, and failure have left him unable to go on. The full implication of Gerd's 'So you came to *my* church after all' is the final stroke. He breaks: he gives way to tears; he is brought to his knees; and he yields to the desire for 'light and sun and gentleness, for tender and serene calm, for the summer kingdoms of this life'. Hot tears melt the frozen grandeur of his will, the icy hold of his resolve; and, like an avalanche released by sudden thaw, his life crumbles and comes roaring down about him.

The essential complementarity of *Brand* and *Peer Gynt* is something which criticism, taking its cue directly from Ibsen himself, has been tirelessly concerned to assert. It has served as a starting point for commentators as far apart in time and attitude as Arne Garborg — who in 1876 called *Peer Gynt* the 'correlating caricature' of *Brand* — and W. H. Auden, who in 1963 related the two dramas through their main characters in the ratio 'apostle and genius'. As succinct a statement as any of this complementarity was given by Philip Wicksteed in his lectures of the early 1890s:

In *Brand* the hero is an embodied protest against the

poverty of spirit and half-heartedness that Ibsen rebelled
against in his countrymen. In *Peer Gynt* the hero is
himself the embodiment of that spirit. In *Brand* the
fundamental antithesis, upon which, as its central theme,
the drama is constructed, is the contrast between the
spirit of compromise on the one hand, and the motto
'everything or nothing' on the other. And *Peer Gynt* is
the very incarnation of a compromising dread of decisive
committal to any one cause. In *Brand* the problem of
self-realization and the relation of the individual to his
surroundings is obscurely struggling for recognition, and
in *Peer Gynt* it becomes the formal theme upon which all
the fantastic variations of the drama are built up.

'*Brand* is *Peer Gynt's* "modsætning" ', Ibsen declared flatly in
a letter to Edmund Gosse in 1872, balancing the peremptoriness
of the statement with a fair measure of ambiguity in the crucial
term: 'opposite', 'counterpart', 'contrary', 'antithesis' are all
terms that might make claim to be the most appropriate translation in this context.

Clearly, circumstances imposed on the two works a relationship of special intimacy. They belong to the same brief and
critical period of residence in Italy, and were published in
successive years. They grew out of a shared locale, a common
raptus, something the importance of which Ibsen himself
emphasized when, in speculating on the way a locality influences
the forms within which the imagination creates, he asked: 'Can
I not . . . point to *Brand* and *Peer Gynt* and say "Look, that was
when intoxicated with wine"?' and in so doing contrasted them
with the beery plays that followed when he moved to Germany.
On their title pages, they are both designated 'A dramatic poem',
a description not given to any other of Ibsen's plays. They are
moreover the only 'dramatic' works of his which were not
composed for the stage. And together they mark the last use by
Ibsen of verse as a medium of dramatic expression. On a number
of occasions in later life, Ibsen used phrases that emphasized or
admitted the close relationship that these works enjoyed. 'Brand
is myself in my best moments,' he once confessed. 'just as I have
also, by self-dissection, brought out many features in both Peer

Gynt and Steensgaard.' And he went on to add that 'after *Brand*, *Peer Gynt* followed as it were of its own accord.' Towards the end of his life, Ibsen returned to this same point in conversation with William Archer, who reported: 'He wrote *Brand* and *Peer Gynt* (which appeared with only a year's interval between them) at very high pressure, amounting to nervous overstrain. He would go on writing verses all the time, even when asleep or half awake. He thought them capital for the moment; but they were the veriest nonsense. Once or twice he was so impressed with their merit that he rose in his nightshirt to write them down; but they were never of the slightest use.' Ibsen also apparently admitted on this same occasion that 'it was much easier to write a piece like *Brand* or *Peer Gynt*, in which you can bring in a little of everything, than to carry through a severely logical scheme like that of *John Gabriel Borkman*.'

That the two works enjoy a close and distinctive relationship, that they were the result of a largely (but not necessarily completely) homogeneous set of assumptions and attitudes, is therefore a commonplace of literary criticism. In itself, however, it is an observation that probably raises more problems than it resolves, and more often than not leaves unexamined the crucial problem of *how* they relate.

Criticism has occasionally found it helpful to think of *Brand* and *Peer Gynt* as two sides of the same coin, for example, or as the positive and the negative of the same exposure. Pondering Ibsen's admission that *both* characters were in their own special way self-portraits, one is reminded of the words of the Thin Man to Peer in the final act of the drama:

Don't forget there are two ways of being yourself. . .
You can either show the straightforward picture
Or else what is called the negative.
In the latter light and shade are reversed;
To the unaccustomed eye it seems ugly;
But the likeness is in that, too, all the same;
It only needs to be brought out.

The unbending, uncompromising, sternly self-disciplined Brand is succeeded by the compliant, opportunistic, and self-indulgent

Peer; dedication to the principle of 'All or Nothing' yields to the easy evasions of 'To thine own self be — sufficient.' Whereas Peer lives his entire life by illusions, Brand finds fulfilment precisely in destroying them. Where Brand speaks in the commanding tones of a genuine prophet, Peer has the plausible tongue of the spurious one: 'Answering prophetwise', he reassures himself in the scene with Anitra, 'isn't really lying.' Where the call of duty binds Brand ever more firmly to the village community despite the urge that he feels to reach a wider world, Peer's abandonment of his responsibilities — even, in the end, that of burying his dead mother — takes him to all manner of foreign parts; in a spatial and dynamic sense, *Brand* is thus centripetal, *Peer Gynt* centrifugal. And where Brand, even under the descending avalanche, forever keeps a hard nucleus of his faith in the Will intact though the outer shell has cracked, Peer Gynt — as his own surprised reflections reveal to him — is onion-like, soft-layered, and with nothing at the centre. Brand's life is a rigorously planned economy; Peer's is *laissez-faire* and private enterprise.

But these recognitions should not be allowed to distract from the fact that there were many things about *Peer Gynt* that betokened a positive reversion to Ibsen's earlier practices, and a partial abandonment of some of those more radical notions to which he had given free rein in *Brand*. And one is reminded of the assurance Ibsen gave to his publisher even as he was writing it: 'It will show no resemblance to *Brand*, and is without direct polemics.' It was, for example — despite the bold declarations of 'To my fellows in guilt' of the previous year — not nearly so challengingly contemporary in theme or setting, and not nearly so audacious in its realism, as his declared programme would have led one to expect. Indeed had Ibsen followed his first inclinations after completing *Brand*, he would apparently have written an out-and-out historical play 'set in the time of Christian IV', as he at first described it to his publisher. Furthermore, there were moments during this year when he was strongly drawn to the theme of Julian the Apostate (which, of course, eventually had its turn in the early seventies); and this would have taken him still deeper into the past and still further away from the contemporary scene. Even when the decision was

taken for *Peer Gynt*, its original setting in time took it out of the
contemporary world and pushed it half a century and more into
the past; only later did Ibsen relent and allow the final scenes of
the drama to 'end close to the present day.'

The suspicion is born that, with *Brand* completed, Ibsen had,
like his scorpion, discharged his venom, vented his spleen, and
now felt better for it. The tension in *Peer Gynt* is notably relax-
ed; the pressure of the passions much reduced. True, any
detailed annotation of the work discovers assaults on a range of
specific and often individually indentifiable targets: the satirical
trouncing of the language fanatics, for example, which left Ibsen
hugely and rather smugly pleased with himself; and his pillory-
ing of Count Manderström, so daringly topical at the time but
today worth no more than a scholarly footnote. Even when one
turns to the broader, diffuser elements of censure, the effect is
uncertain, and the strokes ill-timed. It may well have been that
the public's expectations were at fault. Certainly, Ibsen later
complained that people found much more satire in the drama
than he had intended. The view that Ibsen created Peer with the
intention of amalgamating in one character all that Brand had
repudiated in the Norwegian temperament, making a single
compound of the *lettsind*, the *slappsind*, and the *vildsind* – the
frivolity, the apathy, the irresponsibility — that Brand dedicates
his life to defeating, was widely canvassed, and eagerly —
perhaps too eagerly — adopted. Admittedly, an itemized catalogue of Peer's actions would seem in sum to define a most
reprehensible villain: violent, self-centred, vicious, envious, irresponsible, cowardly, heartless, murderous. And yet, if it really
was the drama's intention to indict Peer, something clearly went
wrong; for whilst Brand was unlovable though admirable, Peer
Gynt is much more the forgivable rogue than the despicable villain. (Perhaps it was too much to expect that a character so given
to *'digtning'*, to invention, to fabulating, to fantasizing, could
for long continue to draw Ibsen's censure).

The ultimate reduction in importance of the role of Solveig's
father within the action also seems to confirm something of the
same attitudinal shift. In the earliest stages of the drama, he was
a *named* character; subsequently he was reduced to anonymity
within the *dramatis personae* as 'a Man newly arrived in the

199

district.' An entire scene in which he was allowed to enunciate a stern philosophy of life, in which he exhorted Peer to deliver himself up to justice and to accept the inevitable seven-year prison sentence in order to settle his account of guilt, was cut out of the play at a relatively advanced stage in its composition. In the same way that any direct and fully argued conflict and confrontation of *Weltanschauungen* had been evaded in *Brand* by modifications to the figure of Einar, so the opposition case against Peer's standards of conduct was largely eliminated from the plan of *Peer Gynt*. It could well be, as Arne Garborg has argued, that Solveig's father was in essence a reincarnation of Brand; if this had ever been the case, he is given no opportunity in the finished *Peer Gynt* to practise his earlier eloquence. Nor, when the targets are the quirks and stupidities of 'national character', is *Peer Gynt* nearly so narrowly focused and exclusively Norwegian as *Brand* is. In the North African scenes, Ibsen extends the satire to embrace also Anglo-Saxon, French, Swedish, and German national weaknesses. All seems to indicate a certain damping down of the emotional savagery with which Ibsen began his exile from Norway, and which marked the earlier months of his residence in Italy. Yet, unexpectedly, the less nationalistic it became, the more national it grew, and the more difficult it became for a non-Norwegian reader to follow. Ibsen's own misgivings on this point found expression in his letter in 1880 to his German translator, in which he stated that, of all his works up to that time, he regarded *Peer Gynt* as the one most difficult to understand outside Scandinavia; few people (he feared) possessed the familiarity with Norwegian literature, people, habits of thought, national character, and landscape necessary for an appreciation of the drama. This seems to have been a strange compensatory side-effect to accompany the more vehement repudiation of things Norwegian of a few short months previously.

Uniquely useful as a kind of tracer element by which to follow through these shifts of attitude and belief is the incident of the youth and the amputated finger. Four stages (one of which is admittedly a sort of nil return) may be distinguished in the fluctuating shape of the incident, and consequently in the purpose it is in each case asked to serve: first, there is the incident as it is narrated in the 'Epic Brand'; second, comes the decision to eliminate it as the 'Epic Brand' is transposed into drama; third, there is the incident as Peer witnesses it and reacts to it in Act III of the drama; and fourth, as an unexpected extension, we are given the churchyard comments, a whole generation later, uttered by the Priest over the grave of the man. In the 'Epic Brand', the incident was pressed into service as a shameful indictment of the Norwegian people: see how this young man will go to any lengths, the story announces, to avoid doing what ought to be his joyous duty of serving as a soldier in defence of his brother Danes. Ignominiously dismissed by the solemn captain, denounced by the whole community, and red with shame, the youth flees the village community; and the memory of this disgraceful scene confirms Brand in the disgust he feels whenever he hears great empty phrases about 'Viking blood' in the speeches on Independence Day. The incident at this stage is unambiguously a device with which to scourge the Norwegian people for their cowardice in evading their obligations. When it came to embodying it in the drama of *Brand*, however, Ibsen clearly found objections to its use. Doubtless he came to realize with time that there were other dimensions to the story, previously unrecognized, that prevented its being used in the way he had first intended: that, after all, it bore witness to a measure of courage of a different but no less valid kind, which thus destroyed its force as a simple parable of non-courage; that one marvelled strangely at the strength of will and purpose that led to an act of this kind, quite apart from its ultimate motive. Such indeed was to become Peer's immediate reaction to the event.

What spunk! An irreplaceable finger!
Right off! And no one making him do it.

When it comes to motive, Peer remembers why this might be: that the boy will by this means avoid being called up to the army. But — and how revealing of the change that had come over Ibsen's attitude to the incident and the significance behind it — he then adds:

201

> That's it. They were going to send him to war;
> And the boy, not surprisingly, objected.

Between this 'not surprisingly' [lit. 'understandably'] and the simpler patriotics of the 'Epic Brand' lies a world of difference.

The final long and quite detailed comment on this incident and its consequences, which is incorporated into the last Act of *Peer Gynt*, then invites a different interpretation, supports a wholly new world of values. The recruiting incident remains much as it was in the 'Epic Brand': the Captain still spits and tells the boy to go; the company make the youth run the gauntlet, 'stoning the boy with silent stares'. But this is not the end of things; and time gives a new perspective to the incident. The man in question devotes himself to the ways of peace rather than the violence of war; he is revealed as one who has led a life of meekness, reticence, humility, quiet endeavour, and great though inconspicuous courage. 'Not even an avalanche could crack his courage', the Priest reports admiringly. The larger abstractions — mankind, patriotism — meant little to him; but loyalty to wife and children, to farm and homestead, fill his life with meaning:

> He was a poor patriot. To state
> And Church, an unproductive tree. But there
> On the brow of the hill, within the narrow
> Circle of family, where his work was done,
> There he was great, because he was himself.

This funeral oration is positioned within a series of offset but overlapping and widening contexts (the fifth Act proper, the drama as a whole, and the collective statement of *Brand* and *Peer Gynt*), and as such it articulates a set of values which contrasts sharply not only with Peer Gynt's but also with Brand's; and it seems to offer evidence of a very considerable semantic shift within the drama as a whole, a shift that eventually left things at a substantial remove from the terminus that was apparently originally intended.

Compared with the hard-edge, blueprint world of *Brand*, with its severe imperatives, its inflexible compulsions, its frozen and intractable topography, the world which Peer Gynt inhabits is one of daunting fluidity, a fairy-tale world of effortless transformation and of disconcerting transpositions. The journey from reality to fantasy and return, from the substance to the shadow and back again, seems to encounter no obvious frontier, to require no particular formalities. Waking and dreaming interpenetrate in a way that was foreshadowed by those lines in the 'Epic Brand' that told of an earlier boy who dreamed: 'The dream bound him to look at himself as the vortex binds one who looks at the stream; and the boy looked at it and could not break free, and was carried round in circles . . . He tried to distinguish — but it was hard to tell — what was truth . . . and what was dream. He slept. Then he dreamed he lay awake.' When it comes to Peer, it is true that he sometimes becomes aware of his day-dreaming, and feels the need to admonish himself: 'Lies!' he tells himself as he wields his axe at the start of Act III: 'It isn't a giant in armour; it's a fir-tree with a craggy bark . . . It will have to stop, this wool-gathering . . .' But at other times, when in this same mood of self-admonition, he also betrays that for him the distinctions are blurred, and that fact and fantasy fuse:

That ride on the Gjendin ridge,
Invention [*dikt*, lit. 'poetry'] and damned lies!
Humping the bride up the steepest
Rock-face — and drunk all day;
Pursued by hawks and kites,
Threatened by trolls and suchlike,
Racketing with crazy wenches;-
Lies and damned invention!

The line between Dichtung and Wahrheit, between fiction and fact, disappears in one great and imaginative universe. Fears are reborn as only nightmare can shape them; desires achieved as only dream can fulfil them. The frustrations of one moment become the fulfilments of the next: if the girls at Hægstad coldly spurn him, the girls at the sæter are ardent and willing; ousted and displaced as a suitor *here,* he is welcomed as a potential son-in-law *there*; ostracized by the valley's wedding guests, he is made a great fuss of by the mountain trolls; disbelieved and

203

mocked by the village youths when he brags of his exploits, he finds enthusiastic credence from the Woman in Green, so that together they can agree that 'black can seem white, and the ugly beautiful; big can seem little, and filth seem clean.' As Aase knows full well, Peer is intoxicated by make-believe as other men are drunk with brandy; his is a world in which wishes *are* horses (except when they are pigs!) and beggars *do* ride. North Africa and other exotic places are only a dream away; things — such as the blowing up of the expropriated yacht — *are* no sooner said than done. A fantasy world seems at times to counterfeit a real one, and at others a real one to mint again the fantastical. Some characters, like the Dovre-Master and the Woman in Green, appear to live a valid life in both; with others, appearances — but only appearances — change, and the Hægstad wedding guests are recognizable again in the trolls. Sometimes it seems, as with the sound of church bells, that reality penetrates fantasy; and at other times, as with the Ugly Child, that fantasy invades reality. Nevertheless, taking the strictest view of the logic of the poem, all these things are merely aspects of a single reality/fantasy continuum, in which fact is a function of fiction, invention a function of experience, and lies and life are one.

The role of Solveig in this world is easily misunderstood. It is often held that she is the only truly stable element in the work, and represents the one genuinely positive virtue: constancy. In a spatial sense, she seems at the end to have remained firm and steadfast, having lived her whole life through in the little forest clearing where Peer and she were to make their home. Admittedly, the drama is not overprovided with positive statements of the kind she is assumed to make. Apart from her father, who is allowed a brief advocacy of confession and expiation as a way of life, and possibly also in some respects Aase, whose deeper loyalty to her son can always be relied on, Solveig is about the only figure who by her actions seems to embody any positive assertion about life's values. The result has been that critical interpretation has tended to burden Solveig with a weight of symbolic significance too heavy for her slight character to bear; and to ascribe a sentimental solemnity to the final moments that relates uneasily to what has gone before. Solveig is by this token seen to be making an almost Brand-like 'all or nothing' commit-

ment of 'love', as offering a counter-statement to Brand's hostile
eloquence on this very theme. When Solveig tells Peer he has
made her life 'a cause for singing' — or, as a more literal
translation brings out even more clearly, has turned her life into
'a lovely song' — there is an echo of the life that Einar and
Agnes lived before Brand came storming into their existence,
when life was a song to be sung together. The way she receives
Peer after a lifetime's absence seems to suggest that her values
are wholly contrary to Peer's: that the great wrong he believes he
has done her is in reality a great right, and that the transformation has been achieved by her faith, her love, her hope. This, it
is suggested, makes her representative of Woman, of 'das Ewig-
Weibliche', an archetypal wife and mother figure finding her
fulfilment as the patient custodian of man's real essence,
preserving, protecting, enfolding: the ultimate refuge where man
at last finds his proper dominion, his redemption, his salvation.
To expect, however, that a character so sentimentalized, so
bloodless, so stylized in her flaxen-haired doll-like unreality, so
absent as Solveig is — to expect that she should carry all this
ponderous significance is merely grotesque. Nor does the
'message' of her life, positive though it is in the *manner* of its
dramatic formulation, carry particularly deep conviction: that
Woman's redemptive role (if such *is* her role) is adequately
performed by sitting and dreaming and hoping a whole life long,
by living on her memories, by cherishing the images of the past.

What Solveig really represents in this last scene is not some
objectively ideal embodiment of Redemptive Woman, but the
realization of Peer's wish-image of Woman at this moment in his
life. What he yearns for, and what his fantasy creates for him (as
it had so often before in his life created for him) is an essentially maternal figure, endlessly forgiving, entirely devoted to
him who will soothe his fears and chase the bogeyman Buttonmoulder away, on whose love and protection he can *exclusively*
count, whose features are compounded of mother and bride,
who can be relied upon to create a cosy intimate world and put
his own Self at the centre.

Such is the mother fixation of Peer (as others have noted
before) that Solveig at this fateful moment takes on not only the
role but also the features of Aase, finally mothering Peer in her

205

lap as he seems almost literally to return to the womb. 'You have mothered that thought of the man yourself', Peer says in the final moments of the drama. 'My mother, my wife, purest of women!' He buries his face in her lap. 'Hide me there, hide me in your heart!' She becomes 'real', is *realized*, only when Peer desires it. He re-creates her for his own comfort; she is as much an escape from the pressing realities of the moment — an old man's realities — as his deathbed ride with Aase had been, and the distorted gratifications of the night with the trolls. Certainly, the Buttonmoulder is not taken in by what goes on. He breaks into Solveig's song to remind Peer that he deceives himself if he thinks this means any real 'escape', and that they will meet at the last crossroads; fantasy may have been Peer's refuge time after time in life, but it is no answer to death. Nor, the Button-moulder seems to imply, is redemption all *that* easy.

It is commonly felt that *Brand* and *Peer Gynt* must together in the end add up to some kind of moral declaration. In the case of *Brand*, this has led to a perhaps disproportionate amount of attention being paid to the closing moments; surely there, it is felt, we should be able to find the essential clue that will permit us to judge Brand's conduct correctly, and thus draw the appropriate moral. If the Voice is thought of as uttering a reproach, as insisting on the necessity (repudiated by Brand) of acknowledging the cosmic force of love, then the stress is seen as having been placed on Brand's guilt, and the discovered pattern of the drama is one of crime and punishment, of blasphemy and retribution. If, on the other hand, the Voice seems to say 'And yet . . .', the emphasis seems rather to be on the merciful intervention of an all-loving God at the very crisis of defeat and destruction, thus making of Brand's career a thing of error and forgiveness, of transgression and redemption. Or, by extension, the total meaning is found synthetically in the kind of ambiguity that holds *both* these interpretations in suspense, and like the 'Ist gerichtet . . . ist gerettet' of Goethe's *Faust*, implies both judgement and salvation. Conversely, when it comes to *Peer Gynt*, the tendency is to concentrate on the cataloguing of Peer's more reprehensible qualities — his mendacity, his irresponsibility and lack of control, his self-centred conduct — and then, by giving special scrutiny to those scenes with the Strange Passenger, the Thin Man and the Buttonmoulder, to work out how the drama invites us to shape our moral condemnation. In all these instances, the criteria are Schillerian: Brand is adjudged a great but morally flawed hero, and the drama such that both the admiration we feel for this hero and also the suffering he endures in working out his destiny have a moral basis; whilst Peer Gynt, though Brand's antithesis and essentially an anti-hero, is nevertheless similarly defined in moral terms.

Yet this seems to leave important aspects of the works only partially, or awkwardly, defined. Although remorse leads Brand in the end to revise certain of his basic beliefs, there is in his recantation none of that sublimity, that defiantly glad acceptance of destiny that is the essence of Schillerian tragedy. In Brand's last cry there is a note of puzzlement, of remonstrance, of querulousness even, and he seems to claim that he somehow deserved better. In *Peer Gynt*, on the other hand, the final moments seem to promise the anti-hero a destiny rather better than he deserves. In both instances the outlines become confused and blurred if the works are thought of as being structured preeminently to making a moral affirmation.

A much more satisfactory interpretation seems to emerge if one takes one's cue not from Schiller but from Hebbel. Exactly how familiar Ibsen was with Hebbel's ideas on tragedy is not very certain. In the present state of knowledge, little more can be said than that Hebbel's theories were closely followed and discussed in the Denmark of their day; that one of his more important theoretical statements — his *Mein Wort über das Drama* of 1843 — grew out of a bitter public exchange which he had in the Copenhagen press with the Danish critic J. L. Heiberg, later director of the Royal Theatre; and that Hermann Hettner's influential monograph *Das moderne Drama*, which Ibsen is believed to have read and studied while on his study tour in Germany in 1852, followed a strongly marked Hebbelian line. How persistent the subsequent discussion of Hebbel's views was in those Scandinavian periodicals known to have belonged to Ibsen's reading in the fifties and sixties is difficult to measure. What can be emphatically said, however, is that Ibsen's dramatic practice as it found expression in *Brand* — and negatively in *Peer Gynt* — strikingly matches Hebbel's theory as he expounded it in the 1840s.

Guilt, both in drama and in what he called the 'life process', was for Hebbel something completely divorced from notions of good or evil, something wholly unconnected with the moral basis of individual action. It derived in his view simply and inevitably and automatically from the exercise of the Will, from the sheer act of self-assertion, from the stubborn, autonomous thrust of the Self ('aus der starren, eigenmächtigen Ausdehnung des Ichs'). For him, as for Brand, it was in large measure a quantitative matter, inseparable from individual action and increasing in direct proportion to the degree of intensity of the individual self-assertion. Guilt, Hebbel insisted, 'does not depend upon the direction of human volition; it is present in all human conduct; and it makes no difference whether we turn towards good or evil, for we may overstep moderation just as much in the one as in the other. It is with this alone that the higher drama is concerned. Not only is it immaterial whether the hero is destroyed in consequence of an admirable or of a reprehensible undertaking, but also — if the most effective result is to be achieved — it is even essential for this to happen as the result of the former and not of the latter.' It was a concept of guilt that made of it an amoral and largely technical thing — a concept which Hebbel only much later discovered was essentially Hegelian.

This was an essential component in Hebbel's view of the 'life-process', and consequently also in his interpretation of the nature of dramatic conflict. Individual initiative, the vigorous exercise of those qualities that in themselves constitute and define individuality, must (he argued) by the sheer nature of things provoke an imbalance, a disequilibrium within the Whole. The more pronounced the individual talent, the more forceful its expression, the greater the tragic dissonance within the wider scheme of things. There is set in train a lumbering, crushing reaction on the part of the 'Universum' — the totality of the age, the environment, the society, the moral climate within which the

individual has his being — as a result of which the individual is
inevitably overwhelmed and defeated, having at most achieved
some slight displacement within the wider framework of life.
There is no doubt that had Hebbel lived only a few years longer,
he would have recognized *Brand* as an almost perfect embodiment of his dramatic theory; indeed it is striking that when
Hebbel attempted in his diaries to find other phrases and
formulations for his theory, he was moved to use the same image
of melting ice that was later to dominate the final moments of
Brand: 'Life is a great stream,' Hebbel wrote in his diary of 6
March 1843, 'the individuals are the drops, but the tragic ones
are lumps of ice which have to be melted . . .'

If this absolves the reader from taking moral sides before
feeling that he can legitimately assess *Brand*, it also deflects
attention in *Peer Gynt* away from the incidentals of Peer's moral
constitution and on to the problem of his individuality, his self-
dom, and the manner of its expression. In other words, to the
topic that Peer himself is endlessly preoccupied with: the
Gyntian Self. By these criteria, Peer then takes his place as a
failed Hebbelian hero. Underlying his conduct generally is the
urge to do what Brand does: assert himself as an individual, be
a 'person-ality', make an impact on those about him, influence
affairs, control human destinies. But there is seemingly no
enduring Self there to assert, no 'stubborn autonomous thrust',
no hard nucleus but only layer after soft onion layer of assumed
personae with nothing at the centre. The Buttonmoulder tells
Peer aphoristically what Hebbel might have said in abstract
prose. In the Buttonmoulder's phrases, Peer has never really
been himself and has defied the purpose of his life; to be oneself
is to kill oneself, or in other words to show unmistakably the
Master's intention in whatever one does; right and wrong, good
and evil, do not enter into the calculations when it comes to
escaping the casting-ladle, for a sinner counts as much as a saint
provided things are done 'on a grand scale'. Or transposed into
Hebbelian terms: that there has been no authentic self-assertion,
and in consequence Peer has failed to participate in the 'Lebens-
prozess', failed to make any positive contribution to historical
development; that those who do properly assert their individuality are inevitably destined for a tragic death by virtue of the

reaction of the 'Universum'; that to recognize this, and act in that knowledge, is just what Peer has conspicuously neglected to do; and finally — as was discussed above — that the criteria applicable in this context are essentially amoral.

Interestingly, this is not the only echo of Hebbelian polemics to be heard in *Brand* and *Peer Gynt*. Within the German-speaking world at mid-century, the grandiose theories of Hebbel, tracing the larger patterns of human destiny through centuries of time, selecting the grander issues of historical development for literary treatment, did not go unchallenged. There was also — by that group of writers who came to be known as the Poetic Realists — a gentler insistence on the values of modest, everyday living, of quiet unspectacular endeavour, of the little things in life. Hebbel himself had to a great extent provoked them to this; at least, he provoked one of his contemporaries, Adalbert Stifter, to draft a reasoned defence of his own philosophy of life and literature, and to commend what he called 'the gentle law' (as an alternative to Hebbel's 'life process') as the essence of authentic living. In response to a somewhat clumsy and heavy-handed epigrammatic poem published in 1848, in which Hebbel accused some of his contemporaries of small-mindedness and lack of vision, of devoting themselves to insignificant themes because they had no understanding of life's cosmic forces, Stifter appended to his collection of short stories, *Bunte Steine*, a preface, dated 1852, in which he set out his own literary credo:

The wafting of the breeze, the rippling of water, the growing of the crops, the swelling of the sea, the green of the earth, the gleam of heaven, the shining of the stars I consider great ... The tremendous tempest, the lightning that destroys houses, the storm that rages in the surf, the erupting volcano, the earthquake that destroys whole countries, these I do not consider any greater than the things above; indeed I consider them smaller because they are only the outer effects of much greater laws ... As with external nature, so with inner nature, human nature. A whole life full of righteousness, simplicity, self-control, reasonableness, activity within one's own circle, love of beauty, combined with a benign calm death I consider great. Powerful and tempestuous emotions, terrible fits of anger, the desire for revenge, the fiery spirit that strains for action, demolishes, alters, destroys, and in its excitement often throws away its own life, I consider not greater but smaller . . .

As Stifter, by this declaration, was to Hebbel, so Agnes was to Brand — not only by the manner of her living and dying, but also by the literal terms of the phrase with which Brand characterizes her: she could discover (he says) the great in the small. In contrast to the strident heroics of Brand, hers is a temperament guided by this 'sanfte Gesetz' of Stifter. Similarly, it is this same set of values that the Priest in his graveside oration is concerned to assert, and which the boy who cut off his finger exemplifies by his later life — a life that stands in conspicuous contrast to the restless, unsatisfied questing of Peer. If it is in fact important to seek for positive moral declarations in these two works, it is surely here in the characters of Agnes and the peasant man that they are to be sought. It is wholly characteristic of Ibsen's art, however, that in both instances this positive statement, though not inconspicuous, is peripheral.

8

Dramas of Transition

The League of Youth; Emperor and Galilean

Between *Peer Gynt*, completed and published in 1867 when its author was thirty-nine, and *Pillars of Society*, the first of the characteristically 'Ibsenite' dramas, lies a Germanic middle age, a decade of dearly-bought but (as one can now see) decisively important experience. The price exacted was the enormous and disproportionate amount of effort that went into the only two plays of these years: *The League of Youth* (1869) and *Emperor and Galilean* (1873), both of which Ibsen felt were clearly to some degree German in their inspiration. From Dresden, whither he had come to live in the autumn of 1868, he wrote after his play was complete: 'The locale has a great influence on the forms within which the imagination creates ... Is there not in *The League of Youth* something reminiscent of "Knackwurst" and beer?' Equally potent was the influence of Germany on *Emperor and Galilean*, except that where earlier it had been social, now it was more specifically cultural: '*Emperor and Galilean* is not the first work I wrote in Germany,' he affirmed later in 1888, 'but it is probably the first one I wrote under the influence of German culture . . . My view of life at that time was still nationalistically Scandinavian, and for that reason I could not properly get to grips with this alien material. Then I experienced that great epoch in Germany, the war year and the subsequent developments. All this exerted a transforming influence upon me in many ways. My view of world history and of human life had hitherto been a national one. Now it widened to become an ethnic one, and then I was able to write *Emperor and Galilean.*'

In a more immediate sense, *The League of Youth* grew out of the anger and exasperation Ibsen felt at the public reception given to *Peer Gynt* — in much the same way as *An Enemy of the People* was to follow the critical attacks on *Ghosts* on a later occasion. *Peer Gynt* had been an experimental drama, an audacious break with the existing theatrical traditions of the day; and both by its verse form and its free play with time and space, it offered itself as something very deliberately non-realistic, intentionally non-theatrical, perhaps even rather self-consciously literary. So that when Ibsen read the review by one of Denmark's most influential critics in one of Denmark's most widely-read papers — Clemens Petersen in *Fædrelandet* — alleging that *Peer Gynt* was not 'literature', his fury knew no bounds. It was not helped by the knowledge that Petersen was a close friend of Bjørnson's, and that Bjørnson had been in Copenhagen about the time that the review had been written. In his rage and disappointment, Ibsen was an easy prey to the suspicion that they were all against him, all those he had left behind in the North when he had set out for Italy three years earlier. He immediately sat down and wrote to Bjørnson in a white heat of passion. He called Petersen's review a 'tendentious crime against truth and justice'. He swore that this drama of his *was* literature; and even if it were not so now, it would surely become so: 'In our country, in Norway, the concept of literature will come to conform to this book.' And he promised he would wreak a most terrible and calculated vengeance:

213

Anyway, I am glad at the wrong which has been done me. I see God's help and providence in it, for I feel my strength growing with my anger. If it has to be war, then so be it! If I am not a poet, I have nothing to lose. I shall try my hand as a photographer. I shall take on my contemporaries up there, individually, one by one, as I did with the language fanatics [i.e in *Peer Gynt*]. I shall not spare the child in its mother's womb, nor the thought or mood behind the words of any living soul who deserves the honour of inclusion.

The following day he read through his letter 'in cold blood'; but in adding a postscript, he recanted nothing: 'Beyond a certain limit, I am quite ruthless. And if only — as I am quite capable of doing — I take care to link my emotional turmoil with a cold-blooded choice of means, then my enemies shall be made to feel that, if I cannot construct, I am well able to lay waste all about me.' The full wealth of meaning behind this 'cold-blooded choice' to act 'as a photographer' is not immediately apparent. One must know something of the weight of contempt with which Ibsen earlier in his career had loaded the term 'photographic'; one must appreciate something of the scorn he had lavished on the public clamour for works that stood 'in photographic relationship to reality' (a dramatic notice of 11 Oct 1857), and of the way in which he tended to oppose the two terms 'photographic' and 'artistic' as though it were obvious they were mutually exclusive. Now, with his threat to go in himself for photography, he was expressing his resolve to descend from the heights of art to his critics' own level, to demonstrate that even in their own debased realistic idiom he could rise superior to them; but in the process he would also let them feel the lash of his satire. Even when in time his immediate anger abated, and his original motives for writing the play merged with others, he nevertheless remained steadfast in his insistence that in this case, and in implied contrast with its immediate predecessors, his play would be realistic and 'stageworthy'.

When, however, over five years later, Ibsen described *Emperor and Galilean* as 'a completely and wholly realistic piece of writing', the sentiment behind his words was profoundly different. On the earlier occasion, his defiance had operated as a kind of excuse for doing something that perhaps in more normal circumstances he would have found inexcusable. Now he spoke from a deep conviction, the same kind of conviction that informed the phrases of his reply to Edmund Gosse, who had ventured to suggest that his new play might have been better written in verse:

> You think that my play should have been in verse, and that it would have gained by this. On that point I must contradict you, for the play is — as you will have noted — cast in a form as realistic as possible; it was the illusion of reality I wanted to produce. I wanted to evoke in the reader the impression that what he was reading really happened. If I had used verse, I would have run counter to my own intentions and to the task I had set myself.

Common to these two plays is then that they are both Germanic (yet how very differently Germanic), and that they are both realistic (yet how very differently realistic). In other respects, it would be hard to imagine two plays more unlike each other, or indeed separately more unlike Ibsen's other plays: the one parochial, locally allusive, comically Holbergian, stuffed with plots and schemes and double-dealing, peopled with caricatured figures of vanity and petty ambition and pomposity, and all rather desperately kept going by a creaking machinery of misplaced letters and contrived encounters and misunderstandings; and the other epochal, distant, heroically proportioned, heavy with cosmic significance, sombrely mystical, chronicling the ineluctabilities of world-historic processes, and proclaiming an earnest if cloudy philosophy.

These were years the immediate yield of which in terms of purely dramatic achievement was dubious. The ultimate returns, however, were of supreme importance: a new and compelling insight into the previously unapprehended potentialities of dramatic realism. When he was on the threshold of his forties, Ibsen had found himself playing the role of realist out of sheer defiance; by his late forties, his conversion to realism was complete and enthusiastic. It is as items documenting the history of this change that the two dramas here under discussion make their most urgent bid for attention.

Despite the fact that the decision to write the realistic and 'photographic' *League of Youth* had been taken suddenly and in anger, the actual composition of the play was carried out with extreme care and attention to detail. Ibsen began work in the summer of 1868, and hoped initially to have things complete by Christmas. In the event, however, he took almost a year over the work, applying himself very diligently (as the draft versions bear witness), particularly to the more technical problems that arose during its composition. Indeed, in one of his progress reports to his publisher, he claimed that this was in technical matters the most carefully revised play he had ever written. When it was finished, there was one point of technique about which he was especially pleased: he had managed — and he wrote to Brandes of his pleasure at this — to compose the entire play without ever once having had recourse to monologues or asides. It was as though, once the decision had been taken to operate in the tradition of the 'well-make play', Ibsen determined that it must be supremely well done technically to forestall its merely being dismissed out of hand. For him, it was rather like electing to do battle on ground not of his own free choosing; and because this in itself threatened to make the play vulnerable, he would need to make it as impregnable as possible in matters more nearly under his direct control.

The medium he settled for was a prose dialogue in a contemporary idiom — a form of language which stood in sharp contrast to the verse rhythms of *Love's Comedy*, *Brand* and *Peer Gynt*, and which was also at some considerable remove from the mannered prose of *The Vikings at Helgeland* and the archaic turns of phrase of *The Pretenders*. The only comparable thing in this line had been the language of *St John's Night*, an early comic play that Ibsen later did his best to disown. The brand of fun he then dealt in turned out to be rather desperately Scribean, as though Ibsen had read it all up in books beforehand. (Actually, while he was busy on the play, Ibsen did send to Copenhagen for a copy of Georg Brandes's *Aesthetic Studies*, explaining that he was seeking enlightenment about the nature of the Comic, a concept he confessed he was a little hazy about.) The pattern of intrigue — with its familiar mixture of crossed letters, secret schemes, and simple exercises in low cunning — showed little that was new, and much that was taken straight from stock.

The local colour is, however, much more acutely observed. So successful and so conspicuous is it that it has deceived many people into dismissing the entire play as simply parochial. This is just what it is not — it *is* parochial, but in a complex and deliberately ironical way. In exploring a specifically local milieu and its tight, in-turned, mean little conflicts, it makes a contribution towards the study of parochialism in its wider essence. (There is no need to stress how so many of Ibsen's later plays came to pivot about this very factor of parochialism at a number of levels — the small town, the remote valley, the little nation — and the consequent crippling effects on the personality.) *De lokale forhold* — a term which it is generally agreed is but feebly translated by the literal 'local situation', and which Ibsen insisted should be translated into German by the phrase 'unsere berechtigten Eigenthümlichkeiten', and which in this edition has been rendered 'by the local proprieties' — provides not merely the setting but also the main butt of the play.

Ibsen was, however, under no illusions about the over-all superficiality of the play he had written: there was no great profundity in it, he admitted afterwards, no strong passion, no particular emphasis on *inner* development. Not that he had entirely disregarded the psychological aspect of things; in particular, he hoped that what he called 'the split personality' of Stensgaard — a character in whom he claimed to have embodied a good deal of 'self-dissection' — would be given its due attention. But it is clear that the main movement of the play is, Holberg-wise, across the surface of life; it is concerned primarily with what Ibsen termed 'the actual conditions of reality', and especially with the repercussions of political intrigue in a small community.

That he had used 'models' on this occasion (something indeed that he was inclined to make a fairly standard practice), he did not seek to deny. It was immediately obvious that he had modelled Stensgaard — that prosaic 'Peer Gynt of politics', as he has been called — to a considerable extent on Bjørnson, though Ibsen later denied it: 'Surely he must be able to see that it was not he who served as a model,' Ibsen wrote a few months after the publication of the play, 'but his pernicious and "thoroughly perfidious" party associates.' True, there are specific details in plenty to support this assertion that Stensgaard is a composite creation, and not merely a grotesque portrait of Bjørnson: there were things clearly reminiscent of the liberal leader Johan Sverdrup, for example; and Stensgaard's multiple attempts to gain a rich wife to sustain him in his political ambitions were unmistakably derived from the public career of Ole Richter. But it was Stensgaard's oratory, and his tendency to be the first to be carried away by this oratory, and his unquenchable faith in his own ability, and (most damagingly) his quickness to assume that he could enlist God Almighty permanently on his side — these were the things that, rightly or wrongly, put people most readily in mind of Bjørnson. The plot emphasizes at every turn that Stensgaard's considerable talents were clearly to be used only for his own self-advancement, and that other people were important for him only to the extend that they could be made to serve his own private purposes; it was the dramatic embodiment of a remark Ibsen made about Bjørnson the same year *The League of Youth* was published: 'For him, only two kinds of people exist: those he can draw advantage from, and those who are possibly a nuisance to him.'

To supplement the realistic detail which his contemporaries thus provided, Ibsen also dredged his memories: memories of his birth-place, Skien, and of his earlier days in Christiania as a young man in his early twenties. The geographical setting of the play corresponded very closely to Skien itself in a number of particulars: the name of Brattsberg had been a well-known name in the locality; not a little of the character of Daniel Hejre came from Ibsen's own father, the bankrupt who dreamed of reinstating himself by his own smartness; and a political campaign which a certain Herman Bagger, a Dane who had settled in the district, had waged in the 1840s in an attempt to get himself elected to the Storting was mirrored in some of the intrigue. Moreover, Aslaksen the printer was linked by name and by circumstantial detail to the real-life N.F. Axelsen, who in the early 1850s had printed the periodical *Manden* with which Ibsen had had some connection.

Yet despite the detailed 'photography', the real targets of the play turned out to be not the prevailing politics of the age but the nature of political life in general, not the day's abuses but the corruptions of political ambition at large, not the politicians of the hour but political man. And although the most conspicuous politician in the play is Stensgaard, it took Ibsen's later plays to confirm what was already apparent in this play under close scrutiny: that the most dangerous of the entire breed is Lundestad, a man modelled on the agrarian leader in the Storting, Ole Gabriel Ueland, prototype for Mortensgaard in *Rosmersholm*, content in his wiliness to be thought a fool if only it helped to further his secret plans, dispassionately weighing up the probabilities uninfluenced either by idealism or by positive villainy, quietly and cynically analysing the motives of his fellows and applying pressure where he found them vulnerable, and manipulating them to his own advantage. Not all the targets in this play were new. Some of them, particularly the bland and yet ruthless opportunism of the politician, had provoked Ibsen to satire before — one thinks, for example, of his operatic parody *Norma, or a Politician's Love*, written in 1851. Some of the other things in *The League of Youth* were, moreover, destined in time to be given an even greater notoriety by him. The fragment of undeveloped tragedy in the situation of Selma, for example — who is driven to tearful rebellion because of the way she has been treated 'like a doll' — later expanded and developed so insistently that it was able to sustain an entire drama. Similarly, a number of other recognizably Ibsenist abuses are stingingly attacked in this play in the authentic Ibsen manner: the easy arrogance of inherited privilege, the pomposity of dignity gone bad, the social frustrations of women, the irresponsibility of speculators, the secret self-interest of so much professed idealism, the emptiness of the big phrase and the hollowness of him who utters it, the hypocrisies of the press whereby no 'good' paper can ever hope to survive, and the iniquity of fathers who seek to fulfil their own ambitions through the unwilling agency of their sons.

Ibsen's own estimate of *Emperor and Galilean* showed a tendency to insist on three main things: that it was realistic; that it was intentionally philosophical; and that it was subjective. He was also, it seems, rather given to thinking of it as his masterpiece.

Except for the fact that it is in prose, its realism is of a kind one perhaps associates more with the eighteenth century than with the nineteenth, more with the realism of Schiller's *Wallenstein* — a realism that derives chiefly from a refusal to idealize — than with the more socially orientated realism that was already becoming visible in Europe in the early 1870s. In this drama, Ibsen looked long and hard at a particular moment in history; like Schiller in *Wallenstein*, he took great pains to try to get an undistorted view of a distant age, to understand the various currents that had been at work, and to see things in a clear light. It was a wholly realistic piece of writing, he wrote to Ludvig Daae, for he had seen the characters before his eyes in the light of their age, and he hoped his readers would do the same. To Georg Brandes, he hesitated to pronounce on what the play was really about; all he did know, he said, was that he had looked hard at a fragment of man's history, and had tried to reproduce what he saw. It was the illusion of reality he wanted to produce, he explained to Edmund Gosse; and because he wanted to evoke in the reader the impression that what he was reading had really happened, he had used prose rather than verse as his dramatic medium, since the form of the language must always be adapted to the degree of idealization that is given to the account. He had kept strictly to history, he declared in one of his other letters to Gosse; he had seen it all occur before his very eyes, and that was how he had presented it.

It is remarkable how to all three correspondents he gave prominence to the idea of *seeing*. This was something intended to emphasize the quality of realism which he had incorporated into the work, to refute any suggestion that he had meant to write a tendentious play, or that he had had it in mind to moralize. He wanted to drive home the point that what he was trying to communicate was truth unadulterated by any suspicion of idealism. Any manipulation he had given to the material was solely to bring out its latent dramatic qualities, he implied, and not to make it serve any particular moral. But he was quick to point out that this matter of *seeing* was not all that simple. There must be some sense of *rapport* between the poet and what he sees; a writer must be prepared by his own experiences, must have had his perception quickened by the events of his own life, by his own thoughts and reactions, before he can really *see* with the degree of understanding that allows him in his turn to communicate successfully with others. In 1874, less than a year after the publication of *Emperor and Galilean*, Ibsen was on a short visit to Norway; and there, in a speech made to a torchlight procession of students, he asked the question: What was it, to write? It had been a long time, he admitted, before he realized that to write was essentially to see; but really valid 'seeing' — and this was for him the real secret of contemporary literature — only occurred when one had oneself experienced, had oneself lived through, what one saw. Everything he had written in the last ten years, he had himself lived through in spirit, he confessed.

This is what prevents *Emperor and Galilean* from being simple dramatic reportage; for Ibsen's explanation of the phenomenon of 'seeing' offered a way of reconciling the objective with the subjective. It was not merely that an apparently uncomplicated chronicle of events could thereby incorporate certain intimate and personal overtones; it also meant that without some contribution from the author and his own personal experience, the essential significance of what he was describing would forever remain inaccessible to him. Such personal relevance was therefore something else that Ibsen kept returning to in connection with *Emperor and Galilean*. To Edmund Gosse, in a letter written while he was still hard at work on the play, he declared that what he was putting into it was a part of his own inner life, things that he had himself experienced in various forms. To another correspondent, to whom he wrote just after the play had been completed and while he was at work making the fair copy, he admitted that in the character of Julian, as indeed in most of what he had written in his more mature years, there was more personal inner experience than he cared to admit in public.

What precisely the relevance of Julian's career was to Ibsen's own situation is not easy to say; in any case, a full answer would depend very largely on what philosophical interpretations are to be put on the events of the play. But Ibsen's torchlight speech of 1874 — the same as was mentioned above — gives a clear indication of where to look for at least one of the points of contact. When Julian reaches the end of his career, what depresses him most in his isolation is the realization that, whereas others have succeeded in making themselves loved by their fellow-men, he has only won a measure of intellectual recognition. To put a distance between oneself and others very often aided artistic achievement: 'I knew very well', Ibsen had written to Laura Kieler in 1870, 'that a life in solitude is not a life devoid of content. But man is nevertheless, in a cultural sense, a long-sighted being; we see clearest at a distance; the details confuse; one must get away from things if one wants to judge.' But, as his words to the Christiania students show, he sometimes had misgivings; the price paid in terms of human affection was terrible, and he often debated anxiously with himself whether his scheme of values was right, wondered with a kind of emptiness whether the sacrifice was worth it. Not only did this give a subjective resonance to something that would otherwise be thinly objective, however; it also emphasized the modernity, the present-day relevance of material that had been taken from remote history. No man, he pointed out, lives in total isolation from his fellows; anything he experiences, he enjoys or suffers along with his contemporaries; and to a large extent his experiences are therefore also theirs. One of the particular reasons why he chose this historical theme was because it was so closely related to the ideological currents he detected at work in his own day. Indeed, after the drama had been completed, he felt that, in some particulars, recent events in Germany and Europe had combined to augment this special relevance, which then resulted in a work of even greater contemporary significance than he himself had imagined.

Nevertheless, the most consciously and deliberately introduced element in *Emperor and Galilean* was its philosophical content. This play was designed to give to the world what he had so long withheld, and which he now felt it was time to provide: his philosophy of life, expounded dramatically. 'The positive *Weltanschauung* which the critics have long demanded of me', he wrote to his publisher on 12 July 1871 shortly after starting work on the play proper, 'will be found here.' By 'philosophy', it is quite clear both from the play itself and from Ibsen's own explanations that he did not mean the elaboration of a system of morals; rather he meant the enunciation of such ordering principles as would help to clarify the problem of Man's evolutionary career, of his path through history, of the role of the individual in the inscrutable processes of the universe. He looked at the characters, at the intersecting plans, at the history, and did not concern himself with what the 'moral' of it all was; on the other hand, he intended the underlying philosophy to be clearly in evidence, and indeed meant it to emerge as the ultimate judgement upon the conflicts and struggles that made up the action of the play.

The groundwork of thought in the drama shows certain obvious and immediate similarities with the Hegelian system. Its world is an arena of dualities: Christianity and Paganism, the flesh and the spirit, the claims of Caesar and the claims of God, the tree of knowledge and the tree of the cross, moral goodness and sensuous beauty, freedom and necessity, the individual and the world. Above all these, and thought of as embracing and reconciling and resolving these opposites, was the great mysterious synthesis of 'the third empire'. It seems unlikely that Ibsen ever made any close, first-hand study of those philosophers whose ideas on occasion erupt into his dramas: of Kierkegaard, of Hegel, of Mill or Darwin. Immediate familiarity with their works on any substantial scale is improbable. On the other hand, Ibsen was greatly receptive to any ideas that were in the air; he was a good listener in company; he was a solitary thinker; and he was a voracious reader of newspapers and periodicals and journals of all kinds. One likely indirect source of his Hegelian ideas is J.L. Heiberg, the man to whom Ibsen in a poem written in the year of his beginning serious work on *Emperor and Galilean* paid homage as a 'great seer'. Heiberg, who up to his death in 1860 had been the leading critic of Scandinavia for the better part of forty years, and who as head of Copenhagen's

Royal Theatre between 1849 and 1856 had exerted a considerable influence on theatrical development there, was also
renowned as the interpreter of Hegel in Denmark. His work *On
Human Freedom*, with its discussion of the roles of freedom and
necessity, was probably already known to Ibsen in his Grimstad
years. Certainly, Ibsen's occasional pieces of dramatic criticism
from the early 1850s clearly show the influence of Heiberg's
ideas; Ibsen met him personally in Copenhagen in 1852, and
generally thought very highly of him.

What is not so generally remarked is that Heiberg may have
served as the link not merely between Ibsen and Hegelian
philosophy, but also between Ibsen and the dramatic theories of
the German dramatist Friedrich Hebbel — theories which show
an astonishing similarity at some points with the ideological
framework upon which *Emperor and Galilean* is built. The bare
facts are that, in 1843, Hebbel (who was technically, as a subject
of the Duchy of Holstein, a Danish citizen) published in the
Stuttgart *Morgenblatt* a short article entitled 'Ein Wort über das
Drama'; this was reprinted shortly afterwards in Danish translation in *Fædrelandet* (in later years, one of Ibsen's regular
newspapers). The ideas put forward by Hebbel in this article
were then severely criticized in some of their details by Heiberg
in the Copenhagen *Intelligensblade*, an attack which in turn
provoked Hebbel to publish an extended defence of his views.
This defence was added to the original article and the whole
thing then published independently in July 1843 with the title of
Mein Wort über das Drama — one of the more significant items
of dramatic theory to come out of nineteenth-century German
literature. In it, Hebbel declared that drama should make
manifest the 'life-process', the resolution of the dualism between
the individual and that great scheme of things of which, despite
his incomprehensible freedom, the individual was still a part; it
was to present the inevitable conflict between the individual will
and the world-will, whereby as soon as the former sought in any
way to assert itself, it released an opposing force from the latter,
which by its inevitable victory restored an overall equilibrium
at the cost of a certain slight re-adjustment in things generally;
dramatic guilt thus became not the result of some sin or transgression but the simple consequence of any act of self-assertion

whatever on the part of the individual. On the basis of this theory, Hebbel defined his own dramatic aspirations as the desire to write a drama that would be social and historical and philosophical at one and the same time, without letting any one of these things preponderate; and in elaborating on this plan, he drafted terms that quite astonishingly anticipate *Emperor and Galilean*:

> A drama is possible which pursues the stream of history to its most mysterious sources, the positive religions, and which — because it manifests in dialectic form all the consequences of the ideas that lie at the root of these religions for the Individual who is consciously or unconsciously affected by them — symbolizes all the historical and social conditions which would in the course of the centuries inevitably develop from all this.

The actual 'Individual' in Hebbel's mind at the time he wrote these words seems in fact to have been Luther — for him, one of the few characters in whose person whole centuries or even millennia of development seemed to be concentrated. But his words could have served equally well for Julian.

The ten Acts of *Emperor and Galilean* follow the career of Julian the Apostate, his rise to imperial power and his attempts to reintroduce the old paganism into the Christianized Roman Empire of the fourth century A.D. The first half, *Caesar's Apostasy*, moves from Constantinople to Athens and to Ephesus, and eventually to Lutetia and Vienne in Gaul, covering the ten years between 351 and 361 A.D.; the second half *Emperor Julian*, embraces the events of the years from 361 to 363 A.D., and moves from Constantinople to Antioch, and thence to the eastern territories of the Empire and to the plains beyond the Tigris. But for the scenes in which Maximus appears, the philosophical implications of the play would not be specially remarkable. The first two Acts define Julian's disgust and dissatisfaction with the evident corruptions of the day. In Constantinople he finds the air of the Christian court unwholesome, suffering anguish of soul and beset by disturbing thoughts; and when a vision seems to command him to leave the city and do intellectual battle in the strongholds of the heathen, he departs gratefully. But in Athens, the corruption which has set in among those who adhere to the older deities is in its way no less dispiriting than in Constantinople. Julian begins to lead the Dionysian life, but he is sickened by the contrast between what he feels must surely have been the ancient beauty of heathen sin and the merely sordid practices of the present. He is compelled to acknowledge that just as the newer Christian truth is no longer true, so the old pagan beauty is no longer beautiful; and he attends eagerly to Gregory's advice to abandon books and the debating chamber as sources of wisdom and to seek it outside, in life, in some new revelation.

By now it is clear that Julian is concerned not in the first place with a search for truth or beauty, but — like so many other Ibsen heroes — rather with a search for a life mission. He is looking for some reliable indication as to what his own role in life is destined to be. With the help of Maximus, he seeks enlightenment from the occult; but the signs are conflicting, seeming to portend three distinct possibilities. First, there is his own interpretation of certain omens and astrological signs that have been vouchsafed to him: that he is destined to rule the earth in company with his half-brother Gallus, the latter as Emperor holding the temporal power and himself as some kind of spiritual head as yet unnameable, but making a fourth in the great line Moses — Alexander — Christ. Whereas all three earlier figures in this tradition had, however, been deficient in some way — either by being physically impaired, or by having to depend on stimulants, or lacking hardiness and vigour — Julian is fully persuaded that he would not possess any such comparable handicaps. Moreover, he believed that he was to be granted what all the others had been denied, namely a 'pure woman', a Bride whom he would lead by the hand to the East and the land of Helios, to a grove on the banks of the Euphrates, there to found a new and perfect race.

A seance shortly afterwards presents two other sets of omens, however. The first comes with a Voice — whether a man's or a woman's, Julian cannot tell — which instructs him that by willing what he must will and by freely submitting to necessity, his mission will be to 'establish the empire'. Maximus explains that this must mean 'the third empire', following the first which has been founded on the Tree of Knowledge and the second which was established on the Tree of the Cross:

> The third is the empire of the great mystery, the empire which shall be founded on the tree of knowledge and the tree of the cross together, because it hates and loves them both, and because it has its living springs under Adam's grove and Golgotha.

A final and much more alarming portent follows immediately on this. It comes when Maximus attempts to identify the three other spirits present at their table during the seance, 'the three corner-stones under the wrath of necessity' as Maximus calls them, and the 'three great helpers in denial'. One of them is identified as Cain, a man who had willed what he of necessity had had to will, who had done as he did simply because he was not otherwise than what he was; the second is named as Judas Iscariot, who similarly had by necessity willed what he had willed — both spirits having thus by involuntary acts of will played decisive roles at crucial turning-points in the world's history. The third spirit cannot be persuaded to manifest itself — something which apparently means that it is still in the land of the living, and therefore by implication possibly Julian himself. This possibility Julian urgently repudiates.

When immediately afterwards the Emperor Constantius sends for Julian to come to Constantinople as heir-elect to the throne (Gallus having been murdered), and also promises his own sister as a bride, Julian at once sees in this the possible fulfilment of several of the more agreeable signs: the establishment of the empire, for example, and the emergence of the 'pure woman', in particular. With this, Julian feels he has found his mission, and he reaches a high peak of confidence and optimism. From this point onwards, the drama follows the slow and inexorable adulteration of his idealism to its terminus in disillusion and defeat. The 'pure woman' turns out to be anything but pure; the Emperor's jealousy and Julian's own compulsion to act forces him to bid for the throne himself. As Emperor, he personally claims the freedom to embrace the ancient pagan beliefs, whilst at the same time he desires to preserve a general liberty of worship for all creeds; but the position soon proves untenable, and inevitably circumstances compel him to harsh and repressive measures against the Christians. He comes to see in their sternly disciplined martyr-spirit the main threat to his own authority as Emperor; he tries to enforce the worship of Dionysos, and Fortuna, and the Sun-King; and in finally attempting to strengthen his position by force of arms, he is killed. He is struck down with the words 'Thou hast conquered, Galilean!' on his lips.

Over Julian's body, Maximus has to admit that he had been wrong; the signs had been ambiguous, and only now was it clear to him how seriously he had been deceived about the role Julian was meant to play. Maximus had envisaged him as a twin-souled mediator, as an emperor-god reconciling the two great kingdoms of the spirit and of the flesh; but in fulfilling his destiny, Julian had contributed towards the great scheme of things in a very different way — negatively. He had in truth been a Chosen One, through whom Necessity had acted — but ambiguously:

> Oh my beloved . . . all the signs deceived me, all the omens spoke with a double tongue, so that I saw in you the mediator between the two empires.
> The third empire shall come! The spirit of man shall reclaim its heritage and burnt offerings shall be made for you and your two guests in the symposium.

Such is the extent of Maximus's error. He had come to place too great a reliance on his own interpretation of the Voice, come to see in Julian the tremendous synthesizing authority who would establish the mysterious 'third empire'. But Julian's was not a positive potential, such as would destine him for the role of a Moses or a Christ; despite all, he had been a 'helper in denial', one who by his career of negation had furthered things, who in attempting to turn back the clock, to revive the past, had nevertheless paradoxically assisted progress and the advancement of Man. Like Cain and Judas — the 'two guests' Maximus here refers to — Julian had been an instrument of the world-will in the incommensurable pattern of events. To play his part, he first had to *will* to play it, but that very act of willing was itself pre-determined. Small wonder that when Ibsen wrote to Brandes in September 1871, he confessed: 'During the work on "Julian" I have in a certain fashion become a fatalist.'

Clearly, then, there are many German overtones in the *Welt-anschauung* which this drama serves. There are perhaps echoes of Lessing's *Die Erziehung des Menschengeschlechts*, for example, with its confidence that a new epoch in religious thinking was at hand, a new and more humanist faith which — taking encouragement from the growth of enlightenment — would evolve out of New Testament thought in the same way as this in its day had developed out of Old Testament ideas. There is also something reminiscent of Goethe's *Faust*, particularly of the role assigned to Mephistopheles in the working of the universe, the role of one who, as Mephistopheles himself puts it: 'Stets das Böse will, und stets das Gute schafft.' Most insistently, however, it reminds one again of Hebbel, especially of that passage in *Mein Wort über das Drama* where he writes of the revision which his theory of drama necessarily imposes on the concept of dramatic guilt:

> One must not overlook the fact that dramatic guilt does not, like Christian original sin, arise only when the way the human will is directed is known; it derives directly from the will itself, from any act of obstinate, autocratic self-assertion; and it is, dramatically, quite immaterial whether the hero comes to grief as a result of admirable or of reprehensible activities.

And finally, of course, it seems to anticipate many ideas that were to become vastly more familiar in time to contemporary Europe through the works of Nietzsche.

What is also essential, however, within this generally Hegelian pattern, is to distinguish between the two separate though over-lapping areas of conflict in *Emperor and Galilean*, both of them productive of dialectic development: the one a clash between the Christian and the pagan attitudes to life; and the other a clash between the individual and the world-will. The first of these not only comes in for extensive dramatic comment in this play, but is also a steadily recurrent theme in other of Ibsen's dramas, both before and after. The Christian view of things (as Julian reports on it, at least) constitutes an extremely powerful philosophy that nevertheless easily becomes tainted, where the spirit conquers and subdues the flesh but where life somehow becomes subordinate to death, where complete fulfilment is denied upon this earth and postponed to some after-life, where sternly dutiful self-discipline kills joy, where martyrdom alone is the ultimate ecstasy, and where all march with their faces resolutely turned towards death. Later in Ibsen, this same spirit was to re-appear in more contemporary guise as, for instance, 'the Rosmer way of life', that philosophy to which the paganly vital Rebecca eventually succumbs — 'ennobled', as she puts it. But, she also confesses sadly, it has at the same time infected her will, sapped her strength of purpose, and killed all happiness. The Dionysian ideals which Christianity had supplanted had originally been devoted to the cult of beauty, to the exaltation of the senses and to the rapture of ecstasy, to the enjoyment of the rich fruits of the earth. It was 'diesseitig' where Christianity was 'jenseitig'. But it also degenerated easily into self-indulgence and licence and harlotry. This is the mode of living that Ibsen returns to in later plays under the term 'livsglæde', *joie-de-vivre*, the joy of life — something which when repressed and shut in, as it is in the career of the late Captain Alving in *Ghosts* for example, turns swiftly to debauchery. It also lives on in Hedda Gabler's visions of Løvborg with vine-leaves in his hair, and her obsession with beautiful death. This Dionysian — or, in some plays, heathenly Viking — philosophy of life is eternally the target for Ibsen's formidable parsons and their like-minded lay brothers and sisters, whose vigilant readiness to denounce the pursuit of earthly pleasure carries the implication that, for them, goodness and enjoyment are wholly incompatible. That both these philosophies were capable of displaying both admirable and reprehensible features, that both of them in their origins had been splendidly conceived but in time had become perverted and corrupt, and that some new revelation was now surely at hand — these made up the nineteenth-century relevance which Ibsen worked into his play, and which he also explicitly referred to in a speech he made in 1887. There, taking his cue from the scientific doctrine of evolution, he announced his confident belief that some new set of concepts — political, social, literary, philosophical, and religious — would emerge out of the old, concepts which would give mankind a completely new potential for happiness. 'More particularly and more precisely,' he added, 'I believe that the ideals of our age, by suffering eclipse, show a trend towards what I have intimated in my drama *Emperor and Galilean* by the term *the third empire*.'

The other main conflict in the drama was not even limited to a merely contemporary relevance, but was (he claimed) timeless and thus eternally valid. 'The play treats of the struggle between two irreconcilable powers in the life of the world, something which will in all ages repeat itself; and because of this universality, I call the book a 'world-historic' play', he wrote to Ludvig Daae in February 1873. This struggle is the one in part exemplified by the title of the work; it is also made the subject of comment by Maximus in Act IV of *Emperor Julian*. When the great primal Creator had imposed order on chaos, he had nevertheless allowed into his creation a second creative power — the power of his creatures to re-create themselves, the will to survive, the urge to self-preservation and self-advancement. These are in essence the two great warring principles in the universe: the Individual and the Whole, Man and God, or — to select particular historical manifestations of them — Emperor and Galilean.

To combine and contain all these many contradictions, it is necessary to discover what Maximus calls 'the twin-sided prince of peace', in whom both 'freedom' and 'necessity' would be subsumed, for whom the spirit and the flesh become one, and in whose essence love and hate are indistinguishable, opposites are reconciled, and the principle of ambivalence is supreme. Only once, in an intense moment of insight, had Julian been aware of the full implications of all this, and he tells Gregory of Nazianzus of his 'great redemptive revelation'. It is:

'That which is, is not; and that which is not, is.'

9

Drama and Society

Pillars of Society; A Doll's House; Ghosts

Pillars of Society appeared in 1877, *A Doll's House* in 1879, and *Ghosts* in 1881. But it is more than chronology alone that orders them thus, as Ibsen himself insisted. 'You say that the translation of *Ghosts* will soon be complete,' he wrote on 14 September 1882 in connection with a plan to bring out English translations of his works in America, 'but I would not consider it appropriate for this play to come out *first*. Of the three works you mention, this one is the most extreme [lit. 'furthest going'], and ought therefore to be the last of the series. This should, I suggest, open with *Pillars of Society*, after which should come *A Doll's House*, since this forms as it were an introduction to, or preparation for, *Ghosts*.' Ordered in this fashion, the plays constitute a series, the

terms of which are a succession of curses, increasing by a kind
of anathematical progression. The things Ibsen thought merited
his abuse, how he abused them and the manner in which his
denunciations became successively more extreme while at the
same time sharing a common alignment — to inquire into these
matters is to ask the crucial questions.

Generally the condemnation in them is directed against those
aspects of contemporary living, and particularly of life as
currently lived in the remoter north of Europe, that put
obstacles in the way of free and unfettered self-realization: the
hypocrisies of commerce, the dead hand of convention, the
compulsion to do the done thing, the fear of what people will
think, the bigotries of institutionalized religion, and all those
related factors which, under the guise of duty or loyalty or
moral obligation, stunt the personality, inhibit a natural
development in the individual, and shut him off from genuine
living. In these three dramas — as also, of course, in so many
other of Ibsen's works, particularly from *Brand* (1866)
onwards — the deeper preoccupations are with a proper
definition of freedom. Freedom, he repeatedly insisted in these
years, was essentially a matter of individual decision and
individual responsibility, something personal which was striven
for without ever being fully realizable, something which steadily
expanded and proliferated as one tried to make it one's own, so
that (as he put it in a letter to Georg Brandes, 17 February 1871)
'if. . . in the course of the struggle [for freedom] a man stops
and says: "Now I have it" — all he does in fact is show that he
has lost it.' Much of the fabric of contemporary society he saw
as made up of out-dated attitudes and opinions, something that
was now quite inappropriate for the new individual. It caught
him in a mesh of prescriptive duties; it saddled him with an
intolerable burden of incumbencies largely obsolescent; it
coerced him and bemused him into a belief that suffering and
joylessness were necessarily predominant in the good life. Above
all, Ibsen was anxious to revise current thinking about what one
owed to oneself; he noted the tendency to suppose that *any*
concern for oneself was unworthy, and he was eager to point out
instead that a proper concern for one's own self was rather one
of the supreme duties.

All three plays document a process of emancipation by ordeal; and all three principals, Bernick and Nora and Mrs. Alving, are driven on from some earlier and more rudimentary stage of personal integrity and freedom (intellectual or spiritual or moral or social) to a more advanced and enlightened one. But they move in echelon, perhaps even in relay; for they have widely separate points of departure, they finish up at different termini, and they cover different ground; only the direction in which they move is common to them. Bernick starts furthest back, in the sense that his career is a sham even by the most common-place standards of public morality, let alone by the standard of 'advanced' thought; and the progress he is able to make is limited by the very nature of his political role in society and the constitution of that society: 'You can't imagine. . . how I've been forced year after year to whittle down any hopes I might have had of living a full and satisfying life,' he says to Lona Hessel. 'What in fact *have* I achieved, however much it may seem? Bits and pieces. . . trivialities. But here they won't tolerate anything else. . . or anything more. If I wanted to take one step in advance of the current views and opinions of the day, that would put paid to any power I have.' Nora, by contrast, comes to the point where she does take a very drastic step ahead of her time; the route of her emancipation begins at a point less remote than Bernick's, in the sense that her life is less obviously inauthentic at the opening of the play than his; her position as the wife of a bank manager, cosseted and seemingly insulated against the more hurtful impact of life, needed a crisis of a different kind to persuade her that she must get away from it all; and she leaves far behind the more conventional ideas of what it was thought proper to do. It is not straining things too far to see Mrs. Alving's emancipation as beginning just here; hers is the career of one who also slammed the door on her husband and ran off into the night, but who was persuaded to return to the path of duty, with all its alarming consequences. The course of her career — of revulsion, of rebellion, and of re-appraisal — takes her so far ahead of her day that even her author dared go no further for the time being. It had been his deliberate intention with this play to extend a few frontiers (as he said), but this was for the moment the ultimate: 'I agree absolutely with you,' he wrote to Sophie Adlersparre on 24 June 1882, 'when you say that further than *Ghosts* I dare not go. I felt myself that the general state of mind in our country would not permit it; nor do I feel any stimulus to go further. A writer must not leave his people so far behind that there is no longer any understanding between them and him. But *Ghosts had* to be written; I couldn't remain standing at *A Doll's House;* after Nora, Mrs. Alving of necessity had to come.'

Bernick, it was suggested above, does not go impressively far in his advance towards the Ibsenist ideal. He may even have advanced less than critics in the past have generally assumed. In the course of the play he is discovered to have transgressed in the past even by the most ordinary standards of mass morality: to have trampled on others in his scramble for power and influence, to have slandered and exploited his fellows for the sake of material advancement. But at the same time there is recognition of the fact that Bernick's deeper crime is not so much the harm he has done to others, but the injury he has thereby done to himself. Johan, with his more liberal outlook, suffers no real hurt from Bernick's lies; and what injury there is, is soon healed by Dina's courage in deciding to run away with him in defiance of public opinion. It is Bernick's own integrity that suffers most from these lies, and he has to be taught the necessity — or at least taught to admit the advantages — of obeying some rather more human compulsion than the pressure of public opinion or the craving for prestige. Under close scrutiny, however, Bernick's moral rehabilitation is a good deal less impressive than he would like it to appear, and even — and this is perhaps the real point — a good deal less effective than either he himself or Lona Hessel believes. In other words, one wonders just how much irony Ibsen meant to be read into the curtain scene. Although Bernick publicly renounces any intention of trying to run the railway for private profit, he nevertheless (one imagines) succeeds in retaining administrative power over it, and at the same time manages very nicely to rid himself of his three earlier collaborators. After it has been made reasonably clear that Martha was done out of her inheritance, he says nothing about making any restitution. And although after fifteen years he finally, under considerable direct pressure, confesses to a youthful indiscretion, to having sheltered behind the magnanimity of his brother-in-law, and to having done nothing to discourage the slanderous rumours that got about concerning Johan, he is nevertheless careful to keep very quiet about the most monstrous thing of all: that he was ready to send a whole ship's company to their deaths merely to save his own respectability. He still seems to be working to the principle that the worst crime of all is to be found out. There is simply no guarantee that the salvage work done on him has brought about any real redemption. At the very moment of confession, indeed, there is in his words an involuntary betrayal of the fact that his thoughts still run on much the same lines as before, that he is still prepared to calculate in terms of what *profit* this might bring him: 'I ask each one of you to go to his home. . . to compose himself. . . to look into his heart,' he says, 'and when we have all calmed down, it will be seen whether I have lost or gained by speaking out.' Indeed, as the play moves into the final moments, and after the carefully phrased admissions, the equally careful suppressions, the sentimental family reconciliation, the gush of moralizing, one waits expectantly for some characteristic dash of Ibsenist cynicism, for the sting of some Relling-like remark such as cuts across Hjalmar's attitudinizing at the end of *The Wild Duck*, for something that would underline the fact that by the sterner principles of *A Doll's House* and *Ghosts* Bernick still has a long way to go.

Where Bernick is reprehensibly culpable, Nora's crime is in essence only a legal offence; it is not a shameful thing to be hushed up like Bernick's, but a source of pride and joy to her, an insurance even against the day when she is no longer young and beautiful, a lien on Torvald's affection. She is, to adapt an idea of Schiller's, a 'sublime criminal', a person whose transgression is against the unfeeling and unsympathetic laws created by male-dominated society, but whose deeper motives are honourable and admirable. It is true that here again the discovery brings things to a crisis, but it is a crisis of a very different kind from Bernick's, and lights up not (as before) the murky parts of a guilty soul but rather the wrongness of her situation as a chattel-wife. Nora's emancipation is much nearer the vanguard of social progress, and her final solution one that took her far in advance of public opinion, and not merely into line with it as Bernick's did.

The implications of *Ghosts* are even more extreme. Nora, in spite of the firmness of her resolution, is left confused; she cannot be sure, she says, how she will turn out, and all she knows is that the attempt must be made. Mrs. Alving's ordeal, or at least the first instalment of what proves to be a double ordeal, is endured in the name of duty. She in the past has done all that convention demanded of her, and more. After running away from her husband, she returned to him; she remained loyal to him guarding his reputation with selfless devotion at enormous cost to herself and her own happiness; she sent her son away from home to escape the evil influence of his father, thereby denying her own maternal instincts, and drawing the accusation of being an unnatural and heartless mother. She puts all her late husband's money into an orphanage to his memory, in order to scotch any possible suspicion about his way of life. And this is the measure of how far *Ghosts* has progressed beyond *Pillars of Society*. Bernick's violence to his own Self is the direct consequence of selfishness, his violation of the standards of common decency; by contrast, Mrs. Alving's offence is her very selflessness. Her crime is a self-inflicted wound, an outrage which she commits upon her own individuality in the interest of a misdirected altruism and for the preservation of appearances. She, the most dutiful of persons, is guilty of dereliction of the most important duty of all: to herself. In living out her marriage, she shows a power of will that is almost inhuman, comparable with Brand's austerely purposeful career; but she comes to realize, as indeed he too is finally instructed, that the warmth of charity was lacking, that she had left no room for 'joie de vivre'. Mrs. Alving's emancipation is indeed a long and painful one, of which only the final rapid stages are presented in the drama. Her first act of rebellion was against the falsity of her marriage and its cruel domination; yet when the opportunity came, her solution was imperfect in that she merely substituted a different kind of domination in place of the earlier one: *she* took control of things as soon as she had a weapon she could use against her

237

husband; she dictated what should be done, and she ran what she was later ready to admit was a sunless, joyless home. Her emancipation, although rooted in the disillusionment that accompanied her marriage, and fed by her reading of 'advanced' books, is left for Oswald to complete. Her attitude to marriage and to the relationship between men and women moves from a general condemnation of the loveless, dutiful relationship as characterized by her own married life, beyond a readiness to condone or approve free-love, to a point where she is prepared to contemplate even an incestuous relationship if she could be convinced it would bring happiness to her son. She is compelled to give drastic revision to her ideas of duty: not merely to reject the loyalty that wives were conventionally expected to show (no matter what the circumstances) to their husbands, not merely to repudiate the idea that children should unconditionally honour their parents, but even to acknowledge a new and terrifying interpretation of a mother's duty as something that must be prepared to countenance euthanasia even, if need be. The most devastating aspect of it all, however, is that her own son is destined to serve as proof that the past cannot be put away by a mere act of will, no matter how prodigious. She cannot run away from the past as Nora could run away from home. She is forced to recognize that the 'ghosts' of the past, whether they happen to be moribund ideas or outworn conventions or inherited characteristics or the latent hideousness of disease, continue to inhabit the living cells of the new, young life, in spite of the most tremendous efforts to deny them; that there are things against which no inoculation of the liberal spirit is proof. In spite of the tremendous advantages Oswald has enjoyed — held by his mother in scrupulous quarantine away from any contamination his poisoned home atmosphere might have for him, given freedom to travel and the choice of a satisfying career, and with everything that had to do with the less admirable side of his father cut as far as humanly possible out of his life — nevertheless his whole career is fated to be nothing more than a demonstration that, notwithstanding, the past *does* live on, and that it can in some cases quite overwhelm. In all this, the pattern is almost Nietzschean in its suggestion of 'eternal recurrence': Mrs. Alving encounters a situation terribly familiar from before, only that now a son substitutes for his father — both of them full of the joy of life, both of them fond of the bottle and with an eye for the women, both of them turning sour in the joylessness of the home she provides; and although she herself has radically changed, although her reactions are different, the pain is the same. Life, coming not quite full circle, completes a spiral turn.

   To live in the present, to live for the future, one must escape from the past. Inevitably, however, the effort to break free brings the individual into immediate conflict with organized society and its institutions, with the established *mores* that derived from past ages and stubbornly lived on. Clearly implicit in *Pillars of Society* is the author's conviction that to lead a life attuned to the degenerate form of contemporary society was necessarily to involve oneself in falsehood; the play is disposed to show that the really magnanimous people, all the liberal minds and the generous hearts, all the more thoroughly integrated personalities, the essentially honest ones are those who got away. They have been able to reach a community with no crippling burden to bear from the past; they found America where the horizons are wider and the wind blows free. Only among those who remained behind does one find the twisted ones, the unfulfilled, the corrupt and the contaminated. Actually Bernick, the chief representative of this false way of living, had had his opportunity: as a young man, he too (like Oswald) had been to Paris, had seen what life was like beyond the narrow valleys of his own country; but the tainting effect of the society he settles down in is inescapable. (This insistence on the tainting effect of society on normally generous minds — and the more generous the mind, the greater the tainting effect — is also something strongly reminiscent of the young Schiller, incidentally). Bernick, it was noted above, explains to Lona Hessel how isolated he feels in the 'shrivelled stunted little community' that provides the context of his life, how each year he has been forced to abandon more and more of the hopes he has had of living a full and satisfying life, because the community would not tolerate any kind of tampering with its set ways. Mrs. Alving

239

says very nearly the self-same thing when enlightenment comes to her, when she realizes what made her late husband lead the kind of life he did: 'There was this lively, happy boy — and at the time he *was* still like a boy — having to eat his heart out here in this little provincial town; pleasures of a kind it had to offer, but no real joy; no chance of any proper vocation, only an official position to fill; no sign of any kind of work he could throw himself into heart and soul, only business.' No opportunity here beyond that of cashing in on things, of making private gain out of what passed for public good, a playing for status, as Bernick did; or of having to make do with substitutes instead of the genuine thing, with a forced gaiety instead of happiness, with the sterilities of routine instead of the satisfactions of honest work, as the late Captain Alving did. If you cannot escape, you must make do with escapism.

Nora, in the more intimate context of her married life, comes to realize the same thing; she too, as she says at the moment of revelation, has known only gaiety, not happiness. And in tracing through the technical treatment of this idea, one becomes aware of the specialized range of meaning that Ibsen is able to attach to the concept of 'home', the symbolic use he makes of it, and the ambivalence that surrounds it: the home country, the home town, the childhood home, the marital home, the family home, the Children's Home, the Seamen's Home. These dramas make a penetrating analysis of the nature of such 'home' conditions, of the conventional organization of domestic and local affairs, and of the assumptions upon which the regulation of home life was currently based. One begins to notice how much of *Pillars of Society* and *Ghosts* is made to turn about the axis *herhjemme/ derute* ('here at home'/'over there'). How to leave home is 'just the thing for a bright lad', and an essential part of the process of self-assertion, a necessary step on the way to self-reliance. To escape from home is to win release from the insidious authority of 'mother (or father) knows best'; it is to flee the place that stunts one's growth, stifles one's breath, distorts one's values, and kills one's opportunities. It gives rise to a particularly obnoxious kind of self-satisfaction; it inhibits the development of a true humility, and it will, if given half a chance, shut the door on the outside world, cut itself off from outside contact, and live on in its own smug self-sufficiency.

The fact that Ibsen himself was, in this special sense, a 'home-less' person has naturally a direct relevance to this aspect of his work, and needs no underlining. At the time of writing these plays, and indeed for the greater part of his creative life, he was a voluntary exile from the North, and he had all the expatriate's eagerness to pass on the lessons exile had taught him — pointing out to the stay-at-homes what they had missed — as well as a strong but guarded nostalgia for his native land. He tended (or pretended) to look back pityingly on those who had stayed put; and behind many of his characters' remarks there is the quietly irritating superiority of one who had been over the hill, who had seen it all and knows what's what, and who insists that they order things better abroad — a quality in his work that in many cases roused the fury of his countrymen quicker than anything else. Ibsen is untiring in his insistence that contact with the outside world broadens the mind and liberates the spirit; and he laboured hard to undermine the assumption he found in so many of his compatriots that geographical remoteness is in itself an admirable thing, providing welcome insulation against the world's wickedness and the sophisticated corruption of the greater nations. And although Ibsen repeatedly and very rightly denied that any of his characters had acted as mouthpieces for him, it is surely true nevertheless that the role of wanderer returned, the role of a Johan or an Oswald, was one that gave him a good deal of vicarious pleasure.

The more specifically domestic aspects of 'home' are taken up and scrutinized in *A Doll's House*. Here, as in its other senses, 'home' is seen as an institution that tends to inhibit the develop-ment of the authentic Self. For a child to be treated by its father as Nora was, for example, or Olaf — as a mere extension of the father's own life, a repository for his own ideas, and perhaps as the ultimate heir to his own life's work — is to suffer a complete eclipse of personality. As Nora puts it, and as the title of the play echoes, it is to endure becoming a doll for the gratification of others, not unlike the way Bernick in his 'home' surroundings becomes a puppet moving not by its own volition but in obedience to the pull of private gain or public esteem, a lay figure to be dressed up with the insignia of office or the

241

trappings of power. For the married woman of Nora's day, the 'home' could be just as disabling as for the child; Nora finds herself reduced to the level of a home-comfort, something that merely contributes to the husband's domestic well-being and flatters *his* ego at the cost of destroying hers. She becomes a possession. Possessiveness is the keynote of such homes; and crisis, it seems, serves only to amplify it: 'For a man [Helmer says], there's something indescribably moving and very satisfying in knowing that he has forgiven his wife. . . . It's as though it made her his property in a double sense: he has, as it were, given her a new life, and she becomes in a way both his wife and at the same time his child.' So immediately marriage becomes a microcosm of the prevailing male-dominated society at large, in which — as the preliminary notes to *A Doll's House* put it — 'a woman cannot be herself. . . . It is an exclusively male society with laws drafted by men, and with counsel and judges who judge feminine conduct from the male point of view.' Nora's inbred faith in authority and in male domination clashes with her natural instincts, and it is very largely this that makes the drama. Relentlessly, Ibsen builds up by such means his case against the 'home': as the source of bigotry and hypocrisy and blinkered vision; as the abode of tyrannical affection and possessiveness; snug, smug places that confine, enfold, demand; ostensibly well-regulated institutions, such as the Captain Alving Home was meant to be, which deservedly burn down; façades, like Engstrand's Seamen's Home, which conceal obscenities; ways of life such as any right-thinking person slams the door on.

Small wonder that strange things happen to truth in such surroundings; the suppressions, distortions, perversions that take place, the garbling and the dissembling that goes on, the sham and the pretence. Consider even *A Doll's House* alone, how much of the lives of the characters is spent in tampering in some way or other with the truth. Suppression first: Nora's big secret is of course the pivot about which the action turns, exploited by Krogstad, shared with Mrs. Linde, and withheld in terror from Torvald. And Rank's mortal secret is similarly a matter to share with some and withhold from others, entering into things by a kind of counterpoint. Then, secondly, both Torvald and Nora need the opiate of day-dreams to help them to bear the reality of their lives: Torvald indulges himself with the pretence that he and Nora are secret lovers, newly and clandestinely wed; and Nora dreams of a rich admirer who will leave her all his money. And while they knowingly day-dream, they also unknowingly deceive themselves: Torvald with an image of himself as the broad-shouldered courageous male, longing only for the opportunity to save his wife from distress; and Nora with a belief that her marriage is a source of genuine happiness when in reality it is nothing but a hollow sham. The fancy dress ball at their neighbour's is not the only masquerade here, nor the tarantella the only performance Nora puts on. All the time she is acting a part, playing up to the role of irresponsible, scatter-brained wife that her marriage seems to have cast her for, masquerading as the helpless little thing so utterly dependent on her strong husband. The entire ménage is based on misrepresentation, deception, falsity, in small things as well as big; it was a fraud that had to be exposed.

Not all three plays seem, however, equally confident that improvement, even using drastic Ibsenist methods, is possible. The degree of optimism built into them steadily diminishes over the range. In *Pillars of Society* the optimism is at its maximum and its most naïve. The suggestion seems to be that merely to have done with falsehood is to create a vacuum which truth and goodness will inevitably rush in to fill; that given light and air and space, the human soul will necessarily grow true and straight and tall, like a tree in a clearing. To clear up and clear out, it seems to say, is the best thing; and that to leave home for the wider world and its more spacious patterns of living is to find an ever-ready solution to the problems of living. Optimism is also there to a considerable degree in *A Doll's House*, but a little dimmed by comparison; the conviction that truth and goodness and self-realization *can* follow an act of breaking free is there, but is not held unconditionally. Nora cannot feel entirely sure that positive gain will follow for her; she hopes to be able to make something of herself, but realizes there can be no guarantee. Yet, as was made clear above, the implications of her career are bright compared with those that follow from Oswald's.

Accompanying these variations in theme are a number of more specifically technical changes of great fascination, particularly in the demands Ibsen made on language. The most conspicuous break with his own past in this respect had actually already taken place, at the time when he deliberately rejected verse as a mode of dramatic speech valid for his own day; but his desire to discover still more about the possibly unsuspected resources of prose dialogue led him unceasingly on. In the intertexture of the three plays here under review, there is clear evidence of Ibsen's continuingly audacious experimentation in the dramatic use of language. Taking as the characteristic intertexture of drama some compounding of the elements of speech, gesture, and situation, one notes in moving from play to play through the series certain distinct changes in the relative importance attached to the separate constituent parts. To claim, *tout court,* that each is allowed dominance in turn — that speech predominates in the intertexture of *Pillars of Society*, gesture in *A Doll's House*, and situation in *Ghosts* — would be to over-simplify and in some measure to distort what is in any event a highly complex matter; but it opens up an approach to the technical nature of these separate dramas that is not without promise.

Clearly the climax of *Pillars of Society* is massively and expansively verbal. The tension that has been built up is discharged not by any sharp encounter of expostulation and rejoinder, not by any quick cut and thrust of impassioned argument, not by any stichomythiac exchange, but — of all things — by a vote of thanks and a speech in reply. Rørlund takes nearly 900 cliché-ridden words to provoke Bernick into speech, and Bernick takes nearly 800 words to reply, both speeches being very largely uninterrupted except by the noises and asides of audience participation and reaction. Could Ibsen have found anything more unpromisingly ponderous, more monumentally rhetorical, more sheerly wordy to accompany the essentially verbal nature of the dramatic mode within which he is here operating? The final confrontation is between men wielding nothing more deadly than a knack for public speaking, a gift of the gab, and indulging themselves in their few well-chosen words. The speech rhythms are — for the dramatic crisis of a modern realistic play — quite astonishingly slow-moving. Prolix, verbose, it is nevertheless a form of climax wholly appropriate to a drama in which so much of the motive force is provided by what is, and was, *said*: where so many of the characters step forward and declare themselves, where the past is brought up to date by gossiping tongues, where rumour is one of the mainsprings of social change, and the liberating effect of public confession is made clear.

To pass from this to *A Doll's House* is to leave what is a predominantly verbal mode of drama for a much more pronouncedly gestural one. It is not merely that the high-point of the whole play, Nora's final exit and her slamming the door, is a 'gesture' of a particularly expressive kind, the first purposeful gesture of the new individualist; nor even that certain incidents and episodes — of which the 'business' with Rank and the flesh-coloured stockings, the practice tarantella, and the change of costume in Act III are the most obvious — are so economically and laconically effective by virtue of their near wordlessness; but that throughout the entire drama there is an exploitation of the dramatic resources of gesture and posture and movement so unrelenting and so ingenious as to make the accompanying words in many cases almost superfluous. The point has been made before that much of (for example) the first Act of *A Doll's House* would not merely have sufficient non-verbal quality to interest a deaf person, but would in fact be in unusually high degree intelligible to him, too: how Nora enters with the Christmas parcels, supervises the delivery of the Christmas tree, takes out her purse and tips the porter with an obvious show of generosity, secretly helps herself to macaroons from a paper bag which she takes from her pocket, stealthily tiptoes across to one of the doors in the room, listens apprehensively, addresses some shouted remarks to the person within, guiltily stuffs the paper bag in her pocket and wipes her mouth as a man puts his head through the doorway; how she drags him across to show him the parcels, meets his reproachful glances, pouts, tosses her head, wheedles; how she plays romping games with the children, how her attitude visibly changes when a stranger interrupts their games; and so on. Nora's role is composed quite differently from Bernick's, is much less an exercise in declara-

245

tion, much less enunciative, less dependent on vocal utterance. To a very considerable extent she enacts what she has to communicate.

It is, however, not until the final moments of *Ghosts* that Ibsen showed how far it was possible to go in reducing the role of speech in the general interdependence of parts. Compared with the verbalistic climax of *Pillars of Society*, compared with the final show-down, the gesturally enriched wrangle, between Nora and Torvald in *A Doll's House*, *Ghosts* reaches its culmination in a situation from which conceptual language has been pared almost clean away, and where ultimately the only gesture is a negation of gesture. The language no longer informs, it marshals; it commands a situation fully realizable only in terms of dramatic production — which may very well explain why, of all Ibsen's plays, it is the one that reads least promisingly, or improves most on being acted. The entire weight of the drama bears down on this one select, refined moment of terror, where words fail and speech has become an idiot's babble and a mother's wounded cry of pain, where gesture has been paralysed by seizure and the torment of excruciating indecision. After the stolid monumentality of *Pillars of Society*, after the daring *bouleversement* of *A Doll's House*, Ibsen built up *Ghosts* to a fateful, final situation, then knocked away the props to leave it desperately balanced on a knife-edge of infinite irresolution and of unspeakable distress.

The other main point of technical interest concerns the dramatic function of a particular kind of Ibsenist character. It is a commonplace to remark that Ibsen's world is populated with characters, many of whom show among themselves a strong family resemblance; and it is always a revealing matter to trace the metamorphoses through which they pass as Ibsen moves on from play to play. *Pillars of Society*, as the first of his 'modern' plays — discounting for the moment the rather ambiguous position of *The League of Youth* — is particularly rich in characters which obviously continued to exert a steady fascination for Ibsen; yet the other plays too provide plenty of examples of how Ibsen continued to modify and adapt for subsequent pieces characters that had obviously meant much to him. One notes, for example, how a good deal of Rørlund reappears in

Pastor Manders, and again in Kroll in *Rosmerholm*; how
Bernick's easy assumption of male superiority comes out again
in Helmer, and his sheer pomposity in Peter Stockmann, the
Mayor in *An Enemy of the People* ; how Hilmar Tønnesen's
comic capacity for self-deception becomes pathetic in Hjalmar
Ekdal in *The Wild Duck*, and vastly more subtle; how the
character of the 'Old Badger' was, in the draft versions, originally part of *Pillars of Society*, but was eventually withdrawn and
kept as Morten Kiil in *An Enemy of the People*; and how also the
mortal sickness of Rank reappears in Oswald, as well as among
the notes of jottings for *The Wild Duck*. But for present
purposes, perhaps the most rewarding thing is to note what
happened, in the three plays here under consideration, to what
might reasonably be called 'the agent'. This is the term by which
is meant the person or force that promotes or initiates or
precipitates the various crises of emancipation — acting upon the
situation in a way not unlike the way (at a more rudimentary
level perhaps) the declared 'villain' of melodrama is traditionally
supposed to act.

In *Pillars of Society* the office is quite unambiguously held by
Lona Hessel, with intentions that are expressly altruistic. The
play is so constructed to allow her to be fed by the dramatist into
the prevailing state of affairs from without; she imposes her
altruism upon an egoist who has forgotten what his obligations
to his fellows should be (however much he may protest to the
contrary), and who has so far neglected the more fundamental
decencies of social behaviour that his career has become the
enactment of a lie. Lona Hessel is the self-appointed agent of
improvement, a kind of 'anti-villain'. She is permitted on her
first appearance to announce her intention of 'letting in some
air'; and is given further opportunity at the end to explain how
she has acted with but one aim in view: to rescue her girlhood
hero from the falsity of the position he had worked himself into.
Her life has been built on devotion to others, first to Johan in
America and now to Bernick; and nowhere is there any suggestion that this is incompatible with genuine self-realization.
Martha's sacrifices, incidentally, are essentially different; for
although admirable in one way, they have inevitably prevented
her from realizing herself completely. (In passing, it might also

be remarked that Gregers Werle in *The Wild Duck* is obviously a later and more complex variation on this idea of the altruistic agent; and, in view of the consequences of his action, he constitutes a kind of anti-villain *manqué*.) The rest of the pattern of *Pillars of Society* is then built round Lona Hessel's design: the developments in the railway scheme, the complications of the shipyard repairs, and finally Olaf's running away all help to increase the pressure that is deliberately and consciously and purposely applied to effect Bernick's rehabilitation.

In *A Doll's House*, on the other hand, the altruism is very largely involuntary, the chief agent in this instance being Krogstad. It is admittedly *through* him that the emancipating ordeal is engineered, but he is no declared altruist; indeed, by a stroke of authentic Ibsenist irony, he represents an egoism of the most conventional and bourgeois kind; he wants, he explains, to preserve at any cost what little respectability he has been able to win since the time of his own misdemeanours. The transformation in the Helmer household is thus obliquely, less obviously, less personally contrived. Yet there still is some slight trace of the Lona Hessel role in the person of Mrs. Linde (and with it, many would claim, a structural weakness in the architecture of the drama). In the last Act there is a moment when it seems the Helmers might be able to withdraw from the brink; if Krogstad were to do what was possibly the most natural thing, and ask for his letter back unopened, matters need never come to a head between husband and wife. But Mrs. Linde has seen 'quite incredible' things in their house, and insists that Helmer be forced to recognize how things are in reality; she dissuades Krogstad from asking for his letter back and thus deliberately precipitates the clash.

In *Ghosts* the agency is vested in Pastor Manders; and much more important than his role as an embodiment of Ibsen's anti-sacerdotal bias is this function of his as an *agent provocateur*: 'A Pastor Manders will always provoke some Mrs. Alving or other into being,' Ibsen once remarked. And a measure of the difference in *Ghosts* compared with *Pillars of Society* is that Bernick's moral improvement comes as a consequence of his capitulating to Lona Hessel's altruism, while Mrs. Alving's comes from a revulsion against Pastor Manders's. To show consideration for others is what Bernick is asked to accept as the surest way of being true to oneself; Mrs. Alving reverses the order, and brings her conduct rather into line with Polonius's advice to Laertes, or with Leslie Stephen's rather more contemporary concern for the 'health of the organism'. Manders's provocation belongs of course in the main to the past, particularly when he 'won a victory' over himself and helped Mrs. Alving to a similar 'victory' by returning her to the path of marital duty; he represents an attitude of mind that cannot accept the idea that circumstances alter cases, and sees only a code of behaviour. He becomes a kind of emancipator *malgré lui*. And the fact that Mrs. Alving undermines her own faith in altruism by obeying the call to duty so unremittingly contributes to the unexpected fluctuations in this play in the validity of first- and second-person responsibilities. Moreover, Manders's provocation is kept deliberately subdued in order not to clash too stridently with the idea of there also being some impersonal agency at work. The sins of the fathers are, in a very literal sense, visited here upon the children; nevertheless the fact that in the end Mrs. Alving is persuaded that these very sins themselves have their origin in the tainting influence of the narrow community her husband was forced to live in, plus the joylessness of the duty-ridden home environment she had created for him, all help to make the crisis seem self-engendered, or at least not imposed on the principals from without, as in *Pillars of Society* and to a lesser extent in *A Doll's House*.

It was because Ibsen was a dramatist and not a philosopher, and also because — as he was never tired of indicating — he was interested in using drama to ask questions rather than supply answers, that he left undefined except by implication those principles he felt might happily govern our actions, either as individuals or as social beings. It would perhaps not be difficult to separate out in his work a broad streak of Utilitarianism, an inclination to believe that what makes people happy is best. Although cynicism is an important ingredient in his dramas, he was never for very long cynical about man's capacity for good; there is below the surface of these plays a certain exhilaration at the thought of destroying all the apparitions, the delusions, the hallucinations of the past; there is a confidence, sometimes clearly expressed and sometimes only intimated, in the possibility of improvement; a belief that although things can go wrong, the potential integrity of mankind is something to be believed in. These dramas make the point that we often give our approval to things too easily, or else allow our unthinking consent. They insist that authority is not something established once and for all, but needs to establish itself ever anew; that filial affection is to be won and deserved, and never merely assumed; that marriage is an association by free choice, and held together by mutual trust; that patriotism needs more to justify it than a mere geographical accident of birth; that religion has to earn individual acceptance; and that social, political, cultural, and national institutions have ultimately to be shaped by individual conviction. The need to judge for oneself what is right and what is wrong is made paramount. Take as little as possible 'on trust' or 'on authority', these plays command; and in particular hold yourself independent of all instruments of human servitude: the codifications of the law, the precepts of dogma, the ingrained responses of habit, the prohibitions of convention, the tyranny of superstition, and the demands of any loyalty that takes itself for granted.

10

Drama and the Person

An Enemy of the People; The Wild Duck; Rosmersholm

It was Georg Brandes who suggested that much of *An Enemy of the People* (1882), *The Wild Duck* (1884) and *Rosmersholm* (1886) might be traced to a point of common origin: the hurt, the distress and disgust Ibsen felt at the hostile reception given in 1881 by the Norwegian public and critics to *Ghosts*. Within a year of this bitterly resented publication, Ibsen had given his answer to those who had abused him: a play (actually begun before *Ghosts* but now splendidly appropriate to the new situation) which traces the bewilderment and incredulity and ultimate exasperation of one who, for publishing unpalatable truths about the polluted sources of the community's economy, is subjected to insult and slander and even physical violence from his fellows. After thus venting his immediate anger, Ibsen in his next play allowed himself a second and more searching look at this phenomenon of a man who makes it his mission to proclaim truth; and *The Wild Duck*, in asking whether it really does add to the sum total of human happiness to put the average person in possession of the truth, redresses a balance. The tertiary stage of exasperation was reached with *Rosmersholm*, a further exploration of the theme of one whose dementia was truth, who like his earlier counterparts had improving designs on his fellows, but whose ultimate achievement is equally unavailing, though not in the same way and not for the same reasons.

Comparable though the three plays may be in this particular respect, they nevertheless vary greatly in quality. *An Enemy of the People* generally ranks as one of the thinnest of Ibsen's maturer works, one which, to use William Archer's phrase, is 'not so richly woven, not as it were, so deep in pile.' Archer goes on: 'Written in half the time Ibsen usually devoted to a play, it is an outburst of humorous indignation, a *jeu d'esprit,* one might almost say, though the *jeu* of a giant *esprit . . . An Enemy of the People* is a straightforward spirited melody; *The Wild Duck* and *Rosmersholm* are subtly and intricately harmonized.' The two latter plays are often to be observed in the critics' estimates vying with each other as rivals for the top place among Ibsen's works: Nils Kjær's characterization of *The Wild Duck* as 'the master's masterpiece' has been echoed many times in the critical studies of recent decades; and it is repeatedly claimed on behalf of *Rosmersholm* that never was Ibsen's constructional skill more confidently or more successfully exploited.

To plot these three dramas against the co-ordinates of technique and ultimate meaning provides evidence, however, of something more than the mere amplification, or even enrichment, of things already there in essence at the beginning; it is to testify also, and more importantly, to a distinct turning-point in Ibsen's authorship, a change of direction arguably no less profound and no less significant than his earlier abandonment of verse as the medium of his dramas in favour of prose. As a rule it was only with the greatest reluctance that Ibsen was ever drawn to comment on his work; his letters to his publisher and to his friends tended to harden into a drily formal, almost communiqué-like phraseology whenever it was a question of reporting progress on his own work: a bare admission that he *was* busy, a hint of whether or not the thing had a contemporary theme, a forecast of the number of acts it would be in, and (for his publisher) perhaps an estimated time for completion, or some indication of the number of printed pages it would fill. Rarely was there anything else of much significance. It is precisely this habitual uncommunicativeness that makes his unsolicited comment on *The Wild Duck* the rather startling thing it is: writing to his publisher on 2 September 1884, he was moved to admit that he thought of this new work of his as something rather special, adding that his methods were new, and that some of the country's younger dramatists might possibly be encouraged by them to launch out along new tracks. It is therefore not without a certain measure of approval from Ibsen himself that one is tempted to consider *An Enemy of the People* as the culmination of a distinct 'period' in the dramatist's career, as something that set a terminus to the line of the development that had begun with *Pillars of Society* in 1887, and had continued by way of *A Doll's House* (1879) and *Ghosts* (1881). There is encouragement also to see *Rosmersholm* as the inauguration of the later mode of composition serving the group of plays that marked the end of his career: *The Lady from the Sea* (1888), *Hedda Gabler* (1890), *The Master Builder* (1892), *Little Eyolf* (1894), *John Gabriel Borkman* (1896), and *When We Dead Awaken* (1899). And — intractable, transitional, between two 'periods' — *The Wild Duck*, composed at a time when its author's dramatic *credo* was profoundly changing.

The pace of *An Enemy of the People* is unusual for Ibsen; elsewhere, at least in the later dramas, the progression is purposefully deliberate, like an exploratory advance over uncertain country which has had careful preliminary study but no close reconnaissance. In this play, by contrast, the advance is conducted with eager exuberance, moving over ground familiar as it might be from regular patrol activity, and not seeming to care greatly if on occasion it happens to put a foot wrong. Part of the terrain had in fact been one of Ibsen's favourite stamping-grounds for over ten years, if not longer: a hatred, carefully nurtured in correspondence and in conversation, of anything in the way of party or association or society or indeed any identifiable grouping that went in for 'majority' practices, that invited majority decisions or accepted majority rule. As early as 1872, he had even talked enthusiastically about undermining the whole concept of statehood, asserting that 'the state is the curse of the individual.' Such political sympathies as he had at the time were reserved for nihilists and anarchists and the extreme left-wing, from a feeling that they at least cared about the big things in life and honestly strove to realize their ideals, whilst the larger parties with their mass appeal struck him as trafficking in nothing but sham and humbug. Organized Liberalism he considered freedom's worst enemy.

To these convictions, the events of the year 1881 — the hostile reception given to *Ghosts* — brought peculiar reinforcement. To his scorn of organized politics was now added a consuming contempt for the press, especially the so-called Liberal press. Ibsen was confirmed in his view that the press as then constituted was no better than a parasite on a grotesque and deformed body politic, for ever talking about freedom, but terrified of the realities of it, for ever proclaiming independence although itself merely the slave of public opinion and organized pressure-groups and its own circulation figures.

Three items, chiefly, 'seeded' his mind, super-saturated as it was by bitterness and contempt for these things; and they provided the nuclei around which the drama eventually crystallized. One was an anecdote, reported to him by a German acquaintance, Alfred Meissner, about a spa doctor who had been persecuted by his fellow-townsmen for reporting, to the great detriment of the tourist trade, a local case of cholera. Another was the incident in February 1881 involving a chemist called Harald Thaulow and the Christiania Steam Kitchens, in which Thaulow was prevented at a public meeting from reading his indictment of the management of the Kitchens and instead delivered an impromptu speech of denunciation. And the third was the personality of his great contemporary Bjørnstjerne Bjørnson.

The life-long relationship between these two men was marked by almost every emotion and attitude except indifference. Never was Ibsen, the self-sufficient, introverted exile, able for long to put out of his mind the image of the popular, rhetorical, extraverted Bjørnson. His feelings were always mixed — admiration, contempt, envy, exasperation, gratitude, affection, resentment, with sometimes one thing preponderating, and sometimes another. At the time when Ibsen was working on *An Enemy of the People*, he had cause to think of Bjørnson with gratitude, particularly for the latter's spirited defence of *Ghosts*; and the courage, the bluff honesty, and the fundamental decency that he acknowledged in Bjørnson reappear also in his created hero, Dr. Stockmann.

But the piquancy of the situation can surely not have been lost on the author. Ibsen *à la* Bjørnson! The opportunities were too good to be missed. And there, accompanying his quite genuine regard and affection for his hero, one finds a good deal of dry mockery, directed in particular against Dr. Stockmann's simple-minded, self-opinionated interpretation of things. (One must beware, of course, of ascribing *all* Stockmann's traits to Bjørnson or even to what Ibsen might have wanted to pin on Bjørnson — the relevance is to be found rather in the author's implicit attitude to his created character, and not in the details.) Dr. Stockmann does not find it easy to relate the immediate problem to any wider context of things; his strength and his weakness lie in his simple directness, his inability to see more than one side of the question; and his brother's remonstrance that the alleged pollution cannot be regarded in isolation as a merely scientific matter but is also political and economic, is not without justification. He lacks any deeper understanding of the motives of human conduct and is even perhaps too easily misled about his own. It is no coincidence that both Stockmann and Gregers have spent much of their adult lives in remote parts, the former stuck away in Arctic Norway as a doctor, and the latter brooding 'up at the works' in Høidal for fifteen years; their conduct lacks the corrective of the 'reality principle', that which could tell them what may be presumed socially possible, and what may not.

It is precisely these temperamental and very human weaknesses in the main character, however, that prevent the drama from degenerating into a theatrical tract; and Ibsen was able to make his Kierkegaardian points about the need for individual decision, the necessity for individual responsibility, and the value of individual courage — especially the courage of one's convictions — and to enlist the sympathies of the audience unambiguously on the side of the lone champion without at the same time making him too offensively virtuous. Against his hero, Ibsen marshals an alliance of vested interest, political hypocrisy, and editorial opportunism: the Mayor, the influential representative of entrenched authority, not without courage of a kind and horribly experienced in the manipulation of others by veiled threat and the promise of favour, who masks self-interest and self-preservation as 'the common good'; Aslaksen, embodying the inherent timidity of public opinion, and making a virtuous 'moderation' out of his essential servility; and Hovstad, hawking his influence to the highest bidder. These are the elements that determine the ultimate shape of the drama, in which principles are balanced against expediency, integrity weighed against quick profits, and the 'individual' involved in a fight against what Hebbel was inclined to call the Idea — the reaction of those who wish to maintain the *status quo* and the inertia and the intolerance of the undifferentiated masses who are their dupes.

Among the earliest jottings preliminary to *The Wild Duck* are two which make special reference to the business of growing up, the transition from childhood to adulthood: one of them compares the advance of civilization to a child's growing up, whereby instinct is weakened, the power of logical thought is developed, and 'the ability to play with dolls' is lost; the other draws a parallel between the revisionary changes in man's attitude to his past achievements and the way in which a child mind is absorbed into the adult spirit. This manifest interest in the phenomenon of childhood and its advance to maturity was not without its personal side. In 1881 Ibsen had begun a short autobiographical account which, however, never got beyond a description of the days of his earliest childhood in Skien. One can nevertheless well imagine how his memories of those days were jogged by this exercise: of his sister Hedvig; of his father who suffered the shame of bankruptcy and who reduced a once prosperous family to something near penury; of the attic at Venstøp (a few miles out of Skien) where the Ibsen family subsequently lived; of the furniture there and the books and the other old lumber left by a previous occupant; and of the puppet theatre, with which as a boy he had been in the habit of devising little entertainments for family and friends. Particular details like these can easily be picked out as having contributed to *The Wild Duck* in fairly obvious ways; but the more reflective items in the preliminary notes about childhood and its problems count perhaps for even more.

One way of looking at *The Wild Duck* is to see it as a dramatic commentary on the shock of growing up. The Ekdal household, seen as an entity, enjoys an innocent and child like happiness until this is upset by its introduction, through the agency of Gregers, to a new and disturbing awareness; it gives an account of the thoughtless, brutal imposition of a new and demanding consciousness upon a ménage totally unprepared to face it, and of the sad consequences; it presents a history of shattered illusions and the destruction of make-believe, an account of what happens when a family's 'ability to play with dolls' — or as Relling puts it, its 'life-lie' — is destroyed.

Its most literal representative of childhood is, of course, Hedvig. Standing fearfully yet expectantly on the threshold of adulthood, taking a secret delight in playing with fire, she has all the genuine imaginativeness of the child, and a naïve and still active sense of mystery; responding intuitively to language's more magical powers, she is greatly impressionable and pathetically sensitive to the moods of those about her. Her death is the consequence of her being caught up in the emotional entanglements of an adult world, the result of confused loyalties; and the senselessness of her self-sacrifice and the pity of her fate are things that the drama is particularly concerned to communicate. Balancing her in the composition of the piece is Old Ekdal, who also enjoys 'the ability to play with dolls', but in his case it is the ability of one who has reached a second childhood. He enjoys dressing-up, wearing his old uniform for private and family celebrations; his enthusiasm for the surrogate reality of the attic is genuine and unassumed. Helped on occasion by the brandy bottle, he can live himself without difficulty into a world of his own imagining; and his sad and — by its rather touching ridiculousness — moving presence is also an important ingredient in the whole. Between them is Hjalmar. Between the representatives of nonage and dotage, between the embodiments of the puerile and the senile is this defining figure of childishness: a child without the innocence or the sensitivity of a child, a big baby, sometimes petulant and querulous, sometimes appealing and charming, happy to let himself be spoilt by the attentions of others, skilled in tantrum but quite ready (as Hedvig knows) to be distracted by some little treat or favourite toy, by a bottle of beer or his flute. He takes refuge from the disappointments and frustrations of life in day-dreams of worldly success, of clearing the family name, which provide him with a kind of substitute purposefulness. He too retains something of 'the ability to play with dolls', but it is a self-conscious, a less wholeheartedly spontaneous thing than that of Hedvig or his father; so that when he uneasily shows the loft and its contents to Gregers, he is quick to shelter behind the excuse that it is for the old man's sake.

What the drama emphasizes is that, before the coming of Gregers, this household was a generally happy one, the members of which had succeeded in amalgamating reality and dream, in bringing them both under one roof as they had conjoined their prosaic studio with their fantastic attic. Access from the one to the other was just too easy. What they do not at this stage realize is that the relative stability of their world depends on Werle's unobtrusive manipulations and the cynical adjustments of Relling. These two are the people in ultimate control, secretly supplying both the worldly goods and the stuff of fantasy without which life *chez* Ekdal would be impossible. Hidden subventions provide the material means to bear reality, inspired suggestions sustain their dream-life. That the Ekdals in return help to satisfy some craving or need in the lives of those who thus manipulate them — serving, one imagines, self-interest or conscience or cynicism or a sense of secret power — is a further integral though subsidiary element in the drama. What is important is that a balanced existence is contrived for the whole family unit, permitting all its members to fulfil themselves as completely as ever they are likely to. This existence is brought into a state of a violent imbalance by the arrival of Gregers, who, seeing or suspecting something of the conspiracy that thus controls the Ekdals, feels that he has a duty to expose it. Applying a moral imperative, he sets out to reveal what he regards as the dishonesty inherent in the whole situation.

Like Hjalmar, Gregers gains extra definition in the play from two flanking characters: his father Haakon Werle, and Relling. To the former he stands in contrast by virtue of his lack of practical sense, his alienation from life as it is really lived. Fifteen years in the backwoods is set against the father's successful business career at the centre of things; his inability even to light his own stove gives heightened emphasis to the quietly purposeful way his father, with his sure grasp of opportunity and his *savoir faire,* has organized his own life and the lives of so many of those around him. With Relling — the soul of cynicism, a maker of dreams for all but himself, whose only solution for his own problems is a good binge — the contrast is on the plane of idealism. He takes his fellows firmly by the arm, and beguiling them with pleasant fictions, leads them quietly away from their own frustrations and the jagged edges of reality; Gregers, by contrast, rubs their noses in the truth. Gregers represents what Ibsen had by now rejected — the principle of making universal demands regard-less of person or situation or circumstance. He is the self-elected agent of his fellows' betterment, trafficking in truth and liberty without any sense of what is appropriate, or of what allowances to make: liberty (wrote Ibsen in one of the preliminary notes) 'consists in giving the individual the right to

liberate himself, each according to his personal needs.'
Gregers's approach is based on an inflexibly abstract view of
life, a theorist's; wanting the best for his fellows, and
convinced of their power to achieve it by heroic methods, he
blunders in with his missionary fervour and upsets what he
does not understand. Human kind, he fails to realize, cannot
bear very much reality.

The compositional pattern of *The Wild Duck* thus poses two
figures *en face*, Hjalmar and Gregers, each with his two
supporting figures: Hedvig and Old Ekdal for the one, and
Werle and Relling for the other. But to resolve what would
otherwise be merely a dramatic encounter into a dramatic
situation, there are cross-references and cross-tensions. Werle
is linked to the Ekdal household by former business association
and (through Gina) by illicit relations and a suspected
paternity; Relling is attached to the Ekdals by his tenancy and
daily association, to Gregers by earlier acquaintance up at the
works; both are tenuously related to each other through Mrs.
Sørby, and so on. The result is a plexus of intimacies,
affinities, bonds, transactions, intrusions, importunities. It was
perhaps to dispose these elements more eloquently and to
control them more effectively that Ibsen seems to have been
particularly concerned during the preliminary stages with what
one might reasonably call 'depth', a certain quality of perspective. The drafts show how some characters were brought
much nearer the foreground, others were stood back, and some
even (like Old Ekdal's wife, for instance) taken out of the
composition altogether. Then there were others whose actual
location seems to have remained very largely unchanged yet
whose focus was altered — like the three guests at Werle's party
who were originally *named* characters and then later became
anonymously typed; or like Mrs. Sørby who in the first
mention was an unnamed middle-aged woman. Hand in hand
with this went a certain reduction in the definition of what was
supplied to the composition by past event; facts in the final
version are not things to prove or determine or demonstrate.
There is no concern to annex certainty, but instead the design
is built up by hint, allusion, suggestion or obliquity generally:
Hedvig's paternity, Ekdal's alleged crime, Werle's treatment of

his former wife, all these things are deliberately blurred in the interests of the design as a whole. Nor must one forget the extra quality of 'depth' that the language is made to sustain, the loading of it with extra and secretly shared significance, as when Gregers talks to Hedvig.

Finally, is it perhaps in some such terms that the Wild Duck itself is best explained; as something arbitrarily interposed, which additionally to its function in the drama as one of the 'Requisiten' serves also to make more explicit the relationship of the other elements 'in depth'. Because it is not difficult in the circumstances to imagine a *human* reaction without it, it gives the impression of being inserted; what really integrates it into the play is the realization that no genuinely *dramatic* reaction is possible without it. Part of its effect on the play is comparable with that produced by the traditional dramatic unities; it concentrates, it holds together a number of otherwise separate things, it permits that density by which art distinguishes itself from the more diffuse nature of life, it helps to compose the drama. To call it a 'symbol', however, is possibly to emphasize unduly the similarity of the many disparate things it is successively made to stand for: Hedvig, in its role as gift from Werle to the Ekdals; Old Ekdal, whom life has winged and who has forgotten what real life is like; Hjalmar, who has dived down deep into the mud; Gregers, who suggests that he too will soon accustom himself to his new surroundings; or the object of Gregers's mission, the thing he will, like some extraordinarily clever dog, save from the depths. It is not so much that there is some kind of identity which all these things share, there is no 'falling together' such as the etymology of 'symbol' might suggest; rather it is that the Wild Duck is at the point of convergence of a series of simultaneous metaphorical equations about life and the living of it, a kind of 'x' quality for which a whole range of variables might be substituted in an effort to find some kind of answer to things. Express your answer (the drama seems to enjoin from those who are tempted to try to solve such problems) in terms of truth and human happiness, and comment on the degree of incompatibility indicated.

One of the contributory sources of *Rosmersholm* was undoubtedly Ibsen's disappointment following his first visit to Norway for eleven years. When in the late spring of 1885 he left Italy for Norway; it was not without the hope that he might find life there congenial enough to make him want to settle; but after only four months he was away again to Munich, sickened by too many of the things he had seen and heard to want to stay in the North. 'Never have I felt more alienated by the *Tun und Treiben* of my Norwegian compatriots than after the lessons they read me last year', he wrote to Georg Brandes in November 1886. 'Never more repelled. Never more discomfited.' Many of the less admirable qualities pilloried in *Rosmersholm* have their origin in this sense of repulsion: the cruel fanaticism of Kroll, whom Ibsen created to represent extreme right-wing thought in Norway; the sacrifice of principles to expediency and party advantage that the left-wing Mortensgaard represents — both of these characters reflecting the disgust Ibsen felt for politicians, a disgust that led him in one of his notes to *The Wild Duck* to suggest that politicians and journalists might serve nicely for vivisection experiments. And there was the ineffectualness of Brendel, who with his visionary dreams and his lack of practical sense mirrored Ibsen's scorn of those who claimed to be poets in spirit, enjoying visions of great brilliance and yet nauseated, they said, by the thought of having to write it all down. Equally there is good reason to suppose that some of the more positive elements also grew out of this visit and out of the contacts he made or renewed: Carl Snoilsky, whose company he enjoyed for several days at Molde, seems to have served in some measure as the model for Rosmer; and Snoilsky's second wife provided something of Rebecca.

Above all, however, it was the pettiness and the self-seeking that he could not stomach, the air of narrow provinciality which to him seemed to characterize such a great deal of Norwegian public and private life. The speech that he delivered to a workers' meeting in Trondheim, only about a week after his arrival in the country, expressed both his impatience with democracy as it was then operating and his conviction that what was lacking was nobility of mind: 'Our democracy, as it now is [he said], is hardly in a position to deal with these problems. An element of nobility must find its way into our public life, into our government, among our representatives and into our press. Of course I am not thinking of nobility of birth nor of money, nor a nobility of learning, nor even of ability or talent. What I am thinking of is a nobility of character, of mind and of will.' These are sentiments one finds, in almost identical phrases, not only among his preliminary notes to *The Wild Duck*, but also allotted to Rosmer at that moment when he seeks to define his mission in life. Democracy is no better than the individuals who constitute it; and some form of *individual* regeneration is necessary if the ruthlessness of the party politician and the brutishness of the masses are to be vanquished.

This is one of the things Ibsen stressed when, on one of those rare occasions when he was persuaded to give an opinion about his own work, he offered an explanation of the meaning of *Rosmersholm*. In response to an inquiry from some grammar-school boys in Christiania, he agreed that the play dealt among other things with 'the need to work', but went on to draw attention to the conflict within the individual between principle and expediency, between conscience and acquisitiveness, between the 'progressive' and the 'conservative' in his nature, pointing out at the same time the difference in tempo in the way these things change. *Rosmersholm* considers the dialectics of change, and the consequences for the individuals concerned, that follow an encounter between a predominantly conservative nature and a predominantly progressive one: Rosmer, contemplative by nature, conservative by family, generous by inclination, of the highest personal integrity, and with his roots deep in a landed tradition; and Rebecca, swept along by her passions, of questionable antecedents, 'advanced' in her thinking, and with a ruthless will-power. He is stimulated by her example to act, to take personal decisions, to commit himself; and she is moved by his example to adopt herself some of the Rosmer scruples. Both of them have a vision of glory as the consummation of their endeavours, a glad cause, stimulating not strife but the friendly rivalry of noble minds, all splendid. But the reality of it is profound disappointment. Rebecca is 'ennobled', but in winning generosity of mind loses her power to act; Rosmer in daring to commit himself to action discovers that he has unwittingly but inevitably involved himself in guilt; and any joy they may separately have had from life is killed.

Between the policies of Rosmer and the earlier Gregers, the difference is fundamental: Gregers seeks to impose a general regulation, Rosmer wants rather to interpose *himself*, to make a personal contribution by mixing with his fellows and helping them to self-help — there is, he says, no other way. One of the reasons for his failure is that he is too fine-grained, too passively receptive, too retiring for the evangelical life. Rosmersholm is a refinery in which all the roughage is extracted from existence — is it not said that Rosmer children have never cried, nor the men ever laughed? — and in which all sense of initiative is filtered away. Rebecca testifies how it kills joy, and some of her remarks show how she suspects it kills sorrow, too; indeed, that it annihilates all the stronger, cruder, and more elemental aspects of life. The innocence of saintliness and the innocence of pathetic gullibility are equally Rosmer's, and he is greatly vulnerable; he has no idea how pitilessly he is manipulated by others, he sees very little of what really goes on. He stands there as one whose authority is largely inherited, taken from the family name; and also whose opinions are 'received', taken from the stronger personalities he yields to: first Brendel who was in the early days his tutor, then Kroll to whom he had turned for advice ever since his student days, and finally Rebecca. When ultimately his faith in Rebecca is destroyed, the ideals she has represented for him also crumble; their validity for him derives only from a faith in their guarantor, and it is characteristic of him that he turns at once to Kroll for a replacement of faith. When Brendel reappears to show himself a broken man, this betokens yet a further assault on what pass for Rosmer's convictions. His ideals, dependent as they are on the borrowed life they take from their sponsors, are not sturdy enough for independent existence, so that when at the end a final claim is made of Rosmer's faith — that Rebecca loves him — he is drawn as by an obsession to demand a living sacrifice, to request that the total personality should underwrite this new proposal.

But whereas Rosmer comes to rely utterly on this 'advanced' woman who has invaded his house, she herself — whose past has been a Nietzschean amoral life 'beyond good and evil' and who has all the instinctive ruthlessness of an animal of prey — falls victim to the insidious power of the Rosmer tradition. She encounters something, a sense of scruple, that turns out to be even stronger than her own pagan will, and she submits to it, numbed, 'ennobled'. The two things — integrity and initiative, innocence and committal, nobility of mind and tenacity of purpose, or however they are termed — seem on this evidence totally incompatible, mutually exclusive; and in this respect the play is profoundly pessimistic. The point where such destinies finally meet and merge is death; when, as Rosmer insists, the two of them become one, one course alone is adequate for *her* to prove her love, for *him* to prove his will, and for both to invite a just retribution for their guilty past.

It is this more than anything that invalidates the traditional question as to whether this play is a Rebecca tragedy or a Rosmer tragedy, for it is both and it is neither. The world that Ibsen constructs in *Rosmersholm* is a world of relationships, a lattice of conjoined characters linked each to each, in which dramatically speaking it is less important to evaluate the constituent elements as discrete phenomena than it is to see how they stand to each other; less important to see how they separately change than it is to see how, in the flux of changing circumstance, the relations between them change; less important to 'place' them by political belief, or psychological type, than it is to note the sightings they separately take on each other, and continue to take (often with unexpected results) in the light of new events; not forgetting that any change in these latticed relationships will be reflected in changes all round, in the sense that Rosmer's relations with Kroll, or Rebecca's, are also functions of their own private relationship, and that any change *there* will have its consequences *here*.

Consider, to take an extreme example, the strangely influential role of Beata, Rosmer's deceased wife, who 'exists' in the play not by reason of her physical presence but solely through the memories and through the assessments of those who remembered her. We know her only through them and what they say: Rosmer, though during her lifetime repelled by her over-passionate nature which he obviously associated with the growing insanity that drove her to suicide in the mill stream, can now think of her with tenderness; Rebecca, who at first speaks sympathetically of her until circumstances make her change her words; Kroll, whose sister she was and who puts first one and then a very different interpretation on some of her last actions; Mortensgaard, to whom she wrote a secret and compromising letter shortly before her death; and Mrs. Helseth, the housekeeper and intermediary between them. Such items constitute bearings, taken from vantage points that can be approximately determined because those who occupy them *appear* and so declare themselves. But of course there is no neat answer. Instead of all converging upon some single point of corroboration, their testimonies are so widely divergent that together they do no more than demarcate an area in which a number of different interpretations of Beata are possible. Allowances have to be made, corrections calculated — for individual bias, for distorted or defective vision, for deceit. How ignorant is Rosmer of the real state of affairs? How unscrupulous is Rebecca? How reliable Mortensgaard? Statements about Beata have not only a demonstrative but also a betrayal value; they are also *admissions*, sometimes involuntary, which provide a two-way link with every other character in the drama, except possibly Brendel. Any change in the relationships among those who make these admissions tends to be reflected there, as well as in their attitude to each other.

Further variables can add to the complexity of the dramatic structure. When, for example, Ulrik Brendel is announced, and before he shows himself, the three people assembled in the living-room line up their minds on this new phenomenon: for Kroll, it is that 'waster' whom he last heard of as being in the workhouse; for Rebecca, it is that 'strange man' of whom she wonders that he is still alive; and for Rosmer — to the astonishment of both Kroll and the housekeeper who cannot think that Brendel is a fit person for the living-room at Rosmersholm — he is, as a former tutor in the house, welcome. Three snap bearings help to locate this as yet unknown quantity. *After* he has made his appearance, and after is has been noted not only what valuation he places on himself but also what by his conduct he involuntarily reveals, the initial bearings can be given some adjustment and thus one's ideas about those who took them refined. The importance of looking to the relations, expressed and implied, *between* the characters and not merely to the characters as independent creations is underlined by the letter Ibsen wrote on 25 March 1887 to Sofie Reimers. Invited to play Rebecca in the first Christiania production, she had begged Ibsen's advice; his answer was that she would do well to note carefully what the other characters said about Rebecca, and not make the mistake of studying the part in isolation. Expanding this, one might say that the truth about the individual characters lies within an area bounded by: what they assert is the case; what they wantonly or unwittingly conceal; what they betray of themselves; and what they draw by way of comment from others. And when it is remembered that it is quite possible for these characters to mislead, to be misled or misinformed, or to be in the grip of instincts or impulses they cannot wholly comprehend, then the unreliability of the raw, untreated evidence is at once apparent. To fit in the separate parts as coherent items in a shifting pattern of event and belief is very largely a question of allotting appropriate values to the various hints, suggestions, and allusions the play is strewn with. What hidden meanings in the opening conversation between Rebecca and Kroll, for example, are subsequently brought to light by the momentary revelation that he had once been infatuated by her? What modifications must be made to Rosmer's implicit allegation that Beata was over-sexed, when his own attitude to Rebecca, and the evidence of the past year of their living alone together in the house, carries the suggestion that he himself was under-sexed? And with such suspicions, should one then begin to wonder where in fact the sterility in his marriage to Beata lay — with her, as she was given to understand, or with him? How much had Kroll suspected about Rebecca before, that his thrust about her one-time relations with Dr. West struck home? And by implanting the idea that she had been guilty of incest, was he merely taking revenge on her with the same weapon she had already employed on his sister Beata: fostering suspicion on a minimum of evidence, knowing just how vulnerable her mind was to such suggestions? All these are things that cause one to look again at remarks that are otherwise deceptively obvious or perversely obscure.

Truth, its establishment and its promotion, is a thing all of these three plays have something to say about. In *An Enemy of the People* truth is provable and demonstrable; it inhabits a few scribbled lines of an analyst's report, it is expressible as a chemical formula. Stockmann, in becoming its spokesman, provokes a bold pattern of communal response to the revelations which, by the authority of science, he is able to make; and the local community is goaded into disposing itself in attitudes of hostility round the main character. Truth lights up the whole as from a central pendant fitting, a naked lamp lowered into the dark places of society, making a composition in strong light and shade. Each individual is the incarnation of the principles he professes, or lack of them; attitudes are adopted and persisted in, word and deed are concerted, and there is plain speaking. In *Rosmersholm* on the other hand, truth is an equivocal thing, being no more than what anybody at any particular time believes to be the case; it is a matter of partly knowing, or not knowing any better; there is no real laying bare of fact but rather a submission of possibilities, no establishment of what in reality was so, but an appeal to plausibility; any authenticity can be substantiated only by stealthy and oblique methods. Things are as they seem, or as they can be made to seem, and genuine motives are buried beneath layer upon layer of self-deception and duplicity; secret shifts and subsidences are for ever taking place in the minds of those concerned, and lighting is dim and indirect and full of flickering cross-shadows, and the wool is pulled over more than one pair of eyes.

The path leading from the earlier drama to the later runs from the outspoken to the unspoken, from bluff honesty to shifty evasiveness, from the self-evident to the merely ostensible, from proclamation to dissimulation, from the ingenuous to the disingenuous, from open debate and public uproar to secret eavesdropping and private intimation, from events urged on by a live issue to events brought up short by a dead woman. By the polluted baths there is enacted a tableau, a positioning of one to many in a generally radial pattern of static relationships, with Stockmann as the hub and cynosure. Beside the millstream, on the other hand, none of the characters is central in the same way, and instead of the build-up of a linear pattern one finds a sequence of positional changes, a ballet of death in which the manoeuvres of the principals trace out a complex pattern of movement. In *An Enemy of the People* the author fashioned a vessel, a parabolic mould, into which he poured his wrath. *Rosmersholm*, however, has no such containing walls; its parts hold together rather on the analogy of particles in a complex magnetic field; they cohere not in obedience to some central solar force but rather because the resultant of all the various and varying attractions and repulsions they exert (or have exerted upon them) moves them the way it does. There is nothing at the centre except Nothing, the great void to which Brendel is finally attracted, and which draws the two anguished principals as though into the eye of a vortex. By comparison with *An Enemy of the People*, *Rosmersholm* seems to dispose over an extra dimension, and to enjoy a dynamic rather than a static existence; it differs from the earlier drama as a mobile differs from a blue-print, the one making a seemingly arbitrary but actually carefully balanced and *necessary* pattern of movement, and the other displaying all the clarity and self-assurance of something that recognizes its own dimensional limitations. By these tokens *The Wild Duck* is photographic, rather, and so ordered as to give an astonishingly successful illusion of perspective depth.

Hand in hand with these changes went an extra care in what Ibsen termed the 'individualization' of character and other 'finesses' attaching to the creation of dramatic dialogue. So, for instance, in conversation with John Paulsen some time in the early 1880s about 'the thousand and one finesses of dramatic art', he is reported to have asked whether his companion had ever considered 'how the dialogue in a play ought to have a different timbre if it was meant to be spoken in the morning from what it would be at night'. In letters written whilst engaged on revising *The Wild Duck*, he stressed that his attention was being given to the 'energetic individualization of character' and the finer formulation of the dialogue; and many years later, when replying to a young Frenchman who wanted permission to translate this play, he returned to this matter and pointed out the great demands the play makes on any translator, since 'one must be extremely familiar with the Norwegian language to be able to understand how thoroughly each separate character in the play has his own individual and idiosyncratic mode of expression'. Ibsen had always been an extremely conscientious artist, painstaking in the care that he gave the successive drafts of his work; now, and especially from *The Wild Duck* onward, he applied his massive revisionary capacity to the problem of the finer delineation of character; the separate figures are now no longer in the first instance the embodiment of general principles or attitudes, but instead personalities whose individuality and uniqueness are emphasized at every point in the drama. They cease to be object lessons, and become instead subjects of study. It is one of the chief fascinations of the draft manuscripts of these plays that they document at a number of points this process of 'individualization'.

Of the *fact* of some fundamental change in Ibsen's writing about the time of these three plays, there is general recognition, although there is not the same unanimity about where precisely to locate the turning point, nor how best to style it. Some critics have seen it as a transition from the 'social' to the 'visionary', from the 'naturalistic' to the 'symbolic', from the 'problematical' to the 'psychological'; there have been arguments in favour of calling the earlier group 'moralist' and for distinguishing *two* later phases, the 'humanist' and the 'visionary'; whilst yet another critic has argued persuasively for regarding the shift as being from a 'demonstrative' to an 'evocative' mood. It may indeed be necessary to relate the change to terms even more fundamental than these, and to see the crux as being a substantial shift in Ibsen's whole scheme of values. Writing to Theodor Caspari on 27 June 1884, Ibsen confessed that he had long since given up making general or universal demands, believing that one could not with any real justification make such blanket claims on people, and added: 'I do not believe any of us can do anything other or anything better than realize ourselves in truth and spirit.' What seemed to matter to him now were particulars rather than generalities; his attention was addressed to private dilemma rather than public abuse, to what was individual and personal rather than typical or representative. He abandoned collective indictment for singular, distinctive investigation; he became less comprehensive in his scrutiny of things, more selective, more penetrative; and with it all went an increasing impatience with the mass mind and all its works.

11

Drama and the Mind

The Lady from the Sea; Hedda Gabler; The Master Builder

Attempts to plot the direction taken by Ibsen's last twelve plays — from *Pillars of Society* in 1877 to the end of his career — began with his great Scandinavian contemporary: the literary critic, Georg Brandes. Dividing these twelve plays six and six, he designated the first group 'polemical', the second group 'psychological'. Many attempts have been made since then to find alternative definitions for the changing pattern: from the 'social' to the 'visionary', from the 'naturalistic' to the 'symbolic', from the 'moralist' to the 'humanist', from the 'demonstrative' to the 'evocative'. The three plays considered in this chapter stand seventh, eighth and ninth in this duodecimal series, and occupy a corresponding position in time: *The Lady from the Sea* was published in 1888, *Hedda Gabler* in 1890, and

The Master Builder in 1892. They clearly have much in common; and, equally clearly, much of what they do have in common represents a new departure.

Throughout his career, Ibsen was given to thinking of the individual as a battlefield, an arena within which are fought out those struggles of will and desire and ability and compulsion in all their multifarious forms. The individual as a point of intersection of forces — social, psychological, moral — is a notion that accompanied Ibsen's search for dramatic form from the very earliest days. Looking back over twenty-five years to his very first drama, *Catiline*, he wrote: 'Many things with which my later writings have been concerned — contradictions between ability and desire, or between will and circumstance, the mingled tragedy and comedy of humanity and the individual — all are already dimly foreshadowed here.' He was fascinated by those forces, within and without the individual, that sought to mould, to dominate, to determine conduct and to direct life; forces that interfered, distorted, coerced.

In the late eighteen-seventies and early eighteen-eighties, in that group of dramas beginning with *Pillars of Society*, Ibsen explored the nature of the interference practised on the individual in the name of the social proprieties, of established convention, of moral obligation, of duty. Even as late as *Rosmersholm* (1886), it is the institutionalized pressures that are emphasized: politics, organized religion, the press. But at one point in this play there is a glimpse of things to come; Rebecca betrays her real motive in coming to Rosmersholm: 'One day Mr. Kroll told me about the great influence Ulrik Brendel had once had over you, while you were still a boy,' she says to Rosmer. 'I thought I might manage to pick up again where he left off.' The domination of the *mind*, and not merely the determination of conduct, is the main preoccupation of the plays that followed.

The three plays in this group represent an attempt to explore the psychic rather than the social conflicts that beset the individual: temperamental incompatibility; the power of suggestion and the aberrations of auto-suggestion; the constraints of hypnotism and magnetism; the 'pull', the 'undertow', the fascination of the will and of the will-less; the struggle of mind with matter, and of matter with mind; the enlistment of 'helpers' and 'servants' in the fight for control of human destiny; the vulnerability of the psyche to dreams and visions; the fear of the staring eye.

In these plays, the health, happiness, liberty, and fulfilment of the individual is under threat from three directions: from the pressure of apparently impersonal and hostile psychic forces that feed on the will and sap its strength; from the schemings of those about him (or her) who seek gratification and vicarious success by subordinating him to their own private and selfish purposes; and from within the individual soul, from the frustrations, the thwarted drives, the twisted or baulked desires under which he suffers. All three types of threat to individual integrity are present and identifiable in all three of these plays, though the emphasis changes; and if *The Lady from the Sea* might be described as a study in the neurotic, then *Hedda Gabler* is a study in the demonic, and *The Master Builder* a study in the erotic.

Built into *The Lady from the Sea* like an armature, giving it strength and rigidity and bracing together its more audacious technical innovations, is a dramatic situation as carefully observed and as naturalistically contrived as anything one might find in this naturalistic age. Stripped down to this bare framework, the play lends itself to definition in the most commonsensical of terms: it is an exploration of the tensions in a household where a middle-aged widower with two growing daughters has married again, and where his second wife is so young as to be not much older than the elder of his two daughters. This situation is provided with a pre-history, the details of which are as carefully worked out and documented as one always expects of an Ibsen play. The second wife is discovered to have come from a family where there is a history of mental illness; moreover, as a lighthouse-keeper's daughter, she has lived most of her life in isolation far out by the sea, remote from people. She comes to her husband not long after an intense emotional experience: an affair with a young seaman who arrived in the district when his ship put in for repairs, but who had to flee in haste after murdering one of the ship's officers. Before he left, he had persuaded her to go through a primitive and rather mystic form of 'marriage', tying their rings together and casting them into the sea. In her new surroundings, geographical as well as domestic, she is profoundly unsettled. Her husband's children shut her out of their lives, their memories, and their secrets; and they allow their resentment of her presence to show in many ways. The elder daughter, having herself run the household for the two years following her mother's death, continues to have charge of things even after the arrival of the new wife. The latter, for her part, despite the anxious affection of her husband, feels deprived, repulsed, unfulfilled, and denied the opportunity of 'mothering' the daughters; left idle for long periods of the day, she turns to the sea for solace. (It is also hinted that the husband, despite his being the local doctor, does not always seem to have enough to do fully to occupy him.) She becomes pregnant, and with her pregnancy begins to suffer with her nerves; after her child is born, she refuses to share her husband's bed; the child dies at the age of four or five months. Once again the emotional shock is severe.

Such are the tensions inherent in the initial situation of the play. A household divided; two private worlds — one the wife's, the other the daughters' — with little direct communication, and only the husband's vain and ineffectual attempts to link the two worlds of the verandah and the summer-house, himself sometimes in one and sometimes in the other, but never really comfortable in either:

ELLIDA. This is known as *my* summer-house. Because I
　　had it made. Or rather my husband had it made
　　. . . for me.
ARNHOLM. And is there where you usually sit?
ELLIDA. Yes, there is where I usually sit during the
　　day.
ARNHOLM. With the girls, I suppose?
ELLIDA. No, the girls . . . generally keep to the
　　verandah.
ARNHOLM. And Wangel himself?
ELLIDA. Oh, my husband comes and goes. Sometimes he
　　sits by me here, and sometimes he's over with

the children.
ARNHOLM. Is it you who wants this arrangement?
ELLIDA. I think that arrangement suits all parties best.
We can talk across to each other ... whenever
we fancy we have anything to say.

Four sets of frustrations interlocked by circumstance, inter-
linked by mutual misunderstanding and distortion: Hilde, the
younger girl, secretly 'idolizing' Ellida, her stepmother, desperately longing for some real sign of affection, deprived of love,
and in her anguish taking a perverted pleasure in being a 'nasty
child'; Bolette, the elder daughter, resentful that she is being
denied her opportunities, and yearning for the chance to read
and to study, to get away from the narrow domestic confines of
her present life; Ellida, sick in mind, victim of her own distorted
vision, twisting the facts to fit her overheated fantasies, a prey
to any suggestion that might seem to confirm or feed her fears,
convinced that her marriage is no more than a commercial
bargain, that circumstances are combining to hold her prisoner
in this stale and airless place while life and its opportunities for
happiness slip by beyond recall; and Wangel, his loyalties
hopelessly divided, helplessly looking on as attitudes harden and
the situation deteriorates, easy-going, asking little more from
life than passive contentment, for too long blind to the real
causes of Ellida's distress, uncomprehendingly suffering from
the withdrawal of his wife's love, and imagining that things
might prove to have a simple, uncomplicated cure — medicine,
moving house, a talk with a girlhood friend — whilst he himself
seeks escape and solace in the bottle. Ibsen has with great
naturalistic skill contrived a situation in which the psychological
interdependence of the people in it is so tightly and intricately
drawn that only the most brutal of shock treatment, the most
intense emotional upheaval can release its hold on them —
'extreme measures', as Wangel calls them.
    This is what, in naturalistic terms, the action might be said to
be about. The characters undergo an emotional and temperamental crisis. Wangel is shocked out of his complacency to the
point where he must declare his love for his wife, his essential
esteem for her as an individual, in the most drastic way open to

him: by giving her complete liberty to decide her own destiny. She who, as long as there seemed to be any constraint upon her — of vow, of gratitude, of contractual obligation, of duty — felt an instinctive need to resist and rebel, now when the future is thrown open to her no longer feels the necessity to resist. With this comes the clearing of the blocked channels of communication; talk, and the unfeigned demonstration of affection and concern among the members of the household, is once more possible. Now comes the possibility of genuine reconciliation, of 'acclimatization'; the earlier paralysing inhibitions between man and wife, between stepmother and stepchildren, are broken down. They no longer act towards each other as the agents of mutual deprivation. They now complement each other, like the pieces of a jig-saw puzzle, previously forced together in a false pattern, and now broken and reassembled in a way that makes good sense.

In all this, a central problem for Ibsen was the technical one of how to extend and enrich the naturalistic mode, over which he had already in the past developed such mastery, to the stage where it could effectively communicate something of these irrational sides of life that now clamoured for his attention: the obscurer warring forces that do battle for the mind, the psychic abnormalities, the neuroses, the mysterious logic by which the deeper layers of the human personality are ordered, the tortuous motives, the ambivalent drives and urges and impulses with their power to hold the individual helpless in their grasp. To externalize this kind of inner drama of the mind is a problem which, today, one might regard as specially amenable to expressionistic techniques; and many have felt that to weight the drama — as Ibsen, operating even in the van of the contemporary tradition, did — with such naturalistic solidities as his stuttering odd-job man, his consumptive artist, his careworn schoolmaster, was to create extra and unnecessary difficulties. Translate the action of the play into choreographic terms, for example (as has been very successfully done), and one discovers that the central conflict in Ellida's mind is of a kind that can, using techniques akin to those of the expressionist theatre, be successfully and economically communicated without any great need of these subsidiary characters. Here is perhaps an index of how firmly, despite his

277

innovations, Ibsen was rooted in the naturalistic tradition. (This is of course not to overlook the many effective functions the subsidiary characters are made to perform, especially by the analogies they offer — the 'contractual marriage' between Arnholm and Bolette, for example, and the possessiveness of the Lyngstrand-Hilde exchange — to the central relationships.)

One answer lay, as indeed Wangel found the key to *his* problem lay, in recognizing and acknowledging the crucial role of the image — which came to represent something as potent in Wangel's existence as it was to be in Ibsen's naturalistic art. To begin with, Wangel observes Ellida's sickness without any true comprehension. He has tried to treat her condition with drugs, which even Bolette realizes can only do harm to her in the long run; he looks for homely treatments for what he takes to be an unhappy but not alarmingly serious state of affairs; he accepts her longing for the sea at its face value, and tries to make it good. It takes time for him to realize the essential gravity of the situation; and it is not until much later, after they have in fact survived the crisis, that he acknowledges her longing for the sea as a symptom of something much deeper seated: 'I'm beginning to understand you . . . little by little. You think in images . . . your mind works in visual terms. Your yearning for the sea . . . your attachment to this man, this stranger . . . These things were nothing more than an expression of your growing desire for freedom. That's all.'

That the sea meant a very great deal to Ibsen personally is clear from many of his utterances of these years. One can only speak of fascination. In this play, the sea is fashioned into an image of great structural complexity. Like the wild duck in *The Wild Duck*, it is made to serve as a point of reference for many different elements in the play. It represents those things in life that are wild and free and primitive, an elemental thing, the cradle of existence before evolution took the wrong turning by coming on to dry land; it is a shrine at which one plighted one's troth; it is a source of vitality and vigour, a link with the great world outside, a highway which in summer brought traffic to the provincial backwaters, and which in winter was shut and barred by ice; a thing beneficent even in its cruelties, as when Lyngstrand speaks of the 'good fortune' of his shipwreck, which

brought him to the study of art; but above all it stands for a
particular *kind* of force, a hypnotic attraction, mysterious,
fearful yet alluring, irresistible, something to which one yielded
in delight and dread, something into which one plunged recklessly yet gratefully.

Were this as far as the sea symbolism went, there would be no
substantial technical advance on the wild duck — a thing there
as a presence, whose essence pervades the entire play, serving as
one term of reference in a whole series of related contexts. The
important technical innovation in *The Lady from the Sea* is that
Ibsen provides for his dominant symbol a second stage: he sets
up the symbol of the sea, fills it with meaning, then personifies
it in the character of the Stranger. By this means he permits the
whole connotative complex which the sea represents to step
forth, to become articulate, to participate. At one level of
interpretation, the Stranger is of course a character, one of the
dramatis personae, possessing a past, a career, a purpose, and a
personality. At another level, however, he is a meta-symbol, a
symbol of a symbol, an embodiment of all that the sea is made
to stand for. At the end of Act III the following tense exchange
takes place:

> WANGEL [*look anxiously at her*]. Ellida! I sense . . .
> something behind all this.
> ELLIDA. There is . . . an undertow [*det dragende*].
> WANGEL. Undertow . . .?
> ELLIDA. That man is like the sea.

Two separate approaches towards an explanation of the role of
the Stranger in the play suggest themselves, both of them finding
their point of departure in naturalistic premises, yet neither of
them proving to be quite adequate when taken in isolation. The
first is that which takes the Stranger as a character *tout court*, the
motivation of whose appearance is sufficiently explained by the
details of the recorded past: Ellida's account of their association,
Lyngstrand's report of his shipmate, the occasion of the ship's
visit. The price of any explanation at this level of naturalism is
to accept a series of chance coincidences so contrived as to
destroy any sense of conviction, any claim to naturalness. The

other way is to 'explain' the Stranger simply as a figment of Ellida's overheated brain, as a hallucination. Ellida has gone through months and years of emotional stress, which have now reached their culmination; her mind responds to the implicit menace in Lyngstrand's projected piece of sculpture; her conversation with Arnholm recalls the past vividly to mind; the cold and dank and remote part of the garden in which the 'encounter' takes place provides a backcloth for the workings of her disordered brain. Her mind — as her husband anxiously points out — is immensely receptive to suggestion; she finds it only too easy to accept the truth of anything that might feed her fevered fantasy. Just as she is ready to give a distorted emphasis to the facts of her marriage, so she could be under severe mental pressure to exaggerate or invent evidence to augment her account of the Stranger, even if only as a kind of defence — the invention of a world peculiar to herself as an answer to the world of the family from which she is excluded. 'I also live a kind of life,' she says to Arnholm, 'from which the others are excluded.' As a dream will embrace and transmute and re-order by its own inherent logic the events of past experience, so (it might be suggested) her imagination creates the sequence of events by the carp pond. By these tokens, she and Wangel and the Stranger might be supposed to be arguing out a dialogue which in essence goes on in Ellida's mind. It might be claimed, for example, that to yield to the Stranger represented suicide by drowning, as a terribly hypnotic solution to the unbearable pressures of her marriage, an answer to her exclusion from their own shared and comfortable world.

To seek an explanation here, however, is to preserve one kind of commonsense explanation of the events at the expense of destroying the consistent naturalism of the action; the scenes with the Stranger can then only be assumed to belong to a different order of theatrical reality from the rest of the play. If we seek too narrowly for strict consistency — either on a purely commonsense plane or on the plane of fantasy — there is much that seems contrived, implausible, illogical, unconvincing. Archer's early dissatisfaction with the ending of the play has been echoed many times since: 'The conclusion of the play . . . depends entirely on a change in Wangel's mental attitude, *of which we have no proof whatever* beyond his bare assertion . . . Too much is made to hang upon a verbally announced conversion. The poet ought to have invented some material — or, at the very least, some impressively symbolic — proof of Wangel's change of heart.' One is led towards the possibility that the play has perhaps deliberately set out to bring together — into a new compound of naturalism — these two separate elements; the naturalism of historical causality, the chain of events of the past years and months, is fused with the psycho-medical naturalism that seeks to explain everything clinically by reference to Ellida's disordered mind. The Stranger is the best exemplification of this: he is not a merely incorporeal vision, yet his presence is possible only because Ellida realizes him, causes him to materialize, *summons* him *à la* Solness; but then neither is he merely the lover returned, because what he *is* is so much less significant than what he stands for. (It is not without bearing on this that whereas Ellida keeps insisting that she is betrothed to the Stranger, the Stranger's own words were apparently that they were both 'wedded to the sea'.) One recalls Ibsen's very firm instructions to the management of that Berlin theatre which tried to give this character a precision of identity he was not meant to have: ' . . I must object firmly to any reference on the playbills to "Ein Seemann" or "Ein fremder Seemann" or "Ein Steuermann". In fact he is none of these things . . . Nobody is to know who he is or what he is actually called. Precisely this uncertainty is the main thing in the method I have adopted for this occasion.' It is in the nature of this creation that he should not be too explicit, too sharp-edged, too concrete; the ambiguity at this level too should be apparent. As a device it might perhaps be compared with, on the one hand, the Boyg in *Peer Gynt*, with which it shares some of the same shadowy indistinctness, the same role of 'realized presence'; and, on the other hand, with Beata in *Rosmersholm* — a presence, though in her case unrealized and insubstantial, working comparably on the main characters and focusing the conflict. (One is incidentally reminded, by the reference to *Rosmersholm*, of some of the parallels between the situation in *The Lady from the Sea* and certain of the earlier schemes and drafts of *Rosmersholm*, particularly the plan for a widower with two daughters, one of them 'near to finding the inactivity and loneliness too much for her; considerable talent without finding any outlet for it'; and the other, younger, one with 'observant dawning passions'). What the crisis leaves Ellida with is a new concept of freedom. Earlier, in what she could only see as the forced detention of her marriage, freedom could only mean escape, rebellion against constraint. When the doors are thrown wide, however, the need to assert this kind of freedom disappears; given nothing to rebel against, rebellion no longer has any meaning. It is the turn of the tide. Freedom, she then sees, is synonymous with the willing acceptance of circumstance. Her final decision is, in the Kantian sense, a sublime act; and her 'freedom with responsibility' a kind of popular paraphrase of the Categorical Imperative. Schiller might well have called her 'eine schöne Seele'.

In only one respect, when *Hedda Gabler*[1] was first published and played, did the play come up to expectation; and that was in those circles in many different parts of Europe where, on the evidence of *A Doll's House*, *Ghosts*, and *Rosmersholm*, it had already been decided that Ibsen was no more than a nasty old man. Here, in *Hedda Gabler*, such people felt they found fullest confirmation. After the London first night the *Daily Telegraph* explained in luscious detail how it had been like a visit to a morgue: 'There they all were, false men, wicked women, deceitful friends, sensualists, egotists, piled up in a heap behind the screen of glass . . . ' Other critics, if less imaginative, were — as William Archer put it — no less denunciatory. The *Saturday Review*, while admitting that Ibsen's new play was free from the mess and nastiness of *Ghosts*, free from the crack-brained maunderings of *Rosmersholm*, and free from the fantastic short-sighted folly of *A Doll's House*, nevertheless fulminated against the 'insidious nastiness of these photographic studies of vice and morbidity', and asked: 'Can any human being feel happier or better from a contemplation of the two harlots at heart who do duty in *Hedda Gabler*?' Robert Buchanan announced that '. . . For sheer unadulterated stupidity, for inherent meanness and vulgarity, for pretentious triviality . . . no Bostonian novel or London penny novelette has surpassed

Hedda Gabler.' The *Pictorial World*, describing the play as 'a hideous nightmare of pessimism', went on: 'The play is simply a bad escape of moral sewage-gas . . . Hedda's soul is a-crawl with the foulest passions of humanity.'

Altogether more serious than this quite comic abuse, however, was the widespread puzzlement and downright disappointment, even among those critics who admired Ibsen and showed a proper understanding of his drama. This ran contrary to all expectations. Where were the famous exposures of folly, where the indications of reform, where the exhortations to truth or liberty or freedom with responsibility? People had come to expect of Ibsen's plays some exploration of the more problematic areas of life, even though it was admitted that simple unambiguous solutions were not to be found there. Now they felt they had been offered a piece of admittedly brilliant but essentially pointless dramatic portraiture: there seemed to be no hint of the play's having any significance outside its own fictive world. Its meaning seemed to stop short at the final curtain; and they wondered uneasily whether perhaps Ibsen was not making fools of his audience with Brack's last words: 'But, good God Almighty . . . people don't do such things.' This seemed to be altogether too near the bone.

Among the play's London critics, Henry James pronounced the word that best defined the reaction of Ibsen's admirers: they felt, he said, 'snubbed'. He himself — a great admirer of Ibsen, as well as of the actress who was currently playing Hedda — could find little more to say on the occasion of its first London performance than that it exercised the mind: 'The play, on perusal, left one comparatively muddled and mystified, but — in one's intellectual sympathy — snubbed. Acted, it leads that sympathy over the straightest of roads with all the exhilaration of a superior pace. Much more, I confess, one doesn't get from it; but an hour of refreshing exercise is a reward in itself.' Praise could hardly have been fainter.

Contemporary opinion largely agreed with James. It was accepted that *Hedda Gabler* must be regarded primarily as a character drama, a psychological study of a bored, upper-class beauty who lives a particularly worthless life and dies a mean and worthless death. In England, two of the most influential

Ibsen critics of the day, Edmund Gosse and William Archer, both formed this particular view, and continued for many years after to hold it: 'I am wholly in agreement with Mr. Archer,' Gosse wrote in his biography of Ibsen in 1907, 'when he says that he finds it impossible to extract any sort of general idea for *Hedda Gabler*, or to accept it as a satire on any condition of society. Hedda is an individual, not a type, and it was as an individual that she interested Ibsen.' In this he echoes Henry James:

> Ibsen is various, and *Hedda Gabler* is probably an ironical pleasantry, the artistic exercise of a mind saturated with the vision of human infirmities; saturated above all, with a sense of the infinitude, for all its moral savour, of *character*, finding that an endless romance and a perpetual challenge . . . . We are free to imagine that in this case Dr. Ibsen chose one of the last subjects that an expert might have been expected to choose, for the harmless pleasure of feeling and of showing that he was in possession of a method that could make up for its deficiencies.
>
> The demonstration is complete and triumphant, but it does not conceal from us — on the contrary — that his drama is essentially that supposedly undramatic thing, the picture, not of an action but of a condition. It is the portrait of a nature, the story of . . . an état d'âme, and of a state of nerves as well as of soul, a state of temper, of health, of chagrin, of despair. *Hedda Gabler* is in short, the study of an exasperated woman . . . . We receive Hedda ripe for her catastrophe, and if we ask for antecedents and explanations we must simply find them in her character. Her motives are just her passions. What the four acts show us is these motives and that character — complicated, strange, irreconcilable, infernal — playing themselves out.[2]

It is a reading of the play still widely canvassed today, and seemingly still of real utility as an aid to understanding. As a recent distinguished Ibsen critic has put it: 'Hedda . . . is a study in a vacuum. Every speech in the play is directed towards the main purpose, the revelation of Hedda's character . . . . As . . . the centre of the play is not a problem but a personality, there is less emphasis on the story — on the links of cause and effect.'[3] The other characters can then only strike us as comparatively unimportant, since to set up any strong character against Hedda would be to disrupt the play: 'Jørgen the painful pedant, Løvborg the debased Dionysus, and Brack the suave bureaucrat, are equally unpleasant and unimportant, and the two minor women's parts are only "feeds".' They are there to display Hedda; beyond this they can have no particular significance.

The assumption behind this interpretation is implicit in much of the criticism which the play has attracted, both for and against. Immediately following publication, it was condemned for the 'unreality', the 'abnormality', the 'inconsistency' of the main character; and just as people felt justified in dismissing the play because by naturalistic premises Hedda seemed implausible, others felt they were somehow defending the play's central essence by bravely insisting — as one did — that he faced a Hedda across the dining table at home every night of his life. And when, later, Freud's map of the psychopathology of everyday life seemed triumphantly to justify a great deal of Ibsen's psychological percipience, this was accepted as further reinforcement for this reading of the play. Nevertheless, to leave it at this seems to leave the play curiously suspended, strangely unmotivated, in Ibsen's *oeuvre*.

Not that one seeks to deny that Hedda's position among the characters is central; nor that one wishes to diminish the degree there of what Ibsen was in the habit of calling 'individualization' of character. Though (it might be said in parenthesis) such 'individualization' seems quite unrelated to anything that might be called eloquence; indeed, in a sense, Hedda must surely be one of the least eloquent heroines in the whole of the world's dramatic literature. This was something that struck Edmund Gosse when he reviewed the play on its first appearance: 'I will dare to say that I think in this instance Ibsen has gone perilously far in his desire for rapid and concise expression. The stichomythia of the Greek and French tragedians was lengthy in comparison with this unceasing display of hissing conversational fireworks, fragments of sentences without verbs, clauses that come to nothing, adverbial exclamations and cryptic interrogations. It would add, I cannot but think, to the lucidity of the play if some one character were permitted occasionally to express himself at moderate length.' The average length of Hedda's speeches — somebody seems to have worked it out — is a line and half; very often her speeches consist of no more than a few words; her longest utterance is about six lines. Superficial examination might suggest that there is almost nothing here but drab everyday speech, something which might explain why her few excursions into imagery — like the bits about 'vine leaves in his hair' — have so startling an impact.

Clearly this is one of Ibsen's more remarkable achievements: his success in creating such an extraordinary — and such an extraordinarily subtly defined — creature as this with such very ordinary-seeming linguistic material. A sample analysis of the dialogue of *Hedda Gabler*[4], in an attempt to show how complex — despite all — its allusive texture is, reveals that the audience is continually being given slight indications, hints and suggestions that betray a state of mind or a habit of thought, many of them so slight that it is almost impossible to separate them out — to say nothing of reproducing them adequately in translation. Yet the price paid for this subtlety is great; for the strain on the audience then becomes almost intolerable. No sooner are suspicions aroused that none of the casualness is strictly casual, that none of the details are essentially trivial, than the search for significance in *all* things is on. One inclines to agree that every detail is then, like Hedda herself, pregnant with consequence; and to agree also that Ibsen's realism is then seen to be dependent for its effect on a suspense that is theatrical in the extreme.

But what, then, if the *character* of Hedda, highly 'individualized' though she might be, is not the real business of the play, not the thing it is chiefly concerned to communicate? A provisional and rather bleak suggestion is that one regards the central character of Hedda not as an end but as a means — a means serving a much more general and characteristically Ibsenist idea. And that consequently the other characters in the play, far from being merely 'feeds' or foils to Hedda, are themselves essential and integral to a full articulation of the statement the play is concerned to make.

There is, in among the draft material of the play, a clear hint of where to look for this 'general idea', the kind of idea which Gosse and Archer and others have found it impossible to detect. The draft material in this instance is very extensive, including a complete draft version of the play, a number of revisions to that draft, together with two notebooks of notes and jottings and trial dialogue. One of the entries in the notebooks (as others before have remarked) leaps at once to the eye; it reads: 'The demonic thing about Hedda is that she wants to exert an influence over another person.' This immediately suggests a rather different way possibly of defining what the play is 'about'. Instead of drawing a portrait, the study of a bored and frustrated and mischievous society beauty, the play documents a campaign. When Hedda discovers early in the play that Thea Elvsted, a silly girl whom she used to despise at school, has been a great constructive influence in the life of Eilert Løvborg, this dissipated, unstable, but highly talented young man, she decides to break Thea's hold and exert the influence herself. If the focal point of the play is here, it then invites consideration not as the record of an 'état d'âme', nor as 'a character study in a vacuum', but rather as the dramatic account of certain proceedings: the history of Hedda's bid for control of Løvborg, of the savagery of her failure, and of its consequences.

Pause in the analysis at this point, and it is possible to recognize in this an aspect of existence that had always roused Ibsen to fury: any interference of this order in other people's lives, any tampering with their liberties or their efforts at self-realization, particularly if done under the guise of altruism or in the name of righteousness, at once drew his anger. Hedda's interference is *personal*, of course; whereas in earlier plays the interference was often impersonal, social, institutional: the pressures of convention, the compulsion to do the done thing, the fear of what people will think, the often inauthentic calls of duty or loyalty or of outdated moral obligation. Though this is not to say that earlier examples of personal interference do not spring readily to mind: Gregers Werle gets his thrill from playing Fate to Hjalmar, for example, very much as Hedda gets hers from playing Destiny to Løvborg; and Rebecca's designs on Rosmer are comparable. One important aspect needs emphasis, however: Hedda may well be seen to function as an agent of interference, but whereas so often in Ibsen this interference is exercised in the name of Christianity, it is exercised in Hedda's case (as perhaps it was also in the case of Rebecca) in the name of Dionysus. Whereas Ibsen's clergymen, his Rørlunds and his Pastor Manderses and their like-minded lay colleagues like Torvald Helmer or Kroll stand by ready to direct their fellows into orgies of self-denial, Hedda is a pagan priestess, driven by a vision of Dionysian beauty, whispering of vine-leaves in the hair and the thrill of beautiful death. The sources of their interfering zeal are very different, the relentlessness of it is common.

This is of course not the only element in what is always admitted to be a very complex pattern of behaviour on the part of Hedda: this baleful influence upon the life of Løvborg. A very similar configuration can also be seen in her relationship with her husband, Tesman; only that in his case one can see how, once the domination is asserted and assured, there is only contempt for the victim. Possible even more interesting than this is the threat she represents to herself. In Ibsen, the Self in its dealing with others is commonly exposed to a double hazard: one from without, the other from within. There is not only the danger of imposed domination from without; there is also the inner threat to the Self that comes from being dependent, of having to live by some essentially humiliating reliance on others, and of having to look to them to provide what the individual Self should supply from within, but cannot. Of the characters who populate Ibsen's plays, many are of this kind — the most immediate example being Hjalmar Ekdal in *The Wild Duck*, who requires his 'life-lie' for his very existence, who looks to others to provide him with regular doses of illusion to sustain his life.

Dependence of a different but recognizably Ibsenist kind is also a feature of that other typical creation: Earl Skule in *The Pretenders*. This, one of Ibsen's earlier works (1864), is a drama which sets out to examine these very factors of inner qualification and disqualification, something which makes of it much more than a simple drama of doubt and faith, which is how it is often described. The deeper implications of *this* drama are not with faith alone, but with the faith that is given to faith; not with doubt alone, but with the doubt that bears on doubt; not with right alone, but with the right to have any rights. Skule is inherently disqualified, and is driven by his own sense of inadequacy to live off others, to try to annex the ideas or the faith of others to make up the deficiencies of his own life.

Of even greater fascination is to observe Ibsen probing the kind of situation that emerges when these two related phenomena coalesce: when these two threats to independent and authentic Selfhood combine to assault the one individual, when the urge to dominate and the necessity to depend are simply two facets of the same thing. This is what it is tempting to select as the main characteristic of the Hedda syndrome. The demonic in Hedda's character — one reminds oneself of Ibsen's jotted note — is that she wants to control another's destiny. But her mischief is not mere villainy; in the last analysis, she does it in an effort to make good some inner deficiency in her own self, to give a kind of borrowed significance to her own life, or to achieve something she was by herself incapable of achieving.

Indeed, it is here that a lot of what used to be thought of as Ibsen's propaganda for Women's Rights now falls into a more meaningful perspective. In a world dominated by the male (which was how Ibsen saw his own age), Woman was often unnaturally deprived by social convention of an adequate opportunity to realize herself; the most she could hope to do, very often, was to make her achievements through the intermediacy, or in the company, of some man. This is the situation that faces Rebecca West, whose kinship with Hedda has already been remarked on above. Her attempts to dominate are very largely a consequence of her own fundamental social dependence: she reaches into other people's lives with a murderous hand, claiming to clear an opportunity for Rosmer to act in freedom, but secretly seeking to control the course of Rosmer's life and in so doing to fill the void in her existence. (It is interesting that in the early draft of *Hedda*, the chief character was originally called Rømer, which was a form of name used in the earlier drafts of *Rosmersholm*.) It is doubtless also in some context of this kind that discussion of the part in Ibsen's life and in the composition of these dramas played by Emilie Bardach should surely take place.

But the closest kinship is probably with Hjørdis, the Viking heroine in *The Vikings at Helgeland;* except that Hedda is, may one say, de-heroized. One tends to think of Hjørdis as possessing a fierce will of her own, yet it is rather the reverse that is true: she is the one possessed. She is (and Hedda is not unlike her in this) dominated by the idea of domination, seeing everything in terms of power and influence: power of will, strength of courage, physical prowess. Even her womanly appeal takes stamp from it; she deliberately translates the act of courtship into an ordeal of strength, not unlike the way in which Hedda exults at the thought of a conflict between scholars. Hjørdis's image of marriage to Sigurd is almost exclusively that of a triumphant alliance of power. Her love, seeking as it does its consummation not in happiness but in greatness, has almost nothing to do with affection, and everything to do with ambition. And her contempt for the gentle Dagny, whose influence over Sigurd she so resents, is a clear anticipation of Hedda's contempt for Thea.

This polarity of domination and dependence, this living upon others, does not in the play stop at the character of Hedda. Indeed, it has been persuasively suggested that in some form or another it pervades the whole action of the play and informs the conduct of many of the other characters.[5] The urge to control and exploit others is never far below the surface of any of their motives. The significance of the part played by these other characters is then seen to be not the negative one of acting as foils to Hedda, but the positive one of functioning as essential elements in the fuller articulation of a very richly developed dramatic statement. The most blatant, and yet in one sense the most honest, example of this is the behaviour of Brack. 'His passion in life', it has been said by Eva Le Gallienne, 'is discovering other people's secrets; this gives him a sense of power. He will go to infinite trouble, to any lengths, to be the one who knows . . . He is obviously a sensualist . . . but one has the feeling that . . . his sensuality has become perverted, impotent . . . and now finds an outlet in watching others, in spying on their lives, on their emotions, in worming his way into the heart of their mysteries, in manoeuvring himself into a position of control over their fate.'[6] (This is, incidentally, a description that one could apply almost without modification to that other impotent sensualist in Ibsen, Bishop Nikolas in *The Pretenders*.) Brack tries to win sexual domination over Hedda, ruthlessly, by blackmailing methods; the one saving thing is that he at least does not pretend he is moved by altruism.

Thea Elvsted is Hedda's rival at her own game. True, she appears genuinely convinced of the altruism of her motives in seeking to help Løvborg; and one might also argue that in the past Løvborg has derived positive benefit from her attentions. But it does not escape notice that she abandons husband and stepchildren with almost indecent haste to run after Løvborg; and that when Løvborg himself is beyond her attentions, she very promptly finds a substitute in Tesman himself, Hedda's husband. If Hedda can take away her man, she can take Hedda's.

What of Løvborg? Is he simply the victim of the interference of others? Not entirely, if we attend again to Ibsen's notes. Here the emphasis once more is on control and on the Self: 'The despairing thing about [Løvborg] is that he wants to control the world, but cannot control himself.' The relevance to the present argument — the interplay of domination and dependence — could hardly be more apposite. In the case of Tesman, the thing is given a delightful academic twist. Like Earl Skule who takes over the 'kingly thought' of his opponent, Tesman takes possession of the manuscripts of his rival: an act of seemingly benevolent usurpation. Yet how devastatingly Tesman betrays himself when, as he and Thea settle down to arrange Løvborg's surviving papers, he cries gleefully: 'This business of getting another man's papers in order — this is exactly in my line.' The words profess altruism; but they are born of a profound sense of inadequacy. Even Aunt Julle is not exempt; however saintly she may wish to appear, she too is not altogether free of the suspicion of living by this now recognizable compound of domination and dependence: no sooner has she been deprived of the opportunity of looking after her nephew and her ailing sister than her altruism reaches out after somebody else to make beholden to her, announcing that 'there's always some poor invalid or other who needs a bit of care and attention, unfortunately'.

Everywhere one finds a complex interrelationship between

domination and dependence, the inauthenticities of an individual's search for self-fulfilment at another's expense, the frustrations of an impotent's will to power. It is in the generality of this idea that one must surely seek the meaning of the particularity that is Hedda's character. When one looks for 'antecedents and explanations' of what happens in the play, it is not sufficient to rummage in some extraordinary rag-bag of qualities called 'Hedda's character'. But is it equally unsatisfactory to think of the particular, i.e. Hedda's character and fate, as merely *exemplifying* some general idea. Rather one must think of the two things as being fused and compounded into an elaborately developed dramatic image, the kind of thing Goethe perhaps had in mind when he contemplated the nature of poetry: 'There is a big difference between the poet seeking the particular for the general, and recognizing the general in the particular. From the former arises allegory, in which the particular serves only to exemplify the general. The latter is, however, the true nature of poetry; it expresses a particular without thinking of the general or referring to it. He who then seizes upon this particular, acquires along with it the general without — or only later — being aware of it.'

Familiar and recognizable now in many of its features, the world of *Hedda Gabler* is a thing of characteristically Ibsenist construction, populated by recognizable Ibsenist creatures: not a loose assemblage of characters that *are*, but a tightly woven mesh of things done or intended, a shifting pattern of event, a series of encounters and conflicts and defeats in a world where life is a relentless living on or living off others. It is an extraordinarily predatory world, a world of wolves, of parasites, of vampires even. Merely to describe the events of the play as strange or complicated or irreconcilable, and to ascribe the oddity to the inexplicable character of Hedda herself, is no explanation at all — or at least not the one that commends itself to anybody familiar with the rest of Ibsen's precisely drawn and rigorously integrated imaginative world.

The complexities of structure in *The Master Builder* are forbidding. Motives turn back in on themselves; the line between the real and the imagined is broken and discontinuous; the symbolism is multi-dimensional; the pattern of tensions labyrinthine. 'I somehow . . . enjoy the mortification of letting Aline do me an injustice,' Solness says at one point to Dr. Herdal by way of explanation of his conduct; and the double twist implicit in this remark is characteristic of the drama in a great many of its aspects.

Somewhere very close to the heart of the drama is the concept of potency. The possession, the lack, the loss of it, the search for it, the submission to it, the stimulation of it, the wonder at it — all contribute to the composition of the play. These things also function at three distinct but overlapping and interrelated levels: artistic potency; sexual potency; and what one might variously call personal potency, volitional potency, or charisma. Because they are quick to take colour from each other, to run into each other, they present a blend of a very subtle kind; because they are so tightly interwoven, one unpicks the weave only at the peril of destroying the pattern. But here and there the texture of the play shows a momentary emphasis on one or the other element, which when pieced together permits an analysis of at least an approximate kind.

Sexual images, indications of potency and impotence, repeatedly obtrude. Solness's career, we learn, has been that of a man who in his past has erected many tall towers, the last time ten years ago at Lysanger. Between that time and the present, however, towers have played no part in his life. Moreover, on that last occasion at Lysanger, there had been a kind of consummation rare in his career; he had climbed to the very top, had reached the heights, and as he stood there a teenage girl had heard harps in the air and cried out in ecstasy; he had (she tells him) put his arms about her, and bent her backwards and kissed her many many times. Now, ten years later, she seeks him out and tries to make him do again what he did then. Her visit coincides with his building another tall tower — the first, it appears, since that earlier occasion at Lysanger, and attached to a house containing three newly-built nurseries, though there are no children 'and never will be'. Why? 'Haven't you ever noticed, Hilde,' says Solness, 'how seductive, how inviting . . . the impossible is?' They talk together, and their talk is of abduction

293

by trolls and vikings, of the thrill of taking women and of being taken, of the ways of birds of prey, and of the pleasures that follow from having a 'robust conscience'. They speak of building together 'quite the loveliest thing in all the world . . . Castles in the air'. When his courage fails, she taunts him with the idea that before they had got halfway his mind would reel. Then:

> HILDE. Let me see you standing on high again!
> SOLNESS [*sadly*]. Oh, Hilde . . . I can't do a thing like that every day.
> HILDE [*passionately*]. I want you to! [*Pleadingly*]. Just once more, master builder! Do the *impossible* once more!

As he makes the ascent and reaches the top, she again knows the thrill, again cries out in delight, again hears harps in the air. But the ascent proves too much for him; he falls, and in falling re-echoes the excitement of her own recurrent dream of falling. There has been a kind of possession: 'My . . . my . . . master builder !' is her last cry of wild intensity.

The tensions between youth and age enunciated here on the sexual plane reappear also in the emphasis placed throughout on the decline of artistic or creative potency. The situation at the opening of the play reveals a measure of creative impotence that contrasts greatly with Solness's reputation as a prolific and successful master builder. The grand designs, the churches and towering spires of the past have yielded to humble domestic dwellings; and the desire to do even this seems to be on the point of drying up altogether. Such work as is done in his office is by the efforts of two men, father and son, whom Solness pitilessly exploits. The decline of creativity with age, and even more urgently the threat to his authority from youth are ever-present elements in his private torment. He waits in terror for the day youth will come beating on his door, crying 'Get out of the way!' He is conscious of draining the energies of others and applying them to his own purposes; he is secretly filled with a sense of his own inadequacy, though he tries hard to conceal it; and with this growing awareness of the realities of the present, he sees even more clearly the way he has used, exploited, misapplied others in the past, especially his wife Aline. He torments himself with the reproach that his own creative life has been based on the destruction of Aline's; that her vocation, her 'talent for building children's souls', lay like a charred heap of ashes, and all in order that his own career could go marching on. His kind of creativity seems to demand the lives of others to feed on; imposes the severest sacrifices on others; leaves a trail of victims. And he fears a terrible retribution.

In all this, however, his personal magnetism, the potency of his will, seems undiminished. As in the past, when he willed the fire and it came, when he willed Kaja and she came, so he appears to will Hilde and she comes — though in most things that concern the relations between Hilde and Solness, reality and imagination, 'Wahrheit' and 'Dichtung' are deliberately confused. That encounter at Lysanger ten years ago — did it 'really' happen? Or did Hilde imagine it? Or did Solness desire it, *will* it?

> SOLNESS . . . All this you've just told me — it must be something you've dreamt. . . . Or, wait a moment! There's more in this than meets the eye, I tell you. . . .I must have *thought* it all. I must have willed it . . . wished it . . . desired it. And then . . . Mightn't that be the explanation? [HILDE *remains silent,* SOLNESS *speaks impatiently*]. All right, damn it . . . ! So I *did* do it then!
>
> HILDE . . . So you admit it?
>
> SOLNESS . . . Yes, anything you like.

Solness's world is — in a limited sense, admittedly — Schopenhauerian; with him the world becomes 'Wille und Vorstellung', will and idea. The kind of will he possesses is the prerogative of an élite; it is effective in its powers of procurement, but is in itself essentially sterile and ultimately destructive both of the exploiter and the exploited. 'Don't you believe,' Solness asks Hilde, 'that you find some people have been singled out, specially chosen, gifted with the power and the ability to *want* something, to desire something . . . so insistently . . . and so ruthlessly . . . they inevitably get it in the end?' But these great desires can only be achieved through the aid of 'helpers and servants', never *alone*, never through their own individual efforts. And the wounds left can never heal; they burn eternally.

Brovik's joyless death is indicative of the fate Solness's victims can expect; he dies embittered, unfulfilled, despairing, deprived of the few words of human comfort from Solness that would have eased his last moments. More terrifying even than this is the death-in-life represented by Aline's existence — an existence from which love has been cut away, and the wound cauterized by fire; an existence eaten away by remorse for something she has no need whatever to reproach herself for. She lives a withdrawn, dutiful, drab, yet anxious life, with three empty nurseries in a cheerless house, finding hidden menace in every move, hidden meaning in the most innocent remark, and bemoaning not the death of her children but the destruction of her dolls, not the loss of life, but the loss of possessions. Her life and Solness's are together a chronicle of mutual repulsion within a confining framework of self-imposed duty and imagined culpability. 'Have you noticed, Hilde,' says Solness, 'that as soon as I come she goes?' To which Hilde replies: 'I have noticed that your coming *makes* her go.' The fetters that bind them to their bleak, cheerless existence seem indissoluble — except, as the play demonstrates, by death.

Solness cries out in anguish: 'Here I am, chained alive to this dead woman. Me . . . a man who *cannot* live a joyless life.' Here is the real measure of the situation from which Solness is tempted to seek release — release, upon the desire for which Hilde so wantonly and urgently and ruthlessly plays. Until, that is, the full pathos of Aline's position is borne in on her; only then does she hesitate in her purpose. The joyless, doom-laden, gloom-ridden nature of the Solnesses' marriage is terrifyingly communicated; yet it is made clear that the terror of it for the people concerned derives less from the actual character of the events themselves than from the construction placed on these events by those who experienced them. 'Schein', the way things seem to them, and not 'Sein', the way things are, is what now determines their lives. Both Solness and his wife declare themselves responsible for the crippling disaster in their lives: the burning of the house, and the death of the children. Yet in each case the guilt is an imagined, a fabricated one; and the assertion, to the other partner, quite inexplicable. When Mrs. Solness reproaches herself, insists on what she feels is *her* guilt because at a time of crisis she claims to have failed her husband, he is both astounded and irritated: 'Forgive *you!*' he says, in exasperation and bewilderment. And when, later in the same poignant scene, Solness confesses himself 'weighed down by a great crushing sense of guilt', Aline can only think he has taken leave of his senses. This is only one of innumerable examples of a form of tension permeating the entire play and giving it much of its characteristic quality: that between the establishable reality of events, what one might take to be 'actually the case', and the partial or defective or distorted view of this reality as seen by the individual characters.

The mental torment of Solness is thus seen to be composed of elements menacingly familiar from Ibsen's previous work. Duty, obligations, remorse, the wish somehow to *expiate* — these are the things that hold Solness to his loveless marriage; fear, a sense of his own inadequacy, a hint of his own failing powers, drive him to subterfuge and aggression in defence of his position; a hope of freedom, the chance of self-fulfilment, and the promise of love form a torment of suppressed desire. The personality of Hilde presses sorely on all these points. She speaks to him of the advantages of having a 'robust conscience', of the heathen courage that defies convention; she urges him to demonstrations of defiance, to acts of self-assertion; and she holds out the promise of an escape to happiness and warm affection. She is his 'princess', in whose honour he will create a kingdom, and who in return will sustain him by her admiration; she is his 'bird of prey', the embodiment of the confident Nietzschean amorality of the wild animal, 'thrilled' by life's encounters; yet she also represents the menace of youth, an agent of that impending destruction of which Solness speaks in fear only moments before she presents herself in his house.

In the haunting exchanges between them which make up so much of the play, Hilde reveals herself as an extraordinarily Ibsenist creation. Like the Hilde Wangel of *The Lady from the Sea* she is thrilled and excited by any hint of the encroachment of death upon life; like Hedda she longs to serve as the inspiration to achievement; and like Rebecca West she is (initially, at least) ruthless in exploiting the sexual situation in pursuit of her objectives. But although the challenge and the response are in the first instance sexual, the series represented by the characters Solness-Kaja-Ragnar-Brovik shows how easily in this world modulations and transpositions are made, and how economically and effectively domination is passed on through a network of personal relationships: from its origins in Solness, sexual power over Kaja is transformed at the second stage into domination over Ragnar (the defeat of youth), which then by a further twist serves to enslave Old Brovik, his one-time professional rival. Perhaps one must suppose that vaguely in Solness's mind is the hope of some similar threefold achievement emerging from his encounter with Hilde: of reasserting his own potency of spirit, of thus silencing the taunts of the younger generation, and ultimately of completely transforming and revitalizing his own domestic happiness. How utterly different, however, from the Solness-Kaja relationship that between Solness and Hilde proves to be, is perhaps one way of saying what the play is about.

Inevitably, the question is debated: how far is Solness the artist's self-portrait? Despite the considerable disparity in age between Ibsen (who was sixty-four when *The Master Builder* was published) and Solness, a number of parallels suggest themselves. There are many who would link the erotic content of the play with Ibsen's own encounters of these years — with Emilie Bardach, with Helene Raff, with Hildur Andersen — and who in consequence have been encouraged to speculate about the state of Ibsen's own marital relations at this time. There are those who would connect the theme of youth's threat to age with the hostility shown by writers like August Strindberg and (more particularly) Knut Hamsun. Here and there are signs that Ibsen is uneasily aware of how the insistent claims of his own dramatic art have imposed sacrifices not only on himself but on those nearest him. He is said to have compared his own 'trade' of dramatist with that of architect; which in turn has evoked the suggestion that Solness's refusal in mid-career to build any more churches and thereafter to devote himself to domestic architecture might symbolize Ibsen's abandonment of poetic drama in favour of social plays. To claim that *something* of the author's life and experience is traceable in *The Master Builder* is of course merely to state the obvious. Did not Ibsen once claim that *all* his plays were rooted in personal experience? What is significant here, as it was similarly with Goethe and *Werther*, is the author's avoidance of tragedy. Ibsen's own disengagement — and one only needs to look at his correspondence with Emilie Bardach for confirmation — was both firm enough and timely enough to assure survival.

12

Drama and
Individual Integrity

Little Eyolf; John Gabriel Borkman; When We Dead Awaken

It took time and the onset of illness to persuade Ibsen of the
inescapable finality of *When We Dead Awaken*, to bring him to
a recognition that with this 'dramatic epilogue' (as he sub-titled
it on its publication in December 1899) all was now said and
done. His first reaction, when he saw the critics reading the term
as a declaration that he was now finished with writing, was to
protest: 'What I intended . . . by "Epilogue",' he is reported to
have said, 'is merely to indicate that the play forms the epilogue
to that series of my dramas which starts with *A Doll's House* and
is now complete with *When We Dead Awaken*. This last work
belongs to those experiences I have sought to describe in the
series as a whole. It forms a unity, an entity, and it is with this
I am now finished. If after this . . . I write anything else, it will

300

all be in a completely different context, perhaps also in a different form.'

When, only a few weeks later, he notably reduced the span of authorship for which he felt this latest play properly served as 'the epilogue' — from eleven works to four — it was doubtless an index of even stronger optimism about what his pen might still be capable of. On 5 March 1900 he wrote significantly to his French translator, Moritz Prozor: 'In essence you are right when you say that the series for which the "epilogue" is the completion actually began with *The Master Builder*.' But the perspectives were soon to change. After a brief but worrying illness, in consequence of which his doctor had temporarily forbidden him to put pen to paper, Ibsen was moved to a more sombre view of his chances of ever again doing serious writing. The phrases he used at the end of April 1900 when discussing with his literary agent how this 'epilogue' could most appropriately be incorporated into the collected edition of his works dwelt on the overriding sense of finality with which he felt the play should now be read: 'Most acceptable for me would be to see an arrangement whereby *When We Dead Awaken* was taken as a concluding item into the collected works, where it organically belongs as a finale to the series.'

It is therefore with endorsement from Ibsen himself that *When We Dead Awaken* presents itself as a possibly triple culmination: to the 'series' of four plays written between 1892 and 1899; to the eleven or twelve 'contemporary plays' extending back over nearly quarter of a century; and to the totality of his life's work since the publication of his first drama in 1850.

To trace — in obedience to the first of these three recognitions — the deeper origins of *Little Eyolf* (1894), *John Gabriel Borkman* (1896), and *When We Dead Awaken* (1899) to a common inspiration which found its initial expression in *The Master Builder* is to award crucial significance to the short poem 'There they sat, those two':

> De sad der, de to, i så lunt et hus
> ved høst og i vinterdage.
> Så brændte huset. Alt ligger i grus.
> De to får i asken rage.

Chapter 12

For nede i den er et smykke gemt, —
et smykke, som aldri kan brænde.
Og leder de trofast, hænder det nemt,
at det findes af ham eller hende.

Men finder de end, de brandlidte to,
det dyre, ildfaste smykke, —
aldri hun finder sin brændte tro,
han aldri sin brændte lykke.

They sat there, those two, in so snug a house
in autumn and in winter days.
Then the house burnt. All lies in ruins.
Those two must rake in the ashes.

For down among them a jewel is hidden,
a jewel that can never burn.
And if they search diligently, it might perhaps
be found by him or her.

But even if this fire-scarred pair ever do find
that precious fireproof jewel, —
She will never find her burnt faith,
he never his burnt happiness.

Best known by Ibsen's own identification of it as 'the first piece of preliminary work for *The Master Builder*', it was precisely dated by him '16 March 1892'. Whether or not it was initially conceived as an organic component of *The Master Builder* itself is uncertain, for in the spring of 1892 Ibsen is believed to have cast aside (and possibly destroyed) the working notes and drafts of the play he was then currently engaged on, and he started anew. (His letters of these months to Hildur Andersen, then studying music in Vienna, would doubtless had shed light here had they survived.) Not in dispute, however, is that this same poem (with two small amendments) was again in the forefront of his mind in the July and August of 1894, in the period when he was deeply engrossed in the composition of *Little Eyolf*. In the draft version he was then working on, the grieving parents in Act III are faced with the anguish of adjusting to a life made desolate by the death of their son; at this juncture Alfred Allmers reads aloud to his wife Rita a poem he has written in his grief. It is 'They sat there, those two'. Alfred begins by assuming an obvious meaning: that it is about himself and Rita. She sees it very differently: as being about Alfred and his 'sister'. Name transference and overlapping identities introduce further ambiguity. And Alfred finally has to concede a complex multiple reference:

> ALLMERS . . . Did you understand that, Rita?
> RITA [*rising*]. Yes. And I also understood that you didn't write those lines about me.
> ALLMERS. Whom else . . . ?
> RITA. You wrote them about yourself and Asta.
> ALLMERS. First and foremost about little Eyolf . . .
> RITA. Oh, no, not about that little Eyolf who is lying deep deep out there . . . You wrote them about that other one. About her whom you called little Eyolf when she was a child.
> ALLMERS. Both to [*sic*] the big one and the little one. And also to you, Rita.

The poem with its ensuing dialogue tersely reinforces the recognition that central to the drama as a whole is preoccupation with shifting human relationships as, merging and dissolving, they move through the stages of superimposition and reassertion, of conflict and resolution. Nevertheless, for reasons which were obviously important for Ibsen at the time, the poem was deleted from the play in the final stages of its revision and replaced by the much longer and more circumstantial account which Alfred gives of his ordeal in the mountains when he lost his way.

As an ingredient thus active in the formative stages of both *The Master Builder* and *Little Eyolf*, yet ultimately rejected from them both, the poem nevertheless retains a special significance. In its laconic account of a man and a woman, unidentified except as 'he' and 'she', who stand in close but undefined relationship to each other in a domestic context of the widest frame of reference (the 'house'), whose lives are struck by disaster and misfortune of an elementally symbolic kind (the 'fire'), in consequence of which the man's 'happiness' and the woman's 'faith/peace' are irrevocably lost, but where something both precious and indestructible (the 'jewel'), though now missing, might just conceivably by shared and patient endeavour be repossessed, the poem articulates in severely abstracted form a preoccupation which recurs in many different forms in Ibsen's work of these years. The world of Ibsen's last plays is the creation of a mind haunted by problems of personal relations in conditions of stress, and by the way these things bear on individual happiness and faith. With the same compulsive anguish that Alfred brings to his poem — 'I had [he claims] to give expression to something which I cannot bear in silence any longer' — these dramas explore the complex interactions, the interdependencies, the shifts and dislocations, the endless conjoining and disjoining of multiple relationships which, though individually often deceptively simple and linear, combine into chains and patterns of daunting elaboration and subtlety. Each discrete relationship is discovered imposing its own peculiar imperatives, raising its own inhibitions, exerting its own special kind of attraction and compulsion. Within this containing structure of interlatticed relationships, this plexus of blood ties and family ties, of parenthood and childhood, of sex and marriage, of youth and age, the inhabitants of the Ibsenist world are subjected to close and intense scrutiny as they stumble in agonized pursuit of happiness and fulfilment.

The kinship links in these late plays — most conspicuously in *Little Eyolf* and *John Gabriel Borkman* — trace an elaborate geometry, an intricate interweaving of ties parental and filial, of sibling and other blood relationships, of affiliate and affinal connections of astonishing variety. Family and kinship obligations are seen occupying a wide band in the spectrum of 'pligt', that larger concept of duty which emerges as one of the dominant motivating forces in these later dramas, exacting from the individual — under pain of 'guilt' — the kind of conduct which convention or tradition or society's expectations impose. (How far Ibsen's preoccupation with 'in-law' relationships was prompted by the recent enlargement of his own affinal connections following his son's marriage to Bjørnson's daughter must of course remain conjectural.)

Prominent is the emphasis given to the obligations and aspirations of parenthood: the rights and duties of fatherhood, the demands and rewards of motherhood are repeatedly appealed to by characters who accord to them a distinctive importance in the business of living. For Alfred Allmers, fatherhood — if one is prepared to accept his protestations — has become the supremely defining element of his life, something with undisputed priority not only over any claims on him by his wife but also over those ambitions he cherished as a writer over the previous ten years: 'From now on it is a father to Eyolf I want to be . . . Eyolf shall achieve the consummation of the family line. And my new life's work shall be that of bringing him to that consummation.' Borkman, though almost completely indifferent to his son for many years, ultimately comes to recognize in the relationship a formidable potential, an opportunity to appeal to Erhart's filial loyalty in the battle for his own rehabilitation: 'Listen, Erhart . . .' he says as his wife and his sister-in-law exert their competing claims on his son, 'What about coming with your father, then? . . . Erhart, will you join me and help me in this new life?' Rubek for his part is served with an affiliation order from his model Irene who insistently, almost hysterically, claims the sculpture 'Resurrection Day' as their 'child' and demands of Rubek that he display a father's solicitude towards it:

IRENE [*silently and swiftly draws a thin sharp knife from her bosom, and whispers hoarsely*]. Arnold . . . have you done harm to our child?

RUBEK [*evasively*]. Harm? I don't exactly know what you would call it.

IRENE [*breathlessly*]. Tell me, what have you done to the child?

RUBEK. If you'll sit down and listen calmly to what I have to say, I'll tell you.

IRENE [*puts the knife away*]. As calmly as ever a mother can who . . .

Motherhood is awarded even greater prominence in these plays — natural motherhood, step-motherhood, foster-motherhood, adoptive motherhood, usurpative or surrogate motherhood, and of course metaphorical motherhood. Rita is as vociferous in repudiating the conventional role of mother as Gunhild is in asserting it. For Rita, motherhood means having *had* the child, not in continuing to minister to it; in her scheme of things, the child is merely an unwanted rival for her husband's affection, and her hostility and aggression mysteriously precipitate the catastrophic events. At the same time, she is also ruefully aware that her place as mother to Eyolf had long ago been usurped by her putative 'sister-in-law': 'Eyolf would never wholeheartedly give himself to me . . . Somebody stood between us . . . Asta, she possessed him. Right from the time that it happened . . . the accident.' Gunhild, in *John Gabriel Borkman*, had also been supplanted, in her case by a twin sister who took over as foster-mother to Erhart after the collapse of the family fortunes; but, in contrast to Rita, Gunhild had been stiffened in her resolve to bind her son to her: 'I alone shall be his mother.' she declares on learning of her sister's plan to adopt Erhart, 'I alone. My son's heart shall be mine — mine, and no one else's.' The force of the words is not lost upon Ella Rentheim who, only moments before, had accused Borkman of cheating her of a mother's joy and happiness: 'And of a mother's sorrows and tears, too. And that was perhaps my cruellest loss.' In *When We Dead Awaken*, Irene too is quick both to interpret and to assess her past life in terms of motherhood: the anguish of serving as 'mother' to the statue, and the pain she suffered from being deprived of real motherhood: 'I should have borne children. Many children. Real children. Not the kind that are preserved in tombs. That should have been my calling.'

The emphasis, once achieved, carries over to a range of other oblique or displaced or deviant parental relationships, which are then made to bear an important motivational burden within the drama. A surrogate mother/son relationship in *Little Eyolf* — Asta's past devotion to Eyolf — is itself reinforced by Borghejm's readiness to play surrogate father to Eyolf during Alfred's absence. A continuing influence on all the Allmers' present lives comes from the family's complex and confused past history of parenthood, legal and natural, from those emotionally intense parentless years which Alfred and Asta spent together when young, and from the fateful impact of the surviving novercal correspondence. In the Borkman household, alongside the natural mother/son relationship, there is also the past foster-mother/foster-child relationship between Ella and Erhart, as well as the proposed adoptant-mother/adoptive-son relationship which provokes Gunhild to such vigorous reaction.

A large part of the continuing fascination which the family held for Ibsen doubtless lay in its function as a natural repository of inherited characteristics. It presented an obvious focus of inquiry for exploring how certain more contingent forces — chance encounter, or friendship and marriage, or the domestic environment generally — combine with factors transmitted through the blood, down the family 'line'. Allmers's half-jesting 'We all have the same eyes' conceals a deep loyalty to the family and betrays a sense of pride in its distinctive features and characteristics, something which can prompt him to say: 'How good it is I have you, Asta . . . Rita is not a blood relation. It's not like having a sister.' In *John Gabriel Borkman* the device of making the two Rentheim sisters twins — which, if one accepts them as 'identical twins', on a mathematical analogy reduces the variables in the situation — permits a dramatically more elegant demonstration of the forces at work within the infrastructure of the family. Even Mrs. Wilton is moved to comment on the relative merits of natural motherhood and foster-motherhood, on blood relationship and non-blood relationship in the domestic context:

MRS. WILTON. I think a good foster-mother often deserves more thanks than one's real mother.
MRS. BORKMAN. Has that been your experience?
MRS. WILTON. Bless you . . . I scarcely knew my mother. But if I'd had a good foster-mother, I might not have become as . . . as badly behaved as people say I am.

Sibling relationships, together with the more distant blood ties and affinal links which radiate out from these, also function as subtle determinants of individual conduct; and there is persuasive evidence in the extant draft material to indicate not only that Ibsen gave earnest and athletic attention to these matters, but also that the alterations he introduced under this rubric were often of the most far-reaching significance, affecting the plays at their deepest levels of meaning.

It facilitates the argument at this stage to take the plays out of their chronological order and consider the (in this respect) somewhat less complicated *John Gabriel Borkman* before the fearsomely convoluted *Little Eyolf*. Ibsen's early plans for *John Gabriel Borkman* did not intend that the two sisters should be twins. In the stage directions of the draft, the unmarried sister 'is older than her sister and resembles her, with traces of past beauty.' To intensify this relationship to twinship at a formative stage in the play's composition marks a deliberate (and, one must assume, purposeful) change of intent: to introduce a modulation, in the interests of the overall balance of motivating forces within the drama, of those expectations which audience and society normally attach to the sisterly relationship. Moreover there was a further knock-on effect transmitted down to a number of the other less immediate relationships in the play: to the Ella-Borkman relation, whereby an already elaborately compounded emotional and affinal relationship — erstwhile lovers who become sister/ brother-in-law — is further complicated by the twinship nexus; and to what would otherwise have remained a simple aunt/nephew relationship between Ella and Erhart, whereby the nephew is required to relate to a 'maternal aunt' who is not a simple 'mother's sister' but the much more intense 'mother's twin sister', which when compounded with an additional element of 'foster-motherhood' yields a total relationship of formidable complexity.

The consequence for criticism of this degree of elaboration is that any attempt to analyse the motivational forces at work in these late dramas is confronted by patterns of interaction of great intricacy. Take, for example, the position of Erhart: not only is he at the climax of the drama positioned at the intersection of five different forces seeking to define his destiny — those of a dominating and hate-ridden mother, an assertive and paranoid father, a mortally sick aunt, a seductive divorcee, and the sexual compulsions of his own youth and emergent manhood — but some of these individual lines of force are also themselves (as we have seen) greatly distinctive in their nature and trace out a highly individualistic pentagon of forces.

Already before this, however, *Little Eyolf* had exceeded in audacity even such kinship complications at these by introducing the total *bouleversement*, through the revelation of past sexual transgression, of what was an apparently established, stable, and even defining relational system. And in the extended attention which he gave to modifying the relational pattern as one draft of the play succeeded another, Ibsen gave convincing evidence of the importance he attached to these factors as determinants of human conduct in the wider world.

Not unlike William and Fanny Price in *Mansfield Park* — of whose relationship it is there remarked that 'children of the same family, the same blood, with the same first associations and habits, have some means of enjoyment in their power which no subsequent connection can supply' — Alfred and Asta are powerfully drawn to each other. In the surviving draft manuscripts, however, the earliest list of characters shows Asta (at this preliminary stage somewhat confusingly called Rita) as simply 'sister' to the character who was eventually to become Alfred, and not (as in the final text) as 'half-sister'. When eventually the change was made from full-sibling to half-sibling relationship — and this may well have occurred at a quite early stage in the play's genesis, possibly even before the opening pages of the surviving drafts were written — the effect was to create plausible pre-conditions for a later fateful denial of blood relationship between Alfred and Asta, and thus to permit a profound change n the basic course of the drama. Moreover when the evidence of Asta's mother's adultery was allowed to come to light, it not only had the result of releasing Alfred and Asta from any ties of blood relationship (with all the consequences which that had for their possible future life together), but it also destroyed any remnants of family affinity between Asta and Rita, and furthermore (posthumously) destroyed Asta's 'aunthood' — though, interestingly, not her usurpative mother-hood — in respect of Eyolf.

Counterpointing this is the progressively diminishing degree of relationship between the Rat Wife and the Allmers family as the draft material took shape — changes in which can again be detected the extreme care Ibsen took to balance the various relationships one against the other. In the earliest plan, the Rat Wife is designated as *Rita's* (or, as it was at this early drafting stage, Johanne's) aunt; this was subsequently modified to make of her Eyolf's aunt (literally 'mother's sister'); and at a later stage still, this was qualified and still further reduced by Miss Varg's own comment in the draft on her situation: '. . . Just send for Aunt Ellen . . . Isn't it strange that everybody calls me Aunt Ellen? Despite the fact that I haven't any living relative — either in heaven or on earth.'

The immediate consequence of this overall revision of relationships was enormously to increase the play's power by admitting into the dramatic action the theme of incipient incest. When precisely this theme entered the play is difficult to determine on the evidence of the surviving manuscripts. Nevertheless, it is not implausible to see the play as having originally based itself on a relatively uncomplicated triangular pattern of husband, wife, and husband's sister, tracing the impact within this situation of certain stresses upon the destiny of the son. (If so, it would have quietly rehearsed the way in which *John Gabriel Borkman* operates with a triangular pattern of husband, wife, and wife's sister, and the way it too impinges on the destiny of the son.)

The progressive modifications to the structure of *Little Eyolf* following the introduction of the incest motif brought a number of new and disturbing elements. The reiterated Asta-Eyolf transferences, the reported transvestite practices of the earlier days, the association of Alfred's betrayal to Rita of these childhood secrets (as well as of Eyolf's crippling accident) with a moment of highly charged sexual passion — all these and more were relatively late additions or adjustments to the play, and must have post-dated the decision to eliminate any blood relationship between Alfred and Asta. Such factors, by their deliberate and pondered introduction, draw attention to the weight of symbolic significance which Ibsen attached to the meta-relationship between kinship obligations and sexual compulsions in the business of daily living.

Running obliquely across kinship links and casual encounters alike is the sexual nexus. To catalogue the sexual relations in these last plays — interpreting the term widely in the sense of how men and women relate to each other — is to identify a very considerable range: marital, pre-marital, and extra-marital, consummated and unconsummated, promiscuous and abstinent, invited and withheld, sensualized and sublimated, overt and suppressed, deviant and incipiently incestuous.

Immediately from the stage directions, and before any word is uttered, it is made obvious that it is the women who are destined to take the sexual initiative, and who are the most obviously endowed physically for the role. By contrast, the men — with the obvious exception of Ulfheim — are for the most part conspicuously deficient in libido. The figure of the married woman of experience and maturity, no longer in her first youth but vital and attractive and strongly motivated sexually, appears in all three plays: Rita in *Little Eyolf*, the 'good-looking woman, blond, fairly tall and shapely [*yppig*], of about thirty'; Fanny Wilton in *John Gabriel Borkman*, the 'shapely [*yppig*] and strikingly beautiful woman in her thirties, (with) generous smiling red lips, sparkling eyes, rich, dark hair'; and Maja in *When We Dead Awaken*, 'quite youthful, with a vivacious face and bright roguish eyes, though she has a slightly weary air.' Moreover, even those women on whom age or personal disaster has left a mark often still give evidence of an earlier physical appeal: Gunhild with her abundant hair and elegant but now shabby clothes; Ella with her thick wavy silver-white hair, who 'still retains some of the great and characterful beauty of her young days'; and the one-time artist's model Irene, now reduced to 'a shadow'.

Not unexpectedly, in the *mélange* of personal relationships — sexual, marital, parental, affinal — it is the women who are most immediately exposed to the claims of loyalties which are generally multiple, often competitive, frequently incompatible, and sometimes totally irreconcilable. Faced in *Little Eyolf* with the competing claims of wifehood and motherhood, Rita (as was seen above) declares herself totally for the former, and in large measure repudiates the latter; Gunhild, by contrast, is bleakly determined to be wife to Borkman in nothing but name, and seeks her entire fulfilment in a mother's relationships with Erhart. *Little Eyolf*, at one crucial moment, pivots about the choice Asta is required to make between a life as wife and helpmeet to Borghejm and a 'passionless' existence as 'sister' to Alfred. There is in all these late plays a readiness to contemplate, sometimes even to adopt, triangular relationships; and the admission in all three plays of the possibility of a *ménage à trois* as a means of resolving a tangled emotional situation is in itself quite striking. Mrs. Wilton, Frida and Erhart go off as a threesome in order that Erhart may have a sexual relationship in reserve; Rubek discusses with both Maja and Irene the possibility of the latter's moving into the household in the villa on the Taunitzer See; in *Little Eyolf* both husband and wife appeal to Asta to live her life with them, an appeal which is still further complicated by what they individually know or do not know of the consanguinity factor.

The men are much less easily moved to passion than the women. Alfred Allmers found on his first encounter with Rita that her 'consuming loveliness' filled him with 'terror'; later he was to discover that to yield to her attractions was — in a literal as well as a metaphorical sense — fraught with crippling consequences, to his child and to his own psyche. Borkman first finds sexual love a commodity easily convertible into commercial currency, but then discovers that love invaded and contaminated by shame turns to fierce hate: 'If Mrs. Borkman had not loved her husband,' Ibsen is reported to have said, 'she would have forgiven him long ago.' When Irene offered herself for cultural congress, giving herself 'with such vibrant desire, such exalted passion' to their aesthetic intercourse, serving him 'with all the throbbing blood' of her youth, Rubek held back from touching her for fear (he said) of profaning his artistic sensibilities, and called the whole thing 'an episode'.

The suppression of sexuality is seen by these men as a kind of victory, a triumph of self-control, a defeat for those darker disruptive forces which would otherwise subvert life's greater, nobler purposes: a child's upbringing, the creation of social wealth, the achievement of art. Their lives are conducted in the name of *duty* — a father's, an entrepreneur's, an artist's — which offers them a double advantage: not only does it serve as plausible justification of their apparently insensitive conduct towards the women, but it also effectively cloaks their own deeper fears and inadequacies. But the imagery which accompanies them in the plays stamps them as 'cold'. The cold numbs them, deadens them, literally kills them. Either, like Allmers, they are recognized as having 'fish's blood' in their veins; or, like Borkman, they are destroyed by the grip of an icy hand; or, like Rubek, they toil at their art in cold, damp cellars away from the warmth of the sun.

One of the defining characteristics of the men, indeed, is that they tend — as much in obedience to society's expectations as to their own proclivities — to seek fulfilment outside the everyday range of personal and domestic relationships, that arena which is in fact the only one open to the women. Borghejm, perhaps the most naïvely ambitious in this direction, is not wholly typical of the late Ibsenist hero, for he is prepared to allow a positive role in his life for a personal relationship on the domestic level. But it is significant that even though his passion for road-building stops well short of obsession, even though his ambition is more a part of the joyous 'game' of life than it is a determined sacrificial undertaking, nevertheless his natural promptings are to see the wife essentially as helpmeet, as sharer of *his* joys and *his* sorrows: ' . . . Nobody to help me in it . . . ,' he says in his unhappiness to Asta, 'Nobody. Nobody to share in the joy of it.' It is a role which Asta too would find wholly acceptable: 'Oh, if only I could be there with you! Help you in times of trouble. Share the joy of it with you . . . ' In those instances where the men find it less easy to reconcile domestic and ambitional claims, ambition usually prevails; and even where this seems to require the savage sacrifice of the love (and even the sanity) of others, there is little hesitation. Borkman's slip of the tongue, which he somewhat shamefacedly but unconvincingly corrects, betrays the scheme of relative values by which these men lead their lives: 'You know very well it was higher motives . . . well, other motives, then . . . that forced my hand,' he says to Ella Rentheim in explanation of how he came to throw her over.

The world of these plays is one that virtually disqualifies women from holding ambitions of the order of Borkman's, Rubek's, or even Allmers's. No women artists, no women writers, certainly no women tycoons are thinkable. The most they can contemplate is public achievement by proxy, through the intermediacy or agency of a man — a husband, perhaps, or a son, possibly a brother. Gunhild can only look to her son to wreak her vengeance and to achieve her reinstatement; Ella needs a man, her nephew, to prevent the disappearance of her family name. For a woman who was prepared to break with home and country and also with the prevailing moral code, it might just be possible — as with Frida — to achieve a career in which the male competition was not severe, like music. Otherwise, there is little for the women beyond a limited extension of motherhood into a more public domain, as when Rita contemplates a measure of social work by mothering the deprived village children.

With passion and ambition distributed in this fashion between the sexes, it is not unexpected to find at the heart of all three dramas a woman's humiliatingly unfulfilled sexuality. Rita, having prepared for her husband's return after weeks of absence by dressing seductively in white, letting down her long fragrant hair, turning the lights low and serving champagne, finds even as she begins to undress that Alfred is more concerned about the state of their child's digestion. Ella Rentheim, wringing from Borkman the monstrous admission that he had once as part of a squalid business deal traded her for a bank directorship, angrily indicts him of that 'truly monstrous crime . . . for which there is no forgiveness.' Irene reveals to Rubek how his self-control as he gazed day after day on her naked beauty had finally driven her to despair and flight and a life of debauchery and madness. Death by drowning, death from seizure, death by avalanche — the direct or oblique retribution which these acts of denial bring is dire.

Nevertheless, a simple affirmation of the more elemental life forces does not always hold out unambiguous promise of fulfilment. Admittedly Ulfheim, hunting his women with the same sporting instinct as he brought to his bear hunting, finds in this a source of pleasure uncomplicated by moral scruple, the pleasure of what Hilde Wangel had earlier called 'a robust conscience'; and Maja, for her part, is also stimulated to glad cries as he and she make their way off the mountain to the receptive valley below. Similarly Mrs. Wilton, though a more genteel seducer than Ulfheim, finds her pleasure — and again a pleasure uncontaminated by conscience — in running away with Erhart and Frida. At the same time, running counter to the idea that a straight surrender to sexual promptings brings simple contentment and as if to emphasize that the causalities of this world are never simple, there is Irene's deep ambivalence at the time of what Rubek called the 'episode' when, by her own confession, she had a sharp and deadly weapon concealed about her person ready to revenge any violation by Rubek of their purely aesthetic relationship.

Such a system of interpenetrating relationships, each with its own peculiar duties and loyalties, obligations and rewards, invaded by motives derived (in the main) from the male endeavour — ambition, a sense of mission, the lust for power, the claims of art, the pursuit of status and esteem — provides the basic pattern by which the fictive life of these dramas is lived. Nevertheless there are two other important elements present to prevent the dramatic event from being a merely or largely predictable consequence of identifiable cause and effect.

The first is that at the deeper and less rationally accessible level of this world there can be seen at work a pervasive influence from mystic or quasi-mystic (or even mock-mystic) forces, a system of 'pulls' and 'currents' and 'undertows' of will and suggestion: forces of which the Rat Wife is the most explicit manifestation, and Mrs. Wilton's throwaway references to her 'spell-casting' the most ironic. The persistent attention which Ibsen had given in the immediately preceding plays — in *The Lady from the Sea*, in *Hedda Gabler*, and in *The Master Builder* — to the power of mind over mind, and the influence of mind over matter, is continued here. The subterranean spirits call to Borkman, stretching out to him their 'twisting, sinuous, beckoning arms' like a greeting from loyal subjects; Alfred and Rita look forward at the final curtain to a visitation by the spirits of those who have departed; Irene lives in a world of shades, herself a 'shadow' watched over by a shadow; the living dead — Borkman whom the cold had long ago killed, Gunhild and Ella existing as two shades over the dead man, Irene and Rubek who had died an earlier death — lead their zombie-like existences, living and partly living. And all the time the secret tides and currents of life are imperceptibly, ineluctably at work. Mysteriously, rationally inexplicable, they act to complement the surface forces of these last plays, and thus to complete a reverberant universe of motivation.

The second (and in its own way decisive) factor comes with the recognition that this is a thoroughly deceptive world. Deceit is endemic; self-deception commonplace; witnesses, particularly where their own motives and conduct are concerned, are frequently unreliable; dissimulation becomes a way of life. It is crucial to realize that one must constantly beware of accepting the characters and their version of events at face value.

The occasion when this most clearly surfaces is in that intensely moving and deeply betraying exchange between Borkman and Foldal, when circumstances finally compel them to admit that they have voluntarily practised mutual deception for as long as they have known each other. Their encounter is a clear invitation to see their two careers as a double melodic line, a two-part harmony in which the one supports, sustains, and complements the other. On the one side is the humble and inadequate clerk whose entire adult life has been sustained only by the dubious promise of an uncompleted play, a tragedy which — in itself a kind of analogue to its author's career — will never be consummated, but which, like Hjalmar Ekdal's invention in *The Wild Duck*, is enough to sustain the level of self-esteem at least at subsistence level. The counterpointing with Borkman's situation is deliberate. His belief in himself as a great captain of industry is underpinned by Foldal in exchange for favours received. An objectively reconstructed and dispassionate account of the events of Borkman's career could only reveal how flawed and inadequate it had been in reality: a simple squalid history of embezzlement, made nastier by his readiness to betray the woman he loved in the interests of sordid commercial gain, followed by a deserved prison sentence which had left him full of excuses and self-justification and illusions of grandeur.

Borkman's and Foldal's exasperated acknowledgement of the

real truth about their relationship gives a pointer to the range of possible deception which the characters in these plays practise on each other and on themselves:

BORKMAN. So all this time you've lied to me.
FOLDAL. [*Shakes his head*]. Never lied, John Gabriel.
BORKMAN. Have you not sat there feeding my hopes and beliefs and confidence with lies?
FOLDAL. They weren't lies as long as *you* believed in *my* calling. As long as you believed in me, I believed in you.
BORKMAN. Then it's just been mutual deception. And perhaps self-deception too — on both sides.
FOLDAL. But isn't that what friendship really is, John Gabriel?
BORKMAN [*with a bitter smile*]. Yes. To deceive . . . that's what friendship is. You are right . . .

One remarks a high incidence of those who, consciously or unconsciously, rationalize their own conduct in deceptive terms, who designate as duty a course of action which at the deeper level is dictated by essentially selfish motives, who devise plausible altruisms in order to escape from situations which either they find distasteful or in which they sense themselves inadequate: Allmers, who ostentatiously addresses himself to his son's needs in order to give second priority to the (to him) alarming sexual advances of his wife; Borkman, who rationalizes his own desire for money and power as a duty to release the slumbering mineral deposits for the benefit of mankind at large; Rubek, who dresses up the 'episode' with his model Irene in sententious references to the holiness of art and the need to avoid profaning it with ordinary humanity. There are those who are blind to or afraid of the realities: pathetically so sometimes, like little Eyolf dreaming of learning to swim and with ambitions of becoming a soldier; culpably so, as with Borkman who refuses to see what is obvious to all: that his plans for a resumption of his business career are hopelessly doomed. Allmers is incapable of facing up to the realities of Eyolf's crippling, and drafts hopelessly unrealistic plans for his son's future. The key element is that in

317

every case the ascription to 'duty' is seen (or at least offered) as a kind of victory, a triumph of self-control, and a defeat of those dark disruptive forces which threaten to subvert man's noble endeavours.

Occasionally it happens that one or another of the characters, generally a woman, will see through the pretence, see through the intellectual and emotional dishonesty, and have the courage to say so. In *Little Eyolf*, Rita indicates already in the draft that she is not deceived by Alfred's grand words when he speaks of his obligations towards Eyolf as representing his 'highest duty' and having 'sacrificed' his career as a writer to this task. It was (she says) not really because Alfred loved his son: 'You were beginning to be consumed by doubts yourself,' Rita declares. 'All that happy confidence, all that hope that you had some great task to perform [as a writer] — this began to desert you. I saw it clearly enough . . . You wanted to make a child prodigy out of him, Alfred. Because he was *your* child. But you never really loved him.' When Ibsen came to revise this exchange, he took the opportunity to work into the final version phrases which even more clearly indicated the disguised and concealed motives that had contributed to the situation: 'Look inside yourself!' Rita exhorts Alfred with some embarrassment. 'And examine carefully all those things lying under . . . and behind . . . the surface.' As the kind of instruction which might equally well have come from Ibsen to his reader, it hints at the restless complexity of the dramatist's intent.

In the case of *Little Eyolf*, there is a particularly high betrayal value attaching to those changes which Ibsen made both to the substance and to the detail of the drafts in order to achieve the final intricate orchestration of the work. As William Archer early saw: revision in the case of this play amounted almost to re-invention, and nearly everything that gives the play its depth, its horror, and its elevation came as what Archer — still perhaps not fully grasping the real significance — rather dismissively called 'an afterthought.' Hermann Weigand's confident italics some years later very properly corrected the balance: 'It is evident', he wrote in 1925, '*that a startling change of plan separates the finished play from Ibsen's original intention.*' The end-product was an artistic and technical *tour de force* without parallel in Ibsen's *oeuvre*, a delicate fabric of nuance and suggestiveness, deeply enigmatic and shot through with the profoundest irony. The value of cataloguing in some detail the various shifts of meaning and displacements of emphasis through the different stages of the play's composition is that one thereby identifies a number of tracer elements which, when plotted, help to define the movement and the direction of the dramatist's basic purposes.

Caution in interpreting the surviving draft is nevertheless essential. As it stands, this draft is in no sense the product of a consistent and fully formed inspiration. Based — as, in accord with Ibsen's usual practice, it surely is — on some earlier set of notes, jottings, scenarios, and trial dialogue, it is the uneven product of a period of some eight weeks' work (from mid-June to early August 1894) at a time when the author's sense of the totality of the piece was still fluid and when substantial thematic changes were being introduced *passim* as they suggested themselves to him. In consequence a number of important new ideas are present on the later pages of the manuscript (for instance, the highly charged reference to the existence of *two* Eyolfs, one big and one little) which are inconsistent with the draft's earlier pages, but which Ibsen was clearly holding in suspense in his mind ready to build into the earlier stretches of the action when the moment came for consolidating revision of his material.

In a curious way the progressive changes to the draft anticipate the account which Rubek was later to give, in *When We Dead Awaken*, of the modifications which he had carried out between phase one and phase two of his statue 'Resurrection Day'. All the evidence suggests that in its first conception *Little Eyolf* was a considerably less ambiguous thing than the complex play it eventually became; and like Rubek's introduction of a great wealth of modifying complexities into a work which in its first stages had been a more unitary and uncomplicated sculptural statement, Ibsen's dramatic invention elaborately revised the motivational patterns in *Little Eyolf* until the new meaning represented a radical displacement of the old. The final version is only the 'same' drama as the earlier version in the sense that the revised 'Resurrection Day' remained the 'same'.

The characteristics which the draft assigned to Hakon

Skjoldheim make of him an essentially different person from the Alfred Allmers he eventually became. Among other things it invested the former with a set of dramatic problems quite unlike those of the latter in a number of significant respects. Skjoldheim starts off as an already *successful* writer, the author of a number of published works which he feels were 'well written' and which he also claims were 'well received'. Of late he had been engaged on a book which seemingly had reasonable expectations of being his best yet, his 'masterpiece'. His motives (at this stage of the draft) for changing course now commend themselves as admirable and wholly selfless: he had been too much concerned with thinking and writing and not enough with *doing*, had been too much given to his own personal and selfish ambitions and indifferent to those of his child. At this stage of the draft, he will now renounce those blinkered, in-turned ideas; and, by devoting himself to his son's welfare, help him towards self-fulfilment and an understanding of 'the art of life'.

In the final text, by contrast, Alfred Allmers has seemingly been working away inconclusively for ten years on a book about 'human responsibility'. The transmutation went through an intermediate stage. At the first revise to the draft, Allmers is made to describe his work thus:

> There I sat writing day after day. And sometimes half the night. Writing that big book [*skrev på den store bogen*] on human responsibility.

For the final version, the phrasing was given a further slight but subtly important revision — the kind of revision which, by its wording, conveys to an alert audience a hint of the spurious:

> There I sat bent over my desk, writing, day after day. And sometimes half the night. Writing away at that great thick book [*skrev og skrev på den store tykke bogen*] on 'Human responsibility'.

As yet, the draft carries no reference to the briefcase full of old family letters which, in the later course of events, were to bear so importantly on the extra-marital adventures of Alfred's step-mother, and consequently on the kinship ties between Alfred and his supposed sister Asta. Nor, in this same connection, is there yet any reference to Asta's recent strange behaviour — a comment by Rita which, in the final text, finds its obvious explanation in the fact of Asta's having by then read the family letters and thus discovered the truth about her relationship to Alfred. Nor is there yet any reference to the orphaned childhood of Alfred and Asta being so evidently 'poverty-stricken'; nor any explicit emphasis on the fact that their subsequent comfortable existence stemmed from Rita's wealth, from her 'gold and green forests'. Furthermore, there is a complete absence of any open or declared hostility on the part of the wife for the 'sister' as a possible rival for Alfred's (or even Eyolf's) affection; indeed, in Act I of the draft at least, the sister is already openly betrothed to Borghejm, and to that extent therefore already emotionally committed elsewhere.

The emergent dramatic conflict at this stage of the drama's composition seems relatively uncomplicated; and when the wife demands her husband for herself unshared, the tensional pattern at this stage seems clearly foreshadowed by the brief exchange in the draft between husband and wife:

ALLMERS. You have a jealous nature. Previously you were jealous of my work. Now you are jealous of Eyolf.

MRS. ALLMERS. I cannot be different from what I am. If you parcel yourself out between us . . . I'll be revenged on you, Alfred!

(The fact that the agent of 'possessiveness' in the marriage situation is now the wife and not the husband — as it was, for example, most obviously in *A Doll's House* — in itself marks a significant change of emphasis in Ibsen's authorship.) The above exchange would then be entirely consistent with the 'willing' of Eyolf's death via the Rat Wife — a member of the *dramatis personae* who is one of the earliest and most persistent in the entire play.

Thereafter, the introduction and the progressive enlargement of what has here been earlier called the incipient incest motif faced the dramatist with formidable structural problems; and it retroactively imposed important changes on a number of existing passages. By the time the draft had advanced as far as Act III, this theme had acquired a central importance. Nevertheless it seems as if certain ideas persisting from an earlier conception of the play continued to influence the shape of the action; and this led to serious psychological inconsistencies in the structure of the play. In the third Act of the draft, it is *Asta* who is anxious to reconstitute the chaste 'brother/sister' relationship. Although she of course knows the real truth about her relationship to Alfred, she still speaks to Borghejm of her 'brother', declaring that she cannot now let him go because she feels she can care for him 'as only a sister can care for a brother'. At this stage in the composition of the play, it is Alfred who sees menace in the proposed *ménage à trois*, a threat that comes from the possibility of his *own* loss of self-control:

> ALLMERS. . . Oh, Asta, I no longer have you. Not the
> way I had you before.
> BORGHEJM [*looks at them in astonishment*]. But I don't
> understand . . .
> ASTA. Oh, but you do, Alfred. Believe me . . . for you I
> will always be the same as I was.
> ALLMERS. But not I.
> ASTA [*shrinks back*]. Ah . . . !

She then evades his embrace as he comes forward to take his leave. Rita, as yet ignorant of their true relationship, urges Asta to remain in their household as their 'child': 'We must have a child who can bring us together . . . Something calm, warm, passionless . . . A child or a sister.' Asta, after her final appeal to Alfred to be allowed to stay has thus been peremptorily refused, thereupon leaves. Rita, from her detached point of observation, thinks she sees through the situation to what is the real but unacknowledged truth: that Alfred has sent Asta away because he fears that she (Asta) could not survive a situation where her own sexual promptings would conflict with her role as 'passionless' sister: 'She too wanted to be all things to you,' Rita declares in the draft. 'Same as me.' But, through ignorance of the real situation she has read the signs wrongly; and Alfred has to confess that in reality *he* and *his* feelings were the sexually untrustworthy factors. Rita's immediate reaction is shock that he could even contemplate incestuous conduct: 'Alfred! You could think . . . desire . . . something criminal! Never in the world!' Her amazement when she learns the real truth is equally prompt, but for entirely different reasons: that Alfred, being thus freed of the prohibitions of sexual taboo, should not at once have seized the opportunity presented by the new situation. A mixture of disbelief and contempt that he could be so ineffectually sexless prompts her immediate response: 'How could you, Alfred? I'd never have been capable of anything like that . . . Oh, but it's just like I say — fish's blood . . .' Then, quickly correcting herself, she compassionately says what she knows he wants her to say and to believe: 'No, no, I don't mean it. It is the great and pure side of you which has won the victory.' It is a clear instance of the readiness of Ibsen's characters to say what the immediate relationship expects of them rather than what they really think. And once again it results in a kind of deception *à la* Foldal.

These shifts left a residue of implausibility in the draft of the drama as it was, and especially in the motivation of Alfred's behaviour. Was he or was he not the kind of man who could remain unmoved by the knowledge that his resident and dearly beloved 'sister' was no longer sexually protected from him by society's taboos? (Alfred and Asta of course represent a reversal of the earlier incestuous dilemma of Oswald and Regine in *Ghosts*, where in the earlier drama the exposure of past misbehaviour *imposes* a taboo on the relationship, whereas in the later one it eliminates it.) Was he or was he not really the kind of 'passionless' person Rita at times accuses him of being? There is some slight evidence to suggest that Ibsen himself momentarily wavered between the two possibilities; and the hesitant revisions to the stage directions which mark Alfred's first appearance seem to document this uncertainty. First, in the draft proper, he is 'a slim, slight figure with a serious expression on his face; thinning dark hair and beard'; after the first revise, his hair is thicker, he is clean-shaven, and his eyes 'sparkle' — clearly a much more assertive character; this was then again revised to restore his beard, to give him back his 'thinning' hair, and to attribute to him 'gentle eyes' — which is how it survived into the final text. The change is reflected in the final revisions to the draft of Act III. Now it is Alfred who begs Asta to stay, and Rita joins in his entreaty: to be sister to him and to 'be Eyolf' to them. Now it is Asta who cannot trust herself in the altered situation: 'Yes, Alfred . . . it *is* running away . . . From you — and from myself.' The changes mean that Rita is now not immediately let into the kinship secret; and in consequence the earlier contemptuous reference by her in the draft to Alfred's 'fish's blood' has now disappeared. Vanished also is her earlier (draft) remark that Asta 'wanted to be all things' to Alfred, and thus by implication usurp her wifely place. The irony of the situation is that now, in the drama's revised form, the remark would have been true.

Running like a thread through the entire sequence of exchanges at the start of Act III in its final formulation — in the first instance between Asta and Borghejm and, subsequently, between Alfred and Rita — is a distinct but suppressed sense of the terror and the ecstasy of the forbidden as it announces itself to Asta, of her aching desire to be with Alfred and her fear of how life might inevitably develop, given the nature of her feelings. When Borghejm innocently — thinking of Eyolf's death — comments to Asta that 'this thing' had changed her whole position *vis-à-vis* the Allmers household, she gives a guilty start since that is precisely how she must have presented the new sexually orientated position to herself. And Rita, in ignorance of the real facts as they related to sexual and blood relationships, again misinterprets the signs. This time she simply assumes that Borghejm is the reason Asta cannot remain with them.

In its final shape, the play thus sets out to demarcate an arena of intricate and tightly drawn linear relationships of a sexual and familial nature. Then two things are allowed to happen: first, disaster, seemingly and mysteriously self-engendered by the situation, invades the scene, imposing one set of adjustments from those who compose it; second, revelations from the past indicate that the world of relationships is in one crucial respect not as it seems. And this requires a further set of adjustments from those concerned. Finally, superimposed on this groundwork of changing and disrupted relationships is an overlay of deception: deceptive appearances, self-deceiving attitudes, feigned motives, false feelings, defensive pretences. Only by paying the utmost attention not only to what is said, but also how it is said, can one begin to resolve the problems of who in these plays can be taken as a reliable witness of events, of whose testimony is suspect, or of what is behind the façade.

If, in those long hours of introspection after the death of Eyolf, Alfred had been able to be totally honest with himself, able to analyse dispassionately and even clinically the true sequence of events and his own part in them, his train of thought might well have run:

As a young man, I knew a great love for my younger half-sister, Asta. The basis of this love was (I now see) sexual, but society's taboos compelled me to subdue and repress my deeper feelings. Together, therefore, we pretended she was a boy. This left its residual effect on my own attitudes to sexual passion. When I first met Rita, who was both rich and very beautiful, my dominant feeling was terror; but marriage to her offered a solution to Asta's and my financial problems, and assured our continuing life close to each other. When my son was born, I called him Eyolf — the nickname I had earlier used for Asta as my pretended brother — in an effort to perpetuate that earlier idyllic relationship. The circumstances of his crippling accident a year later left me psycho-sexually even more reduced than I had been before. Ostentatious self-dedication to my writing protected me to some extent from Rita's passionate demands on my night hours; devotion to our son offered a new line of defence when the book began to lose conviction as a pretext. Both the book and the child inevitably drew Rita's hatred. Then in quick succession two of my defences against the inroads of passion were removed: Eyolf was drawn to his death by drowning; and the blood taboos which had kept my relations with Asta what they were were withdrawn. I tried for a 'passionless' solution:

a triangular relationship based on what the world calls a 'brother and sister ' relationship with both Rita and Asta. But in the new situation Asta feared for her own self-control. I am now left with a 'passionless' existence with Rita, a life in which we devote ourselves to good works, cling to the memories of past happiness, and try to salvage something of value (the 'jewel in the ashes'?) from the collapse.

Instead of this honesty, he pretends; pretends even to himself; pretends that he is sacrificing a writer's and scholar's career in the interests of his son, assigns the blame for Eyolf's death to Rita's unconsciously murderous thoughts, offers a great parade of his grief, does grotesque mental calculations for Asta's benefit to determine how far the currents have taken Eyolf's body out to sea, makes a pathetically inept and spurious suicide attempt, and cruelly torments Rita about her readiness to follow Eyolf into the next world. In short, Eyolf has already become for him what Relling in *The Wild Duck* prophesied Hedvig would soon become for Hjalmar: 'the theme of a pretty little party piece [*et vakkert deklamationstema*]'. Then he'll bring it all up, Relling declares: 'All about "the child so untimely torn from a loving father's heart". Then you'll see him wallowing deeper and deeper in sentimentality and self-pity.'

In a last appeal, Alfred tries by something approaching emotional blackmail to preserve a domestic situation where both women are still available to pander to him. Finally when this fails comes the greatly self-dramatizing account of his mountain encounter with Death; he lingers lugubriously on the notion of dying young, playing unmercifully on Rita's feelings:

ALLMERS . . . I clambered along the precipitous cliffs . . . and enjoyed the peace and serenity that comes from the nearness of death.

RITA [*jumps up*]. Oh, don't use such words about this dreadful thing.

ALLMERS. That was how I felt. Absolutely no fear. I felt that Death and I walked side by side like two good travelling companions. It all seemed so

reasonable . . . so obvious at the time. People in
my family don't usually live till they are old.
RITA. Oh, please stop talking about these things, Alfred!
You did come through all right, after all.

The viciousness of his attitude towards the village children and
their feckless parents is translated by him, wholly in character,
into 'a duty'; and in dressing up this duty in phrases of typical
theatricality, he also at the same time manages to evade any
possible personal commitment or responsibility for himself: 'I've
a right to be hard from now on! A duty! My duty towards Eyolf!
He must not die unavenged. Make it quick, Rita! That's what I
say. Think it over. Have the whole place razed to the ground —
when I am gone.'

The changes imposed upon Alfred in the course of the play's
composition — who naturally as husband, 'brother', and father
is positioned at the very centre of the cataclysmic events within
the household — indicate a strongly marked shift towards the
ineffectual, the impotent, the wordily pretentious, the self-
delusory. The breast-beating, the choked sob, the histrionics,
become progressively more evident as one follows Alfred from
stage to stage in the draft; and the ostensible motives for his
actions become more and more suspect. In contrast to Rita's
impetuous, instinctively 'hot-blooded' but essentially generous
reactions, Alfred is caught out striking attitudes, mouthing
phrases, self-consciously acting a part even at moments of the
greatest pathos. In its final form, the play is a technically
audacious attempt to construct an action on the tension between
a suspect articulation and enactment of motives and causes and
the reality of things inherent in the total situation.

John Gabriel Borkman is concerned to explore the dynamics of
obsession and self-delusion within what is now a recognizably
Ibsenist arena of complex interlocking personal relationships.
Borkman himself lives in a private and solitary world, admission
to which is given only to those who consent to share his
fantasies. He designs a comprehensive personal myth, within

which he casts himself for the central role: that of the *Übermensch* in close contact with those elemental and subterranean powers which inhabit the rich ore-bearing strata of the earth, and whose liberation he is convinced he can achieve. To see him as a great captain of commerce, a Napoleon of industry, is to accept him at his own valuation and to ignore the discrepancy between the portentousness of his phrases and the tawdry reality they conceal. In *his* testimony, a sordid and botched act of embezzlement becomes a heroic undertaking, and simple criminal ineptitude finds excuses for itself in an elaborate myth of betrayal. The spectacle is one of self-administered mythopoeic therapy.

The motives, real and imagined, which led him in the past to do what he did have now fused indistinguishably together in his mind. At one moment, it belongs to the myth that his crime was simply an act of obedience to the call of mystic mineral powers. He claims to have been conscious of a mysterious force of attraction, a 'pull', an inexplicable and irresistible drawing power, a reaching out from the veins of metal ore like spirits of the earth 'stretching out their twisting, sinuous, beckoning arms' to him. At other moments, he traces his actions to their source in a Gynt-like pursuit of his deeper Self: 'Why did I do it?' he asks. 'Because I am me — John Gabriel Borkman.' In this mood, he is the Nietzschean '*Ausnahmemensch*', living by standards different from those that apply to his more 'average' fellow men. On other occasions still he is ready to acknowledge within himself the simple drive of ambition: ' . . . My ambitions in life . . . I wanted to gain command of all the sources of power in this land . . . I wanted control.' Yet even before this particular utterance is complete, he has re-categorized this essentially personal ambition as an agency of social enrichment: 'I wanted to build myself an empire, and thereby create prosperity for thousands upon thousands of others.'

Borkman is clearly constituted as a latter-day 'pillar of society', whose misfortune it was this time not merely to be found out, but to suffer the penalties for his corrupt actions; and the way in which certain features of his conduct echo the earlier career of Bernick is surely designed to call attention to the parallel. Not only does he, like Bernick, callously throw over his

betrothed for her sister (twin-sister in the one instance, step-
sister in the other) for motives of crude commercial gain; not
only does it come easily to him to justify this action by ascribing
it to social or family 'duty'; but also the disparity between the
real and the declared motives is extraordinarily similar in the
two cases. Borkman's excuse that he was acting in the interests
of the well-being of 'thousands upon thousands of others' is of
the same brand of hypocrisy as Bernick's explanation of why he
privately bought up the land over which the branch railway was
to run:

> Don't you see what a boost it will give to our whole
> community? Just think of the huge tracts of forest it will
> open up! Think of all the rich mineral deposits that can
> be worked! Think of the river, with one waterfall after
> another! What about the industrial development that
> could be made there! . . . We, the practical men of busi-
> ness, will serve the community by bringing prosperity to
> as wide a circle as possible.

His obsession with the pursuit of power and wealth reduces
everything to undifferentiated sustenance for his fantasies. In
his mind, the motives coalesce: mystic inducement, willed desire,
and public service. All things are judged, all values determined,
by the one single obsessional criterion: how is thus ambition
served? Of the multiple drives and imperatives which intersect
within his own person, one alone counts; and in awarding an
overriding precedence to this he brutally and insensitively
repudiates all others. When he reviews the evidence for his guilt,
he has no difficulty in finding total — and heroic — justification
for his actions. Contemplating that moment of critical decision
in the past when he abandoned Ella for a bank directorship, he
is quick to use the standard phrases of the heroic: 'I had no
choice. I had to conquer or fall.' But this is not heroic; it is only
heroics. It is nothing more than, retrospectively and spuriously,
putting things in a heroic light. Because he is who he is, because
in his own estimate his talents are extra-ordinary and his
objectives sublime, he feels immune to guilt, even though the
bare details of his conduct show it to have been mean and sordid

in the extreme. Palpably guilty, he acknowledges no guilt, no injury to anybody but himself; all he can see is a self-inflicted wound that cut short a Napoleonic career. His last refuge and defence is always that nobody ever did, or ever does, understand him.

The dreamer returns for his last moments of life to his dream landscape to re-people it and re-stock it with spinning wheels, smoking chimneys, and a toiling night-shift. He prides himself on being 'hard', like the iron ore he worships, and the metallic powers with which he claims allegiance. Even the last mortal pressure on his heart he endures with readier acceptance when he finds that he can correct his identification of the source of it: 'No. Not a hand of ice. A hand of iron.' Yet even this appeal to the values of the mines is suspect; he is himself not a miner (though at times he seems anxious to give the impression that he is) but a miner's son; and all the lyricism of his talk of the singing ore and the liberating hammerblows is largely second-hand, certainly romanticized, and part of the proliferating myth for which he works so assiduously. In the case of this superman *imaginaire*, only one thing is real, one thing great: his obsession. Held to resolutely, stubbornly, it becomes for him the one sustaining element in life. Only when that is destroyed — dismantled in the first instance by Foldal's denial of him and then by Erhart's repudiation — is the life support gone.

Between the initial conception and the final realization of the sculptured 'Resurrection Day' in *When We Dead Awaken*, falls the loss of innocence. At the start, all was simplicity and idealism. Both the design of the work and the early circumstances of its creation were serene, spontaneous, pure, and unsullied. It was to be a single unitary figure, a representation of 'the world's noblest, purest, most perfect woman', a vision of how 'the pure woman would wake on Resurrection Day, not wondering at things new and unfamiliar and unimagined, but filled with a holy joy at finding herself unchanged — a mortal woman — in those higher, freer, happier realms after the long and dreamless sleep of death.' An idealized, uncomplicated, direct expression born of exaltation, a positive vision. The

circumstances were chaste, even reverential; the naked model
was 'a sacred being, untouchable, something to worship in
thought alone'. The pure simplicity of the artist's vision required
a simple purity of conduct and setting. But, for Rubek, the
passage of time brought new and disturbing insights into the real
nature of life. Within the artist grew the realization that he had
something much more complex to express, something more
elaborate and ambiguous:

> RUBEK . . . In the years that followed, Irene, the world
> taught me many things. I began to conceive
> 'Resurrection Day' as something bigger. something
> . . . something more complex. That little round
> plinth on which your statue stood, erect and lonely
> . . . no longer provided space for all the other
> things I now wanted to say . . .
> IRENE [*reaches for the knife, then stops*]. What other
> things? Tell me!
> RUBEK. Things I saw with my own eyes in the world
> around me. I had to bring them in, I had no
> choice, Irene. I extended the plinth . . . made it
> broad and spacious. And on it I created an area of
> cracked and heaving earth. And out of the cracks
> swarmed people, their faces animal beneath the
> skin. Men and women . . . as I knew them from
> life.

In the adjustments thus made to the overall design of the work,
in the relegation of the once solitary sculptured figure to a
congested middle-ground, in the elaborate additions and
accretions of the second stage of composition, was embodied a
newer and sadder honesty, a profounder and more penetrating
yet at the same time more cynical view of the human condition.
Behind its new wealth of de-idealized detail — just as also
behind the 'speaking likenesses' of the new-style portrait busts
to which Rubek turns his talents — is the artist's growing
awareness of the brutalities, the stupidities, and the insen-
sitivities of life as he increasingly came to see it, and of the
soul's torment.

Within the context of the drama, the re-working of the sculpture — as hesitantly described by Rubek — makes a profound shift in the artist's view of life: from an earlier confident belief in simple pieties and a faith in his own capacity to communicate them through art, to a seriously uncertain, ambivalent, and complex view of things in which truth is elusive and where guilt and remorse and a sense of forfeited opportunity and wasted life occupy the central place. Truth and artistic integrity have insisted that these disturbing maturer recognitions be incorporated into the totality of the vision; and it is these later sophistications which have imposed the elaborate revision.

What the drama reveals as it plots this progression from innocence to experience, from simplicity to complexity, is that the work of art which embodies this change has demanded human sacrifice. The creative act had necessitated the exploitation of Irene's humanity, had required the draining of her life's essence, had exacted the death of her living soul. Art functions here as a life-destructive force; and the artist, serving as its agent, had left her disturbed, deranged, unfulfilled, a shadow of her former self, a zombie-like creature enduring a death-in-life existence. Nor was the artist himself exempt from the malignant and corrupting effects:

> IRENE. And when I heard you say — cold as an icy grave — that I was nothing more than an episode in your life . . . I took out the knife. I was going to plunge it into your back.
> RUBEK [*darkly*]. And why didn't you?
> IRENE. Because I suddenly realized with horror that you were already dead . . . Long, long dead . . . Dead like me. We sat there by the Taunitzer See, two clammy corpses . . .

Deprived of its sacrificial victim, art quickly becomes corrupt, and the artist impotent. Even Maja, who staunchly repudiates any claims that art might make on her, who remains unchangingly hostile to the whole ethos of 'cold figures in damp cellars', nevertheless feels threatened by the mere proximity of art, trapped by her association with Rubek, caged in her marriage.

But she retains enough of her independence to be able finally to assert herself, to choose the frankly sensual existence offered by Ulfheim, and thus make good her escape to 'life'.

Not merely art reveals itself here as the enemy of 'life', however. Rubek's crisis of recognition, that moment of truth, of 'awakening' from a living death which is foreshadowed in the play's title, invokes a much wider frame of reference than merely that of artist and model:

> RUBEK. I'll tell you what it was. I began to think that all this business about the artist's mission and the artist's vocation was all so much empty, hollow, meaningless talk.
>
> MAJA. What would you put in its place?
>
> RUBEK. Life, Maja . . . Hasn't life in sunlight and beauty a value altogether different from toiling away to the end of your days in some cold, damp cellar, wrestling with lumps of clay and blocks of stone?

Art, poetry, an ideal, a mission, a vocation, a big business enterprise, anything which demands sacrificial dedication of the order Rubek has experienced and which is required to subjugate 'life' so ruthlessly to its purposes can by this token only be destructive of human happiness, chillingly death-dealing. Images of life, death, and resurrection, and the concepts of living death, death in life, and life after death recur throughout all these late plays — from Allmers's sense of impending 'resurrection' from the deadening pain of Eyolf's loss, and Gunhild's acknowledgement over the corpse of Borkman that 'the cold had killed him long ago', to the accretions to the statue of 'Resurrection Day' and the living-death existence of Rubek and Irene.

Rubek's account of the progressively elaborate remodelling of his statue, the counterweighting of idealism with scepticism, the superimposition of anguished introspection and remorse upon the earlier confident and untroubled harmonies of the original design, thus clearly also has a significance transcending the context of the particular play to which it belongs. In the first place it offers itself as an image of the revisionary procedures to which Ibsen himself subjected his own individual dramas, in consequence of which what might have begun (as in *Little Eyolf*) as the relatively plain articulation of some 'observation' or other he had made about life — to use the term (*iagtagelse*) he was fond of using to describe the initial stimulus that gave life to his dramas — was transformed into an elaborately orchestrated and counterpointed statement embracing all those subsequent doubts and qualifications which had forced themselves upon his attention at the secondary and tertiary stages of composition. Nor, by extension, is it too fanciful to see Rubek's account as a commentary on the totality of Ibsen's own *oeuvre* as it advanced from the relatively undifferentiated idealism and optimism of his earliest dramas of the 1850s to the seemingly often impenetrable ambiguities of the last works.

What these last plays set out to do from their starting point in the poem 'They sat there, those two' was to conduct a rigorous exploration of those sources of human conduct which the ageing dramatist, after the experience of a lifetime, had come to recognize as belonging to the essence of modern living; to communicate something of those forces which he was now persuaded bore most significantly on contemporary patterns of behaviour; and to dissect and lay bare those layers of motivation, those insistent forces at work within and upon the individual, which he, as a compulsive student of human nature and of the fabric of society, felt he could now identify as among the more powerful determinants of his own age. The result is a series of dramatic analyses of extreme virtuosity and daunting complexity, subjecting to scrutiny the dynamics of small and variously integrated and interrelated social groups, and examining the complex interrelations of the compulsions of individual will and desire, the obligations of kinship and family, and the prevailing social and community expectations.

In sheerly technical terms, these dramas stretched the potentialities of dramatic composition to new limits, vigorously exploiting drama's capacity to communicate truths too elusive to be contained within any purely analytical construction. For his purposes, Ibsen developed a semiological system — to call it merely a 'dramatic language' ascribes too heavy a *verbal* component to it to be entirely satisfactory — which combined the qualities of stringent economy with the most delicate subtlety. Into this sign system Ibsen incorporated not merely his own powerful and idiosyncratic variants of drama's traditional elements — speech, action, setting — but also a number of extra semantic devices of a more uncommon kind: the indexing by kinship or relational descriptors of particular imperatives; the encoding of meaning not so much into overt speech as overtly and more elusively into particular speech habits; the locating of action within a carefully defined symbolic topography of setting. The result was a succession of plays of a density and opaqueness resistant to simple analysis, but which in sum constitute a general declaration that great art is, and must inevitably be, destructive: destructive on the one hand of all that is spurious, inauthentic, meretricious, degenerate; destructive on the other of the lives and happiness of those who are sacrificed to it.

These plays establish a gallery of deeply flawed lives, of deficient achievement, of frustrated endeavour. Crippled, guilt-ridden, bankrupt, mortally sick, frigid, impotent, ineffectual, mentally disturbed, these characters exemplify a wide variety of inauthentic living. What little there is in these plays of positive asseveration is generally either naïvely superficial or ironically undermined: Erhart's escape from the 'stuffy air' of the parental home to what he claims will be the 'great, glorious, living happiness' of life in the arms of Mrs. Wilton; Maja's escape from the 'cold damp cage' of her existence with Rubek for the 'free and unafraid' life, the sensual satisfactions, which Ulfheim can bring her; Foldal, finding exquisite joy in his daughter's abandonment of him, and wholly content in those circumstances to be 'run over' by life; and Borghejm who, despite the self-evident fulfilment which his road-building brings, still cannot think of life as anything other than 'a kind of game'.

The genuinely resonant things in these plays belong to a wholly different register: the complex harmonies of guilt and remorse; the profound capacities for self-deception; the dubious therapies indulged in by tormented and obsessed minds. What these plays are concerned to examine is the existential competence of those who would achieve, create, command, initiate — but whose careers merely betray their fatal lack of competence. In Eric Bentley's striking phrase, these are characters who reveal not unexpected depths but unexpected shallows; they contrive obligations which constitute a call upon their time, their energy, their attention, but which in reality are only designed to permit them to follow their own selfish inclination, or to escape from a course of action which they find distasteful, or for which they feel inadequate.

The conventions of irony require the dramatist to signal with greater or lesser clarity the disparity between things as they seem, and things as they really are. The clearer the signal, the broader the irony, and with that the greater the degree of confidence felt by the spectator that an ironic interpretation is admissible. Ibsen's method in these plays is to move closer and closer to the other end of this spectrum: to withhold the more obvious signals, and instead — so imperceptibly, sometimes, as to induce a seriously anxious uncertainty — do no more than drop veiled hints, start vague suspicions that perhaps things are not altogether as they are said by the characters to be.

Borkman, Rubek, and Allmers are all positioned on this ironic scale, but at different points of it; they represent, in this order, a descending series of explicitness. In Borkman, the disparity between the imagined and the real is comparatively emphatic; and when the pathetic swindler and ex-gaolbird characterizes himself as one of the élite, a superman, a Napoleon of industry, the jangled discords of self-delusion loudly invade his protestations. Rubek's progressive betrayal of his ineffectuality is more muted, sadder, in a way more honest. He has, it seems, achieved *one* masterpiece, though he is dubious even about claiming that; since then he has achieved nothing of note, no real 'poems' as he calls them, either in his life or his art — nothing but a few commercially successful but cynically conceived portraits. His life has been emptied of significance; and, as Irene remarks with the percipience of the damned, he too is really 'dead'. Allmers requires a receptive ear rather more finely tuned to differences in pitch between what is said and what is 'meant', and alert to the essential hollowness behind the utterance. When Borkman poses, he strikes a visible Napoleonic pose as he bids his callers enter; when Allmers 'poses', it is only by the slightest of exaggerations, the barest of over-emphases, the faintest falsity of phrase or gesture or reaction that the betrayal manifests itself. The discomfiture which criticism has often shown when confronted by these late plays might well in part trace its origins to this. Where the irony is so finely and accurately metered — in essence a kind of dramatic titration — where the trembling point of balance between the truth of what is said and the truth of what *is* is so audaciously maintained that simple certainty is impossible, it is not surprising that criticism in consequence has found it difficult to adopt a confident stance.

Applying this delicate technique to the task of communicating through drama something of the nature of life's deficiencies and imperfections, Ibsen at once set himself a problem of extreme delicacy and also at the same time exposed himself to immense risk. Put crudely, the problem was this: if, on the one hand, the concern of the plays was to be in large measure with what was flawed, deficient, inauthentic in life, with its discordant notes, its disharmonies, its moments of false tone; and if, on the other hand, his self-imposed technical brief was to reduce the element of overt irony at moments almost to vanishing point, in the belief that thereby unobtrusive irony achieves its most devastating effect; how then — if these two objectives are to be simultaneously realized — does one ensure that the flawed elements are acknowledged as a deliberate part of the dramatist's design and not merely the residual elements of the dramatist's incompetence? If a character's behaviour is designed to be unconvincing, spurious, 'theatrical', how does one prevent the transfer of the audience's censure from the fictive character to the dramatic composition itself, or the labelling as a structural weakness of something which in reality is a virtuoso achievement? It is doubtful whether any other dramatist has exposed himself to this risk so deliberately as Ibsen does in these plays. The natural and defensive inclination of any dramatist is to announce his ironic intent with the minimum necessary explicitness that will insure the work against misinterpretation; Ibsen, by contrast, reduced the ironic gap between what *is* and what *seems* to the point where the irony is left exquisitely poised. The consequence for criticism has been that too often those imperfections deliberately introduced into the plays as part of their controlled realization

337

have been taken as simple ineptitude, by which (to take but one example) the final moments of *Little Eyolf* are taken not as a penetratingly observed and resolved portrait of a falsely sentimental man but only as a passage itself inherently marred by false sentimentality.

Deeply embedded in these late plays is also a large and irreducible measure of self-reproach. The bitterest term of abuse which Irene can find for Rubek is 'poet'. A poet is doubly culpable: not only does he (in common with all artists) mercilessly exploit the human situation for his artistic ends, taking young human life and 'ripping the soul out of it'; but also, when finally the enormity of his conduct is borne in on him, he offers merely *poetic* expiation, makes the stirrings of his conscience into the very stuff of art, and by condemning his created *alter ego* to an infinity of guilt and remorse, thinks thereby to win exoneration for himself. 'Why poet?' Rubek asks in astonishment at this mode of rebuke. 'Because you are soft and spineless and full of excuses for everything you've ever done or thought,' Irene replies. 'You killed my soul — then you go and model yourself as a figure of regret and remorse and penitence . . . and you think you've settled your account.'

As early as 1880, in phrases which have been much quoted since, Ibsen claimed that

> at *digte* — det er at holde
> dommedag over sig selv

- 'to write is to pass judgement upon oneself'. *When We Dead Awaken*, Ibsen's 'epilogue', in setting out to pass judgement on the very act of passing judgement, in condemning those poetic acts of self-condemnation, pronounces upon the author a meta-judgement of extreme severity.

The poet and his age

13

Cultural Conspiracy and Civilizational Change

In his preface to that haunting and visionary — and unjustly neglected — poem *The Anathemata*, David Jones recalled (in 1951) how in the late nineteen-twenties and early 'thirties he and his friends were profoundly concerned in their thinking with something they called 'The Break', something which they recognized as affecting the entire world of sacrament and sign:

We did not discover the phenomenon so described; it had been evident in various ways to various people for perhaps a century; it is now, I suppose, apparent to most. Or at least most now see that in the nineteenth century, Western Man moved across a rubicon which, if as unseen as the 38th Parallel, seems to have been as definitive as the Styx . . . When in the 'twenties we spoke of this Break it was always with reference to some manifestation of this dilemma *vis-à-vis* the arts — and of religion also, but

343

only in so far as religion has to do with signs, just as have the arts. That is to say our Break had reference to something which was affecting the entire world of sacrament and sign.[1]

In the view of this group of artists and thinkers, it was an event which by virtue of its sheer magnitude and its crucial importance represented a fundamental civilizational change.

To turn from David Jones to C.S. Lewis is to reinforce the intuitions of the poet by the analytical insights of the scholar. In his inaugural lecture in 1954 as Professor of Medieval and Renaissance Literature at Cambridge, entitled *De descriptione temporum*, Lewis enunciated the startling proposition that the greatest of all the divisions in the history of Western Man — greater than that which divided Antiquity from the Dark Ages, or the Dark Ages from the Middle Ages — was that which separates our contemporary world from the early nineteenth century:

> I have come to regard as the greatest of all divisions in the history of the West that which divides the present from, say, the age of Jane Austen and Scott. The dating of such things must of course be rather hazy and indefinite. No-one could point to a year or a decade in which the change indisputably began . . . But somewhere between us and the Waverley Novels, somewhere between us and *Persuasion*, the chasm runs.[2]

More recently, a strikingly similar recognition was advanced by George Steiner, who accompanied it with a bolder and more precise dating of the phenomenon:

> The principal division in the history of Western literature occurs between the early 1870s and the turn of the century . . . Compared to this division all preceding historical and stylistic rubrics or movements — Hellenism, the medieval, the Baroque, Neo-classicism, Romanticism — are only subgroups or variants.[3]

The change effected in these years Steiner then calls 'immense'; and he further comments that only now, at the distance of about a century from the event, are we really beginning to grasp it.

In the testimony of these three witnesses — and there are many others who might have been cited in support of this basic conviction — there is eloquent support for the proposition that the last 150 years of Western culture have been the arena of quite unprecedented cultural change. I have recently remarked in another context [4] that our cultural seismologists — by which I mean those whose task it is to record the shifts and displacements and dislocations that have taken place in the history of art and literature and thought — habitually operate with a scale of measurement which recognizes three distinct orders of magnitude. At the lower end of the scale are those tremors of fashion which come and go in rhythm with the changing generations; to the second order of magnitude belong those larger displacements of style and sensibility which mark the emergence of named periods or epochs or movements, like the Quattrocento, the Baroque, Romanticism; and, finally, there is a third category reserved for those overwhelming dislocations, those cataclysmic upheavals, those fundamental convulsions of the human spirit that threaten to undermine even the most solid seeming and substantial of our beliefs and assumptions, our standards and our values. What is asserted by our witnesses therefore is not only that within the last 150 years has there been some 'break', some great divide, the opening up of some 'chasm', some fundamental dislocation, some complex shift of sensibility, but also that in its dimensions — which are only now becoming evident — it can be seen to belong to the third and cataclysmic order of magnitude. To which may be added that, if one is bold enough or incautious enough to attach dates to this phenomenon, it is to the years between 1870 and 1900 that our attention seems to be most urgently drawn.

Within the context of Steiner's comment that, even today and with all the benefit of hindsight and distanced perspective, we are only just beginning to grasp the nature of this event, it is then all the more astonishing to discover a man who, though himself profoundly a creature of his age, seemed nevertheless to have his spiritual antennae so delicately and sensitively attuned

to the mood and movement of the times that he was able —
across all the disturbance and interference of quotidian event —
to detect and respond to those deeper and larger shifts that were
outside the usual range of cultural receptivity, to catch a sense of
things which, in the Wordsworthian phrase, were 'inaudible to
the vast multitude'.

The occasion which betrays this most obviously, the moment
when deeply-felt beliefs surfaced momentarily to find halting
public expression was (improbably) a brief after-dinner speech
on 24 September 1887. The phrases on that occasion were few,
laconic and impromptu; but although not wrought with the care
which the speaker normally gave to public utterance, they were
direct and rooted in a view of life which had been long and
earnestly pondered. They were phrases which recorded the
speaker's belief that mankind had reached a crucial transitional
stage between two distinct epochs; a belief that a profound
evolutionary change was impending in the life of the mind and
the spirit:

> There is . . . one point in particular I should like briefly
> to take up. It has been said that I too, in our countries,
> have taken a lead in contributing to the creation of a new
> era. I believe, on the other hand, that the age in which we
> live might just as well be described as an ending, and that
> from it something new is on the point of being born.
> Indeed I believe that the doctrine of evolution as it is in
> the natural sciences is valid also in respect of the cultural
> aspects of life. I believe that the time is imminent when
> the concepts of politics and the concepts of society will
> cease to exist in their present forms, and that from them
> both will emerge a unity which will, as a beginning, hold
> within itself the pre-requisites of human happiness. I
> believe that poetry, philosophy and religion will merge
> into a new category, a new vital force, of which we who
> are living today can have no clear understanding. [5]

The man who spoke those few spare and yet visionary words,
the man whose intuitions recorded — even if at that stage only
approximately — the movement and direction of the spiritual

forces of the modern world, was Henrik Ibsen.

Despite the post-prandial, throw-away nature of the occasion, Ibsen's phrases of 1887 were not lightly uttered, not born of sudden impulse. The convictions out of which his remarks were born had their roots deep in the events of his own life of twenty and more years earlier, to the spiritual crisis he had himself undergone at the time he quit Norway in 1864 for self-imposed exile (in Italy and in Germany); and, more specifically perhaps, to a quietly conspiratorial encounter in the summer of 1871 with the Danish critic Georg Brandes. In itself, and on the surface, this latter occasion was undemonstratively private, domestic, social; it goes almost entirely unregarded in the literary and cultural histories of Europe. And yet, under more rigorous scrutiny, it reveals itself as an occasion within which much of what was significantly cultural in these years was curiously encapsulated.

It was a short three-day visit which Georg Brandes paid in July 1871 to Henrik Ibsen, who was then resident in Dresden. Brandes was on his way back to his native Denmark after a year's study tour of Europe which had taken him to France, England and Italy. He was then 29; Ibsen 43. They were in many ways strikingly different: 'The Norwegian and the cosmopolitan, the autodidact and the academic, the poet and the critic, the stern moralist and the supple aesthete; the one gruffly buttoned-up, the other naively volatile.'[6] Over the preceding years they had exchanged a few letters; they certainly knew each other's works; but they had never met. Within Scandinavia Ibsen by now enjoyed an established and growing reputation, above all as the author of *Brand* (1866) and of *Peer Gynt* (1867), though his international fame was still some years off. Brandes, though his brilliance as a promising young scholar and critic had won him a measure of recognition in his native Denmark, was as yet without any wider European reputation. The two men had in common a small number of friends, and perhaps a rather larger number of enemies.

Both had looked forward to the meeting with heightened expectancy. Seven months earlier, as Brandes lay recovering in a Rome hospital from typhus fever, Ibsen had set the young man's nerves vibrating with a letter (of 20 December 1870) in the most extravagant terms, calling for nothing less than 'a revolution of the human spirit', and casting Brandes for a leading role in that spiritual revolution:

> World events occupy a large part of my thoughts. The old illusory France is smashed; as soon as the new *de facto* Prussia is also smashed, we shall have arrived with a single leap in a new and emergent age! And how the old ideas will come crashing down about us! And not before time! What we live on today are nothing but crumbs from last century's revolutionary table; and we have been chewing away on those long enough. The old concepts need a new content and new significance. Liberty, equality and fraternity are no longer the same things that they were in the days of the late-lamented guillotine. This is what the politicians will not recognize, and that is why I hate them. They only want specialist revolutions, superficial revolutions, in politics and the like. But that is only tinkering. What is needed is a revolution of the human spirit. And you shall be one of those marching at the head.[7]

Brandes was deeply moved. From his bed he wrote, on 9 January 1871, a poem entitled 'To Henrik Ibsen': a poor dilettante thing, he later admitted, a fragment of 'typhus poetry', a bit of knitting to occupy idle hands,[8] in which he modestly disclaimed any real qualities of leadership, but promised his complete loyalty to one who would be the greater leader in the coming cultural struggle:

> Brother, I found you. What does it matter
> That you are a captain without equal,
> Whilst I am created to fight as an equerry;
> We belong together with all our souls.
> Yes, we will summon men's minds to revolt.
> Boldly to wrench them
> Out of their lethargy,

To inspire, to vitalize,
Let this be our watchword.
Though it is dark, there'll be light for all.
Brother! In time the mists will fall.[9]

Bad poetry it may have been, but the sustaining sentiment was genuine and the ambition real. Brandes later confessed that Ibsen's words had touched his most secret hopes, set his imagination aflame. He felt he had at last, after a period of cruel isolation, found a comrade in arms.[10] Restless, tense, he was impatient for action; above all, he yearned for some vigorous undertaking that would bring life and vitality to the cultural life of his native Denmark and join it to the mainstream of European intellectual life. Moreover, his own career had clearly reached a point of crisis; and he was in desperate need of advice and encouragement.

At their meeting, they greeted each other effusively. Brandes later described the occasion in his autobiography:

Ibsen . . . crushed me to his breast so hard I could scarcely draw breath. I thought he looked handsome. He had an incomparable forehead, clear eyes, long wavy hair. Without more ado, we talked for two or three hours: partly about his work, partly about the state of affairs back home (on which we were in full agreement) and also partly about me.[11]

They met again later in the day, walked out to the 'lovely little Waldschlösslein', drank beer and dined. They confirmed in conversation what their earlier correspondence had already largely established: that they had common cause. As they took leave of each other, Ibsen called out after the departing Brandes: 'You go and stir up the Danes, I will stir up the Norwegians.' As a recipe for achieving Ibsen's 'revolution of the human spirit' this doubtless sounds an excessively modest and indeed rather negative programme. But behind the casual words, both men were conscious in their different ways of an urgent sense of crisis, of personal mission, and of a shared cultural conspiracy.

The meeting found Ibsen in a mood of heightened self-awareness. His mind was in turmoil. Earlier that same year (1871) he had spent several strenuous and draining weeks on the preparation of a volume of his collected poems, selecting and amending and arranging works written at different times over the previous twenty or so years. Having to go through all those earlier states and attitudes of mind, most of which he had by now completely outgrown and even repudiated, had been 'et forbandet stykke arbejde',[12] he said: a tormenting business. It had imposed an anguished process of self-examination and self-discovery; but the task had brought home to him the essential unity of the spiritual and intellectual development he had personally undergone, and it left him even more conscious that what essentially he was engaged on was hammering out a new *Weltanschauung* for himself. But he was also moved to extend and transfer this new awareness from the purely personal level to the condition of society and of mankind as he saw it in his own day. The conviction grew in him (as he was to put it) that perhaps the whole of mankind might be found to be on the wrong track, in much the same way as he realized he personally had been.

The collected poems were published in May 1871. The following month, and only three weeks before Brandes's visit, he at last began the actual writing of his vast new drama *Emperor and Galilean*, the research for which had been going on intermittently over the previous seven years. The new work was to be a uniquely authoritative statement. Forty-eight hours before Brandes's arrival, Ibsen wrote to his publisher (on 12 July 1871) a letter which betrays the real dimensions of his expectations:

> I am hard at work on 'Emperor Julian'. This work will be my masterpiece; it is occupying all my thoughts and all my time. The positive 'Weltanschauung' which the critics have long demanded of me will be found here. [13]

It was to take him all of the next two years of concentrated and unremitting labour to complete: a huge double drama in ten acts. He spoke of it as his 'banner', as a work of supreme universality, a declaration of his own personal philosophy and at the same time a symbolic interpretation of the modern world and of man's place in it, a work which encoded within its historical setting

and the spiritual conflicts of the fourth century A.D. the author's
insights into the predicaments of his own age.

Brandes, for his part, returned home to Copenhagen from
Dresden vibrant with excitement, impatient for action. Later that
same year, on 3 November, he delivered the first of a series of
lectures which that winter took intellectual Copenhagen by
storm,[14] but which in a short time brought the full and crushing
weight of Danish establishment disapproval down on his head. In
so doing, however, he found that he had uttered a literary
rallying cry the like of which had not been known in Denmark
before, and which was very soon taken up in other parts of
Europe. When the lectures were published early in 1872, Ibsen
read them; they disturbed his waking hours, he said, and even
invaded his sleep. With rare vision, he wrote to Brandes on
2 April 1872: 'No more dangerous book could fall into the hands
of a pregnant writer. It is one of those works that place a
yawning gulf between yesterday and today.' He described the
conflict in which Brandes was then engaged as 'a mortal combat
between two epochs'; and he encouraged him to continue the
fight with the words: 'To me your revolt is a great emancipating
outbreak of genius.'[15]

The design of the complete lecture series, the first instalment
of which had had such an immediate and explosive impact, was
an ambitious one: no less than to trace, in six volumes, first the
reaction of the nineteenth century against the literature and the
ideas of the eighteenth, and then the eventual victory over that
reaction. It was a plan that took Brandes nearly twenty years to
execute; and we now know the completed work in this country
under the title of *Main Currents of Nineteenth Century Literature*.
In the history of comparative literature studies, it is one of the
great seminal works.

From the very start of their mutual awareness, it had been the
fighter each admired in the other. Both were quick to comment
in approving terms on the other's courage, the strength of his
conviction and purpose, the intensity of his indignation. The
contemporary cultural scene they both tended to see in terms of
a battlefield, the situation as one of conflict. Intellectual battles

were waiting to be fought, philosophical standpoints to be defended, social abuses to be assaulted. Appropriately, their earliest exchange of letters coincided closely with the publication of the abrasive *Brand*. Among his acquaintances in Rome (where, in the spring of 1866, Ibsen was resident) was a young Dane and close friend of Brandes by the name of Ludvig David. From him, Ibsen learnt of the bitter dispute back in Copenhagen between Brandes and the supporters of religious orthodoxy, a dispute which Ibsen had been following in pages of the Danish paper *Fædrelandet*, of which he was a dedicated reader. The conversation in the small Scandinavian colony in Rome often turned to Brandes. Unhappily the young Ludvig David committed suicide; and in the April of the year Ibsen sent from Italy a long and detailed account of the circumstances to Brandes. It was the first time they had directly communicated. When, to end his letter, Ibsen added a few phrases of a more personal nature, it was characteristically to encourage Brandes in his fight:

> Thank you for your kind words which were conveyed to me. I look forward with pleasure to meeting you personally some time .... Best wishes. Keep up your brave fight. That is something which we in the North need so badly in many respects ....[16]

In his reply — which has not survived but which probably reached Ibsen about the middle of May 1866 — Brandes must surely have drawn Ibsen's attention to his forthcoming review of *Brand* in *Dagbladet*. Though seemingly written in the March, this review was not published until 23 May; in it, Brandes wrote of the reader's 'thrilling, indeed overwhelming, impression of having stood face to face with a forceful and indignant genius'. At the same time, it is clear from the rest of the review and from other pieces he wrote on Ibsen shortly afterwards that, although he admired the indignation, he was not wholly persuaded of the purely literary qualities: compared with the rich poetry of *The Pretenders*, he asserted, *Brand* marked a step in the wrong direction; and Ibsen would need to revise his ideas if he wished to return to the path of true poetry. Nevertheless, Ibsen was grateful for even this faint praise, and later that summer wrote to his publisher in Copenhagen to ask him to convey to Brandes his thanks for the 'warm and friendly criticism of *Brand*', glad no doubt that Brandes had written approvingly of the strength of moral indignation in the work.

The same was true in reverse. When, writing to Jonas Collin the following year, Ibsen commented approvingly on what Brandes had been doing, it was particularly 'the strength of his convictions' that he singled out for admiration, and not so much the precise nature of those beliefs:

> I see from *Dagbladet* that a paper war has broken out in Copenhagen between the philosophers and the theologians. I am not sufficiently familiar with these matters to be able to form an opinion. But I have to admit that there is an unusual power and strength of conviction in Georg Brandes's conduct. I do not know if you are an ally of his or an opponent; but it is clear to me that this man will come to play a big part in the scholarly and cultural life of Scandinavia. Naturally in claiming this I say nothing of my personal attitude to his view. [17]

There had been hopes that they might meet in the summer of 1866. Ibsen wrote from Italy that, now that Brandes had been awarded a travel grant, it was possible that they might be able to meet 'somewhere here in the South', though he suspected that Brandes might well have other plans. Hopes were indeed disappointed; and there the correspondence remained until the summer of 1869.

Nevertheless, and despite the lack of contact between them, Brandes became more and more convinced as the years passed that, in the coming cultural revolution for which he yearned, it would be Ibsen who would take over the role of leader. Increasingly Brandes devoted himself to Ibsen and his work; in May 1867 he wrote reviews of the recently published second edition of *Love's Comedy*; in the November there appeared from his pen a full biographical and critical article on Ibsen in *Dansk Maanedsskrift,* an account which did more than any publication hitherto to establish Ibsen's reputation in Scandinavia. The following month he reviewed *Peer Gynt* in both *Dagbladet* and

Illustreret Tidende. Eventually, in 1868, he revised and consolidated all these pieces to form one section of a collected volume of *Aesthetiske Studier* (*Aesthetic Studies*).

Meanwhile, Ibsen for his part had been following from afar and with intense interest the continuing polemics which had followed Brandes's attacks on the religious orthodoxy of Rasmus Nielsen; and his respect for Brandes's intellectual courage grew with every new development.

What Brandes found himself looking for above all from Ibsen, therefore, was a lead. He had naturally been greatly flattered when Ibsen had written to him as one of those who would be marching at the head of the 'revolution of the human spirit'; but although the thought of playing such a role exercised on him an immense appeal — ever since reading Kierkegaard as a young man he had dreamed of enjoying some exquisite martyrdom in the cause of truth — he suffered an agony of uncertainty about his own innate capacity for achieving this kind of politico-cultural success. He yearned to play the part of some great captain of culture, but — as the poem of homage to Ibsen so readily betrays — he suspected that a more subordinate or supporting role was one more suited to his talents.

It is clear that the fervour and audacity of some of Ibsen's more extreme revolutionary ideas as they found expression in their correspondence startled the young Brandes.[18] There seemed no reason at the time for not accepting Ibsen's expressed views at their face value, despite their uncompromising and occasionally extreme formulation:

The state must go! That revolution I will join. Subvert the concept of statehood; make free choice and spiritual kinship the sole essentials for union and you have the start of a liberty that is worth something. Exchanging one kind of government for another is merely tinkering in matters of degree, a little more or a little less: folly, all of it. Yes, dear friend, all that matters is not to be frightened by the venerableness of the institution. The state is rooted in time; it will reach its limit in time. Greater things than

it will fall. All religion will fall. Neither our moral
concepts nor our forms of art are permanent. What is
there, fundamentally, that we are obliged to hold fast to?
Who can guarantee me that 2 and 2 do not make 5 on
Jupiter?[19]

In such audacious phrases, Brandes found ready encouragement
for thinking that he could enlist Ibsen as a real cultural activist
in the campaign for new values.

At their meeting in the July, Ibsen was nevertheless quick to
recognize in Brandes's condition all the symptoms of personal
crisis, an anguish of spirit such as he himself had undergone only
some six or seven years earlier. Shortly after the meeting between
the two men, and in response to what must have been a disturb-
ingly agitated letter from Brandes, Ibsen wrote to draw attention
to the similarity in their situation:

> I always read your letters with strangely mixed feelings.
> They are more like poems than letters. What you write
> strikes me like a cry of distress from one who has been
> left the sole survivor in some great lifeless desert . . . You
> seem to me to be passing through the same crisis that I
> passed through when I began to write *Brand*.[20]

In the case of both men, the crisis had its origin in their sense
of personal mission. Even in his very earliest days as a novice
dramatist, Ibsen's belief in the high calling of poet or 'scald' had
been very evident. In the breathless Prologue which he wrote at
the very outset of his career to be declaimed at a fund-raising
festival evening in 1851 in support of the recently established
Bergen theatre, he had put the emphasis very firmly on the
public duty of the poet, on his scaldic mission: to proclaim the
nationhood of the people, to affirm its glorious past, to praise its
way of life, to extol the glory of its tongue. [21] Fourteen difficult
years later, and after a severe personal crisis of confidence, the
views that he built into *Brand* were very different in kind but no
less passionate in their intensity; except that now he saw his
mission as being that of the solitary, detached observer, recognizing the realities of life, taking long views, putting the truth

with honesty and courage however unpalatable it might be.

Moreover, at the same time as Ibsen was turning away from the uncritical chauvinism of his earlier works to the admonitory severity of his later ones, and as easy flattery gave way to caustic accusation, he was also widening his horizons from the narrowly and nationalistically Norwegian to the more broadly European. Expatriation had remarkably concentrated his mind; the new awareness of Mediterranean culture had struck him with all the force of a revelation. With the success of *Brand* and *Peer Gynt* and the growth of his reputation, he had found himself invited to serve in new and more public ways: at the opening of the Suez Canal; at the spelling reform conference in Stockholm; on an international art jury in Vienna. His awareness of the European scene had grown much more acute: his experiences in Berlin at the time of the Dano-Prussian war; his period of residence in the Italy of Garibaldi; the anguish of the Franco-Prussian war which made its impact felt even on the streets of Dresden where he was living; the fateful events of the Paris Commune; the change in the status and the role of Rome — all these are things that surface in his correspondence, and it is clear that he pondered them deeply, brooding on the role he sensed he might himself be able to play in influencing the battle for men's minds within the wider Europe.

Brandes, for his part, brought a different set of talents, a different range of experiences, to the Dresden encounter. His was a restlessly brilliant mind which, starting from the more familiar Danish orthodoxies of Kierkegaard in philosophy and of Heiberg in literary criticism, was eager to find a newer, more modern, more relevant set of values. He read insatiably — it is said, for example, that in his last year at school a passion for Goethe led him to the decision to read his works entire.[22] He began as a student of law, but it was not long before his wider reading took him well outside the confines of his law books. The break with the prevailing orthodoxies came in two stages. First, in 1886, came his philosophical heresies, the assault on religious orthodoxy in a book called *Dualismen i vor nyeste Philosophie (On dualism in our most recent philosophy)*, a free-thinker's declaration directed against Rasmus Nielsen's claims to 'mediate' between faith and knowledge. As for his literary criteria, for a long time they remained conventionally Heibergian, and solidly conservative; he found himself able to approve of Ibsen's indignation whilst at the same time condemning his departure from the standards of 'true' poetry *à la Heiberg*. But in the late 1860s a change came over his literary values: he found his admiration growing for the problem-centred plays of Dumas *fils* and Augier; he found himself drawn to the harder, thrusting Mérimée; and he discovered a new affinity with the criticism of St Beuve.

Finally, as the 'sixties drew to a close, he found himself greatly preoccupied first by Hippolyte Taine and then by John Stuart Mill. The direct positivism of their analytical method, the former in literary and aesthetic matters, the latter more in philosophical and moral concerns, appealed to Brandes's forthright mind. Taine, who seemed to offer an escape from the abstractions of traditional German philosophy, was selected by Brandes as the central theme of his doctoral dissertation: *Den Franske Æsthetik i vore Dage (French aesthetics in the present day)*. Eventually, however, it was Mill who above all came to represent Brandes's ideal, and who gave him a design for conduct as well as stimulating him to a new attitude to life. It was an enthusiasm that led to his translating Mill's *The Subjection of Women* into Danish in 1869; and this he followed up by translating *Utilitarianism* in 1872. Above all, Mill appealed to Brandes's own secret dreams of being a man of action. Whilst Brandes was temporarily resident in Paris in 1870, Mill himself happened to be in the city at the same time, and — flatteringly — went out of his way to call on the young Dane in his room. He stayed a full two hours, and by his personality quite captivated the young Brandes. Brandes found Mill utterly different from those other writers and thinkers (Taine and Renan, in particular) whom he had earlier met in Paris. These others seemed to him men of theory, without any real contact with the practical side of life, and as such temperamentally quite unsuited to the kind of public role he himself set such high value on. Direct individual action, apart from what could be achieved obliquely by the printed word, was something quite alien to the two French thinkers; personal intervention in determining the course of events was no part of their ambition. Mill was clearly different. Though in Brandes's eyes in no way inferior as a thinker to these French savants, Mill clearly knew the compulsion to play an active and directly participatory role in society. Brandes has put on record how deeply impressed he was:

> For the first time in my life I met a man who embodied the ideal I had formed of what constituted a great man. This meant having two sides: talent and character, ability and tenacity. The great personalities, artists and scholars I had met hitherto were men of great gifts; but the man who combined these things with great character I had never met . . . Now [in Mill] I found embodied within the one man great tenacity allied to the pursuit of ideas. And this had a life-long effect on me.[23]

Actually — and greatly to his regret — Brandes came in time to recognize that he himself was not really cut out for the stern world of practical politics; nevertheless he determined that he would do everything open to him to influence the larger course of cultural events. He was, he insisted, determined not to be 'a mere scholar, an entertaining author, a literary historian, or anything like that':

> I felt I was made to be a man of action. But the men of action I had come across hitherto had repelled me by their lack of ideas. At last in Mill I made the acquaintance of a man in whom the power of action, of provocation, of perseverance were put wholly at the service of new social ideas.[24]

This was the source of the ideal of the Thinker-agitator that fired Brandes as a young man — an ideal which he came in time to see supremely exemplified in Lassalle, on whom he wrote a monograph; an ideal which even today moves Danish commentators to describe Brandes not as a literary historian or critic but as a 'cultural politician'. It is a designation clearly invited by the opening phrases of his preface to *Hovedstrømninger i det nittende Aarhundredes Litteratur (Main currents in nineteenth century literature)*:

Main Currents, by tracing the development of the literatures of the main countries of Europe through the first
half of the nineteenth century, tells part of the history of
the European Mind. The design of the book is political,
not literary.[25]

It is his way — to adapt the terms he used of Mill — of trying to
turn the academic lecture platform into a popular tribunal.
Certainly, it was not by chance that for the terminal date of his
comparative survey he chose 1848, that fateful and stormy year
in Europe's destiny.

Life style and literary style fused together at this point.
Deliberately, consciously, he set out to perform the role of the
man of action within his own self-acknowledged limitations:
lobbying, proselytizing, establishing contacts, seeking out the
influential figures of the age. His visit to Ibsen in Dresden was
part of the larger design, of which his lectures later that same
year are in a sense a complementary manifestation. He formed
groups, established periodicals; he developed a range of
correspondence with other authors, thinkers, critics and scholars
which in itself served as a kind of marshalling agency, pulling
scattered individuals into concerted action. The title of one of his
most influential books *Det moderne Gjennembruds Mænd (Men
of the modern breakthrough,* 1883) is completely attuned to the
kind of concerted and aggressive cultural advance he sought to
achieve. The printed word, potent though he knew it to be, was
nevertheless inadequate for his deeper purposes. The public
lecture was by its nature at least one stage nearer to the kind of
immediate participation in the pursuit of life's purposes that
Brandes yearned for — admonitory, hortatory, even inflam-
matory, and filled with all the immediacy that belongs to an act
of direct and personalized communication. It was to this, after
some months of anguished self-examination following his first
meeting with Ibsen, that he eventually turned in the November
of that year.

Behind the demonstrative surface of the meeting in Dresden,

there was nevertheless — even as it was taking place — a measure of incipient disappointment, a sense of expectations only partially fulfilled. Although cordial relations were established and maintained, and Brandes even returned to Dresden the following year to pay Ibsen a longer visit, the relationship never developed into the kind of militant alliance that Brandes yearned for. In the first place, Brandes may well have found Ibsen too limited in his range of conversational reference to provide the kind of stimulus which Brandes — who was not without intellectual arrogance — had been hoping for. Less than three years after their first meeting, Brandes could say: 'Friendly though Ibsen was, and always is, towards me, I am too superior to him in education to get any value out of long conversations with him.'[26] But more surprising and even more disappointing was the fact that Ibsen did not turn out to be anything like the urgent activist his letters had seemed to portend. Not only did Ibsen have a deep distaste for any kind of oratorical posturing (such as he associated with Bjørnson); but he also remained distinctly unenthusiastic about joining any communal or concerted effort. He actively shunned alliances or parties or associations of any kind. This at least was something for which Brandes might have been prepared; for one of the more memorable passages in Ibsen's correspondence with him — a passage Brandes was frequently to quote in later career — had been Ibsen's insistence on the paramount need to stand alone, for even friendship was a luxury that a man with a mission could not and should not permit himself:

> Friends are an expensive luxury; and when a man has invested his capital in a calling and a mission in life, he simply cannot afford to keep friends. When one has friends, the expense of keeping them does not lie in what one does for them, but rather in what out of consideration for them one refrains from doing. The consequence is that one's spiritual development is largely stunted. This I know from personal experience; and as a result I was for many years of my past life prevented from being myself.[27]

Nor was this the only aspect of the encounter that left Brandes puzzled and disappointed. There was also Ibsen's unaccountable enthusiasm for *Emperor and Galilean*, the play on which Brandes found him currently engaged. This he found quite inexplicable; and reading between the lines of their subsequent correspondence, it seems that he probably took little pains to conceal his dismay that Ibsen should dissipate his intellectual energies on something so remote as fourth-century Byzantium.[28] Ibsen, sensing that the symbolic meaning of the emergent drama and its oblique but powerful relevance to the contemporary world was lost upon Brandes, clearly did not feel like entering into complex explanations: 'Your last letter on this subject [of *Emperor and Galilean*]', Ibsen wrote crisply, not long after Brandes had returned to Copenhagen from Dresden, 'did not cause me any real concern. In the first place, because I was expecting misgivings of this kind from you; but also because I am in fact treating the material differently from the way you assume.'[29]

To as compulsive a student of human nature as Brandes, the contradictions in Ibsen's nature — or, more accurately, the disparity between what he wrote and what he was ultimately prepared to *do* — were doubtless soon evident. Despite the overt warmth of their meeting, Brandes must quite early have begun to entertain doubts about Ibsen's large phrases, and to wonder about his readiness to match words with deeds.[30] On his return to Copenhagen, Brandes tried to bring things to a point of decision. Possessed by the idea of uttering some great rallying call, of issuing some powerful declaration, of making some gesture that would give focus to the disaffection which he and his generation felt, and yet at the same time himself racked with uncertainty, despondency and indecision, Brandes seems to have made a passionate appeal in a letter to Ibsen, urging him to 'raise a banner'. Brandes's letter itself is lost; but its essential intent can be reconstituted from Ibsen's reply of 24 September 1871 — a reply which can only have been greatly disappointing and even wounding to Brandes:

> So I'm supposed to try and hoist a banner? My dear friend, it would be a bit like when Louis Napoleon came ashore at Boulogne with an eagle on his helmet. Later, when the hour of destiny struck, he didn't need any eagle.

> During my work on "Julian" [i.e. *Emperor and Galilean*]
> I have become a sort of fatalist; but this play will never-
> theless become a kind of banner . . .[31]

The one thing Ibsen's letter of reply did achieve was to bring
Brandes to the point of personal decision, to confirm him in his
own course of action. It helped to persuade him to commit
himself to a socially and intellectually provocative series of
lectures, which he intended should constitute a *political* act of
self-dedication.

The history of the consequences, direct and oblique, of this
meeting of minds in 1871 is a full and continuing one. The
immediate result was that they both, in their own personal and
indeed idiosyncratic ways, proceeded to make declarations which
are startlingly dissimilar and yet strangely related: first Brandes
in 1872 with the opening volume of his *Main Currents of
Nineteenth Century Literature*, analytical, provocative, political;
then, in 1873, Ibsen with his huge double ten-act drama *Emperor
and Galilean*, prophetic, mystic, visionary. Brandes who,
adopting the guise of a scholar's detachment, offered an analysis
in depth of the development of European literature in France,
Germany and England from the French Revolution of 1789 to
the February Revolution of 1848, but who also in so doing
succeeded in forging cultural history and literary criticism into
a powerful weapon for use in the ideological conflicts of his own
age. And Ibsen who, in a work historical in its setting but very
deliberately contemporary in its relevance, made of it the
repository of his own mature and pondered views on life and the
world and the human situation. It was moreover a work which he
repeatedly appealed to as the most fully articulated statement of
his personal philosophy; and it is no surprise to see his Stockholm
after-dinner speech ending with the totally uncompromising
statement:

> More particularly and precisely, I believe that the ideals
> of our age, suffering eclipse, show a trend towards that
> which I have intimated in my drama *Emperor and
> Galilean* by the term 'the third realm'.[32]

Though outwardly and superficially greatly divergent, these two works of Brandes and Ibsen were nevertheless in large measure born of a shared vision and of a common sense of purpose.

And as it had begun, so in the subsequent careers and achievements of the two men it continued. Both of them, in their own distinctive ways, came to dominate those areas of cultural endeavour they had made their own: Brandes in the first instance to become the leading spokesman for 'problem literature' and all that flowed from that, and destined in time to become the intermediary through whom, very largely, both Kierkegaard and Nietzsche won acknowledgement in the wider world as influential thinkers; and Ibsen who, though he abandoned historical drama after *Emperor and Galilean*, continued through the medium of his 'dramas of contemporary life' to offer a comparable analysis of the nature of modern man and his predicaments.

Emperor and Galilean had, it is clear, been an attempt to isolate and identify the ills of the modern world of Ibsen's day, to formulate them indirectly in poetic terms, to embody them in an historical analogue. It was, as we know, destined to be his one and only attempt at such explicitly symbolical definition. Disappointingly, it did not succeed in communicating its deeper meanings in the way that Ibsen had intended, though he never, for as long as he lived, gave up the hope that its message would some day be received and understood. At the time, however, he bowed to the inevitable; and henceforward — over the last quarter- century of his creative career in those plays running from *Pillars of Society* in 1877 to *When We Dead Awaken* in 1899 — his dramatic mode was different. But the deeper convictions out of which his drama grew persisted, as his 1887 after-dinner remarks reveal. Although one would not claim these modern plays as a mere alternative or substitute articulation of what he had tried to say in *Emperor and Galilean*, they did nevertheless spring from the same sense of apocalyptic conviction, a sense so elusive as to be almost incommunicable in direct terms: a belief in impending change so fundamental that the very concepts by which we think, the very images by which we seek to comprehend reality, the mathematics by which we calculate, 'the entire world of sacrament and sign' (to use again David Jones's phrase) were about to undergo the profoundest transformation.

We of the present day, who are still *of* this change, understandably find difficulty in sufficiently distancing ourselves from it to grasp its true shape and dimensions. Ibsen, who was of course even more central to it, was similarly affected. But it was his achievement to detect this thing, to respond to it, to draw attention to it, and to write his dramas in the consciousness of it. Because this consciousness is there only as a presence, however, as a pervasive quality, it is not easy to separate it out for simple scrutiny. Nevertheless the fact remains that anybody who seeks a fuller understanding of Ibsen and his modern dramas in ignorance of this deeper compulsion, this profounder insight, this innate sense of recognition, is forever condemned to a merely partial understanding of their meaning and purpose.

If, now, the reader should be thinking that the link between the two halves of my title — the 'cultural conspiracy' of the Ibsen-Brandes meeting and the 'civilizational change' of the idea of the Great Divide — has been left inadequately realized, let me conclude defensively with an image from Strindberg. In his play *The Father*, the wife Laura finds it utterly absurd, and offers it as self-evident proof that the balance of her husband's mind is disturbed, that he should investigate cosmic phenomena by looking down a microscope at little bits of rock. Impatiently, the husband puts the record straight: it is not a microscope but a spectroscope; they are not just any old pieces of rock but meteoric stones; and the subjection of such specimens to spectrum analysis is an entirely reputable research undertaking. When I contemplate the problems of exploring the larger cultural shifts and displacements of the modern age, I find this image — both in the wife's misconstruction and also in the husband's validation — strongly appealing. I find in it a licence for supposing that one might well be able to identify and set up for examination a selection of cultural 'meteoric stones', that is, individual works or events which are amenable to specific forms of analytical scrutiny and which hold within them encoded information about things perhaps too hugely incommensurable to be sensibly approached other than thus indirectly.

And images beget images; in consequence of which one is prompted to think of the emergence of Scandinavia in these years as nothing less than a meteoric rise, with a consequential scattering of cultural 'meteoric stones' which — given our propensity in this country to think of Europe and its culture as being dominated by Britain, France, Germany and the Mediterranean — have perhaps received less than their deserved measure of scrutiny.

Only one thing, finally, staunches the flow of cosmic images and gives me pause: the sobering realization that Strindberg's hero, in presuming to seek explanation for the cosmically large in the insignificantly small, found in it a policy which, in his own case, led first to a madman's strait-jacket and then to an apoplectic death.

14

Apostasy in Prose

> The principal division in the history of Western
> literature occurs between the early 1870s and
> the turn of the century . . . . Compared to this
> division all preceding historical and stylistic
> rubrics or movements — Hellenism, the
> medieval, the Baroque, Neo-classicism,
> Romanticism — are only sub-groups or vari-
> ants. (George Steiner, *After Babel*, London
> 1975, p.176)

The title of this Symposium is a long one: 'Preludes to Modernism: literature, art, music and thought in the period 1870 to
1914'. Almost, indeed, an Opening Statement in itself.

Nevertheless, it was thought it might be helpful if I were
briefly to sketch out some rough kind of framework within

which, as we listen to the individual papers, the separate con-
tributions might be placed. As I do this, I shall not — deliberately
not — attempt to say anything new. The greater part of what I
shall have to say in the next fifteen to twenty minutes will consist
of references to or quotations from the work of others who have
given their scholarly attention to the period to which this
Symposium is addressing itself. I shall also beg leave to plagiarize
myself here and there where it seemed to me that things I have
said on other occasions might usefully be recalled in this present
context.

[*Here followed a brief introductory statement on the
general nature of the period, indicating some of the more
fundamental changes that had taken place in thought and
in attitudes, and cataloguing some of the more significant
names and achievements attaching to these years. The
widely held view that this period of change was qualita-
tively and quantitatively different from other periods of
cultural change in the history of mankind was noted.*]

Within this period of profound change, drama was of course
not exempt; and the chasm which separates contemporary drama
from the drama of the first half of the nineteenth century —
from Schiller and Kleist, from Hugo and de Musset, from
Grillparzer and Hebbel — is huge. That proposition which,
explicitly or implicitly, serves as the starting point for nearly all
histories of modern drama is also one which focuses the attention
very much on the period between 1870 and the end of the
century. It is a proposition which was given its most succinct
formulation by Kenneth Muir:

The most important event in the history of modern drama
was Ibsen's abandonment of verse after *Peer Gynt* in order
to write prose plays about contemporary problems.[1]

The restless exploration of the resources of prose as a dramatic
medium, the extension of the concept of 'poetry' to embrace
much linguistic territory that was previously neglected or even
despised are things seen as having their origins in this decision of

Ibsen. It is an idea more often asserted than examined; and for an event of such acknowledged magnitude it has (I suggest) had less attention from commentators than it deserves. It is recognized as having been a very deliberate decision, born of a deeply held conviction; and Ibsen's revealing letter to Lucie Wolf some years after the event is regularly quoted in evidence. I remind you that in May 1883 Lucie Wolf, an actress at the Christiania Theatre, wrote asking if he would compose a Prologue to be declaimed at a forthcoming festival occasion in her honour. Let us remind ourselves of the precise terms of Ibsen's reply. No, he said:

> I wish I could comply with your request. Nothing would please me more than to be able to do it. But I cannot; my convictions and my artistic principles forbid me. Prologues, epilogues, and everything of the kind ought to be banished from the stage. The stage is for dramatic art alone; and declamation is not a dramatic art.
>
> The prologue would of course have to be in verse, since that is the established custom. But I will take no part in perpetuating this custom. Verse has been most injurious to the art of the drama. A true artist of the stage, whose repertoire is the contemporary drama, should not be willing to let a single line of verse cross his or her lips. It is improbable that verse will be employed to any extent worth mentioning in the drama of the future since the aims of future dramatists are almost certain to be incompatible with it. Consequently it is doomed. For art forms become extinct, just as the preposterous animal forms of prehistoric times became extinct when their day was done.
>
> A tragedy in iambic pentameters is already as rare a phenomenon as the dodo . . . . During the last seven or eight years, I have hardly written a single line of verse, devoting myself exclusively to the very much more difficult art of writing the straightforward, plain language spoken in real life.[2]

But this was not the abrupt and straightforward decision which many commentaries seem to imply. I shall want to try to show that the factors which were at work in Ibsen's mind at the time he took this decision, the way in which he then found himself — sometimes deliberately, sometimes involuntarily — modifying his dramatic policies and methods in the light of practice and experience, and the residue which these shifts and re-orientations left in his work are elements in an extremely complex act of intellectual and cultural apostasy. I see them as things worth tracing in some of their finer details, not only for the light they shed on the new direction taken by his own drama but also for the impact they had on European drama in general in these years and for long years to come.

The first question to clarify is therefore: which were these years of decision? *Peer Gynt* appeared in 1867, one year after the publication of *Brand*; the first of his prose 'dramas of contemporary life', *Pillars of Society*, appeared in 1877. Ten years of prime life, from the author's fortieth to his fiftieth year. A decade of greatly varied endeavour, in the course of which he published three works of vastly differing quality: a roistering comedy called *The League of Youth* in 1869, a volume of his collected *Poems* in 1871, and his vast 'world-historic' drama, *Emperor and Galilean* in 1873.

Arithmetic alone, if nothing else, indicates how central this last work, *Emperor and Galilean*, is to our present purposes. Completed when the author was 45, it comes almost exactly midway in the period we have selected as crucial: that decade between Ibsen's abandonment of verse after *Peer Gynt* and the start of the cycle of prose plays about contemporary problems. It also, significantly, comes very nearly at the mid-point of Ibsen's creative career as a whole, extending as it does from his first drama *Catilina* in 1850 to his last, *When We Dead Awaken* in 1899.Moreover, the occasion of the publication of *Emperor and Galilean* was the very first time that Ibsen, openly and unambiguously, declared himself on the side of a realistic prose dialogue as the preferred medium of drama and expressed his hostility to what he referred to as 'the language of the gods'. It came in an exchange of letters in 1874 with Edmund Gosse. Gosse had sent Ibsen a review of *Emperor and Galilean* which he had published in *The Spectator*, and in which he had been incautious enough to remark that he thought the play would have been better for being written in verse. Not so, said Ibsen:

> I am greatly obliged to you for your kind review of my
> new play. There is only one remark in it about which I
> must say a word or two. You say that the drama ought to
> have been written in verse and that it would have gained
> by this. Here I must differ from you. As you must have
> observed, the play is conceived in the most realistic style.
> The illusion I wished to produce was that of reality. I
> wished to produce the impression on the reader [sic] that
> what he was reading was something that had actually
> happened. If I had employed verse, I would have counter-
> acted my own intention and defeated my purpose . . . .
> Speaking generally, the dialogue must conform to the
> degree of idealization which pervades the work as a
> whole. My new drama is no tragedy in the ancient sense.
> What I sought to depict were human beings, and therefore
> I would not let them speak the 'language of the gods'.[3]

Emperor and Galilean was planned as a trilogy — three dramas of
3 acts, 3 acts and 5 acts respectively; but at a comparatively late
stage in its composition it was re-modelled as *two* inter-related
five-act dramas — an uneasy structure, which immediately
betrays something of the severely intractable nature of the
material, but also at a deeper level endorses by its form something of the unfinalized, unresolved nature of its message.

Taken together, the ten Acts of *Emperor and Galilean* follow
the career of Julian the Apostate, his rise to imperial power and
his attempts to reintroduce the old paganism into the Christianized Roman Empire of the 4th century AD. The action of the
first half, entitled *Caesar's Apostasy*, moves from Constantinople
to Athens and to Ephesus, and eventually to Lutetia and Vienne
in Gaul, covering the ten years between AD351 and AD361, by
which time the hero had become Julianus Apostata and had
ritually broken with the Christian faith. The second drama,
entitled *Emperor Julian*, follows the events of the years from
AD361 to AD363, tracing the decline of the emperor hero against
a Christianity powerfully reasserting itself, moving from
Constantinople to Antioch and then to the Eastern territories of

the Empire and to the plains beyond the Tigris where Julian finally meets his death at the hands of one of his own soldiers.

After the completion of the work, Ibsen steadfastly and repeatedly insisted on three things about it: that it was highly subjective; that, despite the remoteness in time of its subject matter, its relevance to the contemporary world was both deliberate and of the greatest importance; and that for those who cared to look, his (Ibsen's) own philosophy of life and art was clearly visible there for anybody who could read the signs. To the end of his life, he also liked to suggest that of all his work this was his supreme masterpiece.[4]

Ibsen made a number of separate but abortive approach runs to his material before he finally began writing the version as we now know it. One of the projects which we know he had carried with him when he left Norway in 1864 for what was destined to be a 27 year self-imposed exile was a plan for a tragedy to be called 'Julianus Apostata'.

Between that first unformed plan and the completed drama nine years later lies a period of great turmoil for Ibsen, in which artistic as well as material success was mixed with protracted soul-searching and anguished enquiry and in the course of which his 'world view' — if I may use that term to mean his 'Weltanschauung' — and his artistic credo underwent fundamental change.

I want to suggest that one might identify here three main phases, which I will call (a) the ethical apostasy; (b) the aesthetic apostasy; and (c) the new vision. I must needs speak of them as though they were consecutive, though in reality they were closely intermeshed, with any shift in one area inevitably having repercussions in the others.

The vehemence of Ibsen's repudiation of his tribal ethic — by which I mean that body of beliefs and values distinctive of Norwegian culture and society at the time — is an indication of why he should have found the theme of Julian's apostasy so apposite to his dramatic intentions. On 16 September 1864 he wrote to Bjørnson:

'Here in Rome there is a blessed peace in which to write; at present I am working on a longish poem and I have in

preparation a tragedy 'Julianus Apostata', a work which
I embrace with unrestrained joy and which I am sure will
go well for me. I hope to have both these things ready by
the spring, or at least by next summer.'[5]

The following spring, his plan for a Julian drama was still
alive and active. When he applied back to the authorities in
Norway for a grant to enable him to extend his time in Rome, he
wrote that he would shortly be preparing a substantial drama on
a theme taken from Roman history. In the event, however, it was
not Julian who first served as the bearer of his new convictions,
but Brand: most conspicuously in the poetic drama of which he
is the eponymous hero, but perhaps even more eloquently in the
opening section of the long but unfinished narrative poem which
is generally known as 'the epic Brand'.

It was this poem which, in the most forthright and uncompromising way, announced that its author was breaking with his
own past, turning away from the earlier sentimentalities of
Norwegian national romanticism, in order to dedicate himself to
communicating the truth about *present* concerns. The poem stood
both as a condemnation and as a manifesto, and is probably one
of the most important programmatic statements about his work
and beliefs that Ibsen ever made.

In effect, the poem was a call to Ibsen's fellow countrymen to
repudiate the lying pretence that had been infecting all levels of
public and private life. The past, he insisted, was dead; the
Viking spirit upon which the people so pathetically prided
themselves was no longer a living thing but a rouged and embalmed corpse, pestilential. The ancient grandeur had vanished,
and the modern generation was too puny even to attempt to wear
the trappings of those earlier heroic ages, too feeble to be worthy
of its inheritance. Therefore, the poem declares, he has turned
his eyes and mind away from the soul-dead tales of the past,
away from the lying dreams of the future, in order to enter the
misty, rain-swept world of the present.

So that when Ibsen turned from his narrative poem to begin
work on *Brand* as we now know it, it was inevitable that the new
work should be above all else an act of repudiation and
disavowal, a passionate denial of earlier assumptions and beliefs,

a vehement apostasy. Compounded of distaste, guilt, contempt and frustration, it represented a breakaway from what Ibsen now recognized as a whole world of false values and spurious ideals. It cut free from the past, from an existence of inauthentic living and writing. He wrote as one possessed; and in less than four months the new work — a huge and powerful dramatic statement — was complete.

He was drawn to scrutinize whole areas of his earlier life and career: his own childhood and his relations with his parents, brothers and sister; his earlier authorship, its aims, its purposes, and its disappointing achievements; his earlier unthinking acceptance of a whole range of conventional beliefs and current ideas; the frustrations and humiliations of his professional life in the theatre — 'a daily repeated abortion', he was later moved to call it. He found himself with a new awareness of standards and values fundamentally different from those that continued to serve his contemporaries and countrymen back home. He was moved to contrast the realities of his Italian experience with the defensive fictions of the Norwegian Myth as he had experienced it, notions to which he had himself shamefully given currency by his pen, the lies that told of the decay and effeteness of Mediterranean culture as compared to the gale-swept, invigorating strength of the North. He began to recognize the crippling provincialism of that way of life which had been his lot for half a lifetime and which he now recognized as hollow and empty and based on cruel self-deception. He squirmed as he recalled the active part he had played as a writer in promoting these delusions, in promulgating these lies. He fumed at the realization that chauvinistic social and cultural forces had somehow manipulated him, had exploited his talents in the interests of a spurious and lying ideal.[6]

These passions were however important less for their own sake than as a kind of fuse that set off a veritable explosion of thought and feeling in his own inner life. Things he had suffered and proved on his own nerves, things he had 'lived through' — a phrase Ibsen gave high value to as meaning something different from his merely having witnessed, or experienced from the outside — now combined to impose upon him a fundamental reappraisal: the social pressures, the cultural impositions, the received ideas, the wishful thinking, the public hypocrisy, the individual self-deception, the false assumptions, the spiritual chauvinism, the empty big-mouthed phrases which he now heard as though across the entire length of Europe, were now all distanced and seen for what they really were.

The second stage of his apostasy — what I have called his aesthetic apostasy — was less explosive, more protracted, more diffuse. Ibsen was not unaware that these more obvious changes in values and attitudes would have repercussions elsewhere in his artistic beliefs; and one letter which he wrote from Rome to Bjørnson back in Norway spoke of how he had purged himself of 'aestheticism' — 'det Æsthetiske' — a highly complex concept in Scandinavian thought in this Kierkegaardian era. This, he realized, was something which had up to then exerted a powerful influence over him; now, however, he had come to see that 'aestheticism of this kind ... (is) as great a curse to poetry as theology is to religion.'[7]

In all this matrix of ideas, however, there was one belief where Ibsen's views had conspicuously not yet changed: his view of the role of verse in drama, at least in his own drama. Very shortly after completing *Brand*, Ibsen wrote to Clemens Petersen, one of Denmark's leading critics, to re-assert his own belief that verse was for him the natural dramatic medium:

> You once wrote to me that verse form with symbolic overtones was my natural bent. I have often thought about this. I believe the same myself; and it is in accord with this view that my work (*Brand*) has taken shape.[8]

There seems little doubt that if Ibsen had persisted at this stage with *Emperor and Galilean*, it would have been in verse. As it happens, in the summer of the following year (1866) he still had Julian in his sights, and his correspondence has several references to the possibility of his 'starting in earnest' on Julian. But again another project displaced it — this time the writing of *Peer Gynt*. He started work on this shortly after New Year 1867 and it was complete some nine months later.

Perhaps even at the time — certainly later — Ibsen began to worry a little about the sheer speed and facility which with he had been able to complete these verse dramas: *Brand* in four months; *Peer Gynt*, which, according to its author, 'followed of its own accord', in nine: and both of them unusually long and complex works.

These were years when argument about the concept of 'poetry' and the meaning of 'beauty' led to much earnest and often cloudy public debate in Scandinavia; and from many remarks scattered about his correspondence of this time it is evident that Ibsen brooded much on these and related matters, and especially on how current interpretations of these terms might bear upon his own methods and practices.

In the middle of his work on *Peer Gynt* there appeared in the Danish press a review of *Brand* by Georg Brandes, the young Danish iconoclast whom Ibsen had not yet met but whose views were in time to have a profound influence on Ibsen, on Scandinavian drama in general, and on the spread of literary realism throughout the whole of Europe.

This review, though generally appreciative, must have given Ibsen occasion to pause and ponder. In it, Brandes warmly approves of the passionate intensity of Ibsen's message, the strength of his moral indignation, his hatred of falsehood and deceit. But when it came to the *poetry* in the work, he declared that in comparison with the rich poetry of Ibsen's earlier (prose) work *The Pretenders*, *Brand* represented a retrograde step. Brandes urged Ibsen to abandon the direction he had taken with the earlier (verse) *Love's Comedy* and *Brand* and return to the path of true poetry.

Ibsen must now have found himself wondering whether the bleak honesty of his new vision was best matched by what he was later to call 'the language of the gods', ie verse; and he had to face the question squarely whether the relationship between 'truth' as he now envisaged it and 'beauty' as it was conventionally taken to be was any longer valid.

After the completion of *Peer Gynt*, he awaited the reviews in the Scandinavian press — and especially the judgement of the influential Clemens Petersen — with more than usual apprehension. When it came, it was altogether worse than he had expected. Not because it was generally hostile and dismissive, but because it was compounded of the kind of literary and aesthetic judgements he was most concerned to repudiate. The fury with which Ibsen received this review, and the vehemence of his response, justifies one in quoting at some length from the Petersen review, which began ominously by asking: Was this poetry?

> All poetry is the transmutation of reality into art. Even the most fleeting impressions of beauty in everyday life are precisely this. The view over the harbour when the rain eases and all the boats hoist their sails in the sunlight; the sight of a group of animals, who have stopped motionless in the forest as though Pan were playing for them and who then suddenly, released from their enchantment, go chasing off across the plain; the sight of a man straining with every fibre of his being in quiet self-satisfaction but who nevertheless finds inexpressible joy in it because he is sacrificing himself for something he loves; whenever one encounters something of this kind in real life which leaves on one an impression of beauty and which rouses feelings of poetry, this is due solely to the fact that reality, at such a moment, presents itself to one as art . . . . But if this transmutation into reality is to be successful, so that the raw material of reality is absorbed by art's form and thereby wholly becomes poetry, then art makes its distinct demands, just as reality makes its, and if both demands are not completely met, then the transmutation fails and poetry remains absent, even though there may otherwise be sufficient both of art and reality in the work. But this is precisely how things are in Herr Ibsen's last two works: they might rather be said to have come to terms with these demands than fully satisfying them. Neither *Brand* nor *Peer Gynt* are properly poetry, however great or interesting their immediate effect may be.[9]

Ibsen's fury at this reception was matched only by his dismay — dismay, because what was being urged on him by these and other commentators was precisely what he had after so much soulsearching repudiated: the romanticization of life, the idealized view, the cosily sentimental. He was in despair that there should be so little understanding of his real purposes, and found it equally offensive to be praised for the so-called 'romantic beauty' of certain selected scenes as he was by the alleged uglinesses of others. There seemed to be a kind of smothering, all-enveloping, Boyg-like invulnerability about these critical judgements, deploying as they did their specious notions of 'beauty', 'truth' and 'poetry', which left Ibsen despairing of ever finding any rational way to refute them. He erupted in a long letter to Bjørnson — probably the longest letter he ever wrote in his life — which is deeply eloquent of the depths to which he had been stirred by the article. Defiantly — and prophetically — he declared that *Peer Gynt was* poetry, and would be recognized as such, if not today then tomorrow: 'The concept of poetry in our country, in Norway, will come to conform to the work.'[10]

Ibsen had as little satisfaction from Brandes's review, which also regretted the lack of 'beauty' in the piece:

> If the fine old rule of the French Romantics — 'The ugly is the beautiful' — is really valid, then *Peer Gynt* would be a work of beauty; but if there is any hint of doubt about this rule, then Ibsen's new work has failed totally. That it has failed *totally* does not of course mean that it is unsuccessful in all or indeed in most details. It is in no wise denied that *Peer Gynt* in part contains great beauties, and in parts informs us — Norwegians and everybody — of a number of great truths; but beauties and truths are worth a good deal less than beauty and truth in the singular; and Ibsen's work is neither beautiful nor true.[11]

Later, when his immediate anger had subsided, Ibsen tried in a few lines in a letter to Brandes to give a more sober account of his own views on 'truth' and 'beauty':

> Concerning those particular parts of *Peer Gynt*, I cannot agree with you. Naturally I bow to the laws of beauty, but I don't worry about the rules. You mention Michelangelo; in my opinion, nobody has sinned more against the rules of beauty than he; but everything he has created is nevertheless beautiful; for it is characterful. Raphael's art

has never actually fired me; his figures have their home before the Fall; and in any case, Mediterranean man has different aesthetic values from us. He wants formal beauty; for us, even the formally un-beautiful can be beautiful by virtue of its inherent truth.[12]

The longer term consequences of these upsets were more profound. All this nugatory abstract argument about truth and beauty had nevertheless begun to face him with what was a very real and personal problem: whether the relationship between *what* he felt he now had to say and the medium he had chosen to say it in was the right one. He began to wonder whether the sheer facility with which the verse had come to him did not represent a danger signal, and may even have been detrimental to his achievement. Three short years after it appeared, he was calling *Peer Gynt* 'reckless'; and in 1872 to Edmund Gosse, he repeated the term: 'How far you will find pleasure in it [*Peer Gynt*], I don't know. It is wild and formless, recklessly written in a way that I could only dare to write while far from home.'[13]

Much later in life, in conversation with William Archer, Ibsen recalled the circumstances of those days:

He wrote *Brand* and *Peer Gynt* (which appeared with only a year's interval between them) at very high pressure, amounting to nervous overstrain. He would go on writing verses all the time, even when asleep or half awake. He thought them capital for the moment; but they were the veriest nonsense. Once or twice he was so impressed with their merit that he rose in his night-shirt to write them down; but they were never of the slightest use. 'It is much easier', he (Ibsen) said, 'to write a piece like *Brand* or *Peer Gynt* than to carry through a rigorously consistent scheme, like that of *John Gabriel Borkman*, for example.'[14]

Although his letters from these years make it clear that he had by no means abandoned his Julian project, Ibsen nevertheless found himself side-tracked in the winter of 1868-69 into writing *The League of Youth*, a polemical drama *à la Scribe* aimed directly at those of his contemporaries back in Scandinavia who had infuriated him by their mindless condemnation of *Peer Gynt*. Thereafter, he began assiduously to augment his collection of historical material; and during the summer months of 1869 he gave himself energetically to this task. But once again distractions obtruded. First he began making notes for a 'drama of contemporary life', which if it had materialised would probably have been something not unlike the later *Pillars of Society*; then he spent a number of anguished months selecting from his existing lyric and narrative poems — a task which he described as 'a cursed piece of work'.

The publication of his *Poems* in 1871 can now be seen also as a symbolic act. He had spent several strenuous and draining months preparing the manuscript, selecting and amending and arranging works written at many different periods and times over the previous twenty or more years. Having to re-live all those earlier attitudes and states of mind, most of which he had now completely outgrown and even wholly repudiated, had given him much mental torment. The task had exacerbated his current mood of anguished self-examination and analysis; and it also, fatefully as it happened, forged an inseparable connection in his mind between those earlier discarded values and beliefs and the medium of verse. It was now as though he was anxious to draw a line under this phase of his career and put it behind him. Apart from one or two additional poems which were then later incorporated into the second edition of 1874, Ibsen virtually wrote no more verse for the rest of his life.

Even more significant, however, is the fact that this revisionary self-examination coincided with a new and heightened awareness on his part of impending change of the most fundamental kind. The idea had taken firm root in his mind that some profound shift in the whole course of human destiny was imminent; that the moment was one of those rare transitional periods in history when the world was about to change direction, was ready to repudiate its past and embark on the exploration and the revaluation of its established values, to adopt new systems, new concepts, new modes of thought.

From 1870 onwards, Ibsen's letters — especially those to Georg Brandes — began to carry phrases of enormous portentousness.

Again and again in his correspondence he returned to this sense
of present crisis. Sweepingly, he asserted his belief that the whole
human race was on the wrong track, and that the existing state of
affairs was untenable. He asserted the relativity of all received
truths, the impermanence of all religious, moral and artistic values, and the need to give new meaning to old concepts. He
anticipated the early collapse of many existing institutions and
the abolition of statehood as consequences of the mortal combat
which he saw taking place between two epochs, between — as he
put it — between yesterday and today. Nothing — not even the
most immutable-seeming of truths — could be exempt from
scrutiny: 'Who will vouch for it [he asked] that two and two do
not make five up on Jupiter?' The situation required nothing less
than what he called — in a letter to Brandes of December 1870 —
'a revolution of the human spirit':

> World events occupy a large part of my thoughts. The old
> illusory France is now smashed; as soon as the new *de
> facto* Prussia is also smashed, we shall have arrived with
> a single leap in a new and emergent age! And how the old
> ideas will come crashing down about us! And not before
> time! . . . The old concepts need a new content and new
> significance . . . . This is what the politicians will not
> recognize, and that is why I hate them. They only want
> specialist revolutions, superficial revolutions, in politics
> and the like. But that is only tinkering. What is needed is
> a revolution of the human spirit.[15]

This was the moment, it seems, when *Emperor and Galilean*
began to take on a new and augmented significance for him.
Previously one can well believe that it was the figure of the
Apostate which had exerted the most immediate appeal to one
who was himself engaged on a difficult and misunderstood
apostasy; now, however, it was the historical circumstances of the
age of Julian which began to preoccupy him. He came to see in
those events of the 4th century AD a crisis of destiny in human
affairs such as he was convinced mankind had reached in his own
day. And the more he studied the signs in the contemporary
scene, and the deeper he pushed into his dramatic material, the

closer the relevance between the two epochs seemed to him to be. In October 1872, when he was halfway through the composition of *Emperor and Galilean*, he wrote to Edmund Gosse that the historical subject he had chosen had a much closer connection with the movements of the contemporary age than one might at first imagine; a year later and he went so far as to say that the course of recent events in Europe had made his drama even more timely than he himself had thought possible.

Many years later, in an after-dinner speech at a banquet in Stockholm in September 1887, Ibsen returned to this whole question; he declared his continuing belief that the contemporary age marked an ending, and that something new was about to be born from it:

> I believe that the time is not far off when political and social conceptions will cease to exist in their present forms, and that from both of them there will arise a unity, which for a while will contain within itself the conditions for the happiness of mankind. I believe that poetry, philosophy and religion will be merged in a new category and become a new vital force, of which we who are living now can have no clear conception.
>
> ... I believe that the ideals of our time, whilst disintegrating, are tending towards what in my play *Emperor and Galilean* I designated 'the third empire'.[16]

And there, at last, we have it: that evocative and latterly doom-laden phrase — 'det tredje riget' in Norwegian, 'the third empire/realm' in English, 'das dritte Reich' in German — a concept which, despite the semantic pollution it suffered in the third decade of this twentieth century, has a long and significant history. In Ibsen's drama it is made a central theme, with a total freight of encoded significance which takes one very near the threshold of tolerance.

When the concept of 'the third empire' first enters the play — in Act III — it is interpreted by the mystic Maximos in terms which are almost pure Joachism as we know it from history. It will be remembered that the 12th century Abbot Joachim of Fiore identified three realms: the first being that of God the

Father and the Old Testament, covering the period from Adam
to Christ; the second being that of Christ and the New Testament,
and destined to end as the first realm had done and be superseded
by the third, that of the Holy Ghost. And Joachim's calculations
had told him that this third realm was imminent. In the play,
Julian finds that neither the degenerate Hellenism of the pagan
community nor the degenerate Christianity of the court at
Constantinople hold out any promise of fulfilment, so he seeks
guidance about his true mission from Maximos the mystic.
Thereupon, at a seance, a Voice tells him — with traditional
oracular ambiguity — that his task is to 'establish the empire'.
The gloss which Maximos then puts on it in this imagined 4th
century situation seems a clear invocation of the 12th century
Joachim:

> There are three empires [he declares] ... First, that
> empire which was founded on the tree of knowledge; then
> that empire which was founded on the tree of the cross
> .... The third is the empire of the great mystery, the
> empire which shall be founded on the tree of knowledge
> and the tree of the cross together, because it hates and
> loves them both, and because it has its living springs
> under Adam's grove and Golgotha.

Maximos is thus made to serve as the spokesman for a recogniz
ably orthodox trinitarian doctrine of history, based on the identification of three realms, in the third of which lies the promise
of fruition. What Ibsen has in common with the historical
Joachim is a disinclination or inability to define very precisely
the specific nature of the future ideal era, and leaves its general
nature to be vaguely divined by reference to the two empires
which it supersedes. Where Ibsen differs from Joachim, however,
is that in his account the two first realms — which alone can
determine what the third realm is to be — undergo significant
changes of identity as the action of the play progresses. Specifically, for the early Julian the first two empires are clearly identified as those of Dionysos and Christ; for the later Julian, the
two empires take on the identity of the temporal power of the
Roman Empire and the spiritual force of the Christian church.

Sometimes other — more abstract — dualities seem to represent the two opposing worlds, conceived not as successive entities but as elements unendingly co-existent in time, from the interaction of which an as yet undefined 'third empire' is to emerge: freewill and necessity; the spirit and the flesh; the imperatives of duty and the pursuit of happiness. With so many legitimate pretenders in the course of the play to the first and second realms, the third realm inevitably becomes in this play something dauntingly polymorphous. This proliferation of reference has also, as a by-product, resulted in the recruitment by criticism of almost any thinker from the past whose patterns of thought were in any degree triadic as a mediator here in the search for meaning in the play: Lessing, for example, and Schiller and Hegel and Kierkegaard, with varying degrees of success.

It is neither fitting nor feasible that I should attempt here any wider examination of its multiple functions within the play, its many manifestations, different semantic levels and planes of meaning. Instead I limit myself to isolating for brief comment one particular aspect of its multi-faceted life: that aspect which most nearly concerns the chosen theme of this address.

Let us take the first three acts. In Act I Julian finds the atmosphere of the Christian court at Constantinople unwholesome and unacceptable; he experiences the hypocrisies and indeed cruelties of a Christianity becoming ever more degenerate; so that when a vision seems to command him to leave the city and do intellectual battle in the stronghold of the heathen, he departs gratefully. In the Athens of Act II, the corruption which has infected those who adhere to the older paganism is no less dispiriting; Julian seeks to live the joyous Dionysian life, but is sickened by the contrast between what he feels was the ancient beauty of pagan sin and the merely sordid practices of the present. So that when he moves in Act III to seek wisdom in a life outside these confines, in some new revelation, the drama is seen as having prepared us for a 'third empire' which will supersede the realms of both Christ and Dionysos, and will transcend both hellenic sensuality and Galilean asceticism.

But when the moment arrives for Julian to articulate the lessons he has derived from his experiences in Constantinople and Athens, the terminology he adopts is arresting. As the supremely defining attribute of hellenic paganism, Julian selects 'beauty':

> Why was pagan sin so beautiful? . . . Wasn't Alcibiades
> beautiful when, aglow with wine, he stormed like a young
> god through the streets of Athens by night? Wasn't he
> beautiful in his defiance when he jeered at Hermes and
> hammered on people's doors? . . . Wasn't Socrates
> beautiful in the symposium? And Plato and all the joyous
> revellers? . . .

'Beauty' becomes a kind of single code-word, subsuming all the
characteristic features of paganism in a single counter. The
equivalent code-word in his vocabulary for Christianity is
'truth'. To the world he announces that his mission in leaving
Constantinople was 'to uphold the truth of Christianity against
the pagan lie'. It is therefore natural that his growing spiritual
bewilderment presents itself to him in the form of a simple
specific question: 'I often wonder [he says] whether truth *is* the
enemy of beauty'. And when, tersely, he sums up the reasons for
his despair, his desperate need for some new revelation, he
reaches out for his two code-words.

> The old beauty is no longer beautiful, and the new truth
> is no longer true.

And at once those who can read the signs are aware that behind
and beyond the more immediate ideological conflicts that beset
Julian in his 4th century world there is another dialogue in
progress. Ibsen here puts into the mouth of Julian a formulation
which at once transposes a distant 4th century recognition into a
contribution to mid-19th century aesthetic polemics. Julian's
words silently reverberate with the hurt Ibsen felt at the
insensitive Petersen review of *Peer Gynt* and Brandes's dismissal
of the work as 'neither beautiful nor true'. No longer is he
limited to the halting phrases of his letter to Brandes about the
'laws' and the 'rules' of beauty, in the course of which he found
himself saying things like: '. . . The formally unbeautiful can be
beautiful by virtue of its inherent truth.' Ibsen now enters the
current debate in the one way he really felt competent to

385

contribute: in the dramatic mode.

I have plucked out this one single strand from the enormously complicated weave of *Emperor and Galilean* to give some sort of indication of the obliquity of utterance to be found there. On the one hand we need to take seriously Ibsen's repeated assurance that there was in Julian's career much that echoed Ibsen's own inner anguish of these years; and equally, that the events of those remote 4th century days resonated strongly with what was happening in the late 19th century in Europe.

Emperor and Galilean is then seen to be an encoded declaration of the author's belief in the imminence of incommensurable change. As major components of this change, he identified fundamental shifts in one's understanding of what constituted 'truth' and 'beauty' and also consequently 'poetry', and in the prevailing ways of communicating them. By thus linking the quest for a new kind of truth and a new understanding of beauty with the leading concept of 'the third empire', Ibsen declared his belief that an essential constituent in the new age he so confidently predicted would be a new view of 'poetry', which for him meant above all dramatic poetry. The occasion for him was not one of merely negative apostasy; there was much more to it than the simple repudiation of the past, the de-idealization of content and the de-ornamentation of dramatic language, so that — as he implies elsewhere in his letter to Lucie Wolf — the artist could not then dishonestly 'creep into the nooks and crannies of rhymed verse'. It was something much more positive, much more audacious, yet not easily defined except obliquely through the idiom of drama which was his natural mode of expression.

In both of his prognostications, Ibsen seems to have been proved right by events. Perhaps one would not wish to go with him to the extreme of pronouncing dramatic verse 'extinct'; but — as Kenneth Muir points out — the best plays of the present century have been, and continue to be, written in prose, thus seeming to confirm Ibsen's prophecy that prose would be the principal dramatic medium of the future. Much more to the point, however, is that the new dramatic prose beginning with Ibsen is — if I may recall the phrases I used earlier from C.S.Lewis — prose of a new kind, almost in a new dimension, a prose dialogue which has led more than one Ibsen commentator to speak of the new creation as 'poetic drama in prose'.

As for the second: when Geoffrey Barraclough[17], having identified what he calls the 'great divide' between the contemporary age and that long period of history running from the Renaissance to the age of Bismarck, examined the literature of the period, he found it remarkable that there were people at the time who seemed to be aware of the way things were moving, who sensed the unsettling impact of new forces, and whose perception that the world was moving into a new epoch was not simply an illusion (p.17). *Emperor and Galilean* was born of just such an apocalyptic vision; it was Ibsen's attempt to give expression to *his* sense of the 'great divide' as he felt it on his nerves, to embody it in an historical analogue. Disappointingly, it did not — some would say still *does not* — succeed in communicating its deeper meanings in the way Ibsen had intended. But it lies in his achievement to have detected this thing, to have responded to it, drawn attention to it, and by his own later practice to have made a unique contribution towards its realization.

Notes

Notes to Chapter 1

1. R.L. Graeme Ritchie & James M.Moore, *Translation from the French* (Cambridge, 1918) p.31.
2. E.Stuart Bates, *Modern Translation* (London, 1936).
3. *Werke*, Weimar ed., vol. 41^2, p.307.See also his letter to Carlyle, 15 June 1828, in which he stresses that 'the translator is working not for his own nation alone but also for the nation from whose language he takes the work.'
4. Karl Vossler, *The Spirit of Language in Civilisation* (London, 1932) p.175.
5. Fritz Strich, *Goethe and World Literature* (London, 1949) p.8.
6. *Selected Essays*, 2nd ed. (London, 1934) p.61.
7. *Spirit of Language*, p.176.
8. Cf.Matthew Arnold, *Essays* (O.U.P. London,1925) p.317.
9. See his letter to A.W. von Schlegel, 23 July 1796: 'Alles Übersetzen scheint mir schlechterdings ein Versuch zur Auflösung einer unmöglichen Aufgabe.'
10. An exchange of correspondence in *TLS*, Aug and Sep 1946, ran through some of the more usual graphic metaphors and concluded by likening the translator to 'a restorer of pictures'.
11. *Translation from the French*, p.13.
12. J.P.Postgate, *Translation and Translations* (London, 1922), p.18.
13. Peter Stern, 'The Violet and the Crucible', *Cambridge Journal*, III, 7 (April, 1950), p.397.
14. *The Gift of Tongues* (London, 1943), p.94.
15. Stern, *loc.cit.*
16. *The Philosophy of Rhetoric* (London, 1936) pp.32ff.
17. *PMLA*, LXVII, 6 (Oct 1952), p.6.
18. J.R.Firth, 'Modes of Meaning', *Essays and Studies*, ed. Geoffrey Tillotson (London, 1951) p.118.
19. *Ibid.*, p.125.
20. E.Sapir, *Selected Writings*, ed. D.G.Mandelbaum (London, 1949) p.105.
21. *Ibid.*,p.154.
22. *First and Last Things* (London, 1908), p.16.
23. Hilaire Belloc, *On Translation*, Taylorian Lecture, 1931 (Oxford, 1931), p.37.
24. Postgate, *Translation and Translations*, p.19.

25. H.C.Tolman, *The Art of Translating* (New York, 1901), p.22.
26. But see a full debate in William Empson, *The Structure of Complex Words* (London, 1951), pp.1-83.
27. George Berkeley, *Treatise Concerning the Principles of Human Knowledge* (1710), Introduction, §20.
28. *Ibid*.
29. I.A.Richards, *Principles of Literary Criticism* (London, 1924), p.267.
30. I.A.Richards, *Science and Poetry* (London, 1935), p.28.
31. *Words and Poetry* (London, 1928), p.60.
32. June E.Downey, *Creative Imagination* (London, 1929), p.1.
33. *Ibid*.
34. Firth, 'Modes of Meaning', p.123.
35. Cf.I.A.Richards, *Philosophy of Rhetoric*, pp.62 ff. The possible effectiveness of naturalistic imitation of sound might however be tested experimentally. Givler, in 'The Psycho-physiological Effect of the Elements of Speech in relation to Poetry', *Psy. Rev. Monog.* 19 (1915), pp.1-132 (quoted in Downey, *Creative Imagination*, pp.73 ff.) describes an experiment where 'tonal replicas' of lines of English poetry were devised and it was found that hearer-response was very close to that produced by the original; he concludes that the sounds of lyric poetry were themselves able to arouse 'a mood congruous to that of the original poem, even when torn from their position and their rhetorical anchorage.' If French or Eskimo hearers were to be found responding in the same way to these tonal replicas, this would be a powerful argument in favour of Naturalist imitation.
36. *Radio Times*, Nov 1949.
37. Vossler, *Spirit of Language*, pp.182 f.
38. Louis H. Gray, *Foundations of Language* (New York, 1939), p.141.
39. 'On Translating Plays' *Essays by Divers Hands: Transactions of the R.L.S.*, New Series, V, (London, 1925), p.31.
40. B.Croce, *Encyclopaedia Britannica*, 14th ed., I, p.267.
41. Lascelles Abercrombie, *An essay towards a theory of art*, (London, 1922), p.90.
42. Cf.H.Osborne, *Theory of Beauty*, (London,1952), p.95.
43. Bloomfield analyses an act of speech into A: speaker's stimulus; B: speech; and C: hearer's response; and adds '... Speech utterance, trivial and unimportant in itself, is important because it has a meaning; the meaning consists of the important things with which the speech utterance (B) is connected, namely the practical events (A and C).' (*Language*, British ed., London, 1935, pp.23 and 27.)
44. *Ibid*., p.23.
45. Cf. I.A.Richards, *Principles of Literary Criticism*, p.208.

46. Herbert Read has no doubt that, as between artist and beholder, they do differ considerably, in spite of Tolstoy's contrary view (*What is Art*, sec.v): 'If we must, psychologically speaking, call the resultant state of mind [aroused in us by a work of art] an emotion, it is an emotion totally different in kind from the emotion experienced and expressed by the artist in the act of creating the work of art.' (*The Meaning of Art*, Penguin Books, 1949, p.189.)

47. I use these two terms therefore in the sense given to them by Heinz Kronasser when he writes: 'Der Onomasiologe [geht] vom seelischen Phänomen aus, das seine lautliche Beziehung finden soll, und vertritt so den Standpunkt des Sprechers, während der Semasiologe von den Symbolen für dieselben Erscheinungen ausgeht und so den Standpunkt des Hörers einnimmt.' (*Handbuch der Semasiologie*, Heidelberg, 1952, p.72.)

48. Bates draws attention to the translations into Polish of Tadeusz Zelenski who 'under the pseudonym of "Boy" ... has created his own public, and is read as a Polish writer for his style as well as for the books he makes known...' (*Modern Translation*, p.93.)

49. *Spirit of Language*, p.177.

50. 'Re-creating Brand', *Radio Times*, 9 Dec 1949.

51. Letter to Lou Andreas Salomé, 22 Apr 1924.

52. John Dewey, *Art as Expression* (London, 1934) pp.197 ff.; the terms he favours are respectively 'means' and 'medium'.

53. Richard Hönigswald, *Philosophie und Sprache* (Basle, 1937) esp. pp.136 ff.

54. A.H.Gardiner, *The Theory of Speech and Language* (Oxford, 1932) §§ 65–67.

55. Erich Heller, *The Disinherited Mind* (Cambridge, 1952) pp.187ff.

56. C.S.Lewis and E.M.W. Tillyard, *The Personal Heresy* (London, 1939), p.102.

57. Kenneth Burke, *The Philosophy of Literary Form* (Louisiana, 1941), p.263.

Notes to Chapter 3

1. Letter to Charles Archer, dated 25–28 Jul 1887, reprinted in Charles Archer, *William Archer* (London, 1931) pp.152ff.

2. Henrik Jæger, in a newspaper report of Dec 1887, reprinted in Henrik Ibsen, *Efterladte Skrifter* (Christiania, 1909) ed. Halvdan Koht and Julius Elias, vol.1, pp.xix f.

3. *Ibid.*, p.xxi. The German visitor was M.G.Conrad.

4. In a letter to Bjørnstjerne Bjørnson, 12 Sep 1865 – see *Oxford Ibsen*, vol.III, pp.424 f.

5. In a letter to Edmund Gosse, 30 Apr 1872, see *ibid.*, p.491
6. According to William Archer, *The Monthly Review*, Jun 1906, pp.17 f.

Notes to Chapter 4

1. Raymond Williams, *Drama from Ibsen to Eliot* (London, 1954) p.66
2. Emil Reich, *Ibsens Dramen* (Berlin, 1923, 14th ed.) p.200: Hier wendet sich alles zum Guten, ein wenig zu sehr wie in *Bund der Jugend*. Eine Glücksbotschaft jagt die andere, allgemeine Aussöhnung folgt . . . Nicht äussere Rücksichten, sieghaft vorwaltender Glaube an eine bessere Zukunft bestimmte Ibsen zu einem Abschluss, den auch wir einen guten nennen wollen, nicht aus weichlicher Empfindsamkeit, nein, in trotziger Freude an ritterlichem Streit gegen Verderbtes und Vermorschtes.
3. Halvdan Koht, *The Life of Ibsen* (London, 1931) vol.II, p.134: 'Samfundets støtter' er det einaste av alle verka hans som beint fram rører og kallar på tårene. Elles sluttar stykka hans heist såleis at dei skakar samvetet, herder hugen eller eggar viljen; ein kan harmas eller fælne, seia imot eller samtykke, - det er berre ein ting ein aldri blir: mjuk om hjartet, gråtmild. Så nær som her med 'Samfundets støtter'. (*Henrik Ibsen*, Oslo, 1954, vol. II, pp. 89-90).
4. Roman Woerner, *Henrik Ibsen* (Leipzig, 1909) vol.II, pp.57-61: Ibsen aber wollte hier einmal mit dem Hammer moralisieren . . . Und zum Abschluss ein Nachspiel im Familienkreis von so rührseligem Ernst, so fragwürdiger Aufheiterung, so allseitiger Befriedigung an optimistischen Kernsprüchen, daß es dem vierten Akte Bjørnsons [*En fallit*] lediglich seiner Kürze wegen vorzuziehen wäre. Das künstlerisch geringste von Ibsens modernen Dramen . . . Es ist Ibsens einziges—Tendenzstück. Dies sei betont, nicht um das Stück von den folgenden zu unterscheiden, umgekehrt, damit diese nicht mit ihm zusammengeworfen werden als gleicher Art.
5. *Oxford Ibsen*, vol.V, p.123
6. loc.cit.
7. Eva Le Gallienne, *Preface to Ibsen's 'Hedda Gabler'* (London, 1953) p.53
8. *Oxford Ibsen*, vol.VII, p.490
9. *Ibid.*, p.484
10. Arild Haaland, *Seks studier i Ibsen* (Oslo, 1965) p.82: Til tross for Ibsens merkelige kommentarer, er de egentlige moralske helter - lett karikert - ingen ringere enn Jørgen Tesman, fru Elvsted og den uforliknelige tante Julle.

11. See *Oxford Ibsen*, vol.VII, p.465
12. *Oxford Ibsen*, vol.VI, p.306
13. *Ibid.*, p.324

Notes to Chapter 5

1. Bergliot Ibsen, *The Three Ibsens* (London, 1951) p.17
2. Raymond Williams, *Drama in Performance* (London, 1954) pp.80ff.
3. There is just possibly a tempting, even beguiling, encipherment here, of which it would doubtless be a mistake to make too much. One begins by relating *S*uzannah and *M*agdelene Thore*sen* to *S*igne and *M*argit Gaute*sön*; this might further be linked to *S*uzannah and (her sister) *M*arie Thoresen, who have more than once been likened to Hjørdis and Dagny (in *The Vikings at Helgeland*) and who according to Ibsen's preface of 1883 were transmuted into Margit and Signe in *The Feast at Solhoug*; to which might be added that Ibsen himself, in his letter to Peter Hansen of 28 October 1870, acknowledged that for Hjørdis he had 'used the same model as for Svanhild in *Love's Comedy*'.
4. Otto Lous Mohr, *Henrik Ibsen som maler* (Oslo, 1953) pp.17ff.
5. *Ibid.*, p.19

Notes to Chapter 6

1. It is of interest to note that two years later, in his petition to Parliament on behalf of the Christiania Norwegian Theatre, Ibsen used the same phrase—'a higher combination' [en høiere Forbindelse]— to help him to define the nature of drama; but this time the constituent elements were changed: 'This art [i.e. dramatic art] is by its very nature to be regarded as a higher combination of all these separate art forms, since it manifests itself as a unity of the elements of poetry, painting, sculpture and music.'
2. 'Four Elizabethan Dramatists', *Selected Essays* (London, 1932) pp.109-17
3. *Samlede Værker* (Copenhagen, 1920) vol.i, p.311
4. *Ibid.*, vol.ii, pp.149-50

Notes to Chapter 11

1. The discussion of *Hedda Gabler* here is indebted at a number of points to Jens Arup, 'On *Hedda Gabler*', *Orbis Litterarum*,

Copenhagen, xii, 1957, pp.3-37
2. 'On the occasion of Hedda Gabler', *New Review*, June 1891, reprinted in *The Scenic Art*, ed. Allan Wade (London, 1949)
3. M.C.Bradbrook, *Ibsen the Norwegian* (London, 1946) p.118
4. Arup, op.cit.
5. Arup, op.cit.
6. Eva Le Gallienne, *Preface to Hedda Gabler* (London, 1955)

Notes to Chapter 13

1. David Jones, *The Anathemata* (London, 1952), p.15f.
2. C. S. Lewis, *They Asked for a Paper* (London 1962), p.17.
3. George Steiner, *After Babel* (London, 1975), p.176
4. *Modernism* 1890-1930, ed. by Malcolm Bradbury and James McFarlane (Pelican Guide to European Literature, Harmondsworth, 1976), p.19.
5. *Samlede Verker* (Oslo, 1928-57; hereafter cited as *S.V.*), xv, pp.410f.
6. Henning Fenger, 'Ibsen og Georg Brandes indtil 1872', *Edda,* lxiv (1964),169-208 — a full and indispensable account of their relationship, which reprints much scattered material otherwise difficult of access.
7. *S.V.*, xvi, pp.325ff.
8. Letter to Emil Petersen, 4 March 1871.
9. See Georg Brandes, *Levned* (Copenhagen, 1905), i,p.380.
10. *Ibid.*, p.379.
11. *Levned, ed. cit.,* ii, pp.55ff.
12. *S.V.*, xvi, p.351.
13. *S.V.*, xvi, p.371.
14. Brandes later reported: 'Fourteen days after I had started, my status as a public personality had completely changed. I had become the leading character of the day in the city. The success of my lectures was so enormous that they were being talked about everywhere. Suddenly I had achieved a kind of fame that I had not known before.' He added that, halfway through the lecture series in late December, the audience was packed in like sardines: 'There were something like 500 people packed into a room meant for 200, and the applause was deafening.' (*Levned, ed. cit.,* ii, pp.65-66).
15. *S.V.*, xvii, pp.30ff.
16. *S.V.*, xvi, p.145.
17. *S.V.*, xvi, pp.191f.
18. Brandes's correspondence with friends about this time contains some rather awe-struck comment on the audacity of Ibsen's expressed views.

19. *S.V.*, xvi, p.350.
20. *S.V.*, xvi, pp.373f.
21. *S.V.*, xiv, pp.143ff.
22. How systematic Brandes was in his reading during the years 1859 to 1865 may be gained from the list which he himself compiled of 'Læste Bøger' ('Books read'), reprinted in Bertil Nolin, *Den gode européer* (Uppsala, 1965), a work which gives an authoritative account of Brandes's intellectual development in the years 1871-93 with particular reference to his relationship to English, French, German and Slavic literature.
23. *Levned, ed. cit.*, i, p.310.
24. *Ibid.*
25. Incredibly and inexcusably this Preface was cut from the standard English-language edition of this work: *Main Currents in Nineteenth Century Literature* (6 vols, London, 1923). It therefore remained virtually unknown in the English-speaking world for many years. It may now be found, translated by Evert Sprinchorn, in *The Theory of the Modern Stage*, ed. by Eric Bentley (Harmondsworth, 1976), pp.383ff.
26. Brandes, in a letter to his mother, 18 June 1874.
27. *S.V.*, xvi, p.283.
28. When *Emperor and Galilean* eventually appeared, Brandes confessed privately that he 'couldn't stand the thing'. In a letter to his mother in September 1873, shortly after *Emperor and Galilean* had been published, he compared Ibsens's drama very unfavourably as a source of wisdom with Paul Heyse's *Kinder der Welt,* and added: 'I am sitting here in pain with Ibsen's 'Julian'. Actually I cannot stand the thing, though of course there are some things in it.' He used much the same phrase about it when writing (in Danish) to Edmund Gosse on 22 December 1873: 'This Christmas hasn't brought much. I'd be interested to know whether you felt particularly satisfied by Ibsen's *Emperor and Galilean.* This seems to me improbable, even though competent details are to be found in that work.' Paul Krüger, editor of Brandes's correspondence, nevertheless emphasizes the links between Ibsen's drama, Brandes's literary history and contemporary events: 'Le drame spéculatif d'Ibsen *Kejser og Galilaeer* qui parut le 16 Octobre 1873 réflète l'impression causé par les événements historiques de l'époque: la guerre franco-allemande, la Commune, la lutte de Bismarck contre les catholiques — par la nouvelle philosophie, la critique biblique et les deux premiers volumes de Hovedströmninger de Brandes.' (*Correspondence de Georg Brandes* (4 vols, Copenhagen, 1952-66), iv, p.206).
29. *S.V.*, xvi, p.375.
30. *Cf.* also the views of Ibsen's Norwegian biographer, Halvdan Koht: 'In actuality, Ibsen was the most bourgeois individual

imaginable, a born conservative. The revolution was entirely internal in his thoughts' (*Life of Ibsen*, New York, 1971, p.269).
31. *S.V.*, xvi, p.375.
32. *S.V.*, xv, p.411.

Notes to Chapter 14

This chapter was first given as a paper to the Seventh Burdick-Vary Symposium, held at the University of Wisconsin-Madison, 30-31 March 1984, on the theme of 'Preludes to Modernism: literature, art, music and thought in the period 1870 to 1914.' On that occasion it incorporated an Opening Statement, here given only in the briefest of paraphrase.

1. 'Verse and prose', in *Contemporary Theatre*, Stratford upon Avon Studies, no.4, London, 1962, p.97.
2. *S.V.*, xvii, p.510 f.
3. *S.V.*, xvii, pp.121 ff.
4. See, for example, *S.V.* xvi, p.371; xvii, p.66 and 73; xix, p.229.
5. *S.V.*, xvi, p.102.
6. I consider these matters in rather more detail in the Introduction to the *Oxford Ibsen*, vol.III (London, 1971) see pp.173-177 above.
7. *S.V.*, xvi, p.111.
8. *S.V.*, xvi, p.122.
9. Reprinted in Otto Hageberg (ed.), *Omkring 'Peer Gynt'* (Oslo, 1967) pp.40 ff.
10. 9/10 December 1867, (in *S.V.*, xvi, pp.197 ff.)
11. See Hageberg, *op.cit.*, pp.50 ff.
12. Letter to Georg Brandes, 15 July 1869, *S.V.*, xvi, pp.251 ff.
13. *S.V.*, xvii, pp.41f.
14. *Monthly Review*, June 1906, pp. 17 f.
15. *S.V.*, xvi, p.327.
16. *S.V.*, xv, pp.410ff.
17. *An Introduction to Contemporary History* (London, 1964) p.17.

Index

397